GROWING
FRUIT TREES

The Conservatoire Végétal Regional d'Aquitaine has been working for a quarter of a century to preserve and highlight the region's fruit tree heritage: by collecting and preserving traditional varieties that would have been forever forgotten had they been disseminated into nature, by presenting these varieties to a wide array of people in order that they may be rediscovered, by creating the means for a better understanding of fruits and fruit diversity, as well as the trees themselves and how they perform within their environment, in order to create new relationships with nature for the future, both rooted in past experience and anticipating demand from future generations.

When it became feasible for Aquitaine's Conservatoire Végétal and Éditions du Rouergue—the original French publisher—to publish a work detailing the latest understanding of pruning techniques that respect the natural behavior of fruit trees, Évelyne Leterme, the founder and director of the Conservatoire, naturally turned to Jean-Marie Lespinasse in order to conceive and produce the text. Through a network of acquaintances, technicians, and scientists who were applying, observing, and developing these concepts, they were able to collaborate on this work in a spirit of scientific and iconographic openness and quality.

You may visit Aquitaine's Conservatoire Végétal at www.conservatoirevegetal.com.

For information about permission to reproduce selections from this book, write to Permissions, W. W. Norton & Company, Inc., 500 Fifth Avenue, New York, NY 10110

For information about special discounts for bulk purchases, please contact W. W. Norton Special Sales at specialsales@wwnorton.com or 800-233-4830.

Digital production and composition by Joe Lops
Manufacturing by KHL Printing Co. Pte Ltd
Production Manager: Leeann Graham
Translation by Gregory Bruhn

Library of Congress Cataloging-in-Publication Data

De la taille à la conduite des arbres fruitiers. English
Growing fruit trees: novel concepts and practices for successful care
and management / edited by Jean-Marie Lespinasse and Évelyne Leterme;
illustrations by Jean-Marie Lespinasse; Kitren Glozer, consultant for North America;
authors, Gilles Adgié ... [et al.]
       p. cm.
Originally published in French as: De la taille à la conduite des arbres fruitiers.
Includes bibliographical references and index.
ISBN 978-0-393-73256-6 (paperback)
1. Fruit-culture. 2. Fruit trees. 3. Fruit trees—Pruning.
I. Lespinasse, Jean-Marie. II. Leterme, Évelyne. III. Adgié, Gilles. IV. Title.

SB357.D28513 2011
634—dc22

2010037723

ISBN 13: 978-0-393-73256-6 (pbk.)

W. W. Norton & Company, Inc., 500 Fifth Avenue, New York, N.Y. 10110
www.wwnorton.com

W. W. Norton & Company Ltd., Castle House, 75/76 Wells St., London W1T 3QT

1 2 3 4 5 6 7 8 9 0

GROWING FRUIT TREES

Novel Concepts and Practices for Successful Care & Management

Edited by Jean-Marie Lespinasse and Évelyne Leterme
Illustrations by Jean-Marie Lespinasse
Kitren Glozer, consultant for North America

Authors
Gilles Adgié, René Bernhard, Yves Caraglio, Pierre Chol, Jacques Claverie,
Francis Delort, Bernard Florens, Éric Germain, Charles Grasselly, Bruno Hucbourg,
Pierre-Éric Lauri, Marcel Le Lezec, Jean-Marie Lespinasse, Évelyne Leterme,
Nathalie Moutier, Éric Navarro, Daniel Plénet, Michel Ramonguilhem, Jean-Paul Sarraquigne

Collaborators
Jean Aymard, Henri Azzopardi, André Belouin, Anne Boutitie, Henri Breisch,
Pascal Jargaud, Daniel Lavigne, Jean-Louis Tailleur

W. W. Norton & Company
New York • London

Should fruit trees be pruned?

As irreverent as this question might be, it is worth asking. One man, a contemporary, the son of a grape grower, a state researcher, at once modest and visionary, dared to ask this question and then attempted to answer it through forty years of research as well as professional, friendly, often lively exchange, years of observation and experimentation, all while questioning accepted knowledge and working passionately in the field.

More than anyone before him, he was able to observe and help us understand the world of fruits and trees. His ability to communicate, his pedagogy, and his skillful renderings made visible and accessible to all, in every corner of the fruit world, the reality that he was transcribing.

His friends have come to know Jean-Marie Lespinasse as a man of art.

Our participation in this book was an unanticipated opportunity to show a bit of what he has taught us and to share these teachings, as he would want, with our readers, whether they are arborists, enlightened enthusiasts, or novices of fruit tree cultivation.

We would like to add a stone to his edifice of knowledge, built through a continual exchange of ideas and cemented in friendship.

Gilles Adgié, Jean Aymard, Henri Azzopardi, André Belouin, René Bernhard, Anne Boutitie, Henri Breisch, Yves Caraglio, Pierre Chol, Jacques Claverie, Francis Delort, Bernard Florens, Éric Germain, Charles Grasselly, Bruno Hucbourg, Pascal Jargaud, Pierre-Éric Lauri, Daniel Lavigne, Marcel Le Lezec, Jean-Marie Lespinasse, Évelyne Leterme, Nathalie Moutier, Éric Navarro, Daniel Plénet, Michel Ramonguilhem, Jean-Paul Sarraquigne, Jean-Louis Tailleur.

CONTENTS

• STONE FRUITS • SEEDED FRUITS • DRY FRUITS • OTHER

INTRODUCTION

HISTORY

The donkey and the goat would have been the first animals to practice pruning, starting in the second millennium BCE in Mesopotamia and Egypt. After being subjected to those mammals' teeth, the vine, the first species to be pruned, would come to know the rule of man and his billhook. The Egyptians practiced pruning early on, with their knowledge subsequently being developed by the Greeks and then the Romans.

The billhook and the pruning knife remained the sole tools used for pruning for several millennia. Not until the nineteenth century were they replaced by clippers, which were invented in 1810 by one of Louis XVI's former ministers, Bertrand de Moleville, while he was in exile. He brought his invention back to France when the Bourbons returned to power in 1815. Yet this new tool had a hard time catching on, for it seemed to crush and tear more than cut. This caused Philibert Baron to write in 1858, in his work *Nouveaux principes de taille des arbres fruitiers*: "Before speaking about pruning, I would like to say a few words about the use of clippers and pruning knives, . . . a subject that divides professors and practitioners, the only reason that most people today do not favor clippers is that they don't know how to use them properly." They were gradually perfected, and it was Pierre-Antoine Poiteau who guaranteed their spread and success. *(See figs. 1 and 2.)*

Dozens, if not hundreds, of works have been written on pruning fruit trees. The oldest texts date to the Roman era with Varro, Columelle, and Plin the Elder. These reflect the first observations on cultivation and grafting, sometimes associating completely incompatible species.

In the Middle Ages, the first French publications on the matter, after the invention of the printing press, were translations and compilations of ancient authors and Italian authors. There were few personal studies except in the writings of Ruell in 1536 (*De Natura Stirpium*) and in those of Charles Étienne (*Proedium rusticum*). It was Olivier de Serre who handed down an overview of this knowledge at the end of that era with his *Théâtre de l'agriculture,* published in 1600 and re-edited in 1804 by the Société d'agriculture.

The first treatise on shapes created with an espalier was by Boyceau de la Barauderie, published posthumously in 1640. This was followed by several others, which each presented techniques on structured pruning. We should mention, among others, the abbot Le

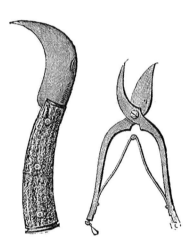

Fig. 1. An engraving from Charles Baltet's *Traité de la culture fruitière commerciale et bourgeoise.*

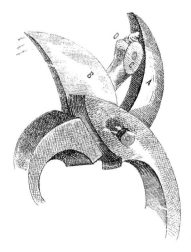

Fig. 2. How to hold clippers: A is the hook, B is the blade (engraving from Philibert Baron's *Nouveaux principes de taille des arbres fruitiers.*

Gendre, in 1652, with *La Manière de cultiver les arbres fruitiers*, in which he discussed nurseries, espaliers, and counter-espaliers, as well as shrubs and tall-stem trees; Merlet, in 1667, with *Abrégé des bons fruits*; and Venette, in 1683, who was the first to observe and describe pear trees in his work *De la manière de tailler les arbres fruitiers*. The posthumous publication in 1690 of Jean-Baptiste La Quintinie's work, *Instructions pour les jardins potagers et fruitiers*, introduced a new period in which advice centered mostly on creating tree shapes according to rules that varied greatly but that constituted a sort of fixed template impeding all freedom in shaping fruit tree arboriculture. That work was later re-edited, recopied, and plagiarized many times over, remaining nonetheless the basis for the field for a half-century. Subsequent major works focused on techniques used at chateaus and nurseries, and those used in Montreuil, but without personal commentary.

Roger Schabol was the first in 1767, in his *Dictionnaire des jardiniers*, to propose bowing techniques based on his observation of peach tree cultivation in Montreuil. This was followed in 1768 by Duhamel du Monceau's *Traité des arbres fruitiers* and then the first volume of Abbot Rozier's *Cours d'agriculture*, which came out in 1785 and remained well known and re-edited for over a century. True innovation started in the early nineteenth century with important observations in plant physiology and numerous publications: Cadet de Vaux in 1805; Sieulle in 1806; Turpin and Poiteau in 1808; Count Lelieur in

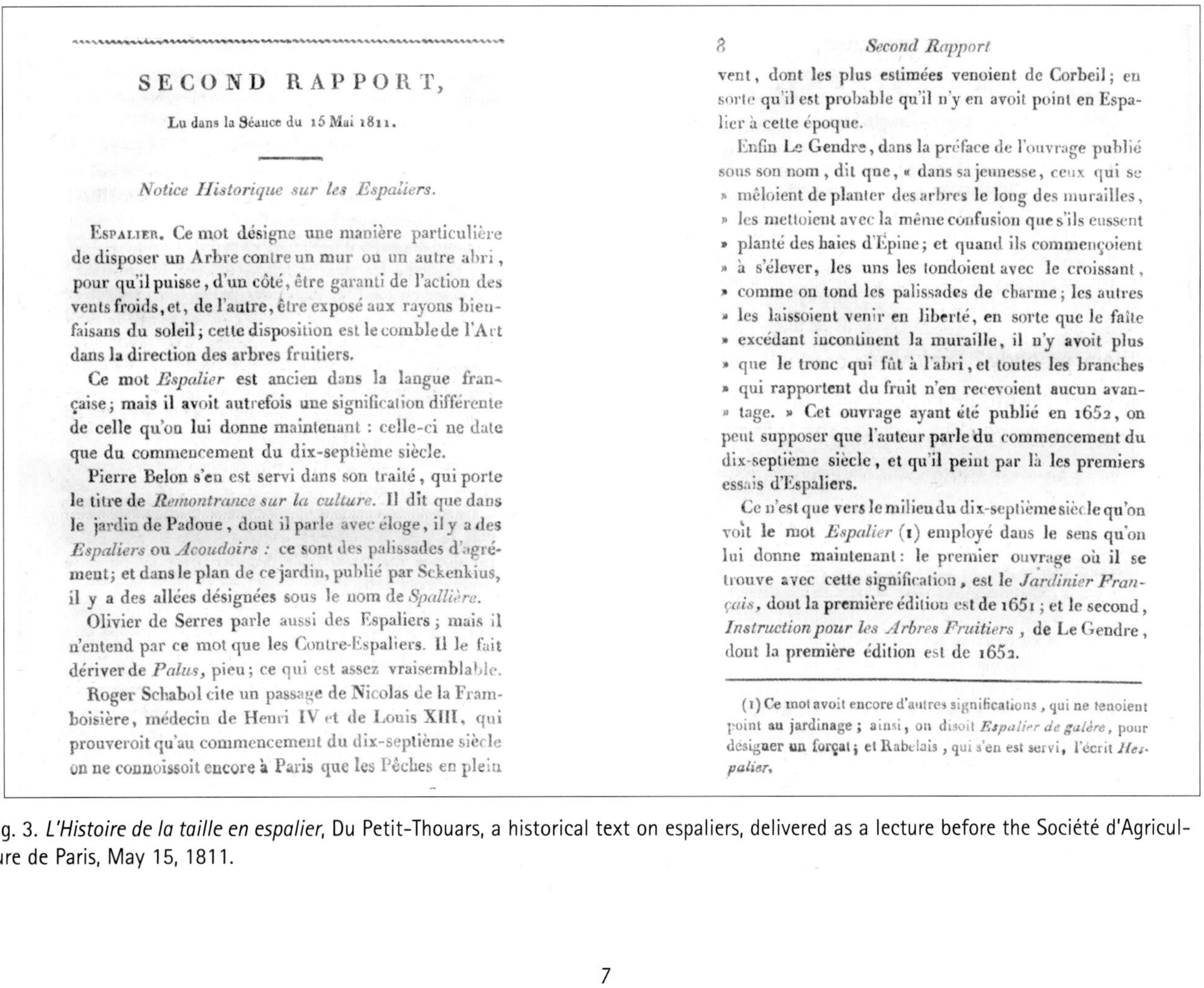

SECOND RAPPORT,

Lu dans la Séance du 15 Mai 1811.

Notice Historique sur les Espaliers.

ESPALIER. Ce mot désigne une manière particulière de disposer un Arbre contre un mur ou un autre abri, pour qu'il puisse, d'un côté, être garanti de l'action des vents froids, et, de l'autre, être exposé aux rayons bienfaisans du soleil; cette disposition est le comble de l'Art dans la direction des arbres fruitiers.

Ce mot *Espalier* est ancien dans la langue française; mais il avoit autrefois une signification différente de celle qu'on lui donne maintenant : celle-ci ne date que du commencement du dix-septième siècle.

Pierre Belon s'en est servi dans son traité, qui porte le titre de *Remontrance sur la culture*. Il dit que dans le jardin de Padoue, dont il parle avec éloge, il y a des *Espaliers* ou *Acoudoirs* : ce sont des palissades d'agrément; et dans le plan de ce jardin, publié par Sckenkius, il y a des allées désignées sous le nom de *Spallière*.

Olivier de Serres parle aussi des Espaliers; mais il n'entend par ce mot que les Contre-Espaliers. Il le fait dériver de *Palus*, pieu; ce qui est assez vraisemblable.

Roger Schabol cite un passage de Nicolas de la Framboisière, médecin de Henri IV et de Louis XIII, qui prouveroit qu'au commencement du dix-septième siècle on ne connoissoit encore à Paris que les Pêches en plein

8   *Second Rapport*

vent, dont les plus estimées venoient de Corbeil; en sorte qu'il est probable qu'il n'y en avoit point en Espalier à cette époque.

Enfin Le Gendre, dans la préface de l'ouvrage publié sous son nom, dit que, « dans sa jeunesse, ceux qui se » mêloient de planter des arbres le long des murailles, » les mettoient avec la même confusion que s'ils eussent » planté des haies d'Épine; et quand ils commençoient » à s'élever, les uns les tondoient avec le croissant, » comme on tond les palissades de charme; les autres » les laissoient venir en liberté, en sorte que le faîte » excédant incontinent la muraille, il n'y avoit plus » que le tronc qui fût à l'abri, et toutes les branches » qui rapportent du fruit n'en recevoient aucun avan- » tage. » Cet ouvrage ayant été publié en 1652, on peut supposer que l'auteur parle du commencement du dix-septième siècle, et qu'il peint par là les premiers essais d'Espaliers.

Ce n'est que vers le milieu du dix-septième siècle qu'on voit le mot *Espalier* (1) employé dans le sens qu'on lui donne maintenant: le premier ouvrage où il se trouve avec cette signification, est le *Jardinier Français*, dont la première édition est de 1651; et le second, *Instruction pour les Arbres Fruitiers*, de Le Gendre, dont la première édition est de 1652.

(1) Ce mot avoit encore d'autres significations, qui ne tenoient point au jardinage; ainsi, on disoit *Espalier de galère*, pour désigner un forçat; et Rabelais, qui s'en est servi, l'écrit *Hespalier*.

Fig. 3. *L'Histoire de la taille en espalier*, Du Petit-Thouars, a historical text on espaliers, delivered as a lecture before the Société d'Agriculture de Paris, May 15, 1811.

1811 (*Pomone française*); and Du Petit-Thouars, who in 1815 made a historic presentation of his work on pruning and techniques studied during that period in his *Recueil de rapports et de mémoires sur la culture des arbres fruitiers lus dans les séances de la Société d'agriculture de Paris (fig. 3)*. These men attempted to develop approaches that involved a less systematic pruning technique. Cadet de Vaux, for example, thought that people should be more respectful of trees by substituting bowing techniques for cutting; he wrote: "Give up the billhook, that damaging instrument." Yet these writers' methods were often criticized by the agricultural societies. There were questions regarding the influence that maintaining the tree in a certain shape plays on reducing fruit production.

Louis Noisette, in 1825, continued in this move toward cutting techniques allowing for more rapid fruit production in his *Manuel complet du jardinier*. Alexis Lepère, a specialist in peach tree pruning in Montreuil for a half-century, published the 6th edition of the *Pratique raisonnée de la taille du pêcher* in 1864, illustrating summer pruning techniques. Yet palmette pruning persisted *(fig. 4)*.

It was the horticultural and agricultural societies that would become the key purveyors of information on the matter. They became a great model without fully questioning systematic shaping. The best thesis on cutting techniques was chosen in competition or by local, regional, and even national agricultural associations. Some have come down to us, especially on vine pruning, and are organized at every geographic level.

Charles Baltet gave a more complete understanding of that era's ideas on cultivation (planting, upkeep, pruning), pomology (the best varieties found in nurseries, region by region), and economy in his 627-page work published in 1884, *Traité de la culture fruitière commerciale et bourgeoise*. His advice on methods for soil preparation, fertilization, anti-frost protection, hay usage, and so on is extremely sensible. He also looked at economic data provided by Hardy on average production volume by tree and species based on shape and age, and he concluded by discussing the great financial interest in fruit tree plantations during that period. Alfred Nomblot, in 1927, in his *Traité d'arboriculture fruitière et de pomologie*, examined a wide array of traditional pruning techniques.

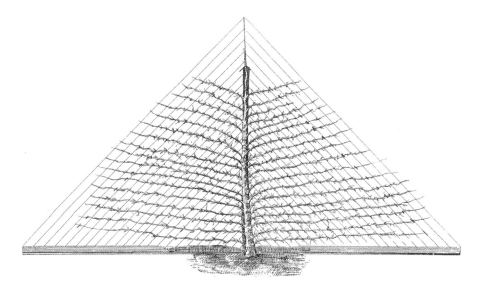

Fig. 4. A plum tree trained as a Palmette on a wire espalier (Philibert Baron, 1858, pl. 12, Fig. 21).

During the twentieth century, a new orientation took hold in terms of fruit tree pruning, thanks to the efforts of people who sought to adapt to the new demands for increased production, and therefore increased fruit production. These new systems were presented in the excitement of modernism and renewal. There was Lorette (Lorette pruning) in 1914, Delbard (Delbard tri-cross) in 1945, Bouché-Thomas (Stop-Thomas fruit hedge, planted at angles) in 1948, Marchand (drapeau Marchand), Ferragutti (vertical cord Ferragutti), Baldassari (Baldassari Palmette then Ypsilon), and Lepage in 1956 (Lepage bowing)—all of whom gave their names to their techniques.

Starting in 1960, bleak economic forecasts led to an improvement in public and private research and by professionals themselves in order to adapt arboriculture to the economy. These efforts included selecting new grafting stocks, developing new techniques for in-vitro propagation, selecting new varieties, cloning, improving plant health, and considerably advancing the phyto-sanitary fight.

Fig. 5. Candelabra form (top) and a Palmette form with horizontal cordons (bottom). Images from *Pratique raisonnée de la taille du pêcher* by Alexis Lepère, 1864.

* Terms in boldface are defined in the glossary at the back of the book.

In the late twentieth and early twenty-first centuries, texts dealing with the latest developments in fruit arboriculture over the past thirty years have been somewhat rare and published almost exclusively for researchers and professionals. The latest information appears in specialized works organized by species, published in France by the CTIFL (Centre technique interprofessionnel des fruits et légumes), in highly specialized articles in research publications, or as a result of scientific conferences.

Novices are often left with works that are disconnected from reality, most often preaching techniques inherited from the seventeenth century. These offer directions on how to use wood to suppress growth as an absolute requirement for obtaining high-quality fruit, as the following confessions about wind-swept trees from 1992 attest: "If you let it grow without pruning it, allowed to follow its whims, it will take on a cumbersome shape. The branches will be dense, impenetrable to air and light. **Epicormic branches*** will form, preventing fruiting. Fruit will remain small, mediocre in quality, and fruiting will show pronounced alternance [**alternate bearing**]. The shape's interior will become bare, yielding only dead wood, and the tree will collapse."

Very few associations allow novices to come together with park and garden professionals. In the Paris region, the old techniques are still taught in places where fruit tree shaping has remained an art, such as the Luxembourg Gardens or the Potager du Roi at the École Nationale d'Horticulture et du Paysage at Versailles, where La Quintinie governed. Jacques Beccaletto described these techniques in the *Encyclopédie des formes fruitières* (Actes Sud, 2002).

THE BENEFITS OF PRUNING

The various techniques outlined in published works are quite diverse, yet they all center primarily on tree shapes. "The shaped tree," the result of "shaping" procedures,

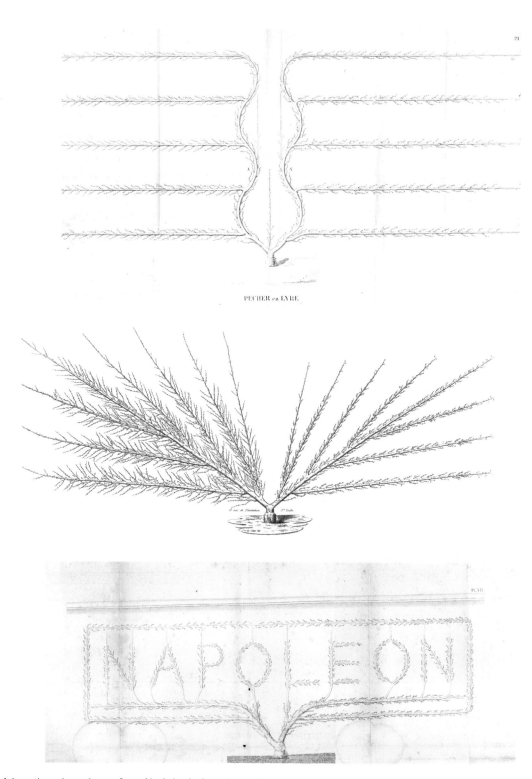

Fig. 6. Top: A lyre-shaped peach tree from Alexis Lepère's orchard. Middle: 12-year-old transplant, 2nd pruning. Bottom: A peach tree executed by Alexis at Montreuil. (Images from *Pratique raisonnée de la taille du pêcher*, Alexis Lepère, 1864)

takes on a specific character worthy of its creative artisanry. Bending the tree to man's will became an axiom and developed through every shape imaginable (or even unimaginable). That is how flexible the fruit tree proved to be; its woody structure seemed ready for manipulation. The aesthetic of very rigidly supported shapes was incontrovertible: horizontal, vertical, or angled bars; simple U palmettes; double U or V palmettes; Verrier palmettes or candelabras—which generally have four branches, though some acquire up to eight, often over a ten- to twenty-year period *(see figs. 5 and 6)*.

Shapes became more numerous in the twentieth century in landscaped parks. Bearing rather poetic names, they included pyramids, spindles, columns, bedposts, tops, boats, and vases, and later vases of various shapes, adapted to productive orchards.

Since fruit trees always end up going to fruit, the anticipated result—the production of fruit—always played a role. But what efforts were involved, how many failures were there, and what was the real result? Certain rather beautiful shapes proved quite unproductive and often only became so after a long period with no fruiting.

Across the rural landscape, the trees ornamenting the countryside, "landscape trees" shaped by the hands of farmers, were not more rapidly productive despite a different range of shaping constraints. Waiting seven to ten years, or even longer for the more reluctant species such as the walnut and the chestnut, was often commonplace and unquestioned. Usually found in close proximity to livestock or farming plots, or even among the crops (among grapes or mixed plantings), and worked over by the animals that passed among them, the fruit trees were not pruned for any garden or orchard aesthetic, but for their large size *(photo 1)*. The trees' crowns were supposed to stand above the crops and animal enclosures, which is why such trees are called "full-wind trees." This allowed for the appearance of monumental trees that dotted the rural countryside for over a thousand years,

which one can only long for today. Yet there have been consequences in terms of varietal selection.

Why is it important to mention that fruit tree selection was influenced throughout the countryside by the trees' cohabitation with domestic livestock? Because the most recent documents on natural fruit tree behavior—the subject of this book after more than thirty years of observation by its authors—have proved that a tree that is rigorously and repetitively shaped will gain height. The process creates a tall, closed frame that slows fruit production. Rural varieties that are not grown in that way have been unfailingly destroyed by livestock grazing on them. Thus, varieties that were naturally fruiting and rapidly productive, but that tended to

1. An older almond tree (Rivière sur Tarn, Aveyron, France).

2. A Basque cherry tree with a natural habit; a Peloa variety grafted onto Maxma, in 7th leaf.

Except for the creepers (vines, kiwi, etc.), which require systematic pruning in today's cultivation circles, we now realize that structuring fruit tree shapes has no scientific reason and no physiological purpose. This book describes new techniques that are starting to replace traditional fruit tree pruning. They will be useful to enthusiasts and professionals alike. No longer thinking that fruit trees should conform to structured, geometric shapes, these twenty-five authors and their collaborators, each treating a particular species in which they have expertise, have come together to discuss these trees' natural development in order to obtain rapid, high-quality fruit production (fig. 7).

Through the coordination of Jean-Marie Lespinasse, who worked at the INRA in Bordeaux from 1962 to 2000 on creating apple varieties, studying types of fruiting, and outlining performance modes within that species, and Évelyne Leterme, the director and founder of Aquitaine's Conservatoire Végétal Régional, fifteen different species are covered here. You will find that by carefully observing the varieties, each one is different and possesses a particular branching and fruiting pattern (photo 3).

hang, were not selected for and have disappeared from our rural heritage.

TRAINING

Why deny the evolution of pruning? Quite simply, because of a cultural phenomenon: the manifestation of our collective memory. For over two centuries, it has been written and reiterated that shaping is a fixed technique that will only evolve by modifying the shapes applied to trees (for various reasons). But we have not yet understood that pruning can be a delicate and harmless procedure that benefits the plant, its shape, and thus its way of growing and producing (photo 2).

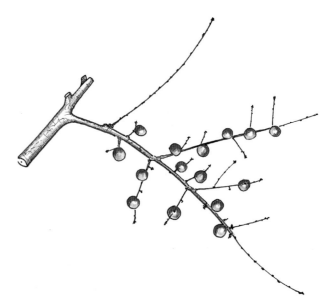

Fig. 7. A fruit branch from a peach variety producing on two-year wood.

3. Mondial Gala® grafted onto an M9 and trained with the solaxe method, three years after planting.

The free and natural approach is most harmonious and efficient in terms of growing trees, inducing fruit production, and maintaining a balance between annual growth and fruiting. The desire to force a variety into a geometric shape hinders its natural processes for branching and fruiting. This requires annual and artificial maintenance of a precarious balance between those parts of the tree that produce growth and those parts where fruit develops—areas whose purposes are dissimilar.

The more severe the shaping, the more dominant the "tree" will be, while the production of flowers, their formation, and their evolution into fruits will remain uncertain and incomplete. If we can respect the tree's natural **architecture**, as well as its mode of fruiting, we will no longer impose artificial shapes.

Our role here is as educators, in favor of each variety's characteristics.

This outlook is meant to restrain us from our "pruning reflexes," which are a throwback to earlier times. For example:

- our desire to systematically train trees to bear fruit near their center, through drastic cuttings;
- our desire to prevent trees from growing vertically, with the use of clippers.

There are many techniques and instinctive interventions that destroy and do not respect nature, with no physiological importance. But more respectful, sensitive methods do exist for cultivating successful fruit trees. We must let the trees do their own work, and guide them along as best we can.

Take a look . . .

ALMOND

Author   Charles GRASSELLY

GENERAL OVERVIEW

Phytogeographical Origins

The almond tree originated in the arid regions of the Iranian plateau—Iran, Afghanistan, Pakistan, and the dry mountain regions of western Kurdistan and eastern Tajikistan, as well as the Tian Shan mountains. Because several wild species grew in proximity to one another, one might think that the cultivated species are the result of natural cross-breeding between certain species whose zones overlapped. However, human contribution, from the beginning of the almond's cultivation, has resulted in types with large fruits (wild species generally produce smaller fruit) and sweet seeds.

Even though almond trees have been in existence since antiquity, their cultivation, which spread from Iran into the Mediterranean basin, has until recently been practiced without irrigation, often in pebbly areas in filtering soil that is well adapted to the trees' root system. Grafting only began in the last century.

The almond's more intensive cultivation, with known **cultivars** being grafted, has only been practiced for about a century in Spain and France, and then in California. Irrigation developed primarily in the latter region and is based, as we will see, on specific rootstocks.

In 1950, most of the world's production (at least that production covered by commercial statistics) came from three areas: Italy, Spain, and California, each producing about 40,000 tons of shelled almonds. Fifty years later, production in those three zones has evolved in the following manner:

- Italy dropped from 40,000 tons to 10,000 tons.
- Spain increased from 40,000 tons to 60 to 65,000 tons.
- California produced 400,000 tons in 2003.

The increase in California's production can be attributed to several factors: the species is well adapted to California's climate (little rain from March to October), well-filtered soil, capacity for irrigation, agricultural systems that are quite a bit more vast than in Europe, an entirely mechanized harvest, and excellent commercial organization with a concentration on processing plants (cracking and sorting).

The low prices found in California, which became even lower as the dollar fell to new lows, caused a substantial increase in worldwide consumption, with markets opening up in countries where almonds had been unknown (such as Japan). California's strong production led to a relative stability of worldwide markets, whereas in the 1950s these fluctuated greatly with climatic conditions in the Mediterranean. California's production has also considerably affected Mediterranean growers, who face elevated production costs in rather different orchard systems. In France, after government efforts in the 1960s to promote this area of cultivation led to the creation of 4,940 acres (2,000 ha) of "modern" orchards, the falling markets of the 1980s nearly halted planting and harvesting at a number of orchards.

As the dollar gained strength in the period from 1985 to 1990, which also saw a price increase for California almonds, more productive **varieties** were obtained (which we will address later) and private commercial affiliations helped keep several French growers in business.

Family and Genus

The almond tree, like most fruit trees from the temperate zone, is a member of the Rosaceae family. For a long time, peach trees and almond trees were considered part of a separate genus, *Amygdalus*, in which the almond tree was known as *Amygdalus communis*. Today we recognize the *Amygdalus* group (peach and almond) as a subgenus within the *Prunus* genus (see Appendix A: *Prunus* Botany). The peach and the almond are thought to have evolved from the same ancestor, and their genetic makeups are sufficiently similar that interspecific crosses have been made—both in the past and currently. At present, such crosses are under development at the University of California–Davis to improve flesh firmness and "keeping" quality on the tree in new peach–almond hybrids that are primarily clingstone peach, but with select almond genes.

The almond species is therefore called *Prunus dulcis* Miller (1768) and not *Prunus amygdalus* Batsch (1801), since precedence takes legal priority. The qualifying term *dulcis* is a bit disappointing since the species produces both sweet and bitter seeds, as do the peach tree, the apricot tree, and the European plum tree.

Climatic Limitations

In central Asia, one finds find almond trees cultivated up to 9,840 feet (3,000 m) in altitude, where they are subject to extremely cold winter temperatures between -4 and -13°F (-20 and -25°C). These trees are quite cold-hardy after dry periods lasting from April to December (non-irrigated). Temperatures as low as -22°F (-30°C) will cause all of the floral buds of some trees to fall off. In those orchards, one does find the exceptional tree showing normal fruiting (from non-grafted seedlings), which gives an idea of the range of the species' physiology.

The almond tree has a definite dislike of humid climates, primarily during its juvenile period. That is why this species, which originated on the Iranian plateau, moved west from that region and not east toward

India with its humid climate and monsoons. Similarly in France, almond trees maintain a distance from the Atlantic coast, yet there again the species' adaptability may reveal a surprise or two. The almond is ideally adapted to the Mediterranean climatic latitudes, and its pests have coevolved from the Mediterranean. Thus, it is relatively low-chill requiring, is highly susceptible to brown rot fungal infections at bloom when it rains, and the fruit's flesh (the hull) is prone to splitting during hot, dry summers. If the flesh dries out and splits, the seed (the almond itself) can be mechanically removed.

The first collection of almond tree varieties was planted by the INRA in 1957 in the Bordeaux region. It included around 180 varieties that, for the most part, became infected with various **cryptogamic** illnesses (apple scab, coryneum, blight). Only one variety proved resistant to all those diseases. From a private collection located in Aubenas in the Ardèche region, that variety was baptized 'Ardéchoise'. Unfortunately, apart from its exceptional resistance, it had several faults and was refused entry into the official French catalog of cultivated varieties.

The almond tree is a species of the light. It only grows well when exposed to the sun. As is typical for fruit trees, even on a well-exposed tree, **basal** or central branches tend to produce fewer and often lower-quality flowers. Within continental zones with cold winters and hot, dry summers, it is sometimes surprising to come across almond trees that are quite healthy, as in the Massif Central of France, in Alsace, and in central Europe, where they seem to benefit from good exposure *(photo 1)*.

1. Older almond trees: an almond tree in Mesher and one in Monpazier, both in France.

The greatest fear for future growers and almond tree owners alike is the risk of springtime frosts. Since the almond tree blossoms early (only after *P. mume*, among the stone fruit), the risk of late frosts remains worrisome. In California, almond blooms in the first two weeks of February. Understanding the planting environment is essential to successful planting. We should bear in mind that almond flowers can only survive frost damage (blackening of the ovary) above 27.5°F (-2.5°C). That threshold may vary depending on what climatic conditions preceded the frost and, obviously, according to species.

When morning frosts are preceded by mild periods that initiated vegetative growth (**budbreak** from **dormancy**), flowers are more sensitive to the frost than when they are preceded by cold days and nights. It is a welcome surprise after frosts of 23° to 24°F (-4 to -5°C) if flowers have not been damaged.

There is a range of sensitivity among varieties. In March 1966, a ground frost of 22°F (-5.8°C) occurred near Nîmes, among the INRA collection, when young fruits measured between 0.39 and 0.78 inch (1 and 2 cm). Most of the varieties showed frost damage on 100% of their fruits. Certain Italian varieties from the Pouilles region, however, showed remarkable resistance. 'Tuono' in particular had 0% damage and 'Cristomorto' only 10%. The 'Ferragnès' and 'Ferraduel' varieties (French creations through the INRA), which had a rate of 20% damage, proved that they had inherited this resistance from their Italian progenitors, whereas another variety, 'Aï', showed 80% damage. (For more freezes and frosts, see Appendix B: Freeze/Frost Damage in *Prunus* Species.)

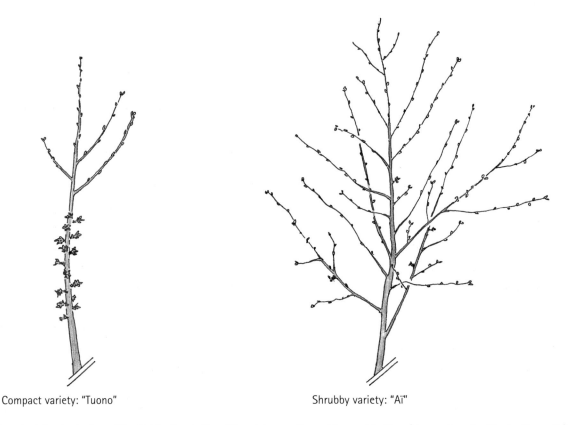

Compact variety: "Tuono"   Shrubby variety: "Aï"

Fig. 1. Branch at the beginning of the 3rd leaf; note the different types of branching and fruiting (observations by Charles Grasselly).

SOIL TYPES

Almond trees are generally grown in deep, loamy, well-drained soils. They can be grown

on marginal soils that are not suitable for most other pomological crops.

Yet we will see in the section "Rootstocks" later in the chapter that by adapting different root systems, one can succeed in growing almond trees in silty, even compact, soil.

TREE MORPHOLOGY

Species Variability

Unlike other species of stone fruit in the *Prunus* genus, such as the peach and the apricot, the almond tree demonstrates an extraordinary range of morphological and physiological characteristics. Here are the reasons why:

- It has a hybrid origin between wild species, and that **hybridization** continues today in the Middle East.
- In some parts of the world, almond is **allogamous**, which means that each seedling is a hybrid.

In regions where seedlings are still widely used, which is the case in numerous countries, certain traits of closely related wild species are found in trees grown in orchards. However, commercially produced almonds in the United States are entirely grafted onto rootstocks, for controlled cropping and fruit characteristics. Selection at the University of California continues for improved disease resistance, drought tolerance, and other desirable characteristics. Elsewhere, the tree may grow tall and straight with few branches, or it may be fuller and hang over *(fig. 1)*; however, a more compact habit is desirable for mechanical harvest, which is the sole form used in U.S. production.

Fruiting occurs in clusters on **spurs** or from individual flowers borne on vegetative shoots *(fig. 2)*.

Fig. 2. Short-branch fructification.

Although the fruit is called a "nut," the entire fruit including the hull is a **drupe**—as are all stone fruits (*Prunus*), olives, and any other fruits in which an outer fleshy part (**exocarp**, or skin; and **mesocarp**, or flesh) surrounds a shell (the pit or stone) of hardened **endocarp** with a seed inside *(photo 2)*. In almonds, however, the hull dries and splits prior to harvest, revealing the fruit's pit.

Fruiting begins in three- to four-year-old trees, with maximum production in six to ten years. Unlike the peach, which is relatively short-lived, almond trees can produce for fifty or more years (however, commercial production is quite low after eighteen to twenty years). Floral buds may produce one flower or two on certain trees. Each almond fruit contains a single seed (consisting of shell and kernel); sometimes two kernels appear within the shell. This condition, called "double" kernel, occurs when both of the ovules within the flower's **pistil** (in the ovary of the pistil) become fertilized. All *Prunus* species have two

2. Almonds at maturity, on the tree.

ovules per ovary, but usually only one is fertilized. "Doubles" are not desirable commercially, and varieties differ in terms of their tendency to produce doubles. The fruit may have a thick shell (as do 'Carmel' and 'Mission') or a "paper" shell (as does 'Nonpareil') that is easy to crack.

To these morphological differences, we may add physiological differences such as extremely early flowering (for example, in December in Nîmes) or extremely late flowering. Almond varieties grown in California begin flowering at the start of February (in the southernmost growing area, such as the lower San Joaquin Valley) and complete their bloom by mid-March (in the northern Sacramento Valley). The bloom time for different varieties is calculated based on 'Nonpareil', the standard for the industry. Maturation periods show quite a range regardless of flowering periods, a common characteristic of other fruit tree species such as

the apple. We can identify four combinations among the known varieties:
- early flowering, late maturation;
- early flowering, early maturation;
- late flowering, late maturation;
- late flowering, early maturation.

The timing of the flowering is a result of the chilling requirements during dormant periods, as well as the heat requirements once chilling requirements have been fulfilled. The timing also varies according to variety; here we can mention the Tunisian varieties in the Sfax region, which have very low chilling requirements and which flower in December in Nîmes. The Italian varieties in the Pouilles region, in contrast, have high chilling requirements and never flower before February 20 in France. Those varieties that do require more chilling are capable, once those needs are met, of flowering at low temperatures ranging from 46° to 50°F (8° to 10°C). Varieties that don't need as much chilling often require higher temperatures in order to flower.

In most Mediterranean countries and in California, later flowering has always been desirable: it poses less risk of frost damage and also allows bee activity. Bees are required for **pollination** and have very little activity below 57°F (14°C). Few almond varieties are **self-fertile** (none in the United States), and even those that are require bee pollination to transfer pollen to the stigma of the pistil for fertilization to occur. In certain areas where there is rarely a risk of frost, varieties with early flowering periods continue to be grown.

PRINCIPLES OF TRAINING

The almond is a small- to medium-size tree with a spreading, open **canopy**, usually 10 to 15 feet (3 to 4.5 m) in circumference in commercial orchards. Even though almond trees are botanically very similar to

3. A fruit branch of a Ferragnès variety in full production.

peach trees and other *Prunus* species, the almond's growth and training are quite particular. The reasons are readily evident. With other fruit tree species, growth is aimed at rapidly producing large, well-colored fruits that are easy to pick, all the while ensuring that their growth will allow new branches to form in the following year. For the peach tree in particular, which must flower on new fruitwood every year, pruning eliminates a large number of branches so as to stimulate new fruitwood, and thinning of young fruits is essential. For the almond tree, in contrast, the fruit's appearance and size are not influenced by the fruit load per branch *(photo 3)*; the goal isn't to produce a lot of flesh, as the husk dries and is not eaten. There is less need to systematically stimulate branch regeneration, as one would do with the peach tree; thus, pruning is a much lower expense with almond. However,

pruning does need to occur periodically, to stimulate new spur production and to allow light penetration into the canopy for more flower production *(photo 4)*. Flowers are borne in leaf axils laterally on spurs or short lateral branches, or laterally on long shoots, and pruning should be selective for flower production.

Starting with a **scion** "headed back" at planting, it is best to promote the development of three or four main **scaffold branches** that will form the framework of a vase shape, and then allow the branching to develop on these scaffolds while thinning them out for light. This will help to promote the largest possible number of flowers. In commercial orchards, trees are planted in rectangular or hexagonal arrangements, with separate rows of pollenizers and main cultivars, usually alternating with each other. Growers use solid rows of pollenizers since trees are shake-harvested,

4. A tree with natural habit. A **reiteration** colonized by fructification.

5. Layered fruiting spurs on old wood.

and this approach makes it easier to harvest without mixing cultivars. Once trees are trained to an open center shape in the first year, they are maintained at maturity by pruning out water sprouts, removing dead and interfering branches, and thinning limbs. Continuing our comparison with the peach tree, we should note that whereas 300 to 500 peaches per tree provide the grower with a profitable harvest (for fresh market peaches, not processing—canning—peaches, where the goal may be 900 to 1,100 fruits per tree), an almond tree needs to produce about 8,000 fruits (for the largest trees) in order to be considered a good harvest. Furthermore, for most varieties of this species, aging fruit organs are formed by overlapping fruit shoots (spurs, *fig. 2* and *photo 5*).

Annual (or biennial) interventions involve simply pruning the excess short- to medium-length branches, thereby preserving sufficient light within the tree's interior. This type of pruning reflects a fundamental criterion of utmost importance: bringing light to the branches. In this way, the tree may reach a height of 13 to 16 feet (4 to 5 m) by four years of age *(photo 6)*.

It is clear that the tree's rapid growth, which relates to its watering and mineral nutrients, will influence its branching. The faster the growth, the longer and more numerous the secondary branches, which would have remained **latent** under slower growth *(photo 6)*. It is not in the grower's interest to over-thin the tree in hopes of promoting faster growth. Keeping an eye on the length of annual shoots, which is the standard practice for California growers, constitutes a fine method allowing for adjustments in pruning density and the use of manure, particularly in terms of nitrogen and irrigation. (See Appendix C: U.S. Standard Fertilizer Equivalents for Nitrogen.) An annual shoot on a one- to three-year-old tree should not measure more than 4 to 5 feet (1.2 to 1.5 m) long. On productive trees, a length of 1.3 to 2 feet (40 to 60 cm) is sufficient *(photo 7)*.

6. An orchard of adult almond trees (8 years).

ROOTSTOCKS

Almond Seedling Rootstocks

When almond trees were first grafted, the initial rootstocks were the seedlings of ungrafted almond trees. These rootstocks present several advantages:

- they are resistant to **chlorosis** in calcareous soils;
- they are resistant to drought;
- they offer increased longevity.
- There are, however, some disadvantages:

- they grow slowly when first planted in an orchard;
- they are highly susceptible to root asphyxiation when there is heavy rainfall on flat terrain or when the soil is silty or clay with few air spaces among soil particles;
- they are susceptible to nematodes in the *Meloidogyne* group;
- they are susceptible to **root disease** (*Armillaria*) and *Phytophthora*.

Improved rootstocks are available for almonds grown in the United States. These have been primar-

7. A scaffold that has developed naturally, with a good balance between growth and fructification.

peaches, plums, and apricots. It has excellent growth, uniformity, and anchorage for young almond trees. It is a low suckering rootstock and has high vigor. This is a newer almond rootstock, and trials are ongoing.

Peach Seedling Rootstocks

Peach rootstocks differ in five main traits:
- resistance to root-knot nematodes;
- tolerance to calcareous soil conditions;
- tolerance to water-logged soil conditions;
- cold hardiness;
- tolerance to peach tree short life (PTSL) associated with the ring nematode.

'Lovell' and 'Nemaguard' are the primary rootstocks for almond in the United States.

'Lovell'—a semi-dwarf rootstock used for almonds, peaches, apricots, plums, nectarines, and prunes. It has good anchorage and vigor, and excellent "wet feet" tolerance. 'Lovell' rootstock prefers well-drained, sandy loam soils and is susceptible to crown rot and crown gall. 'Lovell' also has some susceptibility to bacterial canker and nematodes.

'Nemaguard'—This peach seedling rootstock is root-knot nematode resistant and very vigorous. It is susceptible to root-lesion nematode, bacterial canker, and oak root fungus. 'Nemaguard' rootstock prefers sandy soils.

'Nemaguard' offers certain advantages: rapid growth of young trees, resistance to nematodes (only among certain seedlings), and uniformity throughout orchards. This rootstock is the most often used in California orchards, accounting for more than 80% of trees. In the San Joaquin and Sacramento valleys' deep alluvial soil, roots grow deeper to anchor the tree. In France, along the Costière du Gard, strong winds have been known to uproot almond trees that had been grafted onto peach trees, whereas the same

ily chosen for their resistance to soil-borne diseases such as crown gall and *Phytophthora,* their resistance to nematodes, and their growth habit on certain soils.

'Hansen 536 Hybrid'—used for almonds, peaches, apricots, and nectarines. It has excellent anchorage and is tolerant of salinity, alkalinity, pH, and boron soils, as compared to all other rootstocks. It is moderately resistant to root-knot nematodes. It does require deep and well-drained soils.

'Krymsk 86'—In terms of grafting compatibility, this almond rootstock is compatible with almonds, type of trees grafted onto a different grafting stock were perfectly resistant. Almond trees are more prone to blow over in strong winds than some other fruit trees; storms often occur once almonds have already leafed out, and their leaves offer more resistance to wind—thereby "catching" the wind.

Peach–Almond Hybrid Rootstocks

These rootstocks are more prone to bacterial canker disease when grown on sandy soils, indicating that they are more stressed in soils that do not hold water well.

'Bright's Hybrid'—This rootstock produces large, extremely vigorous, hardy, **self-sterile**, productive, and regular-bearing (not **alternate-bearing**) trees. Created in the past in France as a peach tree rootstock for calcareous soil, these are among the best possible rootstocks for the almond tree since they combine the advantages of both parent species:

- rapid installation and hardiness among young trees;
- good tree development and great longevity;
- resistance to limestone and drought, an aspect inherited from the rootstock's almond tree parent.

Similar selections in California have proven resistant to nematodes; in Spain, growers have had greater success producing rootstocks from hardwood cuttings. The peach x almond hybrid GF-677 rootstock created for the INRA by R. Bernhard and Ch. Grasselly, although sensitive to the *M. javanica* nematode in certain areas of the world, offers the advantage of being the most resistant to humidity among the peach x almond hybrids.

The distance between planting remains a continued source of debate among growers. Considering distances that are ideal for the tree and narrower distances that allow greater production per acre, the compromise is generally between 20 x 16 feet (6m x 5m) and 23 x 20 feet (7m x 6m). (The first measure is "between row" and the second is "within row" spacing.) Almond orchards shaped into 16 x 8 foot (5m x 2.5m) fruit hedges have been attempted in Spain and California, as well as in the Perpignan region of France. After the third-year or fourth-year harvest, those trees lacked adequate light, resulting in little to no flower production in the lowest portion of the canopy.

Plum Seedling Rootstock

'Marianna' (Myrobalan-Marianna plums: P. cerasifera and interspecific hybrids having P. cerasifera as a parent) is a rootstock that can be used with plums, prunes, almonds, and apricots. 'Mariana' rootstock tends to form shallow roots that project outward rather than downward, and root suckering can be a problem.

VARIETIES GROWN IN THE UNITED STATES

Dozens of almond cultivars are grown commercially around the world, with unique selections bred for local growing conditions and marketing preferences. All almonds grown commercially in the United States are found in California, which produces approximately 80% of the world's crop. The top 10 almond cultivars in California are:

1. 'Nonpareil'   6. 'Ne Plus Ultra'
2. 'Carmel'   7. 'Peerless'
3. 'Mission (Texas)' 8. 'Thompson'
4. 'Merced'   9. 'Butte'
5. 'Price Cluster' 10. 'Monterey'

In California, almond cultivars can also be divided by "classification" of nut (seed of the drupe; not a true nut, botanically), which depends on the seed size and shape, the hardness of the shell (exocarp), the ease of skin removal (by blanching), and the ultimate marketing purpose for the seed. The majority of almond production in California falls into the following three major classifications: Nonpareil, California, and Mission. Some varieties may fall under more than one classification since they have characteristics of one type, such as Mission, but are also blanchable, a requirement of the California classification. 'Nonpareil' is the most commonly produced variety: it is easy to shell (the shell can actually be broken by hand), and it has a large kernel and good taste.

The classification Nonpareil includes cultivars with the widest range of uses among marketing categories; they are readily blanched (for skin removal) and cut for

VARIETY	CLASSIFICATION TYPE	HARVEST	SHELL	NUT
'Nonpareil'	Nonpareil type	Blooms and is harvested early.	Soft shell; brown color; high suture opening.	Medium, flat shape; light color; smooth surface.
'Carmel'	California type	Harvested 25 to 30 days after Nonpareil	Soft shell; good shell integrity; fair suture opening.	Medium, narrow shape; slightly wrinkled surface.
'Butte'	California and Mission type	Harvested 25 to 30 days after 'Nonpareil'; versatile kernel applications.	Hard shell; good shell integrity; no suture opening.	Small, short, wide shape; wrinkled surface.
'Padre'	California and Mission type	Harvested 25 to 30 days after 'Nonpareil'; similar to 'Butte'.	Hard shell; good shell integrity; no suture opening.	Small, short, wide shape; dark brown; wrinkled surface.
'Mission'	Mission type	Harvested 40 to 60 days after 'Nonpareil'; strong flavor; not blanchable.	Hard shell; good shell integrity; no suture opening.	Small, short, wide shape; dark brown; deep, wrinkled surface.
'Monterey'	California type	Harvested 40 to 60 days after 'Nonpareil'; high percentage of doubles.	Hard shell; brown color; smooth surface; low suture opening.	Large, long, narrow shape; deep wrinkled surface.
'Sonora'	California type	Harvested 7 to 10 days after 'Nonpareil'; alternative to 'Nonpareil'.	Paper shell; dark brown color; rough surface; high suture opening.	Large, long, narrow shape; light color; smooth surface.
'Fritz'	California and Mission type	Harvested 40 to 60 days after 'Nonpareil'.	Soft shell; light color; good shell integrity; low suture opening.	Small, medium-plump shape; dark brown; fairly wrinkled surface.
'Peerless'	In-shell / Hard-shell	Harvested 7 to 10 days after 'Nonpareil'.	Hard shell; light color; good shell integrity; smooth surface; no suture opening.	Medium, wide shape; fairly wrinkled surface.
'Price'	California type	Harvested 7 to 10 days after 'Nonpareil'; high percentage of doubles.	Paper shell; dark brown color; rough surface; high suture opening.	Small, short, narrow shape; fairly wrinkled surface.

Adapted from the Almond Board of California's "Almond Variety Market Classification," www.almondboard.com.

processed forms. A thin outer shell and smooth kernel allow easy, blemish-free processing. As a result, Nonpareil almonds are used anywhere an attractive appearance or a strong almond identification is important.

The California classification includes a number of varieties that are blanchable and used primarily in manufactured products. California-type almonds have a wide range of shell hardness, kernel shape, skin color, and surface characteristics. As a result, they are quite adaptable and well suited for nearly any process or application.

Mission almonds have hard shells, and their kernels are small, wide, and often plump. The kernel skin is generally darker than Nonpareil and wrinkled, which enhances salt and flavor adherence. Blanching is not as common for this type.

HARVEST AND POSTHARVEST HANDLING

Maturity and Harvest Method

The hull splits at maturity, and nuts physically separate from the tree at this point. Trees are harvested when the hulls of fruit in the interior of the canopy are open, since these split last. The seed coat turns brown during the drying-out process of maturation. Delay in harvest increases the risk of infestation by navel orangeworm.

In California, trees are harvested by means of mechanical tree shakers. The shakers may damage young trees, so they are harvested by hand knocking in the first few years. Nuts are left to dry on the ground for one to two weeks, and then are swept into windrows for harvesting.

Postharvest Handling and Storage

Fruits may be dried and hulled immediately, or stockpiled for fumigation against navel orangeworm after harvest. Nuts are dried by forced hot air until their moisture content reaches 5 to 7%. Nuts are then dehulled and shelled. In-shell nuts can be stored in bins for weeks or months until final processing. Nuts are then shelled and sorted for size and appearance. Last, nuts are bleached for color improvement, then salted, roasted, and/or flavored before packaging.

It is possible to store almonds for months either in-shell or shelled if dry, or for very long periods (years) when frozen. Commercially, nuts for long-term storage are fumigated for navel orangeworm and kept at temperatures below 40°F (4°C).

APPLE

Authors	Pierre-Éric LAURI
	Jean-Marie LESPINASSE
Collaborator	Michel RAMONGUILHEM

GENERAL OVERVIEW

History, Distribution, and Production

Apple trees were present in the Tertiary period. Humans domesticated and improved them very early on. Propagation through grafting has been practiced for at least 2,000 years. Trees were cultivated in Greece around 600 BC, but it wasn't until the eighteenth and nineteenth centuries that the creation of new varieties started, thanks to controlled **hybridization**. Pollen from the flowers of one variety was added to the female reproductive apparatus (style) on flowers from another variety in order to obtain seeds that combined characteristics from both parents. There are an estimated 6,000 named varieties today, among about fifteen primary species within the *Malus* genus—two European, four North American, and the rest Asian. In reality, this number is probably an underestimation when we consider local dessert and cider-producing varieties. Most apples grown in North America are domestic varieties of *M. pumila* Mill., the common apple of Europe.

The apple tree has a great capacity for adapting to a range of soils, temperatures, and rainfall amounts *(photo 1)*. However, it does require a period of cold (which may be partially replaced with dryness or **defoliation** in other climatic zones), allowing for good synchronization of vegetation initiation in the spring. The apple is usually found between latitudes 30° and 60° in both hemispheres, as well as in intertropical areas (such as Indonesia), where it grows in higher altitudes.

France is the second largest European producer,

As for cider apples, no text mentions them until the eleventh century. Even though they are found primarily in four regions—Brittany, Upper and Lower Normandy, and the Loire Valley (except Vendée)—cider apples probably originated in the south, in northwestern Spain and in Basque country.

Cider apples are usually high in tannins and are practically inedible. They are divided into three categories: sweet, bittersweet, and sharp. Annual production is highly irregular due to the difficulty of these varieties in producing for two consecutive years (strong **alternate bearing** in production). Globally, there was a drastic drop from 1965 (2 million tons) to 1990 (650,000 tons). Currently, modern high-density orchards are filling in where older, low-density orchards have disappeared: in 2002, a total of 600,000 tons were produced. Apple juice or cider in the United States is typically made from varieties that have been historically valued for both fresh eating and juice (such as 'Gravenstein', which is largely absent from all but local markets).

WORLDWIDE PRODUCTION

Worldwide production of apple trees averages around 60 million tons, with 30 million from China, 9.8 million from the European Union, and 5.5 million from North America (approximately 700,000 tons exported as fresh market fruit; much less as juice). The United States is not among the top 10 worldwide producers for export. Those producers are, in order: Mexico, Canada, Taiwan, Dubai (UAE), China, India, Indonesia, the United Kingdom, Saudi Arabia, and Thailand. The top 5 producing countries (for both domestic and export markets) are, in order: China, the United States, Poland, Turkey, and Italy. The United States is a net importer of apple juice. The major production states for apple in the United States include, in order: Washington, New York, Michigan, Pennsylvania, and California.

Along with grapes, apples come in third in terms of worldwide production, after oranges and bananas.

1. Apple trees have a great ability to adapt (Cortland variety in Quebec).

after Italy, with an average of 2 million tons per year, from about 133,436 acres (54,000 ha). There are three principal production areas: the Rhône Valley and the Southeast, the Loire Valley, and the Southwest. But this species is also grown in every corner of France, with each region having its own varieties, commerce, and expertise.

Other countries, such as Germany, have extensive family orchards, to the point that irregular production from one year to the next can affect European prices.

Harvest extends from mid-July to early November, and the fruit's ability to be stored makes it easy to enjoy apples all year long. In fact, numerous **varieties** will ripen slowly in fruit bins over the course of fall and winter; others do better in coolers, with temperatures adapted to their ripening cycle. Commercial storage is typically in controlled or modified atmospheres, with ethylene (a ripening regulator) removal or inhibition to regulate ripening. In fact, proper temperature control in coolers can help maintain certain varieties until the following harvest!

APPLE DISTRIBUTION IN THE UNITED STATES

Distribution of apple varieties in the United States is partially based on chilling requirements. Most apple varieties require 500 to 1,000 hours at or below 45°F (7.5°C). Low-chill varieties (requiring 300 to 500 chilling hours) include 'Anna', 'Dorsett Golden', 'Tropical Beauty', 'Beverly Hills', 'Gordon', 'Fuji', 'Pink Lady', 'Pettingil', and 'Ein Shemer'. All these varieties can be grown in home gardens in Southern California, and 'Gala' can be grown everywhere in Southern California except near the coast, where chilling is insufficient. Low-chill varieties may also be found in Texas and Florida. However, many of the red-skinned varieties that can be grown in low-chill areas, like California, may not produce sufficient red coloration for the commercial market. Certain cultural practices, such as the use of white floating row covers (for example, ExtenDay), increase coloration. Some rootstocks lower the chilling requirement; French researchers have found that 'Rome Beauty' apple requires less chilling when grown on M ('East Malling') 26 rootstock than when grown on MM 104 or MM 106 rootstocks.

Cold hardiness can also be a limiting factor in the distribution of apple varieties. Late fall or early winter injuries can occur when the beginning of the dormant season is mild while leaves are present and young trees are still growing, and when temperatures suddenly plunge below freezing for several days. Single-grafted trees that are young (ten to twelve years old or less) are especially susceptible, with the main injury being to lower limbs, limb crotches, and the trunk. (See the later discussion of rootstocks and training for vigor and hardiness.)

Botanical Classification: Species and Varieties

Apple trees belong to the Rosaceae family, the subfamily of Maloideae (fruit trees with seeds) and the genus *Malus*. The pear tree, from the *Pyrus* genus, also belongs to the Maloideae subfamily. The base chromosomal number is 17. Some varieties are **diploids** ($2n = 2x = 34$). Others are **triploids** ($2n = 3x = 51$) and are generally plumper, such as 'Belle de Boskoop' or the family of Reinettes from Canada.

The *Malus* genus includes about twenty-five species that originated in Europe, Asia (from the Balkans to China and Japan; from the Caucasus and Turkistan to Siberia), and North America. The region with the highest diversity of apple trees spans the Caucasus and Turkistan.

For a long time, the apple tree was collectively called *Malus pumila* Mill., named for a species that was endemic to a zone reaching from the Balkans to the Altai Mountains. Yet cultivated apple trees resulted from natural, ancient crossings among several species in the *Malus* genus—especially *Malus sylvestris* Mill., a European species (the cider apple seems particularly marked by this "woodland parent"); *Malus baccata* Borkh., which transmitted its resistance to cold; and *Malus sieversii* Ledeb. M. Roem, which is endemic to central Asia.

For cider apples, it is possible that through hybridization the *Malus sylvestris* transmitted its woodland characteristics to new varieties, developing more robust

2. A variety that naturally bears one single fruit per inflorescence.

trees than those that yield dessert fruits. In the Middle Ages, the Biscaye nobility exported cider to Normandy and down to the Mediterranean. Apple tree grafts and transplants from Biscay were brought to the Cotentin shores starting in the tenth century.

Today we know that different species in this genus can interbreed without difficulty. With domestication, controlled breeding aims to maintain certain characteristics—notably, resistance to diseases. This resistance may be quite specific, as is the case, for example, with apple scab resistance in *Malus floribunda* Sieb., a highly floriferous species used as a pollinator in production orchards and as a decorative garden tree. Others may confer a broader ability to survive harmoniously in nature, a rustic characteristic associated with remarkable fruit quality: this is the case for the 'Reinette de Brive' apple ('De l'Estre').

Characteristics that are more physiological and

naturally transmissible may improve the plant's fruiting behavior. Specifically, this means the possibility of yielding just one fruit per **inflorescence** *(photo 2)*. These varieties will develop a moderate fruiting corresponding to the tree's potential vegetation without the need for much human intervention.

The botanical single species of apple tree therefore doesn't exist. The cultivated apple tree is named *Malus* x *domextica* Borkh., with the x indicating its pluri-specific origin. One may also hear it called *Malus domestica* Borkh or *Malus* Mill.

Numerous varieties are cultivated in French gardens. The range of soil and climate (referred to collectively as *pedoclimatic*) differences in France has progressively caused a varietal selection adapted to each region. Thus, in each region, there is activity associated with preserving each genetic heritage.

In terms of genetic diversity, the largest French conservatories (where protecting genetic heritage and genetic evaluation are the primary missions) include the INRA research stations, the Porquerolles conservatory, the Centre Régional de Ressources Génétiques (CRRG) in Nord-Pas-de-Calais, and the regional plant conservatory in Aquitaine. The latter published an ambitious work in 1995 discussing local and historical cultivation heritage in southwestern France: *Les Fruits retrouvés, histoire et diversité des espèces anciennes du Sud-Ouest* (Éditions du Rouergue). The CRRG in the north published a pomological text in 1996 entitled *Les Pommes du Nord*.

Danon (L'Association Danone pour les Fruits) compiled a full inventory between 1999 and 2001 of all organizations working on establishing the fruit tree heritage of France. This is available at www.patrimoinefruitier.org. There are 253 organizational collections included in the repertory for twenty-one different species, including Mediterranean species and a few rare species. The National Germplasm Repository (USDA) in

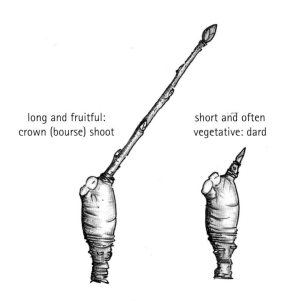

long and fruitful:
crown (bourse) shoot

short and often
vegetative: dard

Fig. 1. An inflorescence (left) and a bourse shoot (right).

Corvallis, Oregon, retains the collection of *Malus, Pyrus,* and relatives in the United States.

Conventional apple tree cultivation is much less rich. Only about twenty apple varieties are grown in France, and much like the rest of Europe, only six varieties account for 80% of production: 'Golden Delicious' (representing 35% alone), the American reds, the bi-colored group ('Gala', 'Fuji', 'Braeburn'), and 'Granny Smith'. The U.S. varieties of traditional top commercial production have included, in order: 'Delicious' (all red strains), 'Golden Delicious', 'McIntosh', 'Rome Beauty', 'York', 'Jonathan', 'Granny Smith', 'Stayman', 'Newton', 'Winesap', and 'Gravenstein'. In the last twenty-five years, newer varieties from domestic (Cornell University, Geneva, NY, and others) and international breeding programs have supplanted many of these in commercial production. The newer varieties include: 'Fuji', 'Gala, 'Pink Lady', 'Jonagold', 'Honey Crisp', 'Idared', and 'Empire'.

"Heirloom" or "heritage" varieties may be found in many local markets, particularly in northern states in the eastern United States.

THE TREE

Floral and Vegetative Characteristics

INFLORESCENCE, FLOWER, AND FRUIT
The apple tree inflorescence comprises two parts that evolve successively as spring growth starts: a **basal** part composed of leaves and vegetative buds, and then a terminal part composed of the actual flowers grouped in a **corymb** *(fig. 1)*.

This inflorescence corresponds to the transformed **meristem** located in a terminal bud. The carrier axis for this terminal bud may be short **spurs** (barely an inch or more, or a few mm) or long shoots (up to 5 feet, or 1.5 m), sometimes as lateral buds on one-year-old shoots. Those with inflorescences are generally shorter. Any continued growth on this inflorescence will only occur through a developing lateral bud located at the leaf axil. This new shoot is called a "bourse shoot" *(photo 3)*. In general, the terminal bud on a very short bourse shoot will remain vegetative in the following year. If

FLOWER

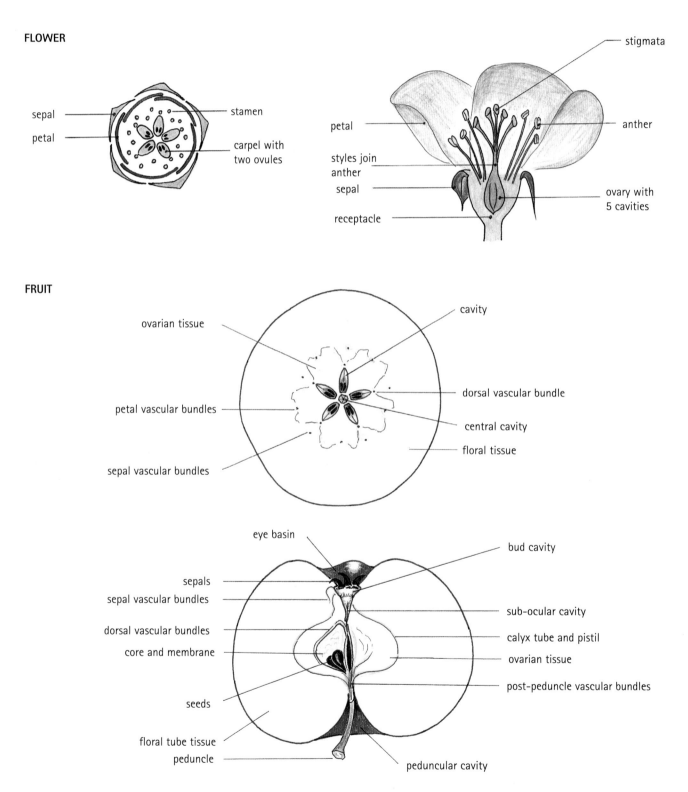

sepal

petal

stamen

carpel with
two ovules

stigmata

petal

styles join
anther

sepal

receptacle

anther

ovary with
5 cavities

FRUIT

ovarian tissue

cavity

petal vascular bundles

dorsal vascular bundle

central cavity

floral tissue

sepal vascular bundles

eye basin

bud cavity

sepals

sepal vascular bundles

dorsal vascular bundles

core and membrane

seeds

floral tube tissue

peduncle

sub-ocular cavity

calyx tube and pistil

ovarian tissue

post-peduncle vascular bundles

peduncular cavity

Fig. 2. Flower and fruit evolution (cross-section and lengthwise).

the bourse shoot is longer (1 to 8 inches or 3 to 20 cm), flowering is more common. This is known as a "crown brindle" *(fig. 1)*.

The apple tree blossom contains male organs (which provide pollen) and female organs (which collect the pollen and bear fruit after **cross-fertilization**). It is considered type 5 (5 sepals, 5 petals, 20 **stamens**, 5 carpels) and has an inferior ovary *(fig. 2)*. Since the apple tree has **self-incompatible** pollen, fertilization is **allogamous**: a flower from one variety will only bear fruit if it is pollinated by another variety. It is therefore necessary to mix trees of different varieties with concurrent blossoming periods. The pollen is transported by insects (in a process known as **entomophily**) such as honeybees and bumblebees.

Apples, like pears, are pome fruits (not **drupes**, as

3. "Bourse on bourse" branching.

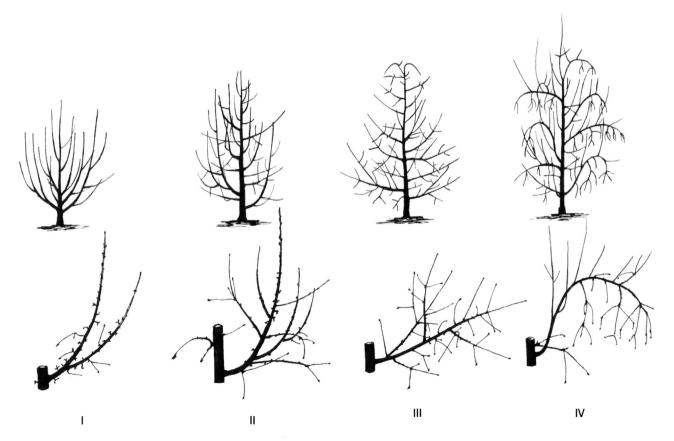

I   II   III   IV

Fig. 3. Four types of training systems.

4. Type IV fructification, Rome Beauty.

stone fruits are), because they form from the union of the ovary (**pericarp**) and the receptacle (extracarpellary tissue below the ovary).

MORPHOLOGY

The characteristics of the wood (more or less flexible), as well as the placement of inflorescences (spur-types vs. non-spur and intermediate types), yield a wide range of shapes—and therefore fruits. Varieties with strong terminal blossoming on long branches ('Yellow Bellflower', 'Reinette du Mans', 'Granny Smith', 'Pink Lady') have a greater tendency to bend than do varieties that fruit on short branches (trees with columnar habits or spurs; for example, 'Reine des Reinettes', 'Api

Rouge', and 'Cassou'). Spurs that are two years old and older begin bearing flowers.

There are four types of trees *(fig. 3)*:

- Type I, the "spur-type," or columnar, trees. These trees have a thin trunk and few branches with short laterals,bearing fruit on their entire length.
- Type II, of which 'Reine des Reinettes' is a good example. As with the preceding type, laterals bearing fruit are short, but here the trunk has more and stronger **scaffold branches**.
- Type III, represented by 'Golden Delicious'. The trunk is dominant in relation to the scaffold branches. There are few short laterals and a more natural bowing of the branches.

5. Leaf thinning and terminal fruiting on type IV.

The Cultivated Apple Tree: A Composite

The variety is grafted onto a root system according to different criteria. This association permits solutions for particular growing conditions:

- for all types of soil, from the lightest (sandy) to the heaviest (clay soils);
- as prevention against excess water from poorly controlled winter stagnation, or the opposite, where soil is highly filtering and very dry;
- in order to determine the tree's final volume. Its height will be based on the rootstock and may reach from 6.5 to 16.5 feet (2 to 5 m). Its volume will be from 71 cubic feet to 883 cubic feet (2 m^3 to 25 m^3).

The indirect consequence: a so-called hardy, vigorous rootstock generally delays flowering, whereas a tree grafted on a weaker rootstock starts fruiting in the second year after planting. In fact, grafted onto any given rootstock, each variety will demonstrate a specific behavior. Growers should discuss varieties with individuals who have a fair amount of experience with them (at botanical conservatories and nurseries or with other novices, etc.). Another effect of less vigorous rootstocks: the higher the grafting point is from the ground, the more it will transmit its less vigorous tendencies to the variety.

Overall, two situations may arise. For less voluminous trees (if available space is limited, 106 to 141 cubic feet, or 3 to 4 m^3), type M9 rootstocks are preferable since they are less vigorous (photo 6). Among them, there are two levels of vigor: the least vigorous, 'Pajam®' 1 and M9 NAKB, and the moderately vigorous, 'Pajam®' 2 and M9 EMLA. This distinction is important, as it permits better balance between growth and fruiting for each of the chosen variety–rootstock unions. These rootstocks are commonly used in production orchards. However, their technical requirements are more demanding (fertile soil, the need to control fruit

- Type IV, represented by 'Granny Smith' and 'Rome Beauty' (photo 4). The trunk and branches are readily comparable; for a few varieties, certain trees may take on a typical dome shape. Basal branches are less hardy because of two factors: bud latency at the base of vigorous branches (photo 5), and high mortality for the more heavily flowering spurs (**extinction** phenomenon). The fruiting zone for type-IV trees is distributed at the tips of branches, which is why these varieties generally display a more hanging (pendulous) habit.

In general, types I and II have a naturally occurring alternate bearing habit. By contrast, type-IV varieties are relatively consistent in their production.

6. Grafting point on an M9 rootstock. It should be 15 cm above the ground.

more cold hardiness: 'Yellow Transparent', 'Hibernal', 'Haralson', 'Canada Baldwin', 'Antonovka', 'Charlamoff', 'Duchess', 'Wealthy', 'Hawkeye Greening', and 'Hyslop Crab'. In addition, 'East Malling' (M16 and M2) rootstocks are more hardy, M9 is moderately hardy, and M4 and M7 are cold-intolerant under these conditions. When temperatures during the dormant season are extreme (-22 to -47°F or -30 to -44°C), 'Golden Delicious' and 'Delicious' **scions** have been killed, even when planted on hardy rootstocks and when fully dormant; but injury was less pronounced or avoided in the upper range of these temperatures when interstocks (above, except for 'Hawkeye Greening') were used. Heavy sod with low N (nitrogen) inputs in late summer (to discourage late growth) reduces the tendency for frost tenderness. (See the appendix, "U.S. Standard Fertilizer Equivalents for Nitrogen") Generally, those rootstocks that induce early maturity in the scion, including M7 and M9, tend to render trees more freeze tolerant of fall freezes than of mid-winter freezes.

PRINCIPLES OF TRAINING

The Basics

As of the past two or three decades, a better understanding of apple trees has allowed us to discover that certain natural behaviors in this species (not provoked by pruning) are rather remarkable. Here are two examples:

- During its first years of growth, the young transplant, when left alone, will construct a solid and harmonious edifice around its trunk. Each variety, in fact, has its own habit and shape. Generally, this natural **architecture of the tree** is better adapted to early and consistent fruit production than are artificial shapes imposed on the tree from pruning (vase/open center, palmette, etc.).
- Later, after fruiting branches develop, fruiting

ing by suppressing excess fruits at the end of May, and regular irrigation).

If you desire a more voluminous tree, you should choose a rootstock from types MM106, M7, or 'Supporter®' 4 PI 80. The root transplant for these more vigorous rootstocks will help in adapting to poorer, more difficult soils and less frequent waterings. The M7 is more rustic and less susceptible to collar rot. There is one small drawback: the emission of root suckers (growing from the rootstock to the ground).

Note that trees grown with these rootstocks require specifically adapted materials *(photo 11)* for the various interventions (pruning, harvest, etc.).

Certain trunkstocks (obtained by "layered" propagation) that provide a double-grafted (layered) tree provide

7. Structural harmony in an apple tree that was never pruned.

we know that the best way to produce a sufficient quantity of high-quality fruit is to let the trees grow freely, balancing growth with fruiting by using our knowledge of the trees' vegetative behavior.

Thus, a different perspective is offered to us: respect the tree and promote its natural functions as it develops and sets fruit. This requires looking at the plant in a different light. It is necessary to observe it and understand it in order to better guide its own abilities. Therefore we switch from "pruning" to "training," from constraining to educating. How satisfying!

More natural training has allowed us to observe the extraordinary diversity of varietal behaviors *(photo 7)*. In particular, we have noticed:

- the erect habit of 'De l'Estre' that delays its fruiting. The bending of its branches may induce earlier blossoming.
- the natural mortality and **dormancy** in a fair number of buds (only one out of four, or 25% of function) on several varieties. This promotes a good natural balance between a branch's strength and its floral buds.
- a great disparity in the number of fruits per inflorescence, with certain varieties such as 'Reinette Dorée' yielding up to five fruits and requiring more thinning. Others are quite the opposite, yielding only one or two fruits per inflorescence.

These three examples demonstrate the naturally advantageous conditions that affect flowering and quality fruit production: branch horizontality, a moderate number of fruit buds, and one to two fruits per inflorescence.

Growers should carefully consider the stages from transplanting the scion to fruiting:

- the development of the tree until it reaches a balance between growth and **fruit set**;
- the fruiting branch and its different modes of fruiting;
- the **spur system's** autonomy and durability.

occurs according to specific modes for each variety (diversity of spur disposition on the branch, number of fruits per corymb, etc.).

Certain varieties may produce satisfactorily every year without any intervention. Others can only do so if we help to control their productivity. Respecting the natural process of tree growth and fruiting means that we need to modify our ways of thinking.

In fact, shaping a tree with clippers transforms and sometimes destroys its natural mechanisms. It forces the tree into an artificial shape and fruiting pattern that are quite contrary to its natural functions. Today

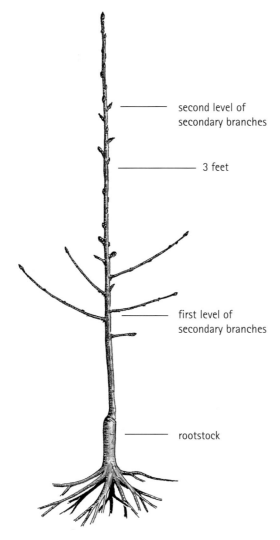

second level of
secondary branches

3 feet

first level of
secondary branches

rootstock

Fig. 4. A grafted scion at planting.

The Tree's Development During
the First Three to Four Years

As we said in the introduction to this book, it is easy today to recognize that humans, in a desire to "shape" fruit trees and "make them fruit," have imposed behaviors on the plant that are quite distant from its natural modes of development. Indeed, each variety has its own modes for branching and fruiting. Using its natu-

ral functions offers us a double reward: starting in the second year, the first fruits appear and we have the pleasure of discovering "the tree itself."

A few words of advice for planting *(fig. 4)*:

- It is essential that planting occur in the fall and winter (dormant season), for apple roots may not stop growing over the winter. The earlier you plant (in the dormant season), the better the conditions will be for springtime growth.
- When buying young scions, make sure they have good roots. This is fundamental. A one-year-old nursery tree, 4 to 6 feet (1.2 to 1.8 m) tall, with a good root system, will establish best and is generally "feathered" in that it already has the first scaffold limbs present. A small tree with a good root system will transplant better than a large tree.
- At planting, renew the cuts on the root system if the roots appear to be restricted by the pot (unless the plant is "bare-root"). If the roots appear to be dry, soak them in water for a day before planting.
- With less vigorous rootstocks such as M9, make sure the grafting point is at least 6 inches (15 cm) above the ground *(photo 6)*.
- Do not pack the soil too densely around the roots; water if the soil is not very moist (which may happen even in winter!), and use stakes.
- Do not cut the scion back. Ask the nursery to deliver it whole.

The first year, upkeep for the young transplant will require a few careful interventions so as to avoid imbalances and to promote structural harmony. First, you should know which type of tree you would like *(fig. 5)*. Depending on whether you keep or suppress secondary branches on the scion, you will cause the tree to either structure itself from its base (multi-axis) or only develop on a single axis (central leader). Looking at *fig. 5*, at left (A) the **secondary shoots** are often present on scions and are "programmed" to compete with the axis. If you

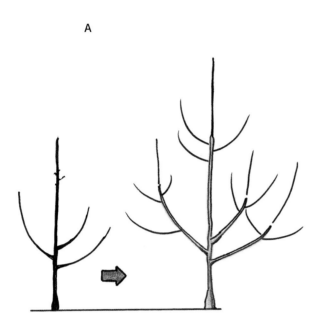

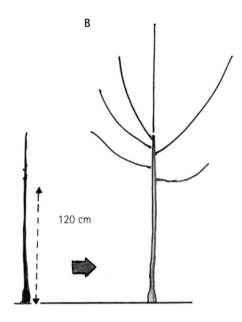

120 cm

Fig. 5. Two possible planting methods.

keep them, your tree will develop several axes or a strong basal structure. A scion without secondary branches may grow young sprouts the first year and at the same level as secondary branches, but these will be less hardy.

As shown at right (B) in *fig. 5*, the suppression of secondary branches during planting up to 3 feet (1 m) from the ground for M9 and 4 feet (1.2 m) for MM106, combined with debudding the basal sections in the spring, will promote growth in the scion's **distal** section. Lateral branchings on the trunk will become future fruiting branches. This is the most natural solution and the easiest shape to obtain. The trees in the collection at the Aquitaine conservatory as well as in the Nord-Pas-de-Calais are trained in this way. Do not let the first shoots bear fruit, except perhaps one for your own pleasure!

CENTRAL LEADER TREES

A central leader tree has one main, upright trunk, called the "leader." Branching should begin on the leader 24 to 36 inches (61 to 91 cm) above the soil surface to allow

work under the tree. The first year, you should select three to four branches, collectively called a "scaffold whorl," from the "feathers" produced in the nursery. The selected branches should be spaced uniformly around the trunk—not directly across from or above one another, or shading will result as the limbs develop. These initial, main laterals will develop into the "primaries" or "scaffolds." Above the first scaffold whorl, you should leave an area of 18 to 24 inches (46 to 61 cm) without branching in order to allow light penetration to the first whorl. Then develop a second whorl of scaffolds at that level. Alternating scaffold whorls and "light slots" will create the central leader structure (resembling a Christmas tree), with progressively narrower whorls moving upward and allowing good light penetration at all levels.

For newly planted trees that have no feathers or that have branches in undesirable configurations, you should wait until just before the buds start to grow in the spring to "head back," or cut, the unbranched central leader to 3 feet (1 m) above the soil surface in order to encourage new lateral branching. Some

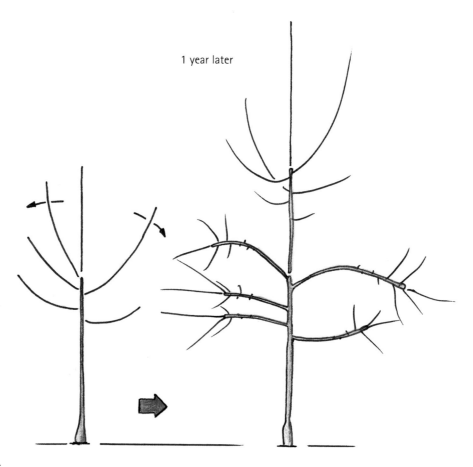

1 year later

Fig. 6. In the second year.

branches may grow mostly upright (the natural tendency for apple). When new growth is 3 to 4 inches (8 to 10 cm) long, identify the most upright shoot that will continue to be the central leader. Leave it, and remove all new shoots growing 3 to 4 inches immediately below this new terminal to prevent competition (or you will end up with a very confused tree!). This will also encourage lateral growth in the area 6 to 14 inches (15 to 36 cm) below the headed **apex** where **apical dominance** by the central leader lessens. Branches that form 6 to 14 inches below the cut tip of the tree are less vigorous, less upright, and easier to train as productive scaffold limbs by bending or spreading.

When the lateral branches (primaries, scaffolds, or the eventual secondaries), or scaffold branches, are 3 to 6 inches (8 to 15 cm) long, they should be spread to a wider **insertion angle** that will provide a stronger framework for fruit production and encourage spur (in spur-bearing varieties) and flower bud formation. You can use toothpicks or clothespins to prop the young branches out to a 50 to 60 degree angle, although commercial plastic spreaders are available from orchard supply companies. This angle will slow vegetative growth, promote lateral branches, and promote **precocity**. Tying down limbs or using hanging weights will achieve the same effect.

During the first and second year, keep all of the

shoots except those that are crossing or in undesirable locations (as well as strong suckers or water sprouts that will compete with the central leader). Then, if necessary, bend any competing branches on the axis *(fig. 6)*. This procedure should take place either in September of the first year, or during blossoming, or in September of the second year, depending on how vigorous the transplant is. Only bend branches that are at least 24 inches (60 cm) in length, and position them below horizontal with string or wire. Do not allow **reiteration** below 3 to 4 feet (1 to 1.2 m). If you've decided on a more structured form with several axes *(fig. 5A)*, do the same for each branch.

Fruiting occurs in the second year in precocious varieties. You can already keep the fruits: their presence stimulates photosynthesis! Here is a good gauge for obtaining a satisfying balance between growth and production: keep five fruits per square foot (cm^2) of trunk cross-section (measuring 12 inches, or 30 cm, from the ground, above the grafting point), or twelve to fifteen apples if the cross-section is 0.38 square inches (2.5 cm^2). Apples in the terminal position of branches should be kept in order to induce natural bowing (in this situation, you may keep two apples per terminal bourse). Then choose from those inserted directly on the trunk; finally, if necessary, those in lateral positions on branches (a single fruit per inflorescence in these last two cases).

During the second and third year, depending on the tree's vigor, let nature take its course. Growth in distal sections and the coming fruiting will already be preparing to slow the axis. For it is fruit that stops the tree, not clippers.

And so you should have understood: oil your clippers and put them aside. Someday they may help in making props for your green peas!

DORMANT PRUNING VS. SUMMER PRUNING

Pruning apple trees during the winter will invigorate the trees and cause them to grow and branch more during the following season (desirable if more vigor is needed, which is rare in mature trees). To promote scaffold branch development, cut the central leader 20 to 28 inches (51 to 71 cm) above the highest usable scaffold whorl in late winter or early spring in regions prone to late frosts. Once growth resumes, training can proceed as described above.

Summer pruning reduces vigor. During summer, prune to remove all undesirable branches directly across from one another on the central leader when they are 3 to 4 inches (8 to 10 cm) long. Select evenly spaced laterals within the whorl to reduce subsequent crowding and crossing. Once the tree has achieved its mature size for the planting density, it is advisable to cut back lateral branches to their desired length during the summer to reduce vigor.

8. The M9 rootstock induces rapid branching.

9. Fruit inhibits growth of the axis, clippers don't.

The Tree's Natural Balance

Varieties are trained as freely as possible based on their own mode of branching. Under such conditions, the tree will reach an optimal height between the third and fifth year, bearing in mind the vigor it inherits from the rootstock. To keep the description of the various stages simple, let's take a look at a subject grafted onto an M9 rootstock. The natural balance between vegetative development and the start of fruiting may be quite rapid (three to four years) if no pruning occurs: the fruit will quickly fill the tree's **canopy**. The terminal parts of the young tree will bend under the apples' weight, and the tree will no longer develop vertically *(photo 8)*.

At this stage, annual shoots will be numerous and just as long at the top as they are at the bottom of the tree, since annual growth distributes itself evenly over all the functional vegetative points. These short shoots are called "crown brindles"; they bear an inflorescence in their terminal bud. Now the tree will attain what we call its "physiological equilibrium."

It is important to keep all of the trunk's lateral shoots, particularly up top. Overly competitive shoots on the axis should be bent at least to horizontal in the first two or three years *(figs. 7A and B)*.

The top of the axis can be handled in the same way when you want to limit the tree's height—for example, to 9 feet (2.8m) *(fig. 7C)*. It is therefore very important

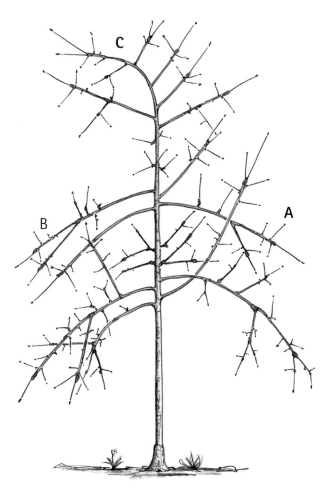

Fig. 7. Shoots that compete with the axis will be bent.

the lateral development of spurs and short shoots on the distal parts of branches, much like a hand at the end of an arm *(figs. 8B and 9)*. This is known as **acrotonic** development. Do not thin out these terminal branchings, as many growers would have you do! Later, in years two or three, when the branch bends under the weight of its fruit, you may lighten the load by removing the most poorly placed shoots and spurs. As fruiting starts up, you will need to control the tree's load (see "Thinning the Fruit" later in the chapter).

At this stage of the tree's development, it is often suggested that you prune for "shaping." This is usually too severe and destroys the tree's early equilibrium *(fig. 8A)* by promoting vegetative growth, or the "structure." The terminal flower gets removed and fruiting becomes secondary. Of course you may, if you wish, choose a particular shape for your tree; but keep in mind that any interventions that are not physiologically based will delay the start of fruiting. The "shape" and the pruning system will ensure nothing.

The Fruiting Branch

After observing the tree's development as it establishes itself (stem development and the organization of primary branchings), you will witness the possibility for obtaining a natural equilibrium between vegetative growth and fruiting in the third or fourth year. Now you should also notice the way in which the branches arrayed around the trunk will rapidly begin to fruit.

The fruiting branch is considered a production unit *(photo 11)*. On a tree grafted with an M9 rootstock, there will be twelve to eighteen branches. Each branch passes through three consecutive stages *(fig. 9)*:

1. The presence of a flower and fruits at the terminal position in the second year. This fruiting halts growth and redistributes it laterally...
2. . . . into buds that will become fruiting organs

not to remove branches that are considered surplus. This would slow down fruiting.

In addition, all of the natural branchings contribute to forming a harmonious canopy, reflecting the balance previously mentioned *(photo 10)*. Later, you can suppress the least vigorous branches that might block sunlight to the tree's center when the sun is at zenith. Yet those eventual removals should occur only after fruiting has become established.

As branches take their place around the axis, they will rapidly yield fruit on their tips *(photo 9)*. This blocks the terminal vegetative shoots and promotes

10. A balanced tree, but be careful of overload.

11. With MM106 rootstocks, fruit branches may reach 2 to 3 yd.

called "spurs." This process is equally assisted by the bending of branches under the weight of their fruit.

3. Fruiting that occurs at the branch bends will create vegetative renewal, an epicormic branch located on the arc: this is a "reiteration" (sucker or water sprout).

Each variety undergoes these three stages in different ways depending on its predisposition for fruiting. Let's examine two extreme cases, 'Reine des Reinettes' and 'Yellow Bellflower'.

'Reine des Reinettes' *(fig. 10A)* is erect and exhibits strong apical dominance: the terminal bud remains vegetative for a long time and dominates lateral buds that cannot become autonomous due to their number. Thus, fruiting is subject to terminal bud dominance and develops from the base toward the summit. This situation generally leads to alternate bearing (too much

fruit in a "+" year and no fruit in a "-" year). In this case, vegetation rules and flowers are not the priority!

For a counter-example, let's look at a variety with a less dominant habit that is quite capable of yielding fruits at the branch extremities—for example, 'Granny Smith' or 'Yellow Bellflower' *(fig. 10B)*. Unlike the preceding case, a terminal flower may rapidly block vegetative growth. This removal of dominance allows lateral buds to become autonomous. However, only the best-placed buds will have this opportunity (one out of three or four). Others will remain **latent** and die off. In this way, the branch naturally controls its fruiting: the tree will sparingly yield fruits every year *(photo 12)*. Fruiting will develop from the tip toward the base of the branch. In this case, flowers dominate and the tree becomes a fruit tree.

These two extremes outline the range of fruiting systems for apple trees. So let's take a look at our garden varieties and try to situate them. To make this

A

B

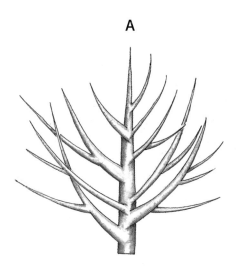
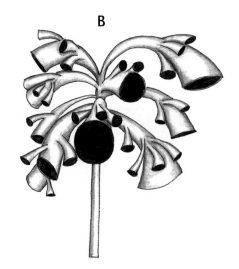

Fig. 8. A tree image (A) and fruit image (B).

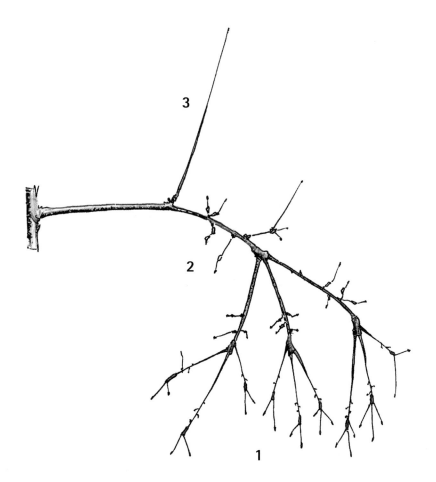

Fig. 9. Three stages of a fruiting branch.

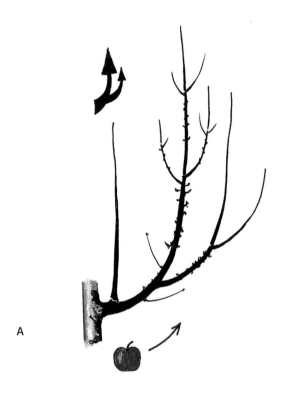

A

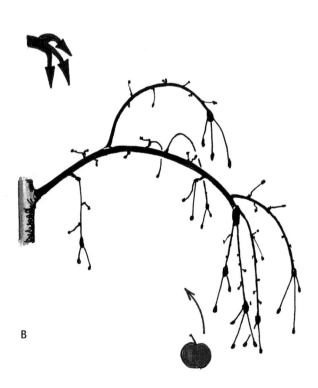

B

Fig. 10. High variability in fruiting habits.

12. Fruit branches with proper distribution of fruit.

easier, *fig. 11* illustrates four modes of spur function. What do we find from A to D?

- The terminal bourse is increasingly present and voluminous, a sign of the progressive hold of the "flower-fruit" organ over vegetation *(fig. 11)*.
- This hampering of dominance by the terminal vegetation allows the lateral bud to become increasingly autonomous and to fruit regularly (via the presence of crown brindles).
- The more autonomous they become, the fewer they will be: latent or extinguished buds are common.

Situations C and D regulate themselves naturally. We must help systems A and B, however, by bending branches and practicing extinction on surplus spurs.

Spurs

The tree...its branches...its spurs...we are reaching our goal: its fruit! Before outlining our role in training fruit branches, let's have a look at the functions of spurs. Their behavior is tied to the fruiting branch's mode of fruiting: the stronger the terminal flower, the more spurs will become autonomous, which will guarantee quality apples and continued fruiting *(figs. 11C and D)*.

To define the spur, let's compare it to two other vegetative growths in the tree: the branch and the epicormic branch. Regardless of the spur's age, it has one or more short shoots that usually terminate in a flower *(fig. 12)*. When this shoot is long enough (3 to

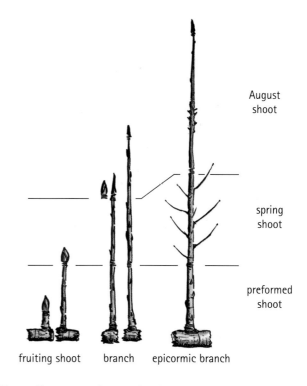

August
shoot

spring
shoot

preformed
shoot

fruiting shoot   branch   epicormic branch

Fig. 12. Three types of vegetative shoots on an apple tree.

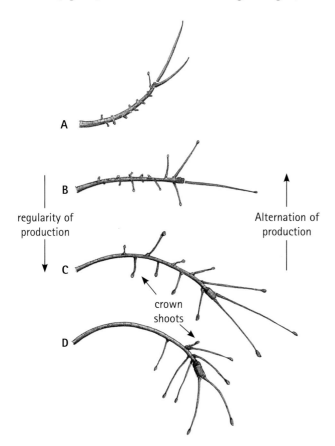

A

B

regularity of
production

Alternation of
production

C

crown
shoots

D

Fig. 11. Location and characteristics of fruiting shoots by fruiting type.

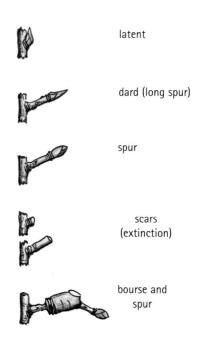

latent

dard (long spur)

spur

scars
(extinction)

bourse and
spur

Fig. 13. Different states of a lateral bud.

49

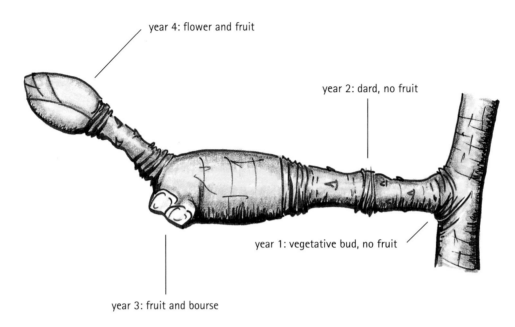

year 4: flower and fruit

year 2: dard, no fruit

year 1: vegetative bud, no fruit

year 3: fruit and bourse

Fig. 14. Chronology of fructification.

5 inches or 7 to 20 cm), it is called a "crown brindle." It is different from a branch in that it stops growing early on, at the end of June, when enough length has developed on the **preformed** shoot in the bud that it grows from.

A branch, which is stronger, often comprises two consecutive shoots that will separately stop growing, particularly when the summer is hot and dry. The first shoot is preformed like the spur; the second is called a "summer shoot." With the epicormic branch or a strong upright sucker produced with bending, we see an amplification and elongation in growth.

EVOLUTION OF THE LATERAL BUD AND SPUR AUTONOMY
- Latent buds will not develop. Over time, you may find a layer of scars on the scales at the bud base *(fig. 13)*. A latent bud will not revive without some interventions: bending or pruning the carrier branch.
- Dards are short shoots from a lateral bud that

goes through one growth cycle and blossoms the next year.
- Each flower spur directly yields a terminal flower on its short shoot.
- Scars are visible marks from spurs that have died (when the surface of the foliar rosette is too small). The rate of mortality has a strong impact on remaining spurs.
- The bourse with a new flower spur: this spur has just produced one or two apples and is preparing for next year's fruiting. The size of the bourse is generally proportional to the size of the fruit it will bear.

THE REGULARITY OF SPUR FRUITING (OR RETURN TO BLOSSOM AND THEN TO FRUIT)
If we do a "reading" of the spur shown in *fig. 14*, we can understand its situation from the two prior years (year 1: wood; year 2: wood; year 3: fruit). This lets us go back in time.

In the same way, it is (usually) easy to predict the spur's situation for the following year; in this case it will be: flower and fruit (year 4).

On an unpruned tree, it is enough to keep about 25% of fruit buds, based on the overall number of buds that the tree bears, in order to obtain a fair balance of growth and fruit. Depending on the variety's mode of fruiting, two different strategies are available:

If spurs are able to produce every year (such as those of 'Belle Fleur Jaune'), as in "fruit–fruit–fruit," then 25% of the tree's buds will suffice for proper and consistent production *(photo 13)*.

If spurs can only alternate production, fruiting every other year (such as those of 'Reine des Reinettes'), as in "fruit–wood–fruit," it will be necessary to have twice as many spurs, or 50% of the tree's buds, since theo-retically 25% will be fruiting and 25% will be producing wood each year.

However, as the tree ages, the spurs on certain varieties will improve and end up producing consistently fruit upon fruit (the family of Canadian Reinettes, for example).

Spring Pruning by Artificial Spur Extinction

Now we have all the information required to understand how the "tree" becomes a "fruit tree":

- To promote growth in the first year, use compost to improve the soil. Don't pack it down, and water when needed (be attentive to any lack of water in the first two summers).

13. Spurs on a Chantecler variety, where fruiting occurs consecutively.

14. Using epicormic branches: they will fruit quickly when bent.

15. Thanks to the chimney, or light well, sunlight penetrates to lower fruits.

- The tree should branch as much as possible: the more shoots there are, the shorter they will be and the more rapidly they will bear fruit. Removing certain branches or their tips with clippers will unbalance the tree and delay fruiting.
- For the most vertical branches, bending will help to induce spurs and will prevent any unproductive enlargement of the tree.

Once the tree is four or five years old, vegetative growth will spread to all of its spurs. This will ensure quality fruit and continued production.

What is left to do? Generally, the apple tree produces too many fruits each year or every other year depending on the variety. Intervention will consist of promoting a fair balance between the tree's vegetative potential and the number of fruits it will bear.

First, take the overall tree into consideration, and monitor two situations that are important to its balance.

Epicormic branches are not generally as numerous if the tree has developed unrestricted (that is, without pruning). However, wherever they are present, it is necessary to control them. They usually develop on two specific points: the top of the tree when its growth has been topped, and along the arcing of stronger fruiting branches *(fig. 15)*. If epicormic branches develop in a relatively empty spot, they can be used as fruiting branches simply by bending them. The next year, the few fruits directly inserted on these branches will be late to develop, but the crown shoots that result from bowing will quickly become functional *(photo 14)*.

Fig. 15. Control of epicormic branches.

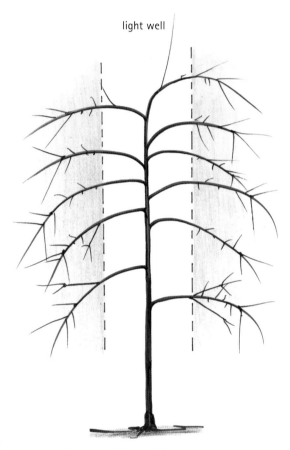

Fig. 16. The chimney , or "light well".

been preserved in their entirety. You have controlled their vigor with bending. Then comes a period when growth "dies down" and fruiting increases dangerously. We say "dangerously" because overabundant production not only will yield low-quality fruits but also will weaken and undermine the tree's structure for several years *(photo 16)*. Thus, you will need to determine the number of spurs that a fruiting branch can yield according to its vigor, and then thin that number by suppressing any spurs that are considered surplus (via extinction).

Here is how to proceed. We know that this balance is obtained when only 25% of buds are fruiting. Yet

16. Too many spurs will reduce fruit quality and unbalance the tree.

If the epicormic branches are too vigorous, they must absolutely be suppressed. This removal should occur under the best conditions at the beginning of autumn after harvest—or better, in high summer—without leaving any "stubs."

Be sure the center of the tree is cleaned. Remove spurs or weaker, shaded branches so that sunlight can penetrate the tree around the trunk when the sun is at zenith. This "chimney" or "light well" can have a diameter of 24 to 47 inches (60 to 120 cm), depending on the variety *(fig. 16, photo 15)*.

Once the tree displays well-balanced vegetation spread over the entire structure, take a closer look at each fruiting branch. These branches have

Fig. 17. An "equilifruit", for measuring fruit size.

we don't want to spend our time counting the buds on each branch. Studies of different varieties have revealed a more rapid way to measure this relationship between branch strength and the number of spurs that it can bear:

- The branch's vigor is determined by the cross-section of its base in square inches (cm^2) (the cross-section is measured 4 inches, or 10 cm, from the branch's insertion point on the trunk).
- There should be five spurs per square inch (cm^2) of the branch's cross-section. An "equilifruit" tool *(fig. 17)* can help you carry out these equations:

branch cross-section per in^2 (cm^2) X 5 =

the number of spurs to preserve

To make this simpler, you can consider the count to be good when you have removed spurs from the light well and the branch bases, as well as any that are poorly placed or poorly lit *(fig. 18)*. Afterwards, you can easily memorize this relationship. Periodic verification of branches will help you figure out if you are attaining your goal intuitively.

This work should be done when the floral buds are swollen enough for you to be able to distinguish whether or not the spur is a fruiting spur, in February or March. Do this by hand, with gloves, since spurs easily break off. In terms of the tree's health, never fear: there is a much lower frequency of fungal parasites on a break than where clippers have cut!

Thinning the Fruit

When fruits are "set" and the underfertilized fruits naturally drop ("June drop"), it is imperative to thin. You can use the Equilifruit tool to determine the number of fruits to leave per branch (four to six per square inch, or cm^2, on the tree's cross-section). As with extinction, you can easily memorize the fruit load to be maintained. In general, you should only keep a single fruit per inflorescence, yet the terminal position is an exception; here you should leave two when each is sufficiently large. The extinction that you performed in the spring will greatly facilitate this operation. If need be, you can clear out a chimney in the center of the tree.

For trees on dwarfing rootstocks, the appropriate leaf-to-fruit ratio (for sufficient photosynthesis to support good fruit growth) is 10:1, with shoot leaves providing better support than spur leaves. More fruit may be allowed to develop on larger trees. In any case, the earlier fruit is thinned, the better ultimate size the fruits will achieve. Thinning can be done by hand, mechanically, or chemically. The last is generally the best option in commercial orchards, although chemical thinning methods may be unpredictable and some varieties are "hard to thin."

Apples should be thinned when they are about the size of a small coin. Remove enough fruit so that those remaining are spaced 4 to 6 inches (10 to 15 cm) apart, leaving a single fruit per cluster. That fruit is often the

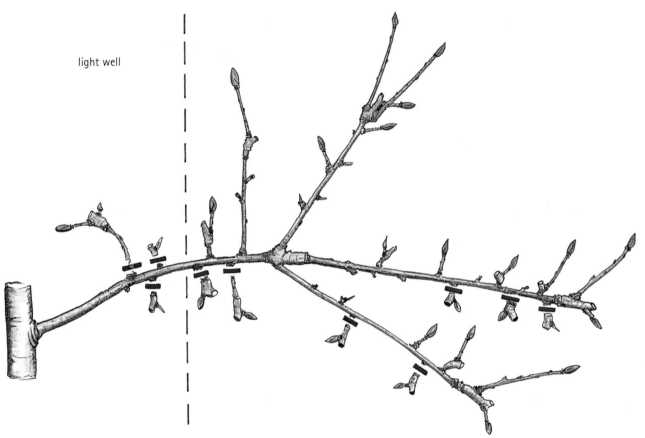

light well

Fig. 18. Extinction: remove poorly placed spurs.

"king" fruit (the first to bloom at the center of the inflorescence), as it is the largest. Thinning promotes better fruit quality, reduced pest and disease incidence, and reduced alternate bearing habit.

Pruning

Any branches that are too weak, as well as those that have bent under the weight of their own fruit and ended up in the light well, will have been removed during the first production years. However, when the tree has balanced out, at four to six years, it is often necessary to reduce the number of branches, depending on the variety's vigor and fruiting mode. Three principal conditions determine the need to remove branches:

- Extinction alone has not reduced excessive fruiting.
- Branches are overlapping and preventing light from penetrating to the fruit.
- A branch has not bent and has become too vigorous, thereby unbalancing the tree.

Branch removal should be modest and should not surpass 10 to 15% of the tree's volume.

APRICOT

Author   Bruno HUCBOURG
Collaborators   Jean AYMARD
             Éric NAVARRO

GENERAL OVERVIEW

History and Phytogeographical Origins

Apricot is native to regions with cold winters. The tree is slightly more cold-hardy than the peach, tolerating winter temperatures as cold as -22°F (-30°C) or lower if it is healthy. In many countries, the limiting factors in apricot culture are: (1) spring frosts, which can destroy the crop, (2) lack of sufficient summer heat for adequate fruit maturation (in colder climates), and (3) inadequate winter chilling in many Mediterranean climates, such as California's. Apricot flowers very early (February to March), and late spring frosts often kill the bud and flowers. A dry climate is best for good fruit production and disease control, but orchards need enough water every year to survive and bear a crop.

Originally from China, where the apricot has been cultivated for more than five thousand years, the apricot tree has undergone a vast geographical dispersion. It was developed in the Middle East, then in North Africa, and then arrived in Europe through Greece, Armenia (where it got its Latin name), and Italy. It arrived in France in the tenth century, having been imported to Roussillon by the Moors, yet it did not reach the Loire Valley until the fifteenth century. The first writings attesting to its cultivation in France come from that period.

The apricot tree most likely arrived in the United States—specifically Arizona and lower California—with the exploration and establishment of the early missions in the early-eighteenth century. Further east in Monticello, Virginia, the apricot tree appeared as early as 1774, when Thomas Jefferson planted seeds he had received from a Florentine wine merchant and recorded them in his *Garden Book.*

Apricot rootstocks have been developed for adaptation to many regions, while grafted varieties have been selected for local and export markets, adaptation to climate, consumer tastes, storability, disease and pest resistance, and compatibility with rootstocks. Numerous varieties have been created in response to local situations (climate, soil, eating habits, etc.). Only the best-adapted varieties have survived in each location. Each variety has specific needs (soil, climate, etc.) that define its **planting zone**. Choosing a variety that is well suited to the environment is essential to successfully growing apricot trees.

Botanical Classification

The apricot tree belongs to the Rosaceae family, in the genus *Prunus.* There are several similar species, the most representative being *Prunus armeniaca* (see Appendix A: *Prunus* Botany).

There are quite a number of apricot varieties, and more continue to arise. They are quite diverse, whether in fruit size, harvest volume, or climatic requirements (chilling requirements, frost sensitivity, etc.).

Worldwide Production

Worldwide production of apricots centers in the Mediterranean countries, Europe, central Asia, America, and Africa. Turkey produces 85% of the world's dried apricots.

World Production of Apricots (in metric tons): 2,681,474
Turkey 500,000; Iran, Islamic Rep 225,000; Italy 199,462; Spain 159,200; Pakistan 121,000; Ukraine 112,000; France 107,500; Morocco 104,350; China 98,000; Greece 80,000; Egypt 79,844; United States 73,660 (*Source:* Food and Agriculture Organization of the United Nations, 2006).

French lands dedicated to planting have multiplied threefold, going from 11,120 acres (4,500 ha) to 37,807 acres (15,300 ha) in a little over two decades. Meanwhile, acreage of apricots in the United States (especially in California) has declined during the same period. U.S. production of apricots occurs in a variety of states; however, historically it has largely been in California. This production has been in continuous decline since the introduction of inexpensive Turkish dried apricots in the 1980s, reduced consumption by U.S. consumers of canned fruit and apricot nectar, and increased urbanization of primary production areas. U.S. production in 2008, as reported by the USDA's Economic Research Service, was forecast at 173.7 million pounds (79 million kg). Washington State is the second-largest producer after California, accounting for 5% of the total U.S. crop (California's production is approximately 94% of the U.S. total). Utah is the third largest producer. About 75% of California's production is for the processing sector, of which more than half is for canning. Early-season California apricots include the popular **varieties** 'Castlebrite', 'Patterson', and 'Earlicot'.

New varieties continue to be developed. French **cultivars** that were released in the 1980s included 'Lambertin' and 'Bergarouge'. Since then, the varietal array worldwide has widened progressively throughout the 1990s and 2000s with the arrival of 'Orangered®', 'Bhart', 'Jumbocot®', 'Goldrich', 'Hargrand®', 'Tomcot®', 'Toyaco', 'Early Blush®', 'Rutbhart', 'Bergarouge®', 'Avirine', and others, with many of the American selections originating from Zaiger Genetics in California. Many "niche" varieties continue to be released, particularly high-sugar, fresh market varieties resulting from crosses of orange cultivars with "white" apricot germplasm from the Middle East and Asia.

Breeding programs have been ongoing at Washington State University, Rutgers University (New Jersey), and Cornell University (New York), and in California (University of California–Davis and USDA Research Station–Parlier), as well as by Zaiger Genetics and other, smaller-scale private breeders in California. Some of the most recent varietal releases in the United States include: 'SunGem' (1994), 'Earlyblush' & NJA82 (1995), NJA97 (1996), NJA150 (2006), 'Helena' (1994), 'Robada' (1997), 'Lorna' (1998), 'Apache' (2002), 'Nicole' (2003), and 'Kettleman' (2005). Breeding characteristics of highest priority are as follows: fresh and processing market use; full flavor; deep color of skin, flesh, and blush; wide adaptability; novel fruit characteristics (such as modified sugar profile, white flesh, and glabrous, or smooth, skin); improved cold hardiness; bacterial resistance; and extended ripening season.

THE TREE

Vegetative, Floral, and Fruiting Characteristics

BRANCHES

The shoot primordium is formed in a terminal or **axillary bud** (found in the axil of a leaf), enclosed in budscales. When the bud "breaks," or starts growth from the dormant phase, the shoot results from this **preformed** growth in the bud. Some preformed shoots stop growing early in the season in a predetermined manner, forming short vegetative branches. This is a form of "determinate" growth—as opposed to "indeterminate" growth, in which there is no predestined end to growth prior to setting a dormant terminal bud at the end of

the growing season. This type of growth corresponds to the "crown shoots" of apple trees. Thus, "extension shoots" continue in one or more successive phases of growth during the same growing season, which is an example of **neoformed** growth (new growth that was not preformed in a dormant bud). Moreover, throughout each new phase of growth in the extension shoot, the number of **internodes** (sections of the shoot between **nodes** of leaf or flower production) decreases relative to that of the previous phase of growth.

A bud forms at the axil of each new leaf as the extension shoot grows in the current season. Depending on the species, the area of growth in the **canopy** of branches in the tree, and the time during the growing season, **axillary buds** will form either as vegetative shoot buds or as reproductive shoot and

1. Sympodial growth.

flower buds. Some vegetative shoot buds will "break" in the following year, creating new extension shoots, while others will remain **latent**. Along the strongest branches (those of largest diameter), axillary shoot buds that have formed in the current year may "break" in that same year and create **sylleptic branching**. For branches with few annual growth cycles, at the end of each growth phase the terminal **meristem** dies off and the next phase of branching arises from an axillary bud just below the original shoot's terminal bud. This results in **sympodial growth** *(photo 1)*. Thus, a branching system arises along a central axis (from the terminal bud) with lateral branches formed from axillary buds. The

primorida of this system can be observed microscopically in the dormant bud.

Suppression of lateral (axillary) shoot **budbreak** is due to inhibition by growth regulators produced by the apical bud—thus, the term **apical dominance**. With increasing distance from the apex of the shoot, the concentration of those growth inhibitors decreases, latent buds of the **distal** sections of the branch system are no longer inhibited, and these "break," creating an **acrotonic** whorl of branches. Break of apical dominance can result in an outgrowth of current-season axillary buds, but this most often occurs in buds formed on one-year-old wood. Pruning eliminates the terminal

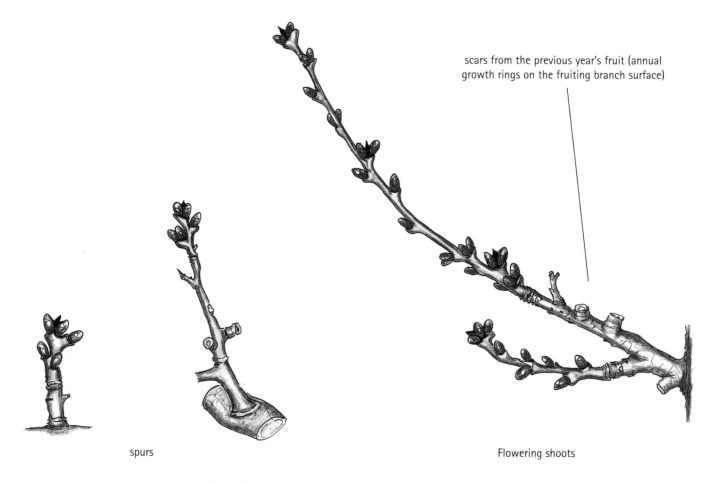

scars from the previous year's fruit (annual growth rings on the fruiting branch surface)

spurs

Flowering shoots

Fig. 1. Short fruiting branches called "spurs", which occur in some species.

2. Spurs.

buds as sources of growth inhibitors, causing lateral budbreak. Bending or spreading of shoots also reduces apical dominance, favoring bud development at the summit of the arc. The tree's response to bending may differ from one variety to another.

Several factors influence the number of growth phases for a single branch: its location on the tree, the tree's health, the variety of the tree, the amount of light interception, and the surrounding conditions. The overall strength of shoot growth is a measure of "vegetative vigor," which can be strongly influenced by the rootstock on which the **scion** (the variety grown for fruit production) is grafted, as well as by fertilizer regime, soil conditions, and water status. In addition to vegetative branches, which form the canopy overall, there are reproductive branches, which can be classified by length into short and long branches. Each type of branch has its own fruiting pattern.

Flowers and fruits form on both one-year-old wood and long-lived short shoots (**spurs**). Spurs are produc-

tive for three to five years, and the highest-quality fruit is borne on younger spurs. Most apricots begin fruiting in their second year, but substantial bearing does not begin until three to five years. Fruits require three to six months for development, depending on the cultivar. The fruits vary in weight from 1 to 4 ounces (30 to 120 gr). Sugar content is 6.2 to 20%, and acids average 0.25 to 2%, which tends to be on the low side for "white" apricots and on the high side for orange apricots. Perception of acids versus sugars tends to be on the acidic side in years when periods of spring fruit development are cooler than average, less due to higher acids than to lower sugars. An average crop from a twenty- to thirty-year-old tree reaches 330 to 1,300 pounds (150 to 600 kg).

The short branches *(fig. 1)* typically go through a single growth phase, creating short flowering twigs called "spurs" and longer flowering shoots. The spurs *(photo 2),* which range from 1 to 3 inches (2 to 7 cm) in length, branch out little by little, primarily bearing flow-

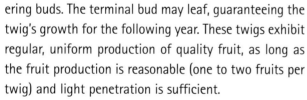

3. A long branch.

4. Replacement or renewal branches.

ering buds. The terminal bud may leaf, guaranteeing the twig's growth for the following year. These twigs exhibit regular, uniform production of quality fruit, as long as the fruit production is reasonable (one to two fruits per twig) and light penetration is sufficient.

Over the tree's lifetime, the twigs will spread more or less rapidly depending on the variety, and their durability will depend on the orchard's upkeep and training methods (light source, optimal density, etc.). Spur life may be several years; thus, pruning out spurs that are productive will reduce bearing capacity.

Flowering shoots are slightly longer (less than 8 inches or 20 cm long), due to their longer internodes *(fig. 1)*. The buds that are present on flowering shoots tend to blossom and produce good-quality fruits.

Long branches *(photo 3)* form over the span of several annual growth phases and have few floral buds along their base. They develop either at the end of the previous year's vigorous branches (one-year-wood), in which case they are known as extension shoots, or on older structures within the tree (**scaffold branches**), in which case they are known as replacement shoots *(photo 4)*. Where there is bending of the shoot or pruning, the tree favors the growth of these replacement shoots. The strongest (known as water sprouts) develop a sylleptic branching system. They may be used for structuring the tree or for renewing it as older scaffolds become less productive. Syleptic branches tend to have few flowers; the more upright, large-diameter branches are the most vegetative and the least reproductive. In certain varieties the

5. Blossoms on a short branch.

weaker shoots are used to produce fruit, via bending to about 60° from vertical or tipping the branch by pruning, thereby enhancing reproductive development.

The quality of the fruit varies according to where on the branch it grows and what type of branch it grows on (see "Thinning Fruits" later in the chapter). The balance of short and long branches defines the type of branching and the fruiting pattern for each variety.

FLOWERING
In winter, floral buds can be distinguished easily from wood buds by their more "rounded" shape and darker color. The floral buds start forming over the summer on growing branches (short or long), beginning shortly after harvest of the current season's fruit. The following spring, each of these buds will produce a single flower. Flowering happens only on one-year-old wood (that is, on a shoot that developed during the prior year), either on spurs or on long shoots. A node may bear one or several floral buds, with or without the presence of vegetative buds (photo 5).

Apricot trees blossom over a span of time. In fact, spurs flower before the long branches do, with flowers along the base blossoming prior to those closer to the tips, in order of formation during the prior year.

FRUITING

For this species, there are two rather dissimilar types of fruiting. Certain varieties only produce quality fruits on spurs. These varieties tend to produce fruit more compactly, as is the case with 'Bergeron' and 'Bergarouge®'. Other cultivars generally produce fruit on long- and medium-length branches, leading to earlier fruiting and a more open tree structure, as is the case with 'Early Blush®', 'Robada®', and 'Tomcot®', as well as with most other cultivars originating in the United States. However, fruiting on "long" branches, as opposed to spur-bearing ones, is also typical of the younger phase in an apricot tree's growth (the juvenile phase); thus, as the tree ages, spurs are the source of most of the fruit production. In spur-bearing stonefruit species, as well as in pears, the better-quality fruit develops on spurs. Fruit quality benefits from a cool spring and a longer development period, both of which promote larger size and higher sugar levels.

POLLINATION AND FERTILIZATION

Apricot trees reflect three types of situations:

- Self-fertile varieties: these are capable of self-pollinating and self-fertilizing. They do not require the presence of another variety, although all apricot trees require bees for the transfer of pollen. Self-fertile cultivars are often quite productive.
- Self-sterile varieties: these are incapable of self-pollinating or self-fertilizing. They require cross-fertilization via cross-pollination, which is obtained by planting two different varieties next to each other that will both flower at the same time and that are cross-compatible.
- Intermediary situations: when there is partial self-pollination, cross-pollination is also needed to ensure sufficient and consistent production.

Fertility is therefore quite different from one variety to another, but placing several varieties in a common area will address any of these conditions. In commercial nurseries in the United States, all cultivars that require cross-pollination should be labeled as to which cultivars are cross-compatible.

The Tree's Development: Morphological Types

Although tree behavior varies greatly among varieties, the natural tendency of the apricot tree is to become bushy, resulting in lower dominance by the initial shoots (primary scaffolds). The type of branching (development of short and long branches), the smoothness of the wood, and the speed of initial production all play a role in the tree's shape, density, and branching mode.

Certain varieties have a very wide structure, such as 'Early Blush®', 'Robada®', and 'Tomcot®' (fig. 2). The latter variety is preferable for open vase pruning systems typical in the United States, so as to maximize light penetration to the tree's center. Others, such as 'Bergarouge®' and 'Hargrand®', have more rigid wood, produce fruit more slowly, and grow in a more erect fashion. Some fall in between. The more erect the training of branches, the slower production will be.

The section located beyond the arching becomes gradually less hardy, producing only short branches where fruit quality will dwindle each year (photo 6). Healthy shoots develop along the summit of the arching, guaranteeing the renewal of sagging branches.

Climatic Limitations and Varietal Adaptation

LETHAL TEMPERATURES

In terms of **lethal temperatures**, the apricot tree in its dormant stage is less sensitive to extreme cold than the peach tree is. The apricot can resist temperatures as low as -4°F (-20°C).

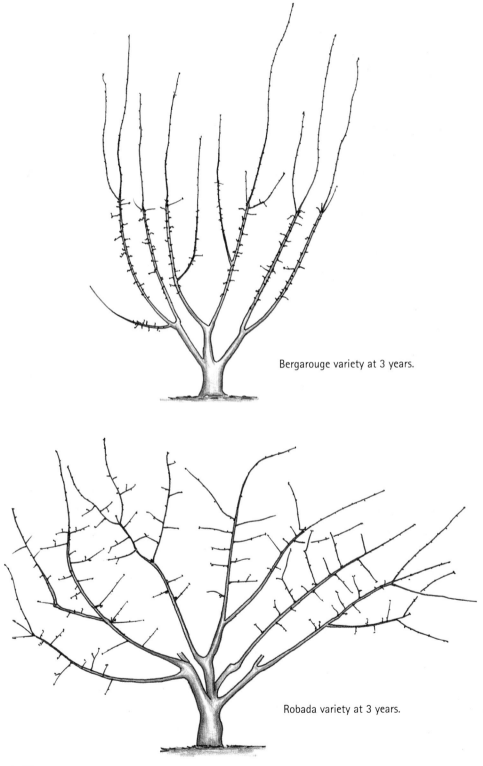

Bergarouge variety at 3 years.

Robada variety at 3 years.

Fig. 2. Two different tree habits.

6. Natural branching on an apricot tree.

SPRING FROSTS

Apricot trees flower earlier than most fruit-bearing Rosaceae, after the almond tree, which means that the apricot becomes exposed to springtime frosts. **Dormancy** release and budbreak occur at the slightest warming as winter ends. In certain regions, such as Valais in Switzerland, where spring thaw arrives a bit later, apricot trees are cultivated where plant growth occurs the latest: on north-facing slopes in slightly higher altitudes. In U.S. regions that experience late frosts, growers tend to breed for and plant late-blooming varieties, while California's emphasis has been on early bloom and early market. (For more on freezes and frosts, see Appendix B: Freeze/Frost Damage in *Prunus* Species.)

Sensitive stages are as follows: 26°F (-3°C) at budding (stage D); 28°F (-2°C) with full flowers (stage E), and 31°F (-1°C) with small fruits (stage I).

COLD REQUIREMENTS

Apricot trees present a broad range of cold requirements. During dormant periods, the more continental cultivars, such as 'Bergeron' and 'Polonais', require more attention than their Mediterranean cousins, such as 'Rouge de Roussillon'. The lack of cold hinders floral growth.

But if the cold arrives early in the autumn, this will also affect the quality of any future flowers: for certain varieties, such as 'Orangered® Barth', the **pistils** (sterile flowers) will die off in the spring if the previous autumn is too mild, regardless of whether cold requirements are met in the winter (Legave—INRA Avignon, France). This may cause the tree to drop buds, flowers, or even young fruits in the spring, which is why it is so important to carefully select varieties that are adapted to one's particular growing region.

If the end of winter and beginning of spring are hot, dry, and sunny, these conditions will be favorable to **fruit set** (pollination, fertilization) and will prevent flowers from succumbing to **cryptogamic** diseases, such as *Monilia* (brown rot of flowers and fruits).

WATER REQUIREMENTS

Traditionally, the apricot tree was cultivated in dry areas (without watering), just like the olive tree or almond tree. The apricot is better suited to these conditions than the apple, pear, or peach tree. Still, it prefers deep, fertile terrain that is well irrigated with filtering soil, where there is no risk of over-saturation.

In more humid regions, such as in the Atlantic climates, apricot trees suffer from bacterial infections in the winter and fungal infections (*Monilia*) when they blossom. There is also an increased susceptibility to spring frosts and, sometimes, root asphyxiation. That is why the number of trees in those regions remains low and why they are usually found in ecologically favorable areas that are well protected.

ROOTSTOCKS AND GRAFTING

Today most apricot trees are propagated through grafting. The rootstock enables the species to better adapt to different soil types. Important rootstock traits are as follows:

- compatibility with the scion
- adaptation to soil and climatic conditions
- tolerance of wet, heavy soil
- ease and uniformity in propagation
- influence on vegetative vigor
- **precocity**, consistent cropping and yield (lack of **alternate bearing**), and fruit quality
- winter hardiness and bloom delay for frost avoidance
- tendency to develop suckers—selecting a rootstock that does not "sucker" is preferred
- sensitivity to disease, pests, and problems at replanting.

The best choices for rootstocks are as follows:

1. apricot seedlings
2. peach (*Prunus persica*) seedlings
    a. 'Lovell'
    b. 'Nemaguard'
    c. 'Nemared'
3. plum seedlings
    a. *Prunus cerasifera*
    b. 'Myrobalan', 'Myrobalan' 29C
    c. *Prunus cerasifera* x *Prunus munsoniana* hybrid
    d. 'Marianna' 2624

Apricots can be grown on their own roots (as "seedlings") or grafted onto peach or plum rootstocks. Seedlings show wide productivity variability year-to-year, while budded trees (apricot scions budded onto rootstocks) are less variable. Apricot cultivars are most often grafted onto plum or peach rootstocks. The grafted scion from an existing apricot plant provides the fruit characteristics such as color and flavor, but the rootstock provides the growth characteristics of the plant.

Rootstock choice, therefore, is primarily determined according to the soil in which the tree will grow, although compatibility between rootstock and scion is sometimes a concern. Specific recommendations for soil types include the following:

- In silty soils, clay loam, or moderately draining soils where saturation may occur (alluvia), the rootstock is often selected from among the plum species: 'Myrobolan', 'Torinel® Avifel', 'Reine-Claude', or 'Mariana'.
- In well-drained or pebbly soil, where there is no excess water, it is best to choose an ungrafted peach or apricot stock.

If a rootstock is poorly adapted to the soil type, the tree may fail. That is why plum rootstocks in pebbly ground make the tree sensitive to bacterial infection, and why apricot or peach rootstocks in dense soil suffer from root or trunk asphyxia. Grafted onto the peach tree, an apricot tree will suffer less often from iron **chlorosis** (yellowing of leaves due to iron deficiency) than the peach tree itself, if grown in the same soil.

The choice of rootstock will also affect the size and stature of the tree, its potential productivity (size of harvest), the quality of the fruit, and its resistance to disease. **Grafting compatibility** between species (apricot–plum) may not always be perfect, depending on the variety–stock coupling; this may weaken the graft union, which will be evident by overgrowth of the scion portion immediately above the graft line. To prevent this from happening, the grafting point must be high enough (10 inches/25 cm or more) above the ground, reducing the risk of bacterial infection.

PRINCIPLES OF TRAINING

The principal elements that guide us in adapting the variety's performance are as follows:

- the variety's fertility (ability to flower and set fruit);
- the effect of bending on varieties with more upright growth patterns, and the number of levels of branching;
- the type of branches that are favorable to quality fruit production;
- the control of fruit loads (thinning).

One must respect certain conditions to obtain regular production of quality fruit. First, allowing a tree to branch out naturally is the most common technique. The use of artificial constraints, such as pruning to conform to a standardized shape, is quite limited. The apricot tree is a fruit-bearing Rosaceae whose natural "shrubby" behavior should be respected (photo 7).

- General rules for pruning apricot trees are as follows:
- Prune trees at planting time to balance the tops with the roots.

7. An orchard of adult apricot trees.

- Prune young trees very lightly.
- Prune mature trees more heavily, especially if they've shown little growth. The tree's canopy should be kept open with considerable thinning-out in order to induce annual formation of fruit-bearing wood. Apricot fruit is borne on short spurs that are short-lived.
- Prune when all danger from fall or early winter freeze has passed, but before full bloom in spring. This will reduce the risk of disease and injury. However, because apricots bloom very early, frost frequently kills all or most of the flowers or young fruits. Delaying pruning until after bloom may be advisable with apricots grown in areas that often get late frost.
- Prune less heavily if there is a light crop or no crop at all.
- Prune the top portion of the tree more heavily than the lower portion, as the top is where most vegetative growth occurs.
- Thin out more shoots toward the end of a well-pruned branch in a mature tree. This will increase fruit size and quality on the remaining shoots.

Pruning too early in the dormant season can lead to several problems:

- increased incidence of Cytospora canker, which enters the tree through pruning wounds (note that pruning close to budbreak when the tree starts active growth leads to rapid healing of pruning wounds);
- increased internal damage;
- increased sunscald of the bark.

Training Systems

The most typical training systems for deciduous fruit trees are the central leader and the open vase or open center. The training system used depends on the fruit crop. Apricot grows and produces best with an open vase (open center) training system. Indeed, allowing ample light within the canopy is essential throughout the tree's life. In fact, the apricot tree is quite responsive to light; flower buds only form where adequate light can penetrate. Allowing enough light also allows better aeration. The different organs will dry more quickly after a rainfall or heavy dew, limiting the development of cryptogamic infections such as *Monilia*. It is possible to obtain improved fruit production by selecting whole fruit-bearing branches in the summer or at the end of winter, followed in the spring by guaranteeing light to excess fruits, rather than drastically pruning the tree's structure.

Techniques Used in Pruning

Pruning should not happen in the winter. It may take place at other times of the year depending on the desired outcome. During dormant phases, pruning is not recommended since the pruning scars will heal more slowly, allowing bacterial pathogens to enter. Final pruning should take place in mid-September.

Growers in some countries practice bending and arching along with pruning. Bending of flowering shoots (long shoots with flowers and spurs) promotes better tree health and control of its structure. This type of intervention may be more efficient than pruning in some training systems. It may be done with saplings in the spring.

Tree Growth

Growers should pay attention to good planting conditions as well as to soil and tree maintenance in the first year. The distance between the trees and other obstacles (other trees, fencing, houses, etc.) should

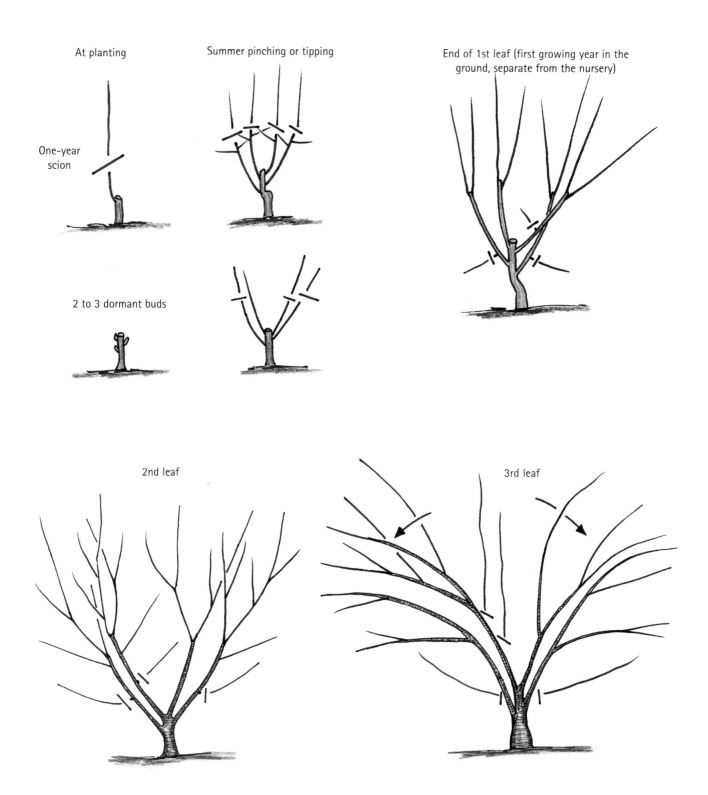

At planting

One-year
scion

2 to 3 dormant buds

Summer pinching or tipping

End of 1st leaf (first growing year in the
ground, separate from the nursery)

2nd leaf

3rd leaf

Fig. 3. The formation of a young tree through thinning and/or bowing (bending).

be greater than the radius of the adult tree's canopy (between 10 and 13 feet or 3 and 4 m). This helps the tree become more vigorous, as does the rootstock–variety graft and the fertility of the soil. For example, a medium-strength variety grafted to a 'Myrobolan' in silty soil may develop a crown over 23 feet (7 m) in diameter. The same variety with an ungrafted apricot tree in "poor" hillside soil will not span more than 17 feet (5 m). So the distance between trees may vary from 17 to 23 feet (5 to 7 m). A balanced and well-thinned tree is only possible if these essential parameters are fully respected.

When planting, remember that the apricot tree's natural branching structure offers an open, shrubby shape, such as with the vase system (eventually reinforced with ties to protect heavily laden limbs from breakage) or a rounded "dome" shape, rather than a single-axis or trellised shape. When planting the tree, be sure to cut it back so that strong young shoots can develop; these will become the future scaffolds for training. The height at which the "heading" of a newly planted tree takes place will determine the height of the trunk, which should be around 2 feet (60 cm) above ground. In terms of planting **dormant-eye trees** (those that have been developed in the nursery to have preformed scaffold buds), sprouts will develop from any buds that are present *(fig. 3)*.

It is desirable to protect cutting scars by sterilizing pruning shears with bleach between trees. Applying "tree seal" to pruning cuts is also an option.

Through May, when young shoots are developing their first early branches, **pinching** (breaking off the tips of shoots) may be necessary in the following cases:

- If the number of shoots that develop after cutting is insufficient (fewer than five), pinching (or tipping) will cause them to multiply.
- If the variety is quite erect, pinching may help to "open up" the tree.
- If there is a range of sprout strengths (that is, if some branches grow more vigorously than others), pinching the stronger shoots will even out their development.

Lower shoots should be removed by means of trimming or pruning.

In the first summer (after harvest), little to no intervention is required other than "clearing" the trunk if shoots start to grow back. A commercial protective wash or copper-based powder may be applied to the trunk, starting from the soil and extending to the joints of future scaffold branches, in order to prevent bacteria from entering into any scars created during trunk growth *(photo 8)*. White latex paint, mixed to half-strength with water, should be painted on trunks to reduce sunscald.

In the second year, the goal is to greatly increase tree development by paying close attention to its nutrition (water and mineral) and to its phytosanitary protection. It is advisable to preserve all scaffolds (to maintain the foliar surface). Do not thin them out or cut them back.

In the summer, you should suppress the lower branches growing horizontally, as well as interior shoots. Do not thin out young scaffolds because branching in the upper third of the scaffolds reinforces training system development. The treatment of trunks and pruning scars should be repeated every autumn.

Obtaining a healthy structure and promoting proper **architecture of the tree** are the primary goals in the third year *(photo 9)*. To that end, different techniques should be applied over the course of the year: bending, spring pruning, and post-harvest pruning. The use of these three techniques will vary depending on the natural habit of each variety.

Bending helps in controlling the vigor of the stronger scaffolds and orienting their development. The branch will not immediately arc into its ultimate position but should be trained to an intermediary position, which should be as pronounced as the strength of the

8. An orchard in southwestern France: a whitewash against bacteria is applied in the autumn.

9. An apricot tree in 3rd leaf, opening into vase form.

tree will allow *(photo 10)*. Tying down or using limb-spreaders are techniques used in bending.

Spring pruning prior to harvest, as well as annual removal of useless shoots *(fig. 4)* will help to better direct growth toward fruiting areas.

Post-harvest summer pruning promotes the rejuvenation of sagging scaffolds that have not bounced back from harvest. It also reduces the number of lower branches close to the ground and other useless branches. In order to allow more light to penetrate, it is important to clean the trunk and the scaffold bases.

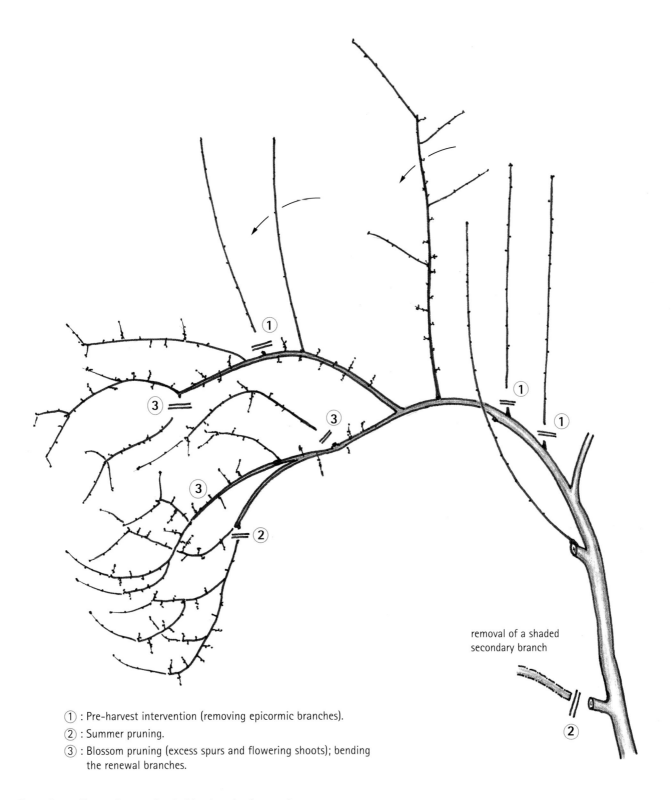

removal of a shaded
secondary branch

① : Pre-harvest intervention (removing epicormic branches).
② : Summer pruning.
③ : Blossom pruning (excess spurs and flowering shoots); bending
    the renewal branches.

Fig. 4. Controlling and promoting fruiting by selective pruning.

10. An apricot tree in 4th leaf, as the scaffolds are established.

Regardless of the variety, scaffolds should not be over-thinned because their branching is "complex," meaning that their natural development should not be inhibited *(photo 11)*. It is important to eliminate any development of secondary branches and scaffolds in the lower section of the tree (to avoid sagging, overlapping, and lack of light). Also, treating the trunk and protecting pruning scars should be repeated.

In the fourth year, the tree is slowly attaining its adult structure *(photo 10)*. It will henceforth produce spurs and flowers on longer shoots. If the tree is normally or highly vigorous, the scaffolds now will assume their ultimate position. Branches growing along the bottom of the tree can be controlled with pruning. Hanging branches that droop below the plane of the soil surface should be removed. They lack strength, and the quality of their spring buds will diminish. Branches that cross over others will intercept light and compete with existing branches. They should only be preserved if you plan on renovating the scaffold branches; thus, it is advisable to prune crossing branches selectively.

Mastering Fruiting

For a productive orchard *(fig. 4)*, mastering the fruiting process and controlling the branching are closely linked to the apricot tree's performance. The variety's level of fertility and the way it branches will determine the type and frequency of upkeep.

PRUNING FOR FRUITING
This should take place just before flowering. The goals are (1) to limit the number of fruits by reducing the number of floral buds, and (2) to improve the quality of the fruit by selecting the best branches for producing quality fruit. Thinning the tree involves removing excess fruits (before the pit hardens) after determining the fruit load capacity for the tree and each of its branches. This quantitative sorting is best combined with a qualitative sorting that involves eliminating fruits that are too small, poorly placed (shaded or in tight clusters), or already starting to rot. Fruits should

11. A "complex" scaffold (primary limb) with secondary and tertiary branching and spurs.

be spaced along shoots and among spurs to achieve an even distribution.

Any medium to long fruiting branches situated in less favorable areas should be removed—from the lower portion of the tree, from within the crown, or any that are hanging. Where there is a high density of branches, thinning out some of them is preferable to shortening all of them *(photo 12)*.

For certain productive varieties with mostly short branches, the selective removal of spurs serves to thin the crop and reduce crop load in subsequent years. Spur removal should take place primarily along the base and under the branches.

THINNING FRUITS

This occurs after fruit set and the eventual dropping of small fruits, but prior to the "pit-hardening" stage, which can be determined by cutting across the tip of the fruit and the seed. Thinning at this time will produce optimal results in terms of fruit size and quality.

12. Adult apricot trees in "Dome" or "elongated vase" form.

13. A branch overloaded with fruit.

in order to prevent contact between fruits at harvest there should be no more than two fruits per cluster. Yet if there is a particularly strong fruit set or if the variety produces a high density of spurs, you may want to maintain only one fruit or none at all *(photo 14)*.

On long branches, fruits that set along the base or central portion of the branches will have better size than those that set toward the ends of the branches. Thinning mainly involves eliminating fruits from the last third of each branch. On the rest of the branch (and as with short branches), it is sufficient to ensure that production is evenly spread, maintaining one fruit per node with a hand's width between fruits *(photo 15)*.

The mistaken impression of low production when the fruits are still small, reinforced by the desire for a "good harvest," often leads growers to thin the tree inadequately. Wherever there is young fruit, you should try to imagine the 2-inch (55 mm) fruit—in diameter—that it will become.

After thinning, it is important to verify whether your calculations for the total number of fruits for the tree have been reached.

PRUNING

The two main types of pruning cuts involve "heading" or "heading back," and "thinning" or "thinning out." Trees respond differently to these cuts.

- Heading back means cutting the plant back to a stub, a lateral bud, or a small lateral branch. Depending on the severity of pruning, heading back promotes a flush of vigorous, upright, and dense new growth from just below the cut.
- Thinning means either removing a lateral branch at the bottom where it attaches or shortening a branch's length by cutting to a lateral large enough to act as a replacement for the terminal limb. A woody plant responds to thinning by becoming more open but retaining its natural growth habit and does not usually produce a flush of vigorous new growth

The goals are (1) to limit the number of fruits in the tree (thereby fostering consistent production of quality fruit), (2) to reduce the possibility of disease (there is an increased risk of Monilia if fruit is poorly distributed in "clusters"), and (3) to guarantee proper tree development by avoiding excess weight *(photo 13)*.

The number of fruits that a tree will bear after thinning depends on its variety and health. On a tree of average vigor, the yield may vary from 750 to 1,250 fruits.

It is quite difficult to visually count the number of apricots on a tree, and usually that estimate comes in low. Only a complete count will give a precise idea of what the tree can handle. Some trees may bear more than 2,000 apricots prior to thinning! The way the fruits spread throughout the tree is equally important; this results from the variety's behavior and its tendency to produce on short and/or long branches.

On short branches (spurs and flowering shoots),

14. Properly spaced fruit distribution with clustered fruit thinned.

15. Production on long branches.

from the cut. Foliage grows more deeply into the tree because more light can penetrate the canopy. Except when trees are newly planted, pruning cuts should be mostly thinning cuts.

Pruning takes place in the spring (at least one month prior to harvest) in order to improve light penetration, fruit quality, and coloration, as well as **floral induction** (the production of new flower buds) in the more shaded spots. Only shoots that may be useful in bolstering saggy scaffold branches should be preserved.

In cases where it is difficult to grow long fruiting branches (as with 'Bergeron' in the Rhone Valley, for example, or with younger 'Orangered®' trees), the best-situated branches should be cut back, preserving three or four buds and promoting the growth of one or more fruiting branches.

SUMMER PRUNING

This promotes branch development and health. The two basic goals of summer pruning are to obtain optimal thinning and to enhance the tree's branching potential. Keep in mind the following points:

Suppressing poorly lit branches and secondary branches around the base of the tree as well as excess scaffolds should always be comprehensive, "all or nothing."

Renovating the scaffolds, if there is reason to, involves cutting back shoots that are two or three years old. It is essential to "anticipate" how the scaffold will be renovated by preserving an **epicormic branch** (a new, vigorous shoot breaking from a location other than a leaf axil and growing mainly upright) two to three seasons prior to removal of the older scaffold.

Removing fruiting organs, especially excess flowering shoots or spurs (because of lack of light or scraping of fruit by shoots), is the last phase of summer pruning. Branch selection will depend on their position within the tree and the quality of their floral buds.

Recently strengthened scaffold branches may be bent if necessary, while the tree is producing sap (that is, actively growing).

Happy harvesting!

CHERRY

Author	Jacques CLAVERIE

GENERAL OVERVIEW

Human beings worked for centuries among the wild cherry trees of Europe's forests in order to tame sweet cherries for cultivation *(photo 1)*. The species rapidly became economically viable and still plays an essential role today in the arboriculture of temperate climates. As it is the first fruit to be harvested each season, it generates substantial profits as well.

Thanks to genetic improvements and selection, today there is a wide range of **varieties** and successful rootstocks, both for the novice and for the professional tree farmer.

Botanical Classification

Within the Rosaceae family, all cherry trees belong to the *Prunus* genus, as is the case with most cultivated stone fruits.

The American botanist Alfred Redher classified these species in 1947 (see Appendix A: *Prunus* Botany). The base chromosomal number for *Prunus* is n = 8, equal to the number of chromosomes inherited from each parent during **hybridization**.

The sweet cherry, *P. avium*, is a **diploid** species (2n = 2x = 16). Certain hybrids of *P. avium* and *P. cerasus* have characteristics of each parent, the best known being the so-called "English" cherry and 'Duke'.

P. avium (sweet cherry) got its name from the sweet taste of its fruit. The group is divided into two subgroups:

1. An older tree in Benauge, France (Belliquette variety).

2. *P. cerasus* fruits (amarelle-type sour cherry), Montmorency sour cherry.

- Bigarreau—sweet fruits with tough skins and white or red skin/flesh ('Burlat', 'Napoleon');
- Morello—sweet fruits with soft skins ('Early Rivers' morello).

Note that morellos are sweet, non-acidic fruits but with soft skins; they should not be confused with proper sour cherries (*P. cerasus*). The bigarreau subgroup represents 95% of all commercial cherries available today. Morellos only exist in their older forms.

P. cerasus (sour cherry) consists primarily of cherries destined for other commercial uses, such as preserves, fruit juice, and pastries *(photo 2)*. Sour cherry is also divided into two subgroups:

- Amarelle—sour cherries with clear juice ('Montmorency');
- Griotte—sour cherries with colored juice ('Griotte du Nord', 'Guin des Charentes').

Several related species are not typically used for their fruit but as rootstocks (*P. mahaleb*, see "Rootstocks" later in the chapter), for landscaping in gardens (*P. canescens*, *P. dawyckensis*, etc.), or for naturalizing—for example, creating a "forest edge" (*P. padus*).

Origin of the Species

The sweet cherry, *P. avium*, originally came from the area situated between the Black Sea and the Caspian Sea. It was spread throughout Europe and Asia by migrating birds, from which it gets its name (birds are from the avian species, hence *P. avium*).

Assorted groups of people also transported the sweet cherry, especially Roman armies during various campaigns. It is believed that the cherry was known during the period 4000–5000 B.C. and that it served as food for humans. Theophrastus gives the first historical data on cherries in the sixth century B.C.; later, the Greek doctor Diphilus mentions that the best are the

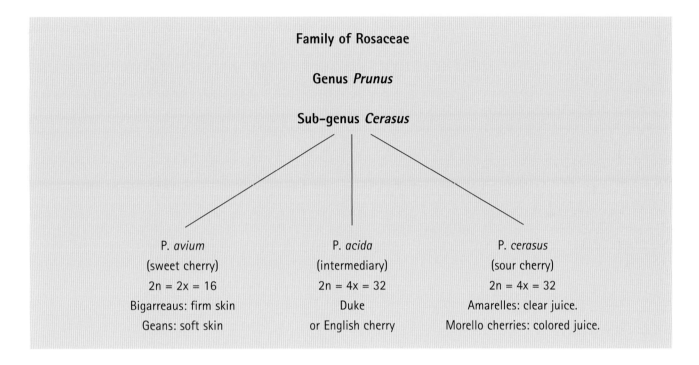

Family of Rosaceae

Genus *Prunus*

Sub-genus *Cerasus*

P. *avium*	P. *acida*	P. *cerasus*
(sweet cherry)	(intermediary)	(sour cherry)
2n = 2x = 16	2n = 4x = 32	2n = 4x = 32
Bigarreaus: firm skin	Duke	Amarelles: clear juice.
Geans: soft skin	or English cherry	Morello cherries: colored juice.

red cherries or those from the kerasos tree, which eventually led to the generic Latin specific *cerasus.*

Pliny the Elder states that the cherry tree must have come to the Mediterranean basin in 73 B.C., when Lucullus was victorious against Mithridates.

But those theories are widely contested today. The cherry tree seems to have already been in place in those countries prior to 73 B.C. Important studies in molecular biology are now under way to retrace the species' dissemination throughout Europe and Asia, as well as to study the different sources of observed variations (the study of gene flow).

Worldwide Production: Recent and Future Developments

At the beginning of the twenty-first century, worldwide production of sweet and sour cherries is approximately 2.5 million tons, 80% of which are grown in the Northern Hemisphere. These numbers are changing rapidly, however, with the emergence of new countries as producers and exporters, such as Turkey, Chile, Argentina, and Australia. Recent plantings have been undertaken in China, which could soon become part of the export market.

European production is currently around 1.4 million tons. These numbers will also change quickly as new plantings become established—notably, in Turkey (where production is expected to be around 400,000 tons). The primary countries of production in Europe are Spain, Germany, France, Italy, and Greece.

French production remained around 100,000 tons for several years but today has dropped to less than 60,000 tons, 30% of which are two-colored fruits for commercial use. This drop can be attributed to several factors: the non-renewal of plantings, the aging ranks of cherry growers, and the various limitations that the species presents (in terms of harvest, selling price, etc.). Recent changes in orchards toward diversifying with newer systems for tree care, as well as new varieties and rootstocks, has not brought France back to its prior level of production. We should point out also that annual consumption of cherries is less than 2 pounds (1 kg) per person, which limits the fruit's economic viability.

These recent modifications and developments will bring about a major transformation in worldwide cherry production. France is currently in competition with Spain for varieties that produce earlier. Spain now produces two times as many cherries as France (120,000 tons), whereas the reverse was true twenty years ago. France exports about 5,000 tons of cherries but imports the same amount, so its commercial balance is neutral.

PRODUCTION ZONES IN FRANCE

The primary production zones are in the southern part of the country. The Rhone-Alpes and Provence-Alpes-Côte d'Azur regions constitute 70 to 80% of production, with all of their fruit going to commercial use.

The southwest, Languedoc-Roussillon, and the Lyon region have seen a drop in production over the past thirty years. There has recently been a significant increase of newly planted areas in Languedoc-Roussillon, particularly in the Costières du Gard, Montpellier, and Pyrénées-Orientales regions, as well as in the Loire Valley. The southwest maintains an average of 10% of national production. There are local cherry producers in several other French regions as well (the Tarn Valley, Itxassou in Basque country, Alsace, etc.).

THE PRODUCTION OF SWEET CHERRY IN NORTH AMERICA

In the United States, commercial production of sweet cherry is dominated by Washington State, California, and Oregon, respectively in order of total production, with much lower production in Michigan and a few other states. British Columbia is also a major producer in North America, particularly in the Summerland area. To the south, Mexico is gradually introducing sweet cherry to commercial production, but its options are very limited with respect to sufficient chilling requirements. As is true of sweet cherry culture elsewhere, the main considerations for successful growth and cropping include sufficient winter chilling, low incidence of frosts at flowering and **fruit set**, and low risk of rain during fruit maturation.

SPECIES-RELATED LIMITATIONS

The cherry tree is a rustic species capable of adapting to a broad range of soil-related and climatic conditions. However, its development is limited by a few physical, climatic, physiological, and economic factors.

Physical Limitations

SOIL

The species is well adapted to deep, uniform soil. Planting in other types of soils may limit its development. The use of different *P. avium* rootstocks allows it to be cultivated in dry or calcareous soils that cause **chlorosis** *(photo 3)* (using *P. mahaleb*) or in mineral-poor soils (using wild cherries or interspecies hybrids).

The main limitation is in adapting to dense, humid soils where there is heavy rainfall. No rootstock is resistant to root asphyxiation; only the use of 'Colt' rootstocks or *P. cerasus* can improve performance in such difficult conditions.

Climatic Limitations

CLIMATE

The sweet cherry tree can adapt to a wide variety of climates. In Europe, it is grown from southern Spain to Norway, but there are some restrictions in terms of temperature, rainfall, and sunlight.

3. A cherry tree showing signs of iron chlorosis.

SPRING FROSTS

As with almost all *Prunus* trees, the cherry tree is very sensitive to spring frosts at the moment of flowering, as well as to "hard" frosts earlier in the **dormant** period. Flowers can withstand temperatures as low as 25°F (-4°C), but the most sensitive stage is when the young fruit starts to form, at which point temperatures should not go below 30°F (-1°C). In high-risk areas, it is imperative to plan for anti-frost protection. (For more on freezes and frosts, including tables showing critical temperatures for sweet cherry buds in the states of Michigan and Washington, see Appendix B: Freeze/ Frost Damage in *Prunus* Species.)

In cherry trees, any significant stress that compromises the trees will contribute to lower cold hardiness and greater susceptibility to either freezing temperatures or lack of chill.

INADEQUATE CHILL

Sweet cherry requires a relatively high amount of chilling, compared to most stone fruits. Various chill models have been developed over the last fifty years, but the one used most often for horticultural tree crops is the Chill Hour (or 45°F) Model, in which one hour at or below 45°F (7°C) equals one Chill Hour. A similar model is the Utah Model, which includes a variable calculation that accounts for more or less effective chilling around the 45°F optimum, with less effective chilling until 32°F or 0°C (no accumulation at freezing) and less effective chilling up to 55°F (13°C). 'Bing', the most commonly recognized variety grown in the United States, reportedly has a chill requirement of 850 to 880 chill hours.

These methods of calculating chill accumulation and chilling requirements are satisfactory for continental U.S. climate zones in all but the warmest areas. In California, sweet cherry growers typically use a model developed for Mediterranean climates that accounts for periodic warming and cooling during the dormant period. What is important to understand, however, is that *minimum* chill requirement does not indicate an optimum for growth, but rather a requirement for breaking rest (dormancy). Nurseries supply varieties that usually have a defined chilling requirement and the USDA zones that are optimum for production. Because California's climate is Mediterranean, a number of low-chill-requiring varieties of sweet cherry (and other fruit species) have been developed for its growing conditions. These may be useful in other areas where chilling accumulation from October through bloom (mid-March in California) is less than 800 chill hours; however, sweet cherry may not be grown subtropically. Breeding programs at the University of California–Davis and by Zaiger Genetics in Modesto, California, have produced many outstanding low-chill-requiring varieties of stone fruits.

RAINFALL
Worldwide, rainfall is the most limiting physical factor in growing cherries since it is so unpredictable during flowering and maturation. During blossoming, rain disturbs **pollination** by preventing insects from flying and by causing damage (blossom brown rot, or *Monilia laxa*). At maturity, rain causes fruits to "crack" *(photo 4)* in sensitive varieties, making them unfit for sale. There is no efficient prevention tool against these climatic occurrences apart from using

4. Fruit that has been damaged by pre-harvest rains.

over-tree canopies, or "tunnels," to protect the trees, but that becomes quite expensive per acre. Moreover, tunnels create humid conditions that increase disease, can cause cracking in very sensitive varieties (such as 'Brooks'), and reduce bee visitation for pollination. The stage when the fruit is most susceptible to rain occurs during the onset of ripening, when fruits start to change color.

Fruit cracking or splitting is the major cause of economic loss, but rain damage also includes fruit softening, discoloration, and increased decay. These problems result in a general reduction of fruit quality, marketability, and consumer confidence. Factors that may influence the severity of cracking include **cultivar**, fruit maturity stage, crop load, fruit firmness, orchard irrigation status, duration of rainfall, and temperature. It is believed that these factors affect fruit turgor by changing the potential for water uptake or the fruit skin's ability to withstand stress. Cherry fruit skin is a mere fraction of an inch thick (approximately 0.2 mm, or three to four epidermal cell layers), and rainwater is taken up readily, swelling the sub-epidermal (flesh) cells more than the epidermal cells.

Conditions that increase the likelihood of cracking (besides more rain) are as follows:
- light crop load.
- greater fruit maturity—darker fruit are more likely to crack than lighter fruit, up to and including mahogany fruit. However, dark mahogany fruit (not a color grade for 'Brooks', other light red cherries, or white cherries such as 'Rainier') tend to crack less, as they are "over-mature."
- irrigation status—water-stressed fruit will swell more with water contact.
- warmer air, more sun.

LIGHT

The species is very sensitive to direct light, which is important for proper fruiting. In the section on fruiting, we will see that **spurs** have a vegetative bud in their center that will only survive if exposed to ample direct sunlight. Where sunlight is reduced, such as within the interior of a dense **canopy**, flower bud production will gradually decrease and spurs will become non-productive. Eventually, "blind nodes" will be obvious along branches, where no production and no branching will form in the future. This loss of productivity becomes permanent unless branches are removed to open the canopy for light penetration.

HEAT

The consequences of high heat during fruit maturation and flower bud development include doubling, spurring, and deep suture disorders.

Excessive summer heat can create anomalies in floral buds, causing the formation of double fruits in the following year's harvest *(photo 5)*. High (approximately 90°F / 32°C or more) temperatures during the last stages of cherry maturation (as the fruits reach maturity) can result in reduced fruit size, softer cherries, and shorter shelf life (a post-harvest issue affected by pre-harvest conditions). Some growers irrigate spe-

5. A double cherry at fruit set.

cifically to cool the orchard (via evaporative cooling), generally by means of impact sprinkler, microsprinkler, or drip irrigation. While this approach may reduce the risks listed above, it can also increase the risks for more fungal infection of the fruit (especially brown rot due to more humid conditions) and the trees (various fungal diseases). It can also cause the fruit to crack if water drenches it—primarily a problem related to impact sprinklers.

Evaporative cooling, if applied over-tree as sprinkling, has potential benefits in reducing doubling, spurring, and deep suturing, which occur when ambient temperatures are high during flower bud formation. Lowering the air temperature through evaporative cooling is a cultural practice that shows potential for reducing risk.

Physiological Limitations

HEALTH

Ever since the time of its forest origins, the species has remained highly vigorous (displaying vegetative vigor at the expense of reproductive vigor). This is a handicap for orchard performance. However, genetic progress along with new rootstocks and changes in growing techniques are helping to control growth in favor of fruiting. Classic pruning is insufficient for controlling vegetative growth; in fact, it even tends to spur it on.

FRUITING

Fruiting is highly dependent on the tree's vigor and is considered rather slow because the juvenile period for cherry trees lasts a long time (generally, three to four years in commercial orchards). In terms of controlling vigor, rootstocks and growing techniques can allow the tree to produce earlier. Dwarfing rootstocks, in particular, and certain standard rootstocks (such as *P. mahaleb*) induce **precocity** (early bearing). Pruning methods that encourage spur development can also aid precocity. Even once trees start bearing, some rootstocks will encourage production of new spurs on two-year-old wood; rootstocks that result in high vigor tend to allow new spur production on three-year-old wood.

GRAFTING

The cherry tree cannot be grown with its own roots since its hardiness is problematic for commercial orchards. Thus, grafting is essential: it permits a choice of rootstocks that are adapted to your specific growing conditions and physical environment. This operation greatly affects the yield of the grafted plant.

Any classic grafting technique may be used with the cherry tree.

Economic Limitations at Harvest Time

Harvesting is done by hand for three main reasons: the fruits are fragile, they are often not firm, and consumers prefer cherries with stems attached (the "peduncle" is the fruit stem). Hand harvest costs in the United States and Europe account for nearly 60% of the selling price.

The creation of new varieties that are firmer and less fragile will permit mechanized harvesting. However, increased firmness in sweet cherry can also be accomplished by the use of gibberellin (GA_3), which growers apply during fruit development in commercial orchards throughout the United States. Mechanical harvest may be aided by the application of ethylene-releasing chemicals (Ethephon or Ethrel), but these cause fruits to soften and can lead to "gumming" in the tree. Ethylene, a naturally occurring plant growth regulator, causes ripening in many fruits as well as abscission (separation or dropping) of plant organs. Therefore, cherries treated with ethylene will separate from their stems, which allows mechanical harvest by limb or trunk shaking and also reduces tearing of the flesh or loss of juice from the stem-end. Although this method is used in the sour (tart) cherry harvest for processed fruit, it is not commercially used for sweet cherry at this time.

Cherries do not have a **climacteric peak**, so the fruit will not continue to ripen after having been picked (unlike the peach, for example). The fruits must be picked at a precise moment: at harvesting maturity, which is determined by color development and soluble solids content, or Brix.

THE TREE: ARCHITECTURE, ORGANIZATION, FUNCTION

Vegetative Development

Becausee they are intricately connected, information on vegetative growth, branch description, and fruiting sites appears in the section "Training the Tree" later in this chapter.

Flowering and Fruiting

Cherry trees bear flowers on floral buds along the base of two- to three-year-old branches and on spurs (see "Training the Tree" later in the chapter).

CHERRY BLOOM STAGES

Most flowers are borne on the short shoots called "spurs," although many can also be borne on long extension shoots. Spurs are important because they can live and produce flower/fruit buds for many years. Spurs take two to three years to form initially, and they primarily appear in the outer areas of the canopy (fruitwood tends to be "lost" in the shaded inner canopy). Thus, their loss through damage, disease, or other means sets back production significantly. Spurs are the main source of flower production in stone fruits in general, with the exception of peach (which has very limited if any spur production). Pears and many apples also produce on spurs.

In sweet cherry, the buds that give rise to flowers are called "trussbuds" (that is, in California cherry culture). They are compound buds containing inside flower buds and leaf buds. Usually, two to several flower buds form inside each trussbud.

CHERRY POLLINATION BIOLOGY

Almost all sweet cherry varieties are **self-incompatible**; thus, they require **cross-pollination** by a compatible cross-pollenizer. In order to "cover" all phases of bloom, it is preferable to use more than one pollenizer. Doing so also reduces the risk of lack of set due to adverse pollen development, which can occur in some varieties either from lack of chill or from rainy conditions at bloom. In all *Prunus* species, bees are required for pollination—even among **self-compatible** species and cultivars—because bees carry the pollen, which is larger and stickier than the wind-carried pollen of species that do not require insect vectors of pollen transfer.

Some growers of stone fruits mistakenly believe that self-compatible means "no bees required'"; however, that is not the case for any stone fruits. Cherry growers are well aware of the need for bees. Recent research on solitary bee pollination of sweet cherry shows promise in adverse weather conditions, but there is no commercial application at this time.

In order for bees to successfully transfer pollen among trees, the following weather conditions are required:

- temperatures at around 65 to 70°F (18 to 21°C) are ideal; bee activity below 55°F (13°C) is very limited;
- winds below approximately 15 mph (higher wind speeds impede bee activity);
- approximately 60% sunlight or more is optimal.

All *Prunus* species have similar flowers. Among the stone fruits, the essential structures in the flower include: **pistil**, **stamens**, nectaries (plant glands that produce nectar), and petals. (These are important attractants, as nectar is a high-sugar food source for bees.) For purposes of pollination and fruit set, the important structures of the pistil are the **stigma** (the upper receptive surface for pollen "capture" and germination), the style (the stalk of the pistil), and the ovary at the base. The ovary contains two ovules, one of which will persist when fertilized to form the seed. The important structures of the stamen are the **anthers** (pollen sacs), the pollen inside the anthers, and the stalk of the stamen. Because these structures form inside the flower bud during the summer before the flowers will bloom, both nutritional and environmental conditions during the time of formation (the period of **floral induction and floral differentiation**) affect how many flowers form and how well developed and functional they will become. However, in *Prunus* species the final development of the critical structures in the flower bud is not complete until the dormant period. The completion stages vary a little from species to species.

POOR POLLINATION AND FRUIT SET

Weather-related factors that can contribute to poor pollination include the following:

- excessively cool temperatures during bloom;
- excessively warm temperatures during bloom;
- rain during bloom.

Very cool periods during bloom impede bee pollination. They also lengthen the time needed for pollen tubes to grow down the style of the pistil to the ovary, in order to fertilize the ovule. Pollen tube growth is temperature-driven; thus, the timing of this event must overlap with the length of time that the ovule remains viable before it degrades and **fertilization** becomes impossible. The "life" of the ovule is also somewhat temperature-related, in that it degrades more quickly in excessively high temperatures than at "normal" ambient temperatures.

The stigmatic surface of the pistil, which receives the pollen deposited by bees crawling into the flower for its nectar and pollen, must also develop "receptivity" to the pollen grains. This means that the stigma, which is made up of secretory cells, must develop for about two days after the flowers open to exude stigmatic fluid. This fluid is the germination medium for the pollen grains. The stigma remains receptive once it is "wet" for about two days, during which time compatible pollen must be deposited, germinate, and produce pollen tubes that grow through the stigma and down into the style.

The period from the start of stigma receptivity through degradation of the ovule is the **effective pollination period**, or EPP. This period can last around two to four days, but the duration is somewhat flexible because it depends on weather conditions. Higher temperatures cause the pollen tubes to grow more rapidly; but excessively high temperatures (above about 78°F or 26°C) cause the ovule to degrade more rapidly, thereby shortening the EPP. If temperatures are too low (under approximately 60°F or 16°C), pollen tubes won't grow

through the style quickly enough to reach the ovule in time to fertilize it. Furthermore, should conditions be warm and windy, the stigma may dry out too quickly and pollen germination will be inhibited.

Fruit set can also be inhibited by post-bloom cool weather and/or rain. Under these conditions, the fruit growth slows down and the sink strength (the demand of developing organs, such as fruits, for photosynthates to drive growth and development) of those fruits is lower; thus, post-bloom **physiological drop** may be higher.

For sweet cherry, floral induction (the transformation of a vegetative bud into a floral bud) begins in early June and finishes at the end of summer. The exact timing of floral induction varies among latitudes and among species; this is true for stone and pome fruits in general. The final development of the reproductive organs (pollen and ovule) occurs during the dormant period shortly before **budbreak**.

The flowering period is relatively precocious, generally occurring in early spring. For each variety, this period lasts about two to three weeks depending on the year. The overall period for all varieties lasts a little over a month.

As mentioned earlier, cross-pollination is necessary for most sweet cherry varieties. Compatibility groups (five have been defined) are based on genetic compatibility among varieties. Research in molecular biology is currently examining allele markers for compatibility. In terms of new varieties, this approach will offer a rapid and trustworthy way for determining which group each tree belongs to.

For the past twenty years, there have been **self-fertile** varieties that don't require a pollinator. The first known variety, 'Stella', was the result of Canadian research (in Summerland, British Columbia). Other self-fertile varieties resulting from these programs are of great interest to growers; however, there are only a few such varieties, and they are generally adapted to latitudes similar to those of British Columbia.

Fruit set, the stage following fertilization, marks the start of fruit growth and stone formation. Models for predicting harvest date are very limited and experimental at this time. Cherries require about two months from full bloom to reach harvest maturity.

Fruit drop, which varies by species and year, often indicates a problem with the tree: excessive weight, a cold period following fertilization, or slowed access to mineral nutrients. The fruit stops developing and drops within several days. Techniques for distributing the number of fruits, discussed in "Training the Tree" later in the chapter, lower the number of droppings through better tree balance.

FRUITING

Fruit evolves into maturity starting with **veraison**, the stage when the fruit changes color. (Another term, "colorbreak," refers to the specific change of pink to red color from straw-colored fruits.) Cherries do not experience a climacteric peak, so they should be harvested at an optimal stage of physiological maturation. Unfortunately, commercial constraints require that harvest be anticipated three to four days ahead of time. In fact, the time of commercial harvesting is defined within each variety by a color code: commercial growers consult a color chart that displays fruit coloration changes from veraison to maturity.

The size of the fruit increases rapidly in the days preceding harvest. Once the cellular multiplication phase is complete, the flesh cells undergo a period of growth but the skin of the fruit does not increase in cell number. Thus, as the fruit increases greatly in volume, the skin becomes progressively stretched; the resulting tension causes "microcracks" in the skin. These are sources of water entry in rainy conditions, leading to fruit cracking. The best size occurs at physiological maturity. In general, the fruit becomes less firm as maturity approaches (though this may not be apparent for firmer varieties). With certain varieties, such as 'Summit', firmness is measured with a FirmTech device (BioWorks, Inc.) and increases as maturity approaches. Excessive heat (over 86°F or 30°C) will hinder firmness. Fruits should be picked early in the morning, hydrocooled, and placed quickly into refrigeration.

PRINCIPAL VARIETIES

A Few Traditional and Attested Varieties

There is a wide range within cultivated varieties in terms of the tree's habit and behavior. Quite a few show two characteristics that are now considered negative: a strong intrinsic hardiness, and a late start to production (seven to eight years for certain varieties). With varietal renewal, many of these cultivars will disappear in favor of new selections that satisfy commercial and agronomic needs.

'Burlat'—A basic variety for more than fifty years, it has accounted for up to 40% of French orchards; but due to some unsatisfactory characteristics (firmness, size), its popularity is waning. Fruits weigh 8 to 9 grams (roughly three-tenths of an ounce), are reniform (kidney shaped), and have weak firmness. The tree is vigorous and erect with few branches; its fruit grows slowly and is difficult to train, even in free form.

'Précoce de Bernard' / 'Bigarreau Moreau'—Same date of maturity as 'Burlat', with firmer fruits and a lower rate of production. Fruits weigh 7 to 8 grams (roughly two-tenths of an ounce) and are rounded or reniform. The tree displays a less erect habit, has more open angles, and is easy to train.

'Van'—'Burlat' + 20 days; fruits weigh 7 to 9 grams and are rounded. The first firm variety, 'Van' was frequently planted but tends to produce smaller fruit when over-cultivated. It is a vigorous tree, semi-erect with dense branching. Rapid fruiting and the ability to produce on vertical branches allow its cultivation with vase training.

'Stark Vigorous Giant'—'Burlat' + 15 to 20 days; fruits weigh 8 to 9 grams, have good firmness and excellent quality, and are rounded to reniform. It is a vigorous tree that spreads out and displays average branching with very open angles: this is the ideal type of tree for training (axe, solaxe).

'Hedelfingen'—'Burlat' + 25 days; fruits weigh 7 to 8 grams and have an elongated heart shape. Being the latest variety to fruit, it is rapidly losing popularity. The vigorous tree is erect with a high number of branches; fruiting branches hang. This tree is quite adapted to training, particularly with the axe method.

'Lapins'—'Burlat' + 25 to 28 days; fruits weigh 7 to 9 grams, are slightly elongated, and display good firmness. It is a very vigorous tree, quite erect, with low branching. It is extremely difficult to train.

'Reverchon'—'Burlat' + 25 days; fruits weigh 7 to 9 grams, are typically heart-shaped, and display excellent firmness. This tree is slow to fruit and has low productivity. It is quite vigorous, has an erect habit with very few branches, and is very difficult to train (bowing is not effective).

'Napoleon'—A two-color variety meant for commercial use. 'Burlat' + 20 to 25 days; fruits weigh 7 to 8 grams and are rounded. The tree is an erect variety with sharp angles, which make it well adapted to vase training for mechanical shaking.

New Varieties Currently in Production

'Summit' is currently the most planted new variety with one of the largest fruits. Other new varieties include the vigorous 'Arcina® Fercer' *(photo 6)*; 'Duroni 3', which is difficult to pollinate since it flowers quite late; and 'Noire de Meched-Badascony', which is well adapted to training.

6. Arcina® Fercer

Future Varieties

Programs in genetic improvements are under way worldwide, especially in France (INRA UREFV Bordeaux) and Canada (Summerland Station). These have yielded several new varieties that professional growers are beginning to plant. Besides size, firmness, and agronomic quality, research goals include more rapid fruiting as well as broader or hanging habits. We can mention the new INRA selections 'Ferprime-Primulat®', 'Folfer', and 'Fertard'; Delbard nursery and garden varieties 'Earlise® Rivedel' and 'Bigalise® Enjidel'; and the Canadian-produced 'Satin® Sumele' and 'Sweetheart® Sumtare'.

For these varieties, studies on the best methods for training either have been completed or are in process within an experimental framework.

TRAINING THE TREE

An orchard's success results from three main factors:
- rapid fruiting;
- regular production;
- maintaining quality and size.

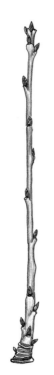

Fig. 1. A one-year-old vegetative branch on a young tree, yielding only wood buds.

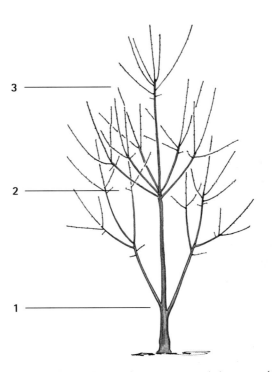

Fig. 2. Rhythmic growth on an unpruned cherry tree (natural habit): this is an example with three levels of scaffolds in whorls.

To reach those goals, two important technical aspects should be considered:
- the choice of training method;
- the techniques for balancing fruit loads and regulating fruit size.

Before addressing these issues, it is important to be familiar with the tree and how it performs.

Knowing the Tree and Its Performance

TREE ARCHITECTURE

In its natural state, without human intervention, the sweet cherry tree (*P. avium*) produces a vertical trunk bearing branches at regular intervals that form **verticils** (growth that is **rhythmic**) *(figs. 1 and 2)*. Growth is **monopodial**, the terminal eye being the site of prolongation (unlike the walnut tree, which displays **sympodial growth**).

Growth is also **orthotropic**, or nearly vertical. Only after a few years does natural bending begin as a result of the weight of branches, leaves, and fruits. In terms of the tree's **architecture**, there are significant differences among varieties *(fig. 3)*.

Branches located in the **distal** sections of structural branches stand more erect and are hardier as a result of the species' strong **acrotony**. The terminal bud on each branch plays an important role in the branch's future structure: this bud controls and inhibits inferior buds. As vegetation renews each spring, this bud loosens its inhibiting action, allowing five or six inferior eyes to sprout as well. The **proleptic** branches form verticils *(fig. 4)*. Their number diminishes as the tree ages. After six to eight years, no more verticils form and the tree

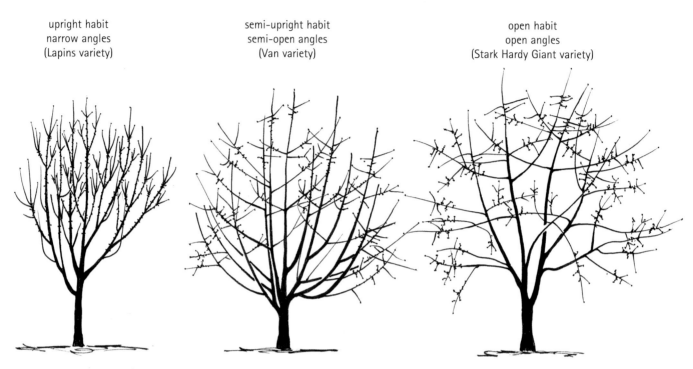

upright habit
narrow angles
(Lapins variety)

semi-upright habit
semi-open angles
(Van variety)

open habit
open angles
(Stark Hardy Giant variety)

Fig. 3. Three types of natural habit.

reaches a point of balance favoring fruiting. At this point, the juvenile period has ended.

Depending on the climate and growing practices, **sylleptic** or **secondary shoots** may appear. They develop on the branch at the same time as the terminal bud, at sharp **insertion angles**. For this reason, it is recommended that they not be used as fruiting branches.

VEGETATIVE STRUCTURE OF THE BRANCH
Observing the branch at the end of its annual growth cycle, we discover two distinct zones whose functions determine subsequent pruning techniques *(fig. 5)*. The **basal** or **preformed** zone at the base of the branch consists of the eyes that are already present in the bud before it begins another growth cycle. This zone comprises eight to ten eyes that will produce floral buds and thereby guarantee one part of production. The absence of vegetative buds in this zone may cause barren areas in the following year.

The **neoformed** zone, which is separated from the preformed zone by a longer (or sometimes shorter) **internode**, forms as the branch grows and elongates. The number of its buds will depend on the tree's health, the zone's position on the tree, and the tree's variety. As the tree ages, this zone tends to shrink; thus, pruning for renewal is necessary. The eyes situated on the terminal sections are close together, while those in the **median** section are farther apart. This is due the branch's growth pattern, which is more rapid early in the growing season and slower toward the end.

All of these buds will produce the cherry tree's characteristic organs: spurs or short branches.

The transformation of buds into spurs should occur near the summit, if possible; colonization of the rest of the branch will be complete after a few years. Training techniques should allow this transformation to accelerate.

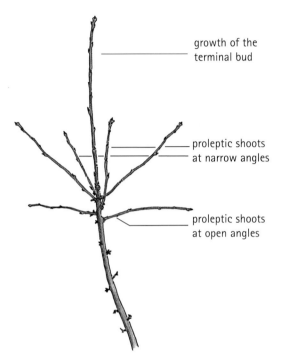

Fig. 4. A terminal vertical shoot demonstrating apical dominance by suppression of other laterals.

growth of the terminal bud

proleptic shoots at narrow angles

proleptic shoots at open angles

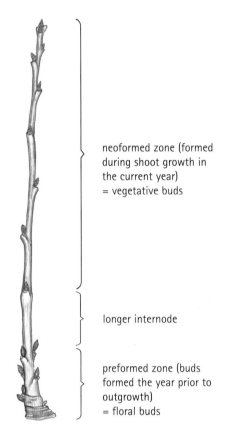

neoformed zone (formed during shoot growth in the current year) = vegetative buds

longer internode

preformed zone (buds formed the year prior to outgrowth) = floral buds

Fig. 5. A one-year-old vegetative branch yielding floral buds at its base.

FRUITING AREAS

The cherry tree's fruiting is relatively simple *(fig. 6)*. Only two types of production occur: on the simple flowering eyes along the base of the one-year branch, and on the spurs. Production by the flowering eyes along the base (in the preformed zone) will only happen once but may yield quality fruits. Training of the cherry tree can promote this type of production, but it means that the tree must constantly renew its branches. This is the principle that many growers follow in choosing shorter pruning techniques.

Spurs *(fig. 7)* comprise seven or eight floral buds along a stem containing a vegetative bud whose function is to guarantee continued production by elongating annually by a few millimeters (sometimes up to a centimeter or more—just a fraction of an inch). New techniques in training trees are based on the potential productivity of these spurs and their ability to last for several years, as long as there is no damage in the meantime.

The Fruiting Branch

Branches grow year after year as the terminal bud develops. As several elongations or growth units with spurs succeed one another on a single branch, a fruiting branch is formed *(fig. 8)*. These branches should be evenly spread and balanced on the structural axes

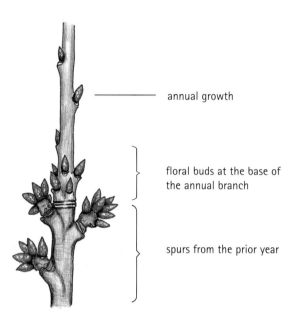

annual growth

floral buds at the base of
the annual branch

spurs from the prior year

Fig. 6. Fruiting sites: floral buds borne at the base of the 1 year old, vegetative shoot and spurs with floral buds.

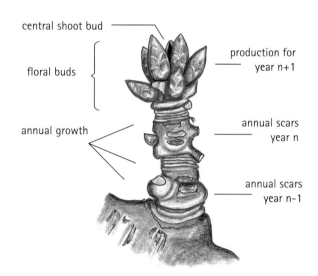

central shoot bud

floral buds

annual growth

production for
year n+1

annual scars
year n

annual scars
year n-1

Fig. 7. Multi-year function of a spur (from the end of summer to blossoming).

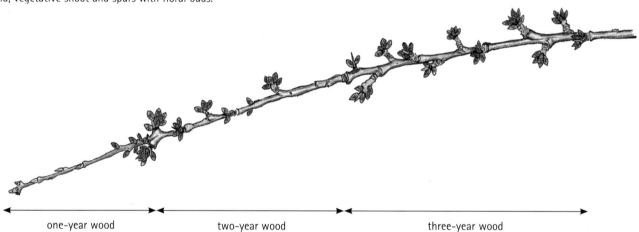

one-year wood   two-year wood   three-year wood

Fig. 8. A three-year-old fruit branch.

(trunk, **scaffold branches**). They should also receive ample light to ensure long-term survival.

WHICH BRANCHES SHOULD BE USED FOR BEARING FRUIT?

Any branch can become a fruiting branch *(photo 7)*. However, it is preferable to first make use of verticil branches,

being careful to remove those that have a narrow insertion angle. In order to balance the tree, it may be necessary to aid in branch growth along more barren zones, particularly in medial and basal zones. For weaker varieties, two techniques are useful when vegetation begins:

- making deep incisions above the bud that you wish to induce *(photos 8 and 9);* it is possible in this way

7. A fruit branch in production.

8. An incision.

to choose the level and direction of future fruiting branches;

• treating with growth regulators, which will promote several new growths along the structural axes; pruning then consists of removing poorly placed branches.

It is possible to combine both incisions and growth regulators.

Keep in mind that using secondary branches is quite difficult since they are merely **reiterations** of the principal axis. Their insertion angle is so narrow that it would require intense bowing to control their development.

THE ROLE OF BENDING IN TRAINING THE FRUITING BRANCH

By observing productive older trees that are growing naturally, we can see that a large number of fruit-bearing branches are inclined at a less-than-horizontal angle, with some even hanging down. This is natural bending.

All training techniques share the goal of obtaining the greatest number of ideally placed, productive branches. That is the role we should maintain with artificial bending.

The goal is to very rapidly induce the transformation of vegetative buds into spurs and to reduce

9. Vegetation resulting from an incision.

10. Bent branches: a colony of spurs.

competition between vegetative growth and fruiting *(photo 10)*. Bending may be achieved in several ways, each with the same rate of success:

- through the use of weights;
- through the use of thread or wire;
- through basal torsion of the branch;
- through the use of other tools (toothpicks or clothespins to increase the angles of young shoots).

The most favorable period for training branches is just after harvest, when the branches have grown to a length of 24 inches (60 cm) and **lignification** has begun. The ideal angle of inclination is between 120° and 135° in relation to the vertical axis.

Fruiting and Quality Control

Different techniques for training fruiting branches based on the variety–rootstock coupling will promote a more rapid production of abundant, even excessive, fruits. In fact, 10% of the tree's flowers are all that's needed to guarantee a sufficient commercial return (between 4 and 8 tons per acre, or 10 and 20 tons per hectare). Commercial fruit quality—which is determined by the fruit's measurement in millimeters (24 to 32 mm or more, or 0.9 to 1.25 in) or by its average weight in grams (between 8 and 15 g, or 0.02 and 0.5 oz)—is negatively proportional to overall production: high production creates smaller fruits, and vice

11. The principle of renewal pruning (shortening).

12. An example of pruning.

13. Vigorous fruit as a result of pruning.

versa. It is necessary to thin out the tree's overall fruit numbers in order to achieve a commercially optimal fruit size.

Two methods from two different "schools" are currently in practice: renewal pruning and artificial **extinction**.

RENEWAL PRUNING

This is the traditional technique that growers use. It consists of suppressing a large number of fruiting areas by means of winter pruning *(photos 11 and 12)*. In practice, the procedure suppresses the upper third of fruiting branches and can be performed on either older branches (four to five years) or younger branches (one

to three years). This method of shortening the branch has two disadvantages: it must be repeated annually; and it causes an imbalance within the tree's structure if done to excess, for uncontrolled reiterations promote the growth of spurs *(photo 13)*. Renewal pruning should take place after harvest in order to limit these secondary effects.

EXTINCTION PRUNING OF SPURS

A more efficient method involves extinction pruning (also called "artificial extinction") of spurs by manually or mechanically removing a certain number of them *(photo 14)*. Determining how intensely to do this requires an understanding of overall production and the

14. The principle of extinction of fruiting by spur removal.

15. An example of manually removing excess spurs.

desired size of the fruit. This is necessary to maintain a good balance between branch strength and fruit production. The principle is to remove any spurs that are judged to be in excess *(photo 15)*—notably, those in the distal areas of the branch, those that are poorly placed, or those that have low access to sunlight (usually underneath the branch). For complete effectiveness, the whole tree must be pruned. This may take place at the end of winter, in February, or just before flowering (at the end of March through the beginning of April).

Studies conducted in recent years demonstrate that at least 30% of spurs should be extinction pruned for the best results. Up to 60% may be pruned in this way depending on specific goals (such as obtaining very large fruits). Indeed, extinction pruning of spurs will cause a significant improvement in fruit size. With 'Burlat' and 'Summit', weight can increase up to 1.5 grams (or 2 to 4 mm in diameter). Moreover, on trees that have been pruned with the artificial extinction method, fruit ripens three to four days earlier, especially with precocious varieties.

Since extinction also creates space along the branch, the resulting aeration lowers the risk of **cryptogamic** infections (*Monilia laxa* and *Monilia fructigena*, among others).

THE "CHIMNEY" OR "LIGHT WELL"

The cherry is extremely sensitive to light, which is a necessary element for flower production and the tree's survival (more than fifteen years in sunny regions). Apart from positioning the branches and spurs to receive maximum light, it is important to allow ample light to reach the center of the tree. To that end, it is necessary to space the growth and branches around the main axes to a distance of 12 to 16 inches (30 to 40 cm). This technique, which can be combined with any of the training methods, is known as a "chimney" because it creates a light well within the tree.

Toward a New Type of Tree and the "Pedestrian" Orchard

Recent rootstocks have led to less vigorous trees, and the modern pruning techniques outlined here have helped to create new tree shapes (the two main types being multi-axis and solaxe). As a result, the look of orchards has changed.

THE MULTI-AXIS METHOD

Being based on the vertical axis method, which is widely known and practiced among tree growers, multi-axis involves spreading the tree's intrinsic fullness over a certain number of axes, generally between four and six *(fig. 9)*. The number of axes chosen depends on the vigor of the variety–rootstock coupling. The choice of axis should be based on more open insertion angles and position on the trunk in order to create more volume. Growers should follow the procedure outlined below:

- Plant an uncut **scion**, with no pruning.
- At the end of the first year in the orchard, cut back the trunk to a height of 16 inches (40 cm).

- During the second year of growth, choose four to six axes that have not been cut back. Select ones with a more open insertion angle.
- During the third year, in the spring, make incisions or apply growth regulators. In the summer, select future fruiting branches and begin bending them.
- In the fourth or fifth year, practice extinction pruning on productive branches.

Beyond this, maintenance will involve removing possible reiterations that cannot be used as well as cutting back productive branches to promote renewal.

THE SOLAXE METHOD

The solaxe training technique is based on the same principle as that for single-axis structures: spreading the fruiting branches around the axis *(fig. 10)*. This

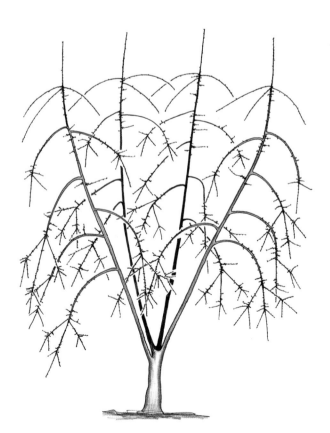

Fig. 9. Multi-Axis.

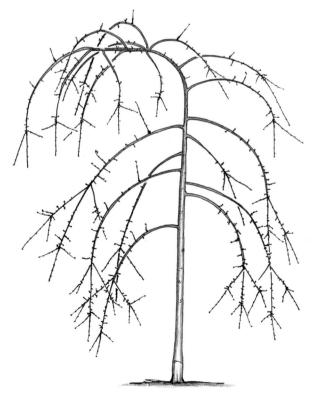

Fig. 10. Solaxe.

16. An orchard with solaxe training.

technique, which was developed for apple trees, has become successful with cherry trees thanks to the use of dwarfing rootstocks such as 'Tabel® Edabriz' and 'Gisela 5®' *(photo 16)*. The technique is relatively simple to perform. It aims to control the tree's development in order to promote rapid production. Growers should follow the procedure outlined below, which occurs entirely in the first year:

- Plant a whole scion, with no pruning.
- At the end of the first year (or the second if growth has been slow), train the axis toward a horizontal position.
- Remove branches that are inserted lower than 3 feet (1 m) high on the trunk.
- Make incisions or apply growth regulators.
- Select future branches with an eye toward even distribution along the primary axis and inclined branch.
- Systematically bend branches downward to an angle between 120° and 135° from the vertical, including the terminal verticil *(photo 17)*.
  - Begin extinction pruning on branches that have started to produce.

As with the multi-axis method, future maintenance

17. Flowering shoots hanging lower than horizontal.

will include pruning reiterated branches and suppressing branches that have produced for a few years, in order to ensure renewal. An orchard based on this system is known as a "pedestrian" or "semi-pedestrian" orchard, since all pruning and harvesting can be done from the ground *(photo 18)*.

ROOTSTOCKS

In order to be cultivated, cherry trees must be grafted. Experiments in developing trees from their own roots have resulted in overly vigorous trees. As varieties

18. A pedestrian orchard (Feugarolles, Lot-et-Garonne, France; pedestrian orchards can be harvested from the ground).

evolve toward less vigor, new attempts in this direction may occur.

The use of rootstocks allows the species to adapt to different soils and, more important, to modify the grafted variety's natural behavior by controlling vigor and fruiting. The primary problem with grafting has to do with the rootstock and the graft: **grafting compatibility** is not always perfect, and that can cause the tree to die quite rapidly or abruptly after several years in the orchard.

Propagation can take place in one of two ways: (1) vegetative, or (2) asexual propagation: cutting, layers, in vitro; sexual propagation, with seeds: commercial bundles, or controlled and certified selections.

The grafting operation, which is an important and delicate process, may be undertaken at various periods depending on the seedling's vegetative state. The grafting can take place in summer, during the "sleeping" eye phase, or in spring or winter, during the "growing" eye phase. Grafting techniques vary greatly, but the most common are as follows:
- budding, which is done in the summer;
- cleft grafting or bark grafting, which is done in the winter.

The primary rootstocks used for cherry trees belong either to the subgenus *P. cerasus* or to one of the interspecies hybrids *(photo 19)*. These species are specific to the cherry tree and are not commonly used as rootstocks for other *Prunus* species (apart from a few cases of compatibility with *P. mariana* 'Myrobolan'). The currently available range allows the cherry tree to grow in varied pedoclimatic conditions, with a range of staged sizes from the very vigorous to the almost dwarfed.

The primary species include *P. avium, P. mahaleb, P. cerasus,* and their interspecies hybrids.

P. AVIUM

P. avium is the oldest of the species used, better known as the "franc" or wild cherry. The level of vigor is quite high, and fruit induction is quite slow (seven to eight

19. Point de greffe Burlat sur Sainte-Lucie SL 64.

years). Most propagate vegetatively, but some selections are diffused as seeds and present a high level of homogeneity. The wild cherry tree is still grown in nurseries for arboricultural purposes, especially in regions with poor soil quality (the Ardèche plateau in France, for example). It is also used for producing seedlings for amateurs (top-grafting and landscaping).

There is a good level of grafting compatibility. Lifespan, though much lower today, still may reach up to sixty years.

Propagated rootstocks include the following:
- F12-1: vegetative propagation, quite vigorous, slow fruiting.
- 'Pontaris® Fercadeau' and 'Pontavium® Fercahun': a wild cherry tree with homogeneous seedlings, slightly less vigorous than the F12-1, more rapid fruiting.
- "Common" wild cherry trees: depending on their place of origin, there is a range of heterogeneity.

P. MAHALEB

P. mahaleb was the second species to be used and is still widely in use today. It is commonly known as the

'Sainte-Lucie' because it was grown and developed by monks at the Sainte-Lucie convent in eastern France.

This species is related to the subgroup of *cerasus* and is subdivided into its own subgroups. Of those subgroups, the small-leaf versions are used as rootstock since they seem to be fairly compatible for grafting. The main problem with this species is its range of variance in terms of compatibility for grafting union: several types prove immediately incompatible, while others may not manifest a lack of affinity until much later, sometimes four to eight years later. This is known as delayed compatibility.

P. mahaleb creates a less vigorous graft than *P. avium*, starts producing more rapidly (in the fourth year), and has a higher level of production.

This rootstock is particularly well adapted to dry or calcareous soils in the Mediterranean, yet it also displays adaptability to a range of other soil types. It is, however, quite sensitive to soil dampness, which can cause rapid asphyxiation of the root system. This limiting characteristic prevents it from being used in soils with standing water or in denser soils that are more compacted or subject to heavy rainfall.

Propagating the rootstock happens in one of two ways:

- vegetatively through branch or leaf cuttings, in winter or in autumn (semi-woody cuttings);
- with seedlings: there are two types of commercial seedlings—those known as "common," which should be avoided since they present a high level of heterogeneity and a low level of compatibility for grafting union, and "certified" seed, whose agronomic performance is well known.

Propagated rootstocks include the following:

- INRA SL 64, from the 'Sainte Lucie' group: vegetative propagation, average to fuller vigor, excellent compatibility for union with virus-resistant varieties.
- 'Ferci pontaleb®': propagation from seed, homogeneous descendance; same characteristics as the SL 64.
- "Common" 'Sainte-Lucie' seedlings, which should be avoided due to their excessive heterogeneity, their low affinity, and their susceptibility to viral infection.

P. CERASUS

P. cerasus as a species offers the advantage of reduced vigor as well as rapid and high production. Still, production should be monitored so that the size of the fruit doesn't suffer.

This species was selected for its rustic character and its adaptability to different soil types. There are frequent cases of union incompatibility, so it is important to choose certified stocks that are guaranteed. The main representative is 'Tabel® Edabriz', which propagates in vitro. It is considered a veritable dwarf rootstock that has helped growers to reconceptualize orchards. Vigor is reduced by 30 to 50%, and a good level of production is induced rapidly.

Interspecies Hybrids

Within the *cerasus* group, a certain number of crosses have been created using botanical species related to the cherry tree. This has helped in developing a range of new rootstocks. Many are still under evaluation, but certain candidates show promise.

Propagated rootstocks and those still being tested include the following:

- 'Colt': a *P. mahaleb* x *P. pseudocerasus* hybrid, quite vigorous, rapid fruiting, resistant to moist soil.
- 'Maxma Delbard® 14 Brokforest': average vigor, rapid fruiting, the most widely used rootstock today.
- 'Gisela' Series: new rootstocks that are quite promising but still under evaluation.

CHESTNUT

Author   Jean-Marie LESPINASSE
Collaborators   Anne BOUTITIE
             Henri BREISCH

GENERAL OVERVIEW

With the chestnut tree *(photo 1)*, we meet the great family of Fagaceae in which a number of species (beech, oak, and chestnut) have a clearly woodland character (or **phenotype**) and a vast and varied geographic dispersion: from northern regions (deciduous species) to tropical regions (non-deciduous). (See Table 1.)

History and Phytogeographical Origins

Historically, the chestnut tree—or at least its ancestor *(Dryophyllum)*—existed in the Tertiary period 8.5 million years ago, as the fossil record (leaves and chestnuts) in the Ardèche region of France attests. Closer to the present, in the Quaternary period the chestnut tree was quite present in Europe (fossil pollen dates back 5,000 years), and its growing area shifted from the north to the south before spreading back northward after successive glacier retreats.

Next came the period when chestnut trees were progressively cultivated. The first traces of the chestnut being cultivated for its fruit were found to the east of the North Sea in the Caucasus region and in Azerbaijan (J.-R. Pitte). Cultivating the chestnut for its fruit implies grafting and possibly transporting **varieties** as grafts. This type of cultivation spread across Asia Minor (Turkey) toward Greece, then into Roman Italy, and finally into France. Historians have not resolved whether Romans introduced grafting techniques into Gaul or whether the Gauls were already familiar with them. The Gauls

1. A chestnut grove in Limousin, France.

did eat chestnuts, and chestnut trees did exist, at least in the wild. From there, fruiting chestnuts were developed by means of grafting, with periods of accelerated development occurring repeatedly. The last one dates to the eighteenth century *(photos 2 and 3)*.

The apogee of European production took place in the nineteenth century: 500,000 tons in France (which was the worldwide rate of production in 2002). In North America, the eastern half of the United States was covered with native chestnut trees until an Asian blight fungus destroyed them in the early 1990s. Starting in 1880, a rapid decrease of European production began that has lasted until today (less than 10,000 tons), with two slower periods during the two world wars. The causes for this decline are multiple and overlapping:

	Genres	
	Deciduous leaves	Persistent leaves (Evergreen)
Chestnut trees	*Castanea* (7 species)	*Castanopsis* (134 species), *Chrysolepis* (2 species)
Oak trees	*Quercus*	*Cyclobalanopsis, Lithocarpus, Quercus*
Beech trees	*Fagus and Nothofagus*	*Nothofacus*

Table 1. The *Fagaceae* family.

2-3. Grafting points on older chestnut trees (Langon, France).

- The rural exodus toward new industrial centers of growth.
- The arrival of ink disease around 1880, caused by a soil fungus, *Phytophthora cambivora*, followed by another species, *Phytophthora cinnamomi*. Trees killed by the ink are of no value for carpentry, but they proved so profitable to the tannin-extraction industry that many healthy chestnut trees were felled and sold for tannin (J. Reyne).

Agricultural developments in other areas, the green revolution for feed and grains, the expansion of potatoes as a universally grown vegetable in acidic soil, and progress in arboriculture: peach trees and cherry trees in the Ardèche and Cévennes regions pushed the chestnut trees out into uncultivated, remote, hilly, and more acidic land areas.

Later, in the 1950s, a new disease known as chestnut blight, caused by the fungus *Cryphonectria parasitica*, brought on new ravages in an era when there were not as many growers working with chestnut trees.

Finally, after abundantly using them as "breadfruit," people abandoned chestnut trees and took no steps to protect them.

In France, chestnut trees grow in older geological regions characterized by primarily acidic soils: mainly in Brittany, Limousin, the Ardèche region, the Cévennes, the Montagne Noire region, the Pyrenees foothills, the Maures regions, Estérel, and Corsica. In Spain, the chestnut mostly grows in the northwest in Galicia and Leon; in Portugal, in the northeast in the Trás-os-Montes region; in Italy, in many areas, especially in Campania (Avellino) and Piedmonte (Cuneo).

Current worldwide production is only about 500,000 tons. China is the major producer (40%), followed by Korea (15%) and various others producing less than 1 to 10%. In the United States, production in Oregon and Washington State is estimated at 300 acres (121 ha). California's production is estimated at 600 acres (243 ha), with about half of that acreage bearing by 2009. Most U.S. plantings are only ten to fifteen years old; 'Colossal' is by far the most common chestnut variety planted here. However, growers are also trying 'Dunstan', 'Skookum', 'Layeroka', 'Myoka', and similar varieties. Varieties grown today are primarily chestnut blight resistant.

Early and Current Growing Techniques

The development of chestnut orchards occurred during three periods, from a technical point of view:

- Initially, a very long period involved the grafting of wild samples: natural seedlings that "self-selected" until they grew large enough to be grafted beyond animals' reach. This method is still in use today.
- The planting of grafted plants and rootstocks, followed by on-site grafting in the eighteenth and nineteenth centuries, allowed for natural selection; but the arrival of ink disease caused extensive tree deaths.
- The grafting and layering in nurseries and planting in orchards began in the 1970s. (The twentieth century marked the arrival of seeds from Japanese chestnuts, *C. crenata*, which were used in attempts to re-grow chestnut trees that had been devastated by ink disease at the end of the nineteenth century; but those chestnut trees proved to be quite sensitive to frost. Finally, hybrids were created with the native *C. sativa*, such as 'Marigoule', 'Marsol', 'Précoce Migoule', and 'Bournette', and more recently 'Bouche de Bétizac' in France, and various hybrids elsewhere.)

Upkeep often involved the following activities:

- periodic thinning out of tough branches;
- tilling the soil at the tree base;
- mowing of grasses and ferns prior to harvest;
- creating berms in order to bury fallen leaves.

Top grafting occurred in two cases: to alter the variety, or to use an intermediary variety when the desired variety grafted poorly to the available rootstock—which happened frequently with chestnut trees, even within a single species.

Botanical Classification

The genus *Castanea* belongs to the family of Fagaceae and contains seven deciduous species that grow in temperate zones. Three are of definite interest for their fruits:

- *C. sativa* in Europe and Asia Minor;
- *C. mollissima* in China;
- *C. crenata* in Japan and Korea.

Other species have smaller fruits:

- In North America: *C. dentata*, the most woodland variety of all of them (almost completely destroyed by chestnut blight), and *C. pumila*, or "chinquapin," a shrub. Both produce tasty fruits.
- In China: *C. henryi*, a woodland variety, and *C. seguinii*, a shrub.

C. pumila and *C. henryi* are peculiar in that they only create one fruit per burr, whereas other species have three.

Species in the *Castanea* genus are **diploids** (2n = 24 chromosomes). Numerous interspecies hybrids have been created in various countries—for example, between *C. sativa* and *C. crenata* in Europe, and between *C. dentata* and *C. mollissima* in America.

Pedoclimatic Limitations and Varietal Adaptation

The ideal soil for chestnut trees is slightly acidic, deep, well filtered, with no stagnant water, and cool in summer. Careful choice of the **planting zone** is essential for successful cultivation, since chestnut trees are more demanding than most other fruit tree species. The ground must be tested to a depth of 24 inches (60 cm) to guarantee that it is healthy (not asphyxiating) and adequately loose. Chestnut trees won't grow in calcareous soils, where they develop **chlorosis** and die, or in heavy and poorly drained soils, where standing water can be a problem. However, it is important to provide calcium to the trees, especially if the soil is more acidic. Chestnuts will tolerate low pH soils very well, but not highly alkaline soils. Growers can acidify soils by adding elemental sulfur or aluminum sulfate to achieve a pH of slightly below neutral. Soils that are extremely acidic, below a pH of 5.5, should be remedied with active limestone to a pH of about 6.5.

The chestnut tree requires a microclimate that is free of frosts. Although the European species *C. sativa* is resistant to different types of frost, hybrid chestnuts may be sensitive to springtime frosts in frost-riven areas such as shoals, as well as strong winter or autumn frosts since the trees produce sap long into the autumn if temperatures are high enough.

Chestnut trees grow to an altitude of 1,312 to 1,640 feet (400 to 500 m) in southwestern France, 1,640 to 1,969 feet (500 to 600 m) in southeastern France, and up to 2,625 feet (800 m) in Corsica. In France, several native varieties have adapted to hillside growth at an altitude between 656 and 1,312 feet (200 and 400 m). Chestnuts grow successfully in the California Sierra foothills.

Currently, in California the principal **cultivar** is 'Colossal', with pollenizers chosen from among 'Silverleaf', 'Nevada', 'Eurobella', or 'Colossal' seedlings. A new pollenizer for 'Colossal' is 'Okei', a vigorous tree with abundant pollen and large nut size, but light bearing. Other new cultivars that produce nuts of excellent quality and very large size are 'Fowler' and 'Montesol'. Many other cultivars and hybrids are grown throughout the United States in very small numbers.

Vegetative and Floral Characteristics

The vegetative cycle of the chestnut tree is slightly different from that of other fruit trees: **budbreak** occurs a bit later in April, blossoming in June, fruit production from mid-September to late October, and leaf drop rather late in November. April flowering allows the tree to avoid most frosts, thereby guaranteeing annual production.

Vegetative growth on the branches is characterized by terminal bud abscission: the branch grows throughout the spring and then stops (often in June), the **apex** dries out and falls off, and the last lateral bud remains as the terminal bud *(photos 4 to 6)*. This process, which reflects **sympodial growth**, has significant consequences: when the shoot apex falls, it allows several lateral buds to grow, thereby creating a moderately **acrotonic** branch structure:

- The final three to five buds on a branch grow the most when they are freed up by apex abscission, which occurs at the end of the preceding growing season.
- Younger trees display strong **orthotropic growth**, producing more vertical and more vigorous shoots. These juvenile characteristics include the fact that one of the shoots will be quite vertical and will act as the leader (for up to three or four years).
- Adult trees display a weaker orthotropic tendency. There is no more leader, and shoots stop growing vertically.

In very particular cases, there is a more **basitonic** pattern of growth. This is evident when lateral branch development occurs around the trunk after a feeble growth period, when a transplant does not quickly succeed (a frequent phenomenon), or when a grower has pruned the trunk too much in an effort to raise the **canopy** higher. If basitonic branches are poorly

4-6. Apical abscission (from top to bottom: growing apex, drying, fallen).

placed, they should be removed early in their growing season in June and July, as they can become quite vigorous and sap the tree's energy (see "Training Chestnut Trees" later in this chapter).

Basitony also occurs when a chestnut tree is cut down to ground level, as the tree can easily spread out into several shoots from the base of the trunk. This characteristic is widely exploited in forest areas (copses) and where layering causes vegetative propagation. Basitony always results either from a growth anomaly or from human intervention.

Natural **extinction** of fruitfulness regularly occurs on chestnut trees when there is low sunlight. Branching results in an increase of terminal buds with an average multiplying coefficient of 3 (see the next section). This proliferation of vegetative spots causes an excessive development of fruiting areas that the tree cannot support except in the strongest of growing situations. That is why, if this system functions well while the tree is young, the rate of propagation lessens through progressive natural bud extinctions as soon as the tree's growth slows. This means that the weaker and more poorly lit branches and their laterals will no longer produce burrs. They will only yield male catkins, and then only leaves, and will end up drying out.

Chestnut tree **phyllotaxy** *(fig. 1)*—the arrangement of buds in the order they grow around the branch—may be of two types:

- 1/2: starting from a bud, one complete rotation must be made in order to count two buds and end up directly above the first (an example of **amphitony**);
- 2/5: two turns must be made in order to count five buds.

The 1/2 layout, called **distichous**, often occurs on hybrid varieties with the Japanese chestnuts along the **basal** section of branches and along young, vigorous branches. It creates a baffling palmette shape. In fact, the **architecture of the tree** is well organized; in the

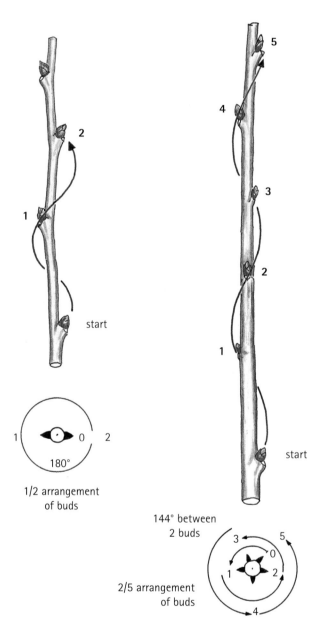

start

1/2 arrangement
of buds

144° between
2 buds

2/5 arrangement
of buds

Fig. 1. Chestnut tree phyllotaxy.

send out a main root that rapidly disappears in the second year, leaving room for a branching root system that burrows at an angle of 30° to 45°. Seedlings that are created by layering or cutting have a broader root system, one that eventually conforms to the variety's specific angles. Today's fruiting chestnut trees are large structures that have close ties to their forest origins. Most vegetation problems result from shallow soils in chestnut orchards. A minimum depth of 24 inches (60) cm is absolutely necessary.

A Glance at Chestnut Variability

Some chestnut trees may exhibit forest-like tendencies, such as abundant vegetation, straight trunks, minimal fruiting, small-sized fruit among C. dentata and C. henryi, and many trees from the C. sativa species. Alternatively, other chestnuts may behave much more like a fruit tree, with average vigor, a broad span, intense branching, abundant fruiting, and larger fruit sizes among C. crenata, C. mollissima, and numerous varieties selected from the C. sativa species.

The tree's shape may range from quite erect ('Bouche Rouge') to spreading ('Bournette') or even weeping if the fruit load causes the branches to bow. Chestnut tree architecture is rarely based around a central axis. In most cases, the axis only exists for the first three or four years.

There are a few different fruiting patterns:
• little fruit, only on a few branches;
• an abundance or even an excess of fruits (as with the *spicata* type, which exhibits a succession of female flowers on androgynous catkins and very small fruits);
• a good distribution of fruit with one to three burrs on each terminal bud; this is the case for selected fruiting varieties.

For most trees, one branch will produce three to five

following year it will develop branches that are perpendicular to the palmette branches.

The 2/5 layout mostly occurs toward the **distal** ends of the branch. It is widely dominant on fruiting branches of C. sativa varieties.

Chestnut trees root deeply. The young seedlings

7. A branch in bloom.

8. Spanish chestnuts (left) and chambered sweet chestnuts (more than one ovule within the exocarp; right)

'Précoce Migoule', exhibit simpler branching: one or two branches create a more erect shape with scattered branching ('Marsol'). These latter varieties, despite their low degree of branching, maintain good productivity, bearing four to six burrs per branch compared to two or three for other varieties.

Sensitivity to climatic changes—winter frosts, springtime frosts, cold requirements in winter, heat and light requirements in spring and summer—as well as susceptibility to diseases and pests also vary greatly within the *Castanea* genus.

Annual Cycle of Vegetation, Phenology, and Floral Induction

At budbreak in April a green shoot appears, rapidly followed by the start of the first catkins. Chestnut trees have both male and female flowers, making them **monoecious** *(photo 7);* but if those flowers are clearly separated into two types of inflorescences, they are **diclinous**.

Chestnut flowers are found in two kinds of catkins,

shoots in the following year; these grow from the last three to five **axillary buds**.

Shoots four and five, when they exist, do not generally fruit but die off rapidly. The third shoot will often fruit one year and then have its laterals die off. As for the first two shoots, they generally continue to create productive branches. That is the case for numerous interspecies hybrids such as 'Marigoule', 'Bournette', 'Bouche de Bétizac', and most varieties of *C. sativa*. A few hybrid varieties, such as 'Marsol' and

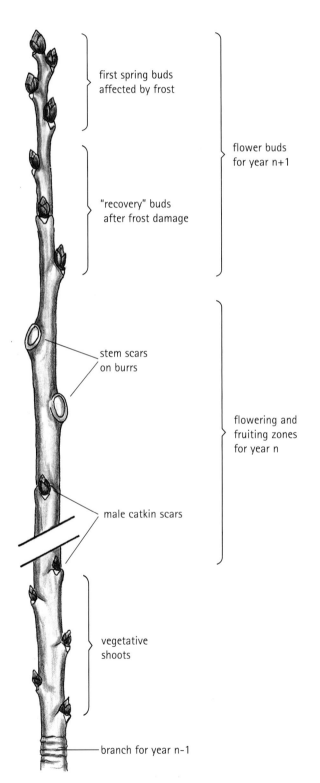

first spring buds
affected by frost

"recovery" buds
after frost damage

flower buds
for year n+1

stem scars
on burrs

flowering and
fruiting zones
for year n

male catkin scars

vegetative
shoots

branch for year n-1

Fig. 2. Fruiting branch in winter.

the first of which has only male flowers blooming prior to emergence of female flowers. At the base of the second type of catkin (androgenous or bisexual), small clusters of female flowers may be found in a green prickly inflorescence that resembles the fruit. Two or three female flowers within the inflorescence together form a two- to four-lobed prickly calybium, which fuses during growth to make the brown hull covering the fruits.

Fruiting occurs on growing branches that are the result of the last three or four axillary buds on the previous year's branches, thus displaying acrotony *(fig. 2; photo 9)*.

Floral induction, or the formation of floral primordia within the bud, occurs during the summer prior to blossoming for unisex male catkins and some of the androgynous catkins (which will have started to produce shoots), but not for the pistillate flowers that grow at their base. These will only form, by sexual differentiation, after budbreak in April or May, shortly before flowering. Together, the cold winter temperatures and the warm spring temperatures determine female flower formation, with the different varieties exhibiting different requirements. When those climatic conditions are

9. Sympodial branching and fructification on a Bournette.

not met, male flowers grow at the base of the androgynous catkins instead of the pistillate flowers.

Pollen may be transported by the wind when the air is dry (around the Mediterranean) or by insects. Bees collect nectar and pollen from male catkins but are not attracted to flowers that have **pistils**; therefore, most **pollination** is by the wind. The pollen also attracts other insects such as cantharids, which are small, elongated, orangey beetles.

The chestnut tree is **self-incompatible**, meaning that in most cases it doesn't pollinate itself. Therefore, several genetically different varieties need to be grouped together based on good genetic compatibility and similar flowering periods *(fig. 3)*. Varieties that belong to pure species such as *C. sativa* or *C. mollissima* are generally good pollinators. Interspecies hybrids are less efficient since they are less compatible.

Male catkins do not always carry pollen. Its quantity and quality are generally proportionate to the length of the stamen filament. Catkins on some commercial cultivars, such as 'Colossal', produce only a few or no staminate flowers; and other cultivars may shed pollen before the female flowers are receptive, thus giving rise to self-incompatibility. The pollen parent can influence the pollinated nut, particularly its size, via a phenomenon called "metaxenia." This is a condition in which pollen from a tree with large nuts may contribute larger size to the nuts of trees that ordinarily bear smaller nuts. There are three distinct types of male flowers:

- **longistaminate**—from 5 to 7 mm long, containing a lot of fertile pollen;
- **mesostaminate**—from 3 to 5 mm long, containing little pollen of average fertility;
- **brachystaminate**—from 1 to 3 mm long, containing practically no pollen; pistillate flowers often don't open at all, and the flowers are then considered **astaminate**.

Pistillate fowers generally produce three flowers (sometimes more, up to seven). Each flower is topped with **stigmata**, the visible parts of the pistil, which spread out during the period of full blossoming and pollen receptivity. The diameter of a growing inflorescence (denoting a future burr) ranges from 12 to 16 mm (roughly half an inch).

The flower contains about six ovules, not all of which are fertilizable. When a single ovule is fertilized, a whole fruit develops (this is the "marron" or "round" category). When several are fertilized, a partitioned fruit develops that contains several kernels (this is the "châtaigne" or "sweet" category) *(photo 8)*.

From blossoming at the end of June until September–October, the fruit grows. At maturity the spiky husk, or burr, opens or "cracks." This is the moment of **dehis-**

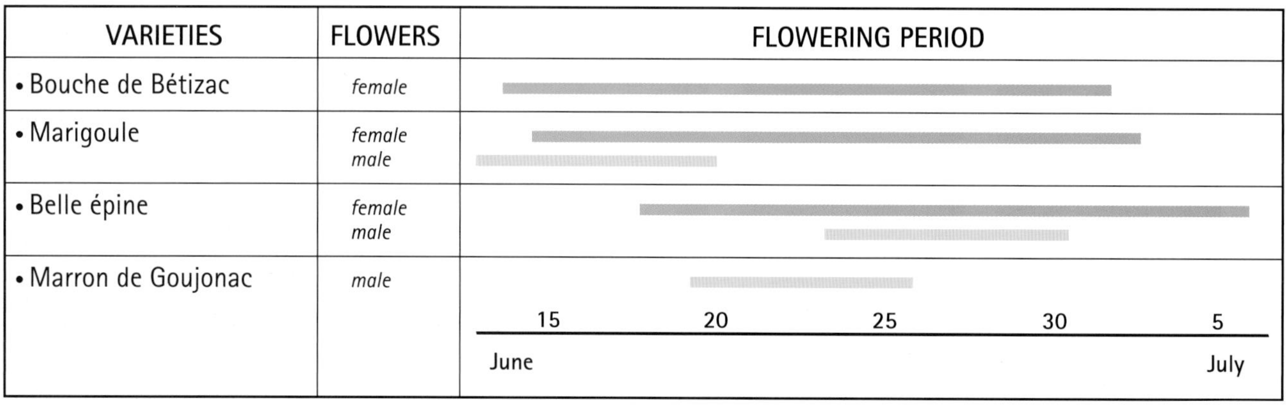

VARIETIES	FLOWERS	FLOWERING PERIOD				
• Bouche de Bétizac	female					
• Marigoule	female male					
• Belle épine	female male					
• Marron de Goujonac	male					
		15	20	25	30	5
		June				July

Fig. 3. Examples of flowering dates (Dordogne, 1995).

10. Fruit burrs on a Bouche de Bétizac.

cence *(photo 10)*. The burrs either release the chestnuts, which are seeds called **achenes**, or drop with them.

It is common to see a second wave of blossoming at the end of the summer and sometimes a third that will not affect the next year's flowers. Only the terminal bud is concerned (the others don't reach budbreak) when it prematurely comes out of **dormancy** and the new fruiting shoot that it creates, which is normally short, gets tipped by a new bud.

Description of the Fruit

The fruit has two main envelopes: outside is the **pericarp**, a sort of plant skin that belongs solely to the fruit. Inside, a thin skin, the seed coat or **endocarp**, called a "pellicle" with high tannin content (thus, bitterness), results from the fusion of one reproductive

nucleus of pollen grains with those of the embryonic sac. The embryo or nut (the edible part), consisting of two cotyledons and the radicle, results when the second reproductive nucleus of the pollen grain fertilizes the **oosphere**.

The pollen grains that fertilize the ovules may come from different trees, a phenomenon that explains the differences in color, texture, taste, and composition from one fruit to another on a single tree. For the same reason, when chestnuts are sown, their seedlings are heterogeneous.

Ripe chestnuts are 52% to 55% water. They are essentially made up of starch. Their protein levels are average (there is no gluten), and they are low in lipids. They have a good amount of potassium, vitamin C (well preserved in roasted chestnuts), and gamma-aminobutyric acids (GABA), an interesting neuromediator. However, the chestnut husk is a bit hard to digest since it contains a fair amount of insoluble fiber: cellulose and lignin. Because of chestnuts' high water content at maturity, storage of the fresh nuts must be like that of starchy foods such as potatoes or corn, as they are highly perishable from mold or other sources of decay. Preservation methods include drying, freezing, and canning. Chestnuts contain high-quality proteins and much starch, unlike other nuts that are usually more than 50% fat.

SOIL AND PLANT PREPARATIONS

Preparing the Soil for Planting

For successful planting, it is essential to choose good soil. It is advisable to follow the steps listed below:
- Loosen the soil, deeper than plowing depth (24 to 31 inches or 60 to 80 cm), using a clawed tool: a ripper or a chisel.
- Add some active limestone.
- Balance out minerals and trace elements on the basis of a soil analysis.
- Till, providing organic elements.
- Plant early, using stakes to help the plant stand up; make sure it is sheltered from wind.

Plant Quality

Achieving good-quality chestnut trees is difficult. Propagating this species through grafting and farming presents many pitfalls. The buyer must choose seedlings that are well rooted for their height: they must show abundant roots that have spread and branched out. Avoid seedlings that only have a single vertical root (main root) that will not grow. This is a sign that the tree is a seedling and not a selected rootstock.

Planting

Chestnut trees are hard to transplant. This should be done as early as possible from November to January. Position the roots in shallow ground in well-aerated, friable soil in order to benefit from the first increases in temperature toward the end of winter. The hole should therefore not be too deep, about the height of a spade, but wide enough to allow the roots to spread out. Prune the roots minimally, cutting away only what broke when the tree was uprooted. Do not pack down the soil, since rain will take care of that. It is important, however, to prop the tree and protect it from animals (rabbits, deer, etc.).

Upkeep After Planting

In the first year, be sure to water after the ground has dried out, even in March if it is a dry year. Most often, this is around May–June.

Be vigilant about weeding. Several methods are possible:
- hoeing—recommended in the first year.
- mulching—a useful technique in many ways. Mulch carries organic matter that the tree responds well to and prevents groundwater from evaporating. It also maintains the roots close to the surface, which is ideal in shallower ground. Plastic mulch is not recommended for the first year because it may promote many soil diseases. The risk subsides in subsequent years.
- chemical weeding—this may involve products designed for chestnut trees or for all fruit trees. Avoid any product containing aminotriazole (or amitrole), and remove any vines from the base of the trunk prior to spraying.

Remember that watering is fundamental. A healthy dose of water should be a grower's major preoccupation throughout the season.

TRAINING CHESTNUT TREES

There are three distinct periods in the life of a chestnut tree:

- a juvenile period, from planting to fruiting, lasting three to five years.
- an adult period characterized by active fruiting and regular vegetative growth, and lasting a long time: eighty years or more. It may be much shorter in poorer conditions, such as shallow ground.
- a senile period, in which the tree often reaches the age of 130 or 150, when fruiting continues with a reduction in fruit size, greatly reduced vegetative growth, and higher branch mortality corresponding to the death of some of the root system. The tree can no longer withstand parasites and will die off. However, some trees in shallow ground that may only be twenty-five years old will act like old trees, producing only short annual shoots (see "Reconditioning Old Chestnut Trees" later in this chapter).

Different techniques for upkeep are adapted to each of these three periods.

To begin with, a basic principle: any pruning must be fully justified. For example:

- stalling future mass pruning by promoting branch dispersion;
- improving accessibility to the trees in an orchard (for weeding, irrigation, harvest) by cutting out branches that are too low;
- facilitating phytosanitary maintenance around the trunk and **scaffold branches** (against chestnut blight) by removing leafy twigs toward the center of adult trees;
- increasing the size of fruits that are deemed too small in terms of variety potential by thinning out (assuming that the tree has been fruiting for several years),

- major aging of the tree: extreme thinning or **topping**.

Managing a Young Tree: From Planting to Age Four or Five

Upon planting, it is useful to take note of the tree because it might be necessary to cut its height back by about half if any of the following unfavorable conditions are present: the stalk is tall for its root system, the soil is of only average quality, or steps have not been taken for proper maintenance (hoeing, weeding, fertilization, irrigation). In contrast, in favorable conditions when planting occurs when the tree's height is proportional to its roots, cutting back is not necessary—though this is not usually the case.

Do not loose sight of the fact that young trees have undergone major stress at planting and that the chestnut tree is fragile for transplanting. Also, in order to promote springtime renewal, it is advisable to limit the number of growing buds to three or four.

Since the chestnut tree can easily become basitonic, with strong, vertical shoots growing from the base of its trunk, it can rapidly develop a shrubby shape once its trunk growth is established. The ideal tree grows well on its own and develops a balanced structure. Plantings will succeed or fail on the basis of the following factors:

- seedling quality;
- soil choice and preparation;
- care provided in the first years.

These factors will determine the tree's health and growth rhythm for the first three or four years. Let's look at three extreme cases:

- If all factors are favorable, the shoot is strong and there is almost nothing to remove except a few branches that will hinder future growth—those that are too low or overlapping.
- If growth starts rather slowly and if interventions

invigorate the tree at age two to three years with growth of low branches in an untimely fashion, you should cut these with clippers during summer pruning to promote trunk growth.

- If vigor is low, the tree is "not growing." It may be tempting in this case to prune (cut back) in order to promote a vigorous shoot. Yet that is wishful thinking. Only appropriate care to the soil and roots can improve the situation.

In fact, there is no single rule for tree training, other than training with a single trunk to facilitate mechanical harvest by shaking: the grower must be able to adapt to any situation. Summer pruning (during the leafy growing season) may serve to guide the tree to a productive and practical architecture, primarily during the first two years. On its own, the tree tends to have a rather fruiting-oriented habit.

- To help it along, it is necessary to do three things:
- favor a central axis by removing or bending competitive branches *(fig. 4)*;
- remove overlapping or competing branches (when they are separated by less than 8 in or 20 cm on the axis);
- choose as the lowest branches (4 to 5 ft or 1.2 to 1.5 m above the ground) those that are growing in the right direction or that will be the least hindrance during later phases (20 to 31 in or 50 to 80 cm above, perpendicular to the first level).

WHEN AND HOW TO PRUNE
The main idea is to prune the starting shoots in the spring to reorient the tree's vegetative growth toward future perennial branches *(fig. 4)*. To do that, it is advisable to pinch any badly placed shoots in May in order to temporarily stop their growth. In June and July, when the shoots are longer and the tree has enough leaves, you can remove unwanted shoots at their base or at their second leaf.

Take the time to imagine that remaining shoots will be future scaffold branches: they should not grow at too narrow an angle and should be well distributed around the trunk. In years two and three, stick to the same principles but with very few interventions: privilege the axis by removing or bending its competitors. Until the third year, shoots are solely vegetative *(fig. 5)* and don't bear flowers, other than perhaps a few male catkins.

Training the Adult Tree

A tree in production will not need pruning as long as its fruit size is satisfactory. The un-pruned tree will

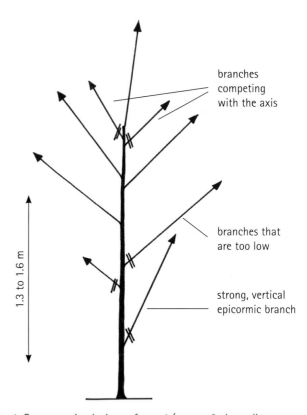

branches competing with the axis

branches that are too low

strong, vertical epicormic branch

1.3 to 1.6 m

Fig. 4. Green pruning in June of year 1 (or year 2, depending on the height of the tree). Remove lower shoots from the selected trunk. Promote the axis by removing or bending any competitive shoots. Keep the more open lateral shoots. Remove epicormic branches from the base of the trunk (they are a sign of poor development in the upper portions).

118

produce the maximum amount of fruit. If this amount starts to hinder fruit size, thinning out can take place during the winter. Thinning out consists of removing whole branches that are two to four years old (most often three years old) in order to leave fewer fruiting ends, and therefore fewer fruits, so that those that do remain are larger.

What branches should you remove? Obviously, the least vigorous branches should go, meaning those whose distal points aren't long enough to get sunlight. Chestnut fruiting is completely dependent on light. In other words, you should anticipate for natural branch selection. If you do not thin the tree out, the branches that can't compete for light will stop producing and dry out.

You may find it necessary to remove certain lower branches that, under the weight of foliage and fruit, end up getting in the way of upkeep. In that case, only one large branch on each tree should be cut in a given year.

These thinning techniques will have little effect on the tree's architecture, which will evolve into a ball (half-sphere) that is hollow inside *(photo 11)*. Due to the lack of light, fruit won't grow toward the interior.

If trees get in one another's way, overlapping branches will stop producing. This indicates that they are too close to one another based on their cultivated variety and the soil make-up. During planting it may be hard to ascertain the soil's capacity, which is based primarily on how deeply the roots will flourish. But now you may need to adjust planting distances by removing every other tree or drastically thinning out the trees.

You can choose between these two options on the basis of the tree's vegetative state:

- If the tree's rate of growth, measured in the annual shoot length, is still high (more than 8 in or 20 cm), it is advisable to remove every other tree or every other row.
- If the rate of growth has fallen, it is preferable to drastically cut back all of the trees in a growing area (see the next section).

Reconditioning Old Chestnut Trees

When a chestnut tree reaches senility or simply shows a significant drop in production, it may be necessary to intervene at least by thinning the tree out, although completely cutting it back would more likely extend its productive life by a few years. Factors to consider are the length and quality of its last annual shoots *(fig. 6)*.

Thinning should be rigorous enough to promote the growth of new young branches. This work should be done by a professional tree thinner.

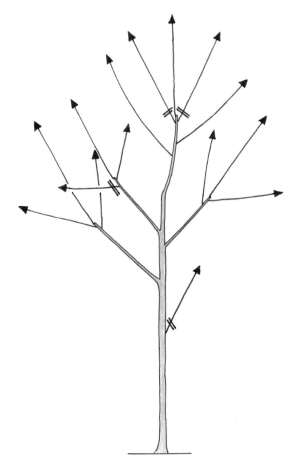

Fig. 5. Green pruning in June of years 2 and 3. Limited interventions: cut (or bend) 2 or 3 of the branches competing with the axis, cut poorly located shoots.

11. Six-year-old chestnut tree, *Castanea sativa*.

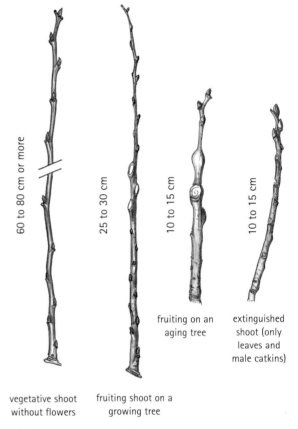

Fig. 6. Different types of branches.

Begin by eliminating non-grafted shoots from the base of the trunk.

Cutting the tree back consists of topping the tree *(fig. 7)*, which involves cutting all of its branches and adjusting the length of the cut to the tree. This cut should be located above the grafting point in order to preserve the variety (in the past, it was typical to graft at a height of 7 to 10 ft or 2 to 3 m). Next, in order to promote new branches that will best fill in the space and receive enough light, you should use the existing scaffolds and cut far enough away from the axis, and always above a bifurcation. This branching zone has more **latent** buds than other areas, and they will respond quickly to cuts made locally. As much as possible, try to cut in the younger wood, where bark is smoother.

It is a good idea to preserve young horizontal branches that have grown between the grafting point and the cutting level, as they will help draw sap during the first years and can then be removed.

The process of thinning branches can be performed during the second or third year according to the following criteria:
- orientation—choose the least vertical shoots that are growing outward from the tree, separating any that are competing;
- how solidly is the shoots are attached—privilege shoots that are growing near cuts on young

wood; those growing on older wood will be less secure and will require more time to become sufficiently solid;

- level of health—eliminate all shoots affected by chestnut blight.

Beyond these measures, you may carry out a second thinning six to seven years after cutting the tree back.

Cutting back will be more efficient in terms of high-quality fruit production when the soil is maintained at the same time. This will involve adding mineral and organic compounds, watering, and adding soil over roots that have become exposed due to erosion (on sloping land). (See Appendix C: U.S. Standard Fertilizer Equivalents for Nitrogen.)

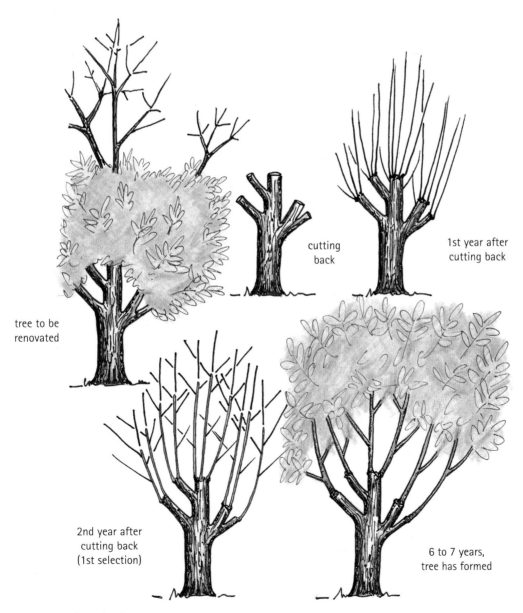

tree to be renovated

cutting back

1st year after cutting back

2nd year after cutting back (1st selection)

6 to 7 years, tree has formed

Fig. 7. Thinning methods for older chestnut trees.

FIG

Author	Yves CARAGLIO

GENERAL OVERVIEW

The fig tree belongs to the botanical family of Moraceae. This family, which is not naturally common in France, nonetheless includes some well-known trees such as the mulberry tree, known for its fruits and as an indispensable food source for silkworms. Moraceae are widely represented, primarily in the tropics, but they are most commonly found from northern China down to New Zealand.

The main characteristic of this family (among its criteria for recognition) is the presence of a white or colorless latex ("milk" flow) wherever a wound occurs on any part of the plant.

History and Phytogeographical Origins

The fig tree is recorded in fossil sediments from the Oligocene epoch (35 million years ago). Its strong early presence in the Mediterranean basin suggests a Middle Eastern origin (Turkey, Syria). Its current distribution relates partly to its origins and partly to its broad and ancient diffusion via the cultivation of its fruit. Traces of that cultivation have been found throughout every civilization in the Mediterranean vicinity (up to 1500 BCE). The fig's current distribution has increased tremendously since cultivation was imported to the American continent—first into North America, and then into South America (Brazil, Venezuela, Argentina).

Worldwide fig production numbers around a million tons, with the majority coming from the Mediterranean basin and being dominated by Turkey (27%, mostly as dried figs). France contributes a modest 3,000 tons, far behind Spain, which is the number one European fig producer with 60,000 tons. Turkey's production typically is between 250 and 300,000 metric tons annually. U.S. production is less than 50,000 tons annually. Most of the production is in California.

In France, fig trees are above all found close to family gardens and are subject to occasional picking, since wider planting and cultivation is relatively recent. French orchards occupy about 1,483 acres (600 ha), located mostly in the Solliès-Pont and the Tarascon regions. Production centers primarily on two **varieties**: 'Dauphine' and 'Bourjassotte Noire'.

Spanish missions first imported figs to Mexico and then California. As the Franciscan missionaries planted fig trees in the mission gardens, their efforts gave rise to the first dark purple California figs, which they named 'Mission' figs. During the California Gold Rush, settlers brought a wide variety of figs to California, the most popular of which was 'White Adriatic'. The first dried figs were shipped by rail to the East Coast in 1889. The twentieth century saw the introduction of 'Smyrna', but all its fruit dropped. In 1890, **caprification** was shown necessary to set fruit.

Thereafter, caprifigs were imported with the fig wasp needed for **pollination**, and commercial production in California began in 1899. The 'Smyrna' fig was renamed 'Calimyrna' in honor of its new homeland. The 'Calimyrna' fig is golden-brown. By 1931, California had 57,278 acres (23,180 ha) of figs, with virtually all production located in the central San Joaquin Valley. California's dried fig production has averaged 28 million pounds (almost 13 million kg) over the last five years. Today, all dried figs harvested in the United States are grown in California's Central Valley; most of the fresh figs are grown there also.

Botanical Classification

The botanical name of fig trees is *Ficus carica* L. The Latin word *ficus*, meaning "fig," comes from the Greek word *sykon*, meaning "narrow." *Carica* refers to the ancient Akkadian word designating a dried fig. Figs belong to the Moraceae family, which includes about 1,500 species classed into 52 genera, one of which is the Ficus genus detailed by Linneaus.

We are familiar with a few of those genera, such as Brousonetia (*B. papyrifera*, the paper mulberry, a small ornamental tree), Morus (*M. alba*, *M. nigra*, mulberry trees for fruit and silkworms), and Maclura (*M. pomifera*, the Osage orange tree, an ornamental tree). The Ficus genus itself includes about a thousand species that grow primarily in tropical zones. Its origin would have been in the Assam basin in Asia. The biological types (growth types) are quite varied. As a result, there are fig trees, creepers, chokers, shrubs, and even **epiphytic** figs. This diversity of types is not the only peculiarity among fig trees. Their mode of reproduction, which is strictly associated with tiny wasps, is another (we will address this in more detail below in relation to *Ficus carica*).

Among the various species, some are grown indoors as decorative plants—such as *Ficus elastica*, commonly called "rubber" fig because of its abundant latex. Another, *Ficus benjamina*, reaches gigantic proportions in its area of origin (Southeast Asia), where it is known as the banyan tree. Regardless of the species, the fig tree is easy to recognize by its fig, or "syconium," which starts as an **inflorescence** before becoming a fruit.

Ficus carica L., the only temperate species, is also the only species in cultivation today. In contrast, the Egyptians also grew *Ficus sycomorus* L. and already practiced artificial pollination by placing blossoming branches in trees. All figs are edible. Certain figs are succulents—such as *Ficus auriculata* (Asia), which smells of strawberry. Even if humans don't cultivate this species widely, they tend to pick from their own trees (in Asia and America). Birds, monkeys, and bats eat the fruits in abundance, broadly spreading the seeds.

Soil and Climate Limitations

By nature, the fig tree is not very demanding and adapts well to all types of soil. Nonetheless, it develops best in sandy, fertile areas, with a strong preference for calcareous soils. Ideally, fig plants should have a well-drained, loamy soil with plenty of organic matter, but they will tolerate average to poor soil as well. Once established, they are somewhat drought tolerant. Figs tolerate soils with a pH ranging from 5.5 to 8.0. Growers with acidic soils should apply active limestone to bring the pH up to the fig's preferred level of 6.0 or 6.5. Alkaline soils will also support figs.

Well adapted to dryness, this species can also handle additional water. In fact, it demonstrates impressive branch development when well irrigated. During maturity, extra water will cause fruits to burst, so that

should be avoided. Moreover, fig trees are sensitive to root asphyxiation in areas that are saturated with water.

The primary limiting factor in nature is cold. Indeed, fig trees are limited to growing areas that are quite sunny and located for the most part at an altitude of 1,969 feet (600 m) or less. Figs are easy to grow in warm climates, but they produce their best fruit in Mediterranean climates with hot, dry summers and cool, wet winters. Although they are a subtropical species, mature trees are fully cold-hardy to 15 or 20°F (-9 or -7°C).

The plants need plenty of sun (eight or more hours per day) and heat, which helps to ripen the fruit. Growers should be sure not to apply fertilizers too late in the growing season, since doing so would encourage new growth that would be susceptible to frost. Chilling requirements for the fig are less than 300 hours.

Heavy rains and excessive or sporadic watering may cause the fruit to split. The amount of splitting varies from variety to variety, but a good rule of thumb is that the riper the figs, the more they will split and sour.

1. A Fig tree with trunk and as a shrubby clump.

TREE MORPHOLOGY

The Tree's Development

The fig tree's **architecture** naturally organizes around a primary axis, spreading its erect branches in regular and annual stages. The primary axis, or trunk, slows its growth over the years, giving the tree a natural ball shape with the lower branches tending to bend and eventually touch the ground *(photo 1)*.

Depending on its growing conditions, the tree may develop around several trunks, making the plant look more like a shrub than a tree. This shrubby shape may also result from other phenomena, such as natural layering. In this case, the branches or twigs touching the ground take root; once that happens, the ends of each branch start to grow upward and behave as another trunk. As the process gets repeated, the tree ends up creating an enormous hedge.

Fig trees grow quickly to 15 to 30 feet (4.5 to 9 m) in height, with an equal **canopy** spread. The root system is typically very shallow without a taproot, and it can readily spread to three times the diameter of the canopy.

Flower Growth

Flowers form at the axils of branches' first leaves during May and June, starting as small green spheres. These structures grow either in pairs or singly on the sides of buds. They are closed inflorescences giving rise to a multiple fruit (the "syconium"): the flowers are located within. There is an opening toward the exterior called an "ostiole" *(photo 2)*. Thus, the multiple fruit is derived from many ovaries and fused receptacles of many flowers.

The inflorescences grow at the base of branches that have not yet developed. The branch will later form from the small bud *(fig. 1)*.

Aside from all the first leaves on a shoot, any of the leaves can bear one or two inflorescences in their axils.

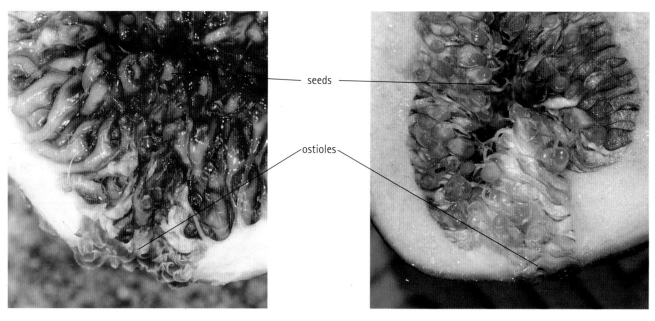

seeds

ostioles

2. Figs from domestic fig trees.

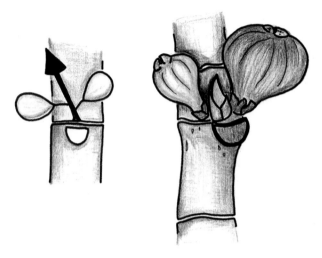

Fig. 1. Flower placement.

3. CapriFig tree, winter figs.

But when the closed inflorescences—the figs—will appear depends on the leaf position on the shoot. In general, the first four or five leaves begin to develop around the end of May. Other leaves that grow later will yield their figs in the following spring, after winter **dormancy**.

POLLINATION: A COMPLEX SYSTEM WITH A PARTICULAR POLLINATOR

In the case of the "common" fig, the flowers are all female and need no pollination. However, there are two other types: the "caprifig," which has male and female flowers that require visits by a tiny wasp, *Blastophaga grossorum;* and the 'Smyrna' fig, which requires **cross-pollination** by caprifigs in order to develop normally (via caprification).

Only the first are of direct interest to us. In fact, they are often the only ones that people know because they are the trees that produce the delicious fruits we enjoy so much. The other ones, wild fig trees known as caprifigs or male fig trees, are present in nature and more or less abundant depending on the area. Often disliked or even removed, they do not produce "good figs" but rather spongy, inedible figs—sometimes called "goat figs," from which arose the name "caprifig." Their fruits house the pollinator insect, the blastophagus wasp. These "male" fig trees are easy to recognize by their leafless winter silhouette with growing figs *(photo 3)*.

To speak of the fig tree without mentioning its system for pollination would be a huge loss in terms of discovering the mysteries of nature as well as in terms of understanding and managing fruit production, which is obviously a worthwhile goal.

So here is the (abridged) story of the "male" caprifig, the domestic "female" fig tree, and the blastophagus (the pollinator wasp).

In winter, everything is calm. Insects and fig trees are at rest, awaiting the month of April to reawaken. The fig tree sprouts a new shoot (growth unit) while

stamens

female blasto-
phagus wasp
entering the
Fig through the
ostiole

galls

4. Details of a fig in autumn.

the enclosed larval insects in the existing figs on the caprifig trees continue their development. New adult insects emerge from the figs to begin the reproductive cycle that will create a new generation of insects in July. During that period, the female blastophagus wasps are loaded with pollen, visiting the fruits of the caprifig trees, pollinating and laying eggs within the fig flowers *(photo 4)*. They also pollinate the hundreds of flowers on domestic 'Smyrna'-type fig trees (female fig trees), thereby allowing ovules in the fig seeds (summer figs) to develop; however, in this case the shape of the flowers prevents the wasps from laying their eggs.

Those figs will become edible figs: autumn figs. This kind of pollination is necessary for varieties known as the 'Smyrna' type (or 'San Pedro', which has both "common" and 'Smyrna'-type figs), while other varieties (known as the common domestic type) naturally develop fruits without requiring pollination: these are the **parthenocarpic** variety. In areas where the pollinator insect doesn't exist, it is important to produce this second varietal type; in fact, it is this type that is exclusively produced in the United States. Very few caprifigs, 'Smyrna' figs, or 'San Pedro'-type figs grow in the United States.

Since the fig tree's inflorescence is closed, we can-

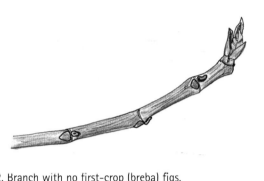

Fig. 2. Branch with no first-crop (breba) figs.

not observe the flowers or their state of receptivity to pollen without destroying the fruit. The coloration of the caprifig epidermis allows us to estimate the flower's state. When the fig has a shiny, light green epidermis, this indicates that the female flowers have not been visited by the blastophagus. A dull, dark green surface signals the presence of a blastophagus in the fig (pollination activity). A shiny fig coat marks the end of the female flower's receptivity phase.

Fruiting

The domestic varieties of fig trees (those producing edible fruits) fall into one of two groups according to their ability to produce one or two fig harvests per year.

In the first case, the varieties are called "uniferous" because they produce a single crop. The figs, which come out in the spring and early summer, undergo an uninterrupted evolution. They develop along the **pre-formed** section of the branch in the winter bud *(fig. 2),* thus breba figs grow on "current season" or "annual" branches. The breba crops's long season of growth allows them to ripen in the same year they arise, generally starting in August. These are autumn figs. They grow along the bottom two-thirds of the annual shoots and often appear in successive waves. Their maturation period extends over three to four weeks. They reach maturity at the end of June or beginning of July in

A Bit of Advice on Planting

• Seedlings started from cuttings are the most common type and the best rooted, but seedlings can also be created by means of layering.

• Planting with bare roots in the autumn will facilitate spring resumption, as long as there is a sufficient root system. Bare-root planting may be done until March, with sufficient water.

• Planting in containers is also possible for the first two to three years of growth (maximum).

• It is best to plant fig trees in areas protected from wind and not in areas with a high risk of frost. In colder regions, plant fig trees next to a wall with southern exposure.

• Depending on the growing technique, the tree should either be headed back to about 2 feet (61 cm) at planting or left alone.

• Even though this species requires a fair amount of water, avoid watering during maturation (notably in September–October) since this will weaken the epidermis and cause the fruits to burst.

• The recommended planting distance is 10 to 20 feet (3 to 6 m) within the row with 16 to 23 feet (5 to 7 m) between rows, or approximately 200 trees per acre *(photo 5).*

5. Grove of fig trees.

southern France, and about the same time in the Central Valley of California.

The second kind of variety, called "biferous," yields first-crop figs (the breba crop as well as autumn figs. Breba evolution is halted by winter. They reach maturity at the end of June or beginning of July in southern France. These are the breba figs. Their maturation period extends over two to three weeks *(fig. 3)*. Thus, the common fig bears a first crop, the breba crop, in the spring on the last season's growth. The second crop, the main crop, is borne in the fall on new growth. In cold climates, spring frosts often destroy the breba crop.

In reality, there is not always a clear separation between the two groups, and there is a continual gradient between strictly biferous varieties and uniferous varieties. The physiological factors causing maturation with one or two harvests are still unknown.

Some common figs, such as 'Barnissotte' and 'Verdal', drop all or nearly all the fruit buds of the first crop but mature a good second crop. Others, such as 'Franciscana' and 'Dottato', have practically complete parthenocarpic development in both crops. The expression of parthenocarpy is incomplete in some varieties, apparently being affected by the environment.

Varieties are generally grouped according to external and internal color:
- skin green or yellow; pulp amber or white;
- skin green or yellow; pulp various shades of red;
- skin dark (various shades of red, brown, or violet to black); pulp white or amber;

Fig. 3. Branch with first-crop (breba) figs.

- skin dark (various shades of red, brown, or violet to black); pulp various shades of red.

Some lighter-skinned figs may have characteristic vertical stripes.

ADVICE ON CHOOSING THE VARIETY

The following varieties are available in the United States (synonymous names appear in parentheses). Some nurseries may have other varieties as well.

STANDARD VARIETIES

'Adriatic'—Originated in central Italy. Small to medium fruit; skin is greenish, flesh is strawberry colored. Good, all-purpose fig. Good fresh but especially good for drying. No breba crop in most cases. Large, vigorous tree leafs out early; is subject to frost damage. Prune to force new growth. Ripens late September–October. ('Fragola', 'Strawberry Fig', 'Verdone', 'White Adriatic')

'Black Mission'—The most dependable variety for the home orchard. Purple-black skin with red flesh. The first crop (breba) matures in late June; the second crop matures in August and September. Easy to dry at home. Single best all-round variety for South, North, coast, interior. Brebas are prolific, fairly rich. Tree is very large, so plant at maximum spacing. Do not prune after tree reaches maturity. Commences growth midseason. ('Beers Black', 'Franciscan', 'Mission')

'Blanche'—Medium to large fruit; skin is yellowish-green, flesh is white to amber, very sweet, lemon flavor. Light breba crop. Valuable in areas with short seasons and cool summers. Slow-growing, dense, hardy tree. ('Italian Honey', 'Lattarula', 'Lemon', 'White Marseille')

'Brown Turkey'—Originated in Provence. Medium fruit; skin is purplish-brown, flesh is pinkish-amber. Good flavor, best when fresh. Large fruit of excellent quality. Produces a small breba crop every year and a second crop in August–September. Small, hardy, vigorous tree. Prune severely for heaviest main crop. Does best in southern California. ('Aubique Noire', 'Negro Largo', 'San Piero')

A Few Pruning Precautions

• From a health standpoint, due to the presence of a **medullar** gap within the stem (pithy wood), scars from cutting may have difficulty healing and fungal infestation may affect the plant (photo 6).
• To resolve this problem, intervention in the spring is required to promote healing while vegetative growth is under way. In fact, besides the latex that flows from cut sections, fig trees have another peculiarity: a rather hollow pith. It is compartmentalized, as is the walnut tree's, and only the section corresponding to where winter bud growth has stopped will be filled (fig. 6).

6. Wood cross-section.

'Celeste'—Small to medium fruit; skin is light violet to violet-brown, flesh is reddish-amber. Very sweet, usually dried. Light breba crop. Tightly closed "eye" (ostiole), good for Southeast. Small tree is productive, hardy. ('Blue Celeste', 'Honey Fig', 'Malta', 'Sugar', 'Violette')

'Conadria'—The first artificial hybrid fig. Medium fruit; skin is pale green, flesh is strawberry red. Mildly sweet. Good fresh, excellent dried. More productive than 'Adriatic' but of lesser quality. Light breba crop. Tree is vigorous, tends to excessive growth under irrigation, does best in hot climates.

'Croisic'—The only edible caprifig. Fruits very early, only brebas are useful. Fruits are pale yellow, small, pulp is nearly white, without a lot of character. Tree is low, dense, spreading. For Pacific Northwest. ('Cordelia', 'Gillette', 'St. John')

'Desert King'—'San Pedro' type. Large fruit; skin is deep green, minutely spotted white, pulp is strawberry red. Sweet, delicious fresh or dried. Commonly matures good fruit without caprification near the coast. Tree is highly vigorous. Hardy, best adapted to cool areas such as the Pacific Northwest. ('Charlie', 'King')

'Excel'—Large fruit; skin is yellow, flesh is light amber. Fruits are practically neckless, blocky. Very sweet. Excellent, all-purpose fig. Light breba crop. Similar to 'Kadota' but more productive. Tree is vigorous, and does well in most parts of California.

'Flanders'—A seedling of 'White Adriatic'. Medium fruit; long neck, skin is brownish-yellow with violet stripes, flesh is amber. Strong, fine flavor. Excellent all-purpose fruit. Good breba crop. Ripens late. Tree is vigorous but requires no great pruning. For south coastal California, San Joaquin Valley

'Genoa'—Medium fruit; skin is greenish-yellow to white, flesh is yellow-amber. Sweet, good fresh or dried. Light breba and main crops. Tree is upright, requires constant annual pruning. Best adapted to cooler regions of the West. Very late in northern California, continuing to ripen even after first frosts. ('White Genoa')

'Judy'—A probable seedling of California 'Brown Turkey'. Large, broad fruit are brown to black with pink pulp.

'Kadota'—Medium fruit; skin is yellowish-green, flesh is amber, tinged pink at center. Rich flavor. Resists souring. Produces both breba and a second crop with moderate pruning. Tree is upright, requires annual pruning to slow growth. Requires high temperatures and a long growing season to perform well. ('Dottato', 'Florentine', 'White Kadota')

'Len'—A seedling of 'Black Mission'. Fruit is smaller than 'Mission', black, pulp is pink, quite sweet.

'Osborn'—Performs well only in cool coastal areas. Produces breba and second crops. Purple-bronze fruit with amber flesh. Very prolific.

'Osborn's Prolific'—Medium to large fruit; skin is dark reddish-brown, flesh is amber, often tinged pink. Very sweet, best fresh. Light breba crop. Tree is upright, bare, will grow in shade. Ripens late. Only for California's north coast and the Pacific Northwest. Fares poorly in warm climates. ('Arachipel', 'Neveralla')

'Panachee'—Small to medium fruit; skin is greenish-yellow with dark green strips, flesh is strawberry, dry but sweet. Best fresh. No breba crop. Requires long, warm growing season. Ripens late. ('Striped Tiger', 'Tiger')

'Smyrna'-type—'Calimyrna' variety figs require cross-pollination by the caprifig male to produce a crop.

'Tena'—Small fruit; skin is light green, flesh is amber. Fine flavor. Good fresh or dried. Good breba crop. Bears heavily. Tree is strong, dense. For coastal California and interior southern California.

'Ventura'—Large fruit; skin is green, flesh is deep red; long neck. Excellent flavor. Good fresh or dried. Good breba crop. Ripens late but matures well in cool areas. Compact tree.

'Verte'—Small fruit; skin is greenish-yellow, flesh is strawberry. Excellent fresh or dried. Good breba crop. Small tree. Recommended for short-summer climates. ('Green Ischia')

'Violette de Bordeaux'—This very productive tree produces two crops of purplish-black figs with strawberry-colored flesh. Very good quality, rich flavor. Grows well in the Pacific Northwest or on the East Coast in a sunny location. ('Negronne')

Choosing Varieties Based on Production Type

- Biferous such as 'Dauphine' or 'Cottignane' ('San Pedro' types), 'Dorée' or 'Longue d'Août' ("common" types);
- Uniferous such as 'Bourjassotte Noire' or 'Col de Dame Noire' ("common" types).

Choosing Varieties Based on Flavor Quality or Personal Affinity

- White: 'Marseillaise', 'Longue d'Août', 'Dottato', etc.;
- Black: 'Noire de Bordeaux', 'Noire de Barbentane', 'Noire de Caromb', etc.

GUIDELINES FOR UPKEEP AND TRAINING

In this section we describe the first years of fig tree growth by discussing the biological characteristics of its development that relate to planting and training.

YEAR 1: THE START OF THE FIRST BRANCHES *(fig. 4)*
When planting a fig tree, you should "head" the tree back by about one-half. This will allow it to focus on developing roots and becoming well established. Heading back will also help the fig tree grow side branches for a more compact tree. When growth has become sufficient within the planting year, the lateral branches will grow fairly well. Several branches will put out five to ten leaves at the axils. They may appear at the axils of the first leaves on the shoot, close to the ground. The higher and more vigorous leaves may be preserved,

contributing to the tree's infrastructure. In the next winter after transplanting, it is best to start pruning fig trees for "fruiting wood." This is wood that you will be pruning to keep the fruit healthy and easy to reach. Select four to six branches to be fruiting wood, and prune away the rest.

The first axes, including the trunk, will lengthen considerably and may start to produce figs. These should be removed. In order to restrict the length of stems while the tree is growing, summer **pinching** (tipping of branches) may be advisable. Early intervention, however, will cause the initial axis to regenerate, while late intervention will slow bud growth below the pruning area. The optimal period for pinching is at the end of the active growth phase—that is, when the stem is no longer producing new leaves.

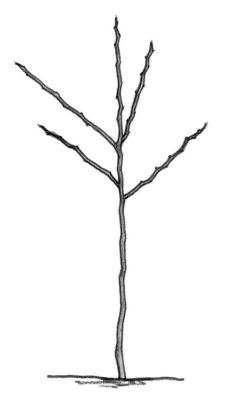

Fig. 4. First year shoots.

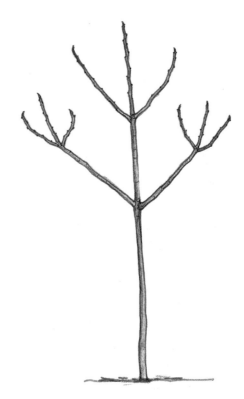

Fig. 5. Second year shoots

YEAR 2: DEVELOPING THE TRAINING SYSTEM *(fig. 5)*

If top growth is considerable in year 1 (the first growth year), it is a good idea to keep the lateral axes upright so that new branches will develop near the trunk (between 16 and 28 inches, or 40 and 70 cm). After the tree is established, the best time to prune will be in the dormant (winter) season when the tree is not growing.

Start by removing any branches that are not growing out from your selected fruiting wood (see Year 1 discussion), as well as any dead or diseased wood. If any suckers are growing from the base of the tree, remove these as well. Also remove any secondary branches that are growing at less than a 45° angle from the main branches. This step eliminates any branches that may eventually grow too close to the main trunk and will not produce the best fruit. Cut back the main branches by one-third to one-quarter. This step helps the tree put more energy toward the fruit that will be produced next year, yielding larger and sweeter fruit.

With fig trees, the leaf insertion point on the stem is accompanied by a ring-shaped scar, which is a remnant from the dropping of two small leafy parts (budscales) that protect the young leaves on a bud. The scars may be

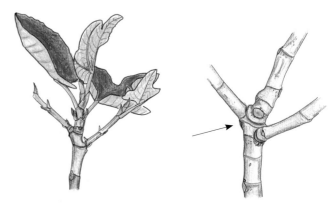

Fig. 7-8. Monopodial and acrotonic development with inter-annual growth.

quite close on the stem, indicating that there had been a winter bud and therefore revealing the age of the axis. These breaks in growth are where stems and branches grow. Their development continues once spring vegetation resumes (unlike in year 1, branching is immediate, an expression of the cutting's root health) *(fig. 7–8)*. Growth—that is, elongation of the stem as well as the start of new leaves—takes place for a period ranging from fifteen days (in spring) for the shorter branches to several months for the longer axes. Leaf production drops accordingly from thirty or more down to a dozen. Stems range in character from heavily marked and hanging (as with 'Bellone') to compact and sturdy (as with 'Pastilière'). These axes will then branch out and produce figs in the summer at the axils of present leaves.

YEAR 3: START OF BEARING *(fig. 9)*

Due to the proliferation of growing points, axis growth starts to slow. Branches in turn start to bear regular branches, which will tend to grow more than the carrier branches themselves and begin to form successive bowing *(fig. 10)*. At this stage, flowering becomes regular along all the axes.

To maintain a good balance of vegetation and fruit production, shoots should not grow to more than

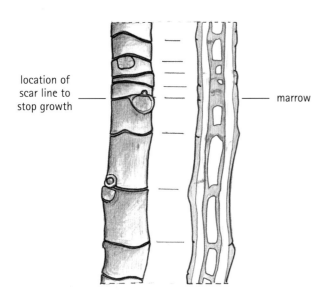

location of scar line to stop growth — — marrow

Fig. 6. Bark and internal spine of fig tree.

Fig. 9. Third-year shoots.

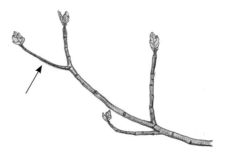

Fig. 10. Hypotonic bending.

12 to 16 inches (30 to 40 cm, or about ten to fifteen leaves). Summer pruning, in June, may be one way to regulate axis growth while also reducing production sites. In light of this information, and depending on the variety and desired fruit type, growers should consider the eventual consequences of cutting the axes. In fact, new axes caused by pruning will hinder the development of fig flowers, whereas reducing the number of new axes will promote the development of autumn figs.

Additionally, with weaker growth cycles, more pre-formed figs in the winter buds will set, leading to more autumn figs. To prevent this from happening, in terms of biferous varieties, hand removal of figs in the autumn or removal of the terminal bud in winter will favor fruit production.

The choice of growing methods on a given axis helps to form a full-grown tree (with branches growing around a trunk). The fig tree has a natural propensity toward shrub behavior and may produce growth around several axes in its efforts to form a shrub. This tendency allows main axes to be renewed as development continues. Later, removal of one of the axes will allow the structure to periodically reju-

venate (every three to five years, depending on the health of the tree).

This growing method helps the tree maintain reasonable dimensions, since a fig tree that is happy in its surroundings may continue to grow to phenomenal proportions. Depending on soil fertility and available space, growers should provide considerable room between trees by planting in a 16 by 23 foot (5 by 7 m) space instead of a 10 by 16 foot (3 by 5 m) space.

Reconditioning the Tree

Fig trees are quite soft-wooded and can easily blow over in high winds.

In case of any damage to the tree (from frost, wind, etc.), it is possible to make significant cuts to recondition it. Intervention may even go so far as coppicing, since fig trees react well to this method as long as it occurs before vegetation starts to grow back. Be sure to use clean tools, however. Since cutting is significant, there is a considerable risk of rotting and fungal infection.

Pay attention to how the scar is healing for one to two years, depending on axis health. Numerous new shoots will develop, from which you should select one or two axes depending on your desired growing method. In any case, you will have to continue to remove new shoots for the following two years.

TABLE GRAPE

| Author | Gilles ADGIÉ |
| Collaborator | Daniel LAVIGNE |

GENERAL OVERVIEW

History and Phytogeographical Origins

The vine is a climber that can take root in any corner of the world except in the most extreme locations (the poles and deserts). No one knows the exact origin of the vine (*Vitis vinifera*), but it likely came from Asia Minor or the area around the Caspian Sea. Certain studies show that grapes were cultivated more than 7,000 years ago in western Asia, with the purple grape first being domesticated in the region that is now Turkey. Representations found at Egyptian burial sites depict grape cultivation in 2375 BC. There is also a long history of grape production in China.

Table grapes and wine grapes have been linked throughout history since the days of antiquity. Corinthian grapes were discovered in Greece, for example, next to different wine **varieties**; and still today, certain types of table grapes can be made into wine or juice.

The Importance of Table Grapes

The table grape occupies an undeniable place in world production. In 2000, 12 million tons were consumed fresh and 60 million tons were destined for grape products.

Table grape production in Europe yields 2,300,000 tons, with Italy alone producing 66% of those, mostly of the 'Italia' variety. France produces table grapes on 23,475 acres (9,500 ha), accounting for 3.3% of Euro-

1. A fruit bowl of Chasselas Doré grapes.

pean production. Thirty-seven percent of the French market is dominated by the varieties 'Chasselas' *(photo 1)*, 'Muscat de Hambourg', and 'Alphonse Lavallée'; the other 63% are purchased from abroad. The average French person consumes about 8 pounds (3.5 kg) of grapes per year.

Production in the United States includes wine, raisin, and table grapes. The majority of all three types primarily come from California (91% including all types, 13% of which is for fresh market), although both Oregon and Washington are also major wine grape producers, well behind California. California produces 99% of all table grapes and 100% of all raisin grapes in the United States. Some varieties used for raisins are also sold as fresh table grapes. Annual per capita consumption of table grapes in the United States is slightly over 8 pounds (3.5 kg) per person. Approximately 30% of table grapes produced in California are exported overseas to more than sixty countries (not including Canada). The top export markets for California table grapes are Canada, Mexico, China, the Central American region, and Australia. More grapes are produced for juice, with a large percentage coming from New York, Michigan, Ohio, Indiana, Arkansas, and other eastern states.

Yields in the United States are typically twice those of any other country because so much more acreage is used for table, juice, and raisin production than for wine. (**Berries** for wine are much smaller and have thicker skins than those used for other purposes.)

Statistics issued by the United Nations' Food and Agriculture Organization for 2004 placed the United States as fourth in the top twenty producing countries, accounting for only 8% of the total world production (Italy accounted for 13%). Estimates for that year from the U.S. Department of Agriculture found U.S. production at 5,429,500 metric tons or 11.9 billion pounds (5.4 billion kg). The industry was then valued at $2.9 billion, making it the highest-value fruit crop in the United States, on 800,000 acres (323,750 ha) in California.

As of 2009, California's acreage planted in table and raisin grapes was 700,000 (283,281 ha; roughly 16% of the state's total grape acreage), although not all of that acreage was yet bearing. An estimated $1.2 billion was the table grape crop value for California in 2009, with 10 to 15% loss of the potential crop to sunburn on fruit from high temperatures in the major growing area of the San Joaquin (85% of acreage) and Coachella (14% of acreage) valleys. The crop was estimated at around 925,000 tons, which is average for annual yields.

Family—Genus

The table grape belongs to the family Ampelideae and to the genus *Vitis*. The grape family includes three principal groups: the European species *Vitis vinifera*, several North American vines, and **hybrids** developed from *Vitis vinifera*.

VITIS VINIFERA
The European species *Vitis vinifera* is produced in France as both a table and a wine grape. This is the most highly cultivated species, furnishing 95% of grapes.

The first *Vitis vinifera* for table grapes were introduced to the area now known as Los Angeles in 1839

by William Wolfskill, a former trapper from Kentucky. In the mid-1800s, Colonel Agoston Harazszthy brought 100,000 table grape cuttings to California by wagon and planted them to provide fruit to the miners of the California Gold Rush. In the 1860s, William Thompson, an English settler, first planted 'Thompson Seedless'—now a popular eastern Mediterranean grape—in what is now the Yuba City area of Northern California. In 1869, R. B. Blowers pioneered freight transport of fresh table grapes to eastern markets, beginning with Chicago. Each grape cluster was individually wrapped in paper bags in 22-pound (10 kg) boxes (the current industry "standard" box is 19 pounds or 8.5 kg).

Vitis vinifera **cultivars** grown in California for table grapes comprise more than sixty varieties. The top fourteen producers (according to roughly 550 farmers) are as follows:
- 'Autumn Royal'—August-November; large, blue-black, oval-elongated; seedless
- 'Crimson Seedless'—August-January; medium-large, red, cylindrical; seedless
- 'Flame Seedless'—May-December; medium-large, red, round; seedless
- 'Princess'—Jun-November; very large, green, cylindrical; seedless
- 'Red Globe'—June-November; very large, red, round; seeded
- 'Ruby Seedless'—April-December; medium, red, oval; seedless
- 'Scarlet Royal'—July-November; large, red, oval; seedless
- 'Sugraone'—May-August; large, green, elongated; seedless
- 'Sugranineteen'—September-December; very large, red, oval-elongated; seedless
- 'Sugrathirteen'—June-September; large, blue-black, elongated; seedless
- 'Summer Royal'—June-October; medium, blue-black, round; seedless

- 'Sunset Seedless'—September–November; large, red, oval-elongated; seedless
- 'Thompson Seedless'—June–December; medium-large, green, cylindrical; seedless
- 'Vintage Red'—September–December; medium-large, red, oval-elongated; seedless

Of these, 'Crimson', 'Flame Seedless', and 'Thompson Seedless' are the top varieties produced, with other green seedless (such as 'Perlette' and 'Princess') rapidly advancing on the market share of 'Thompson Seedless'. Other common table varieties produced in California include 'Perlette' (green, seedless), 'Emperor', 'Flame Tokay', and 'Muscat'. Virtually all of the acreage is treated with plant growth regulators to increase firmness, size, and keeping quality.

NORTH AMERICAN GRAPEVINES

The second group is of North American origin. It includes the following:

- *Vitis labrusca*, the North American table and grape juice grapevines (including 'Concord'); native to the eastern United States and Canada;

sometimes used for wine (sweet and normally only marketed in the eastern United States).
- *Vitis riparia*, a wild vine; native to the entire eastern United States and northward to Quebec.
- *Vitis rotundifolia* (muscadines), used for jams and wine; native to the southeastern United States from Delaware to the Gulf of Mexico.

Among *Vitis labrusca* varieties (wine and table) cultivated in the United States, we can identify the following categorized by use:

- Wine: 'Catawba', 'Concord', Delaware', 'Isabella', 'Ives', 'Niagra', and 'Noah';
- Red and purple table: 'Autumn Royal', 'Beauty Seedless', 'Bluebell', 'Canadice', 'Catawba', 'Christmas Rose', 'Concord', 'Crimson Seedless', 'Emperor', 'Fantasy Seedless', 'Flame Seedless', 'Fredonia', 'Niagra', 'Reliance Seedless', 'Ribier', Rouge', 'Ruby Seedless'.

In addition, the following *Vitis rotundifolia* selected varieties (wine and table) are cultivated in the United States: 'Red', 'Black Beauty', 'Black Fry', 'Dixie Red',

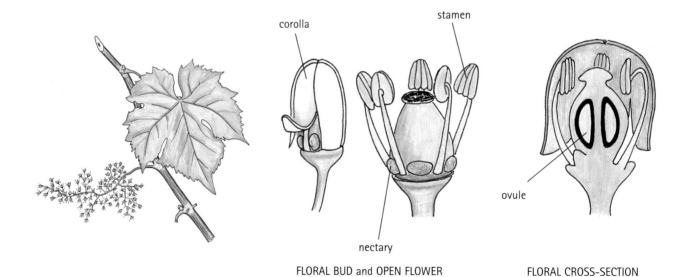

FLORAL BUD and OPEN FLOWER   FLORAL CROSS-SECTION

Fig. 1. Stage 1: Full blossom (source: Georges-François Charmeux).

'Early Fry', 'Flowers', 'Fry', 'Fry Seedless', 'James', 'Scuppernog', 'Sugargate', 'Tara', and 'Thomas'.

FRENCH HYBRIDS

In the third group, we find hybrids or "French hybrids" that were developed from *Vitis vinifera* grapes. The species *Vitis vinifera* almost disappeared from France in 1863 because of an accidental import. A miniscule aphid-like insect known as *Phylloxera vastatrix* arrived with plant material from North America, eating the roots and destroying the vines. American varieties are tolerant, unlike the *vinifera* species. The pest was first found in California in 1850.

Other species used as rootstock include *V. berlandieri, V. rupestris,* and *V. riparia.*

Limitations

Some main varieties are susceptible to countless parasites and diseases (such as vine moths, blight, powdery mildew) and to wood diseases (such as esca, eutypiosis, black dead arm). Thus, it is important to plant healthy plant material.

- Temperature: in France's climate, neither extreme hot or nor cold temperatures are strong enough to cause the vine to die or even slow its development.
- Frost risks: spring frosts may affect nascent buds (frost at 32°F or 0°C). A second bud, sometimes called a "counter-bud," located at the base of a frost-damaged bud, may provide a better yield.
- Risks associated with dryness: in certain years, such as in 2003, light or pebbly soils will cause the vine to suffer enormously if there is not enough water—notably, during root installation after the transplant. All vineyards in California are irrigated; therefore, this problem is not present there.
- Soil types: there are no soils that are incompatible with grapevines, yet some are more favorable to specific varieties. For example, 'Chasselas' performs well in argilo-calcareous soils and 'Muscat' in loamy soils.
- Risks associated with hail: since grapes are grown at a single level, there is a good risk of losing them in a hailstorm.
- Risks associated with rain: rainfall close to harvest will hurt quality by causing the fruits to burst (crack). Rain during **berry** maturation also greatly increases the risks from fungal diseases.

GRAPEVINE MORPHOLOPGY

The grapevine is a rustic plant with a strong development *(fig. 2)*. It's a climber whose root system is often quite strong and can colonize broad stretches of land.

THE TRUNK

The trunk **lignifies** after its first few years of flexibility. It is covered in bark that thickens each year.

THE BRANCH

This climber bears buds at each **node**, separated by a lignified section called an **internode**. Leafy bud shoots

2. A blossoming cluster (stage 1).

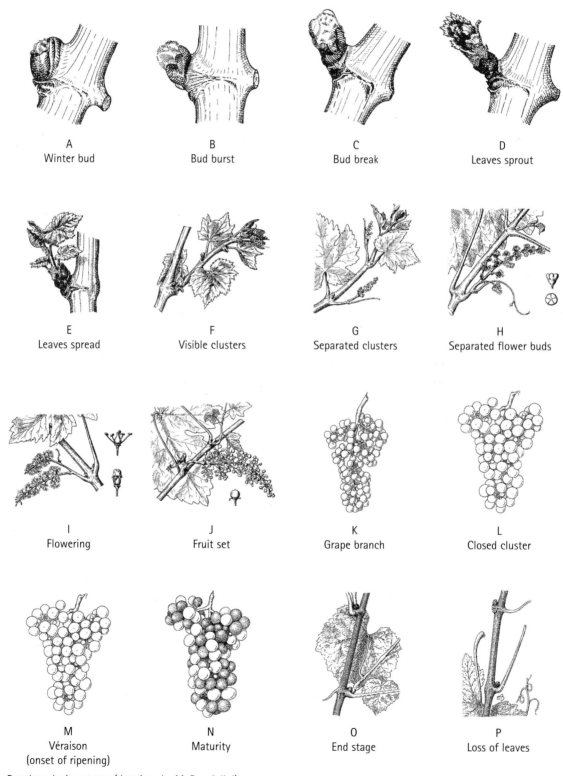

A	B	C	D
Winter bud	Bud burst	Bud break	Leaves sprout
E	F	G	H
Leaves spread	Visible clusters	Separated clusters	Separated flower buds
I	J	K	L
Flowering	Fruit set	Grape branch	Closed cluster
M	N	O	P
Véraison (onset of ripening)	Maturity	End stage	Loss of leaves

Fig. 2. Benchmark vine stages (drawings by M. Baggiolini).

yield vine shoots that will fruit in the same year they start growing, as long as they are located on the previous year's wood.

On these vine shoots, each node bears a leaf. The vine shoots at the top of the branch help to fix it in space. Grape bunches develop mostly on the first two or three nodes near the base of the vine shoot.

LEAVES

Leaves vary in shape and size according to species and cultivar, a trait unique to the vine's **ampelography**. Muscadine grapes have small (2 to 3 inches or 5 to 7.5 cm across), round, unlobed leaves with dentate margins. *Vinifera* and American bunch grapes (*V. rotundifolia*) have large (up to 8 to 10 inches or 20 to 25 cm in width) cordate to orbicular leaves, which may be lobed; varietal differences exist in the depth and shape of the lobes and the spaces between them (sinuses). Leaf margins are dentate. DNA **genotyping** is used to identify both the origins of cultivars (especially wine cultivars) and their identity; this work is occurring at various locations, including the University of California-Riverside and the University of California-Davis. In fact, this method was used to discover that Sauvignon blanc and Cabernet franc are the parents of Cabernet Sauvignon and to

confirm that Crljenak Kasteljanski is identical to Zinfandel. Leaves are almost always palmate and relatively intricate. Adult leaves are found on current-year branch shoots. On **epicormic** branches or **side shoots**, the leaves are different, often more intricate than the other leaves.

FLOWERS

The flowers are **hermaphrodites** that can self-fertilize *(fig. 1)*. They are grouped into **inflorescences** that form the grape cluster *(photo 2)*. The cluster is made up of a **rachis** and berries. **Floral induction** takes place in July of the year preceding harvest and occurs in the young buds around the branch base. Heat (stable temperatures) and light are necessary for floral induction to take place.

FRUIT

Grapes are berries *(fig. 3)*. They are round, slightly elongated, and relatively fleshy. They grow in clusters (bunches) of various sizes, with numbers ranging from a few to 300 grapes. Color varies with the different varieties: from milky white to golden for 'Chasselas', or midnight blue to black for 'Black Muscat'. California table varieties are classified as green, red, and blue-black or black.

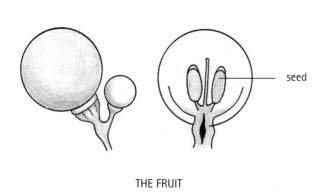

THE FRUIT

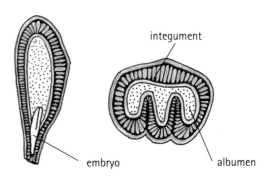

THE SEED

Fig. 3. Grape-berry (source: Georges-François Charmeux)

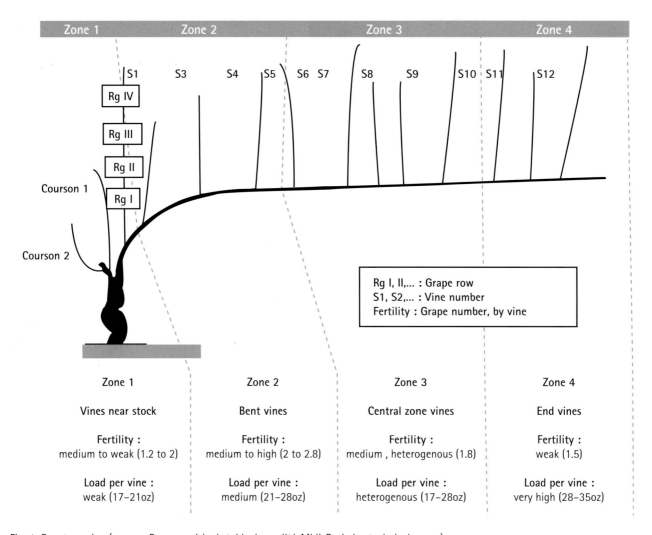

Fig. 4. Guyot pruning (source: *Pour un raisin de table de qualité*, Midi-Pyrénées technical group).

Surrounding the juicy, sweet pulp is a relatively fine skin, which is thinner or thicker depending on the variety. This skin is covered with a thin, powdery film called *pruine* (French) or "bloom," which contains the yeast cells that are responsible for turning grape juice into wine.

The pulp contains zero to four seeds depending on the variety. Seedless grapes, or "apyrene" grapes, have very soft seeds that might even be imperceptible.

Species Variability

The species displays wide variation, particularly in terms of certain fruit characteristics:

- color: black, white, pink, or two-toned;
- seeds: may or may not have seeds;
- the shape of the cluster and berry: shouldered or cylindrical clusters; round, oval, or elliptical berries;

• sugar content in the grapes: from 14° to 22° Brix.

For wine grapes, there are a multitude of cultivated varieties that present a wide range of flavors.

Annual Vegetative Cycle

This cycle is composed of six periods:
• winter repose: known as **dormancy**, this state is defined by the lack of bud growth.
• bleeding: droplets form at the tips of the vine shoots, signaling the change from inactive to active growth. This sap flow indicates that root activity has started back up.
• **budbreak**: the buds swell, the scales split open, and the **floss** (fibrous covering) that was protecting the bud through the winter starts to sprout.
• branch growth: as soon as temperatures warm up in the spring, vegetative growth becomes quite rapid. Flowers appear early along the base of the yellow shoots.
• flowering and **veraison** (color change in the ripe-

ning fruit): flowering occurs in June, and veraison starts in August.
• leaf drop: the wood lignifies, the leaves fall, and the pruning season begins.

THE FOUR SEASONS OF TABLE GRAPE CULTIVATION

Winter

PRUNING
This intervention is a moment of closure for the preceding harvest, in preparation for the harvest to come. We will take a look at two examples: Guyot (or **cane**) pruning from southwestern France, and Cordon de Royat (or unilateral) pruning from the southeast. In California, table grapes are either "cane" or "head" pruned—systems similar to those described for France (see the following discussion).

Guyot pruning. In southwestern France, the most popular pruning method is the Guyot method *(fig. 4)*, in

3. Guyot training with a saw.

4. Double Guyot training, terrace cultivation.

which choosing the vine shoot for future canes has a major impact on production. Observing the vine shoot's characteristics, particularly its diameter, will help you to evaluate the vine's balance and take stock of how well your pruning is working. More concretely, you want the future cane to be fleshy (about the thickness of a pencil).

Guyot pruning involves only keeping long renewals (canes) and a renewal **spur** with two buds *(photos 3 and 4)*. In the case of 'AOC Chasselas de Moissac', Guyot pruning seems to induce better elongation and more flexible clusters. The prettiest clusters generally grow on vine shoots toward the end of the cane.

Advantages of the Guyot method are as follows:
- Vigor is more easily controlled.
- It is possible to balance the length of the cane with the trunk's vigor.
- Clusters are of better quality: their length and flexibility conform better to the criteria for 'AOC Chasselas de Moissac'.

However, there are several disadvantages:
- Mechanical pre-pruning is not possible.
- The necessary manual picking is long and tiring.
- Clusters become heterogeneous, especially in the middle of the cane.
- Spur clusters are often bunched tightly.

Cordon de Royat pruning. In southeastern France, this is the most popular method for pruning. It consists of keeping a perennial **scaffold** and pruning back the annual shoots to two buds, or eyes *(fig. 5)*. The method is popular for its simplicity. In fact, before pruning you can pre-prune mechanically, effectively removing a majority of the vine shoots from the trellis.

Advantages of this method are as follows:
- It is well adapted to varieties in which pollen viability, and thus fertilization, are impaired by rain.
- Mechanical pre-pruning is possible.
- Pruning time is shorter.
- Vine shoots become more homogeneous.

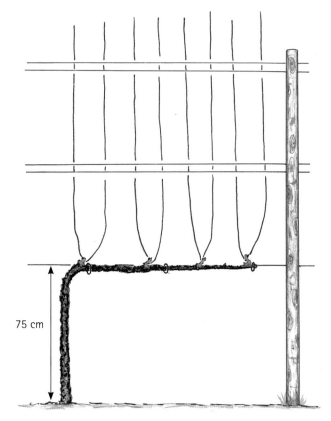

Fig. 5. Cordon de Royat training.

- Vine shoots can be removed mechanically.
There are two disadvantages:
- Clusters are shorter and more compact.
- This type of pruning is poorly adapted to 'Chasselas' grapes.

Training systems and pruning in California's table grapes. In the United States, most grapes are trellised and grown in long, narrow rows spaced about 9 to 15 feet (3 to 4.5 m) apart depending on the training system. Vines are usually spaced 3 to 8 feet (1 to 2.5 m) apart in the row. Muscadines are spaced further apart in the row (about 20 feet or 6 m) due to high vigor, but row spacings are not appreciably different.

Pruning takes place in late winter when vines are

dormant. It involves only the previous year's growth, or one-year-old shoots.

Training refers to the permanent parts of the vine, not the one-year-old wood, whereas pruning is done to shape (train) and regulate growth. Two basic training forms are used: "head" and "cordon." In head training, the permanent part of the vine consists of the trunk and a bulbous "head" at its top that bears fattened stubs of vines that have been pruned off. Spurs or canes develop directly from the head. Thus, with head training, the only permanent parts are the trunk and the head. In cordon training, in contrast, the permanent part of the vine consists of the trunk and one to four long, straight arms (cordons) trained along a trellis wire. Spurs or canes are spaced at regular intervals along the cordons.

No training occurs in the first year in most vineyards, thereby allowing maximum development of both the leaf area and the root system. (Some vines may be trained up to a stake for support.) At the end of the growing season, growers prune back the vines when dormant, so that all shoots are removed except a single, strong, well-placed vine. This is cut back to two buds.

Vines that will be drip-irrigated in the San Joaquin Valley and those grown in the Coachella Valley are more likely to be stake-trained in the first year, when very good, uniform growth is anticipated and an intensive investment in training is desired. The shoots and clusters must be thinned during the second year in order to produce a modest crop that is proportional to the vines' capacity. While the purpose of first-year training is to generate early income, the differences in individual vine vigor account for less uniform training up the stake in the first year; moreover, budbreak and shoot development along the new cordons (the vine "arms") may be erratic.

In the second year, all growth should be directed up the stake in a single shoot (trunk) for permanent development. As numerous shoots will emerge from each vine in the spring, shoot selection requires removing all but the longest shoots—those that have grown to 8 to 12 inches (20 to 30 cm) or more. Growers then choose the main shoots (two or three of the most vigorous, upright cordons) and remove all others. The shoots retained are tied over to the stake. Once the main shoot has reached 12 to 18 inches (30 to 46 cm) in length, growers remove the remaining ones. The main shoot must be tied up about every ten days to prevent breakage.

The placement of pruning cuts reflects a choice between *spur* versus *cane* lengths of pruned shoots. The former yield a shorter stub than the latter. We can describe three types of pruning: spur versus cane pruning, spur pruning with bilateral cordon training, and head training.

First, let's consider *spur versus cane pruning.* Differences in fruit quality between cane- and spur-pruned vines appear to be related to crop load effects, as well as to cluster location on the cane. Growers manage cropping by leaving the requisite number of buds on several short stubs of cane or on a few longer cane shoots. Short stubs with few buds are considered to be spurs, whereas longer pieces of one-year-old wood are considered to be canes. Spur pruning is advisable for cultivars that fruit from buds found at the base of the previous year's wood and for those that are excessively vigorous, such as muscadines. Cane pruning is advisable for cultivars, such as 'Thompson Seedless', that do not produce fruit on shoots from the base of the previous year's wood, and for cultivars that are low yielding and lacking in vigor.

The second type of pruning involves *spur pruning with bilateral cordon training.* Beginning in the second year, the trunk is topped at 18 inches (46 cm) above the lower cordon training wire in a double-wire trellis system; the purpose of **topping** is to induce uniform, strong cordons. Cordons are formed from two lateral shoots at the top of the trunk. Growers train the cordons on a wire about 20 inches (51 cm) below the cross arm of the trellis. It is advisable to delay topping with vigorous 'Flame Seedless' vines until 2 feet (61 cm) or more of growth extends beyond the cordon wire. Because 'Flame Seedless' has very long internodes that may still be elongating between the trunk and the shoot tip at this time, growers typically allow that growth to slow or stop before topping.

Once the top lateral shoots have been selected for the cordons (usually two) and tied to the wire, it is time to remove all the remaining lateral shoots down the trunk. If the lateral shoots are vigorous enough to grow past midway to the adjacent vine by midsummer, they can be tipped at this point. The procedure will stimulate additional lateral shoot development on the permanent branch canes.

It is important to control excessive vine vigor (such as in 'Flame Seedless'). Excessively long internodes and erratic budbreak are two signs of this problem.

Bilateral cordon training is not recommended for some varieties, such as 'Autumn Royal', due to inadequate productivity when too few spurs are retained per vine. Cane pruning can cause over-cropping in this case, with reduced berry size and color.

5. A trunk with its cane/cordon.

The third system, *head training,* is useful for cane-pruned (not spur-pruned) vines such as 'Thompson Seedless'. The main trunk is topped when it has grown 18 inches (46 cm) beyond the desired head height, which depends on trellis design. The top of the main shoot is secured, and lateral shoots are allowed to develop only from the top third of the trunk. The fruiting canes are then wrapped onto the trellis wires, enabling good sunlight penetration for fruitfulness in the following year.

It is important to avoid over-cropping during vine training, as vines and spurs can be permanently weakened. You can accomplish thinning by means of proper pruning, shoot thinning, and cluster thinning.

REMOVING VINE SHOOTS FROM THE TRELLIS SYSTEM
In general, this manual operation takes place soon after pruning with the Guyot technique. It consists of removing the vine shoots. This is a relatively slow process, since vine shoots often attach themselves to the wires by smaller stem tendrils (small vegetative organs next to the buds), and it is necessary to pull hard in order to remove them.

Clippers are useful for cutting the vine shoots into several pieces to facilitate their removal. Vine shoots also may be broken or burned, though many people in France still use them for grilling meat. In any case, it is preferable to fully remove them for the health of the vine.

BENDING
With Guyot pruning, "bending" is the operation that closes the season leading to budbreak. This intervention consists of bending the retained vine shoot onto wire once pruning is complete. This will become the cane *(photo 5).*

Bending can occur until the moment of budbreak. Since sap is already circulating, the wood will be more flexible and easier to bend. But bending can also take place rather early in winter, as long as there is enough humidity in the air to make the wood somewhat flexible.

It is advisable to position the cane horizontally and wrap it two or three times around the wire. The tip can even be attached to maintain its position.

WHITEWASHING
To prevent ferric **chlorosis**, growers in France brush on a mixture of citric acid and iron sulfate no more than twenty-four hours before pruning. This practice is not necessary in California, as iron deficiency in grape vines is not a problem there.

DISEASE AND PEST MANAGEMENT
To prevent wood diseases (esca, eutypiosis), it is advisable to brush a protective fungicidal wash onto pruning scars. For larger pruning scars, you may want to apply a second coat. The final wound will need to be covered with a sealant.

The University of California–Davis makes the following recommendations for Eutypa management in grapes:

- Prune late in the dormant season to promote rapid healing of wounds.
- Remove and burn infected wood inside the vineyard and dead wood in adjacent vineyards and orchards to reduce the spread of the pathogen.
- Cut out and remove dead arms and cordons from the vineyard during dormancy.
- Completely remove all cankers, pruning below each canker on the vine or trunks until no darkened canker tissue remains.
- Make large cuts directly after a rain because the risk for infection is lowest at this time, as the atmospheric spore load has been washed out temporarily (or is at its ebb).
- Practice double pruning of cordon-trained vines so that final pruning cuts can be made quickly

and late in dormancy, thereby reducing the chance of infection. For additional protection, consider treating pruning wounds.
- In table grapes, note locations in the vineyard that show poor budbreak in spring. Examine these areas in fall for disease damage. Mark locations of vines with poor growth for future confirmation and management.

Spring

REMOVING SIDE SHOOTS (SUCKERING)
This procedure takes place in May, after budbreak. Removing side shoots **(suckering)** consists of manually removing all the buds growing on a vine trunk, since these will not yield fruit. However, for various reasons (excessive trunk growth or disease such as Eutypa) it is sometimes necessary to maintain a side shoot for possible replacement use later. That intervention would take place during the next winter pruning.

DEBUDDING
Performed in May, debudding consists of selecting and promoting the best-placed buds by removing surplus buds from the cane or vine stock. This action promotes several beneficial outcomes:

- it aerates the vine shoots by suppressing double or undernourished buds;
- it simultaneously promotes better photosynthetic activity in foliage, inducing better grape coloration;
- it helps to protect against botrytis.

This operation is comparable to shoot **extinction** on apple trees or other fruiting species *(photo 6)*.

On a vigorous vine, you should keep the maximum number of buds in order to weaken the vine. On a weaker vine, you should decrease the number of buds. Balance will be completed by thinning the clusters.

6. Young grape shoots (vines/canes).

TRELLISING THE VINE SHOOTS

In terms of table grapes, this is the longest and most time-consuming operation. It takes place from May to July and needs to be done three or four times with Guyot and Royat methods.

Trellising aims to create a balanced distribution of vegetation, notably at the height that clusters grow. This aeration will be quite beneficial to cluster quality and simultaneously will help protect against botrytis, the grape's number-one enemy. Different trellis arrangements are available to growers.

In California. Head-trained, cane-pruned varieties and quadrilateral/spur (cane-pruned) varieties, such as 'Crimson Seedless', are usually trellised with a "Y" system (open gable). This large and expansive system can increase the vine capacity and yield potential of vigorous vines, in comparison to the standard California "T" system. The primary advantage of "Y" systems is that they allow more canes or fruiting wood to be retained per vine without a proportional increase in **canopy** density (a shading problem). Up to twelve canes per vine are normally retained on "Y" systems. Berries in these varieties tend to achieve larger size and color than if cordon-trained, spur-pruned, and planted on the standard California "T" trellis—but only when well managed for good light interception by the fruit. The "Y" system combination increases cluster numbers and total yield, but it is more intensive and expensive to manage.

When using the standard California "T" trellis, the quadrilateral cordon-trained/spur-pruned system offers several advantages over the head-trained/cane-pruned system. Spur pruning is less complicated than cane pruning, requiring less time and expense. The canopy tends to have clearly defined areas of fruit production; thus, cluster thinning and harvest are also less costly in time and money. Microclimate management practices, such as thinning of **basal** leaves for better light penetration and air movement, are facilitated; and where colored fruit are grown, pigmentation is better developed. Better air movement is especially important for reduced humidity in late-maturing varieties. Growers using the standard "T" trellis typically retain 8 canes on head-trained vines, whereas they retain 28 to 36 two-

7. Stapler.

bud spurs on quadrilateral cordon-trained vines (that is, 7 to 9 spurs per cordon).

Regardless of the pruning method, it is easier to cover the standard "T" system with plastic (to protect fruit from fall rains) than the open gable system.

In France. The most popular technique today for 'Chasselas' production is the double-wire method *(fig. 6)*, consisting of two wires spaced 2 inches (5 cm) apart. These wires stretch across the top and middle of the post. The double wiring helps to stabilize the vine shoots by interlacing them. It is a quick operation, but it needs to occur at precise moments once the shoot has grown 4 to 8 inches (10 to 20 cm) above the base wire. If the procedure occurs earlier, the vine shoots will not take; if later, they will break from bending onto the wires.

Another technique involves vine staplers: if shoots develop heterogeneously, the more developed vine shoots can be attached to the trellis with vine staplers *(photo 7)*. Several models are available, including the Max Tapener or Stopfil stapler that affixes the vine shoot with an elastic band or a plastic band held

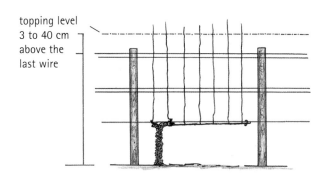

topping level
3 to 40 cm
above the
last wire

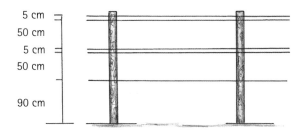

5 cm
50 cm
5 cm
50 cm

90 cm

Fig. 6. Position of trellis wires: upper and middle wires are doubled (source: *Pour un raisin de table de qualité*, Midi-Pyrénées technical group).

8. Crimping pliers.

enting their flow toward the berry clusters. It should also cause a uniform increase in berry size. Girdling must be done on balanced vines with a normal load of soft grapes. The procedure removes the bark, phloem, and cambium; prevents the translocation of carbohydrates to the root system; and thereby affords greater nutrition to the growing fruit until the girdle heals.

Annular incision

together by a staple. Unfortunately, these staplers don't always work properly and are a bit heavy.

Summer

GIRDLING

This operation aims to produce plumper grapes and to advance grape maturity by about ten days. It should always be done on vines that show a satisfactory balance of growth and fruiting.

The incision is made during **fruit set** (bloom + 10 to 14 days), when the grapes are about the size of a pea, to increase berry size. Using crimping pliers *(fig. 7; photo 8)* or double-edged girdling knives of varying widths, make an incision around the cane after the third vine shoot (starting from the trunk). The first three vine shoots are not affected by the incision and may be part of your subsequent winter pruning.

The faster maturity will only affect those clusters on any vine shoots beyond the incision. This annular (ring-shaped) incision causes a temporary interruption of sugar and hormone flow in the xylem vessels, reori-

Crimping pliers

Fig. 7. Annular incision and its tool.

Repeating girdling at veraison (color break) enhances fruit color and maturation. Research on 'Flame Seedless' in California has shown that the increased berry size may also reflect the vine's improved water status due to reduced transpiration; if this is the case, then we can say that proper girdling decreases the impact of soil water deficits—thus, water stress—at fruit set when berries are undergoing rapid cell division and enlargement. However, results vary by cultivar; moreover, berry size increase may also cause reduced coloration in red grapes. Double girdling generally involves re-opening the original girdle with a narrower girdling knife.

There is no counter-indication against practicing this method for several consecutive years on four-year-old vines and older. The practice should not cause any weakening or degeneration.

REMOVING SIDE SHOOTS

This process takes place at the end of June or in early July. It consists of manually removing the young side shoots located at the leaf axils at the base of the vine shoot. This is essential for aerating the grape clusters, which is in turn essential for preventing botrytis. Removal of side shoots also helps to improve coloration in the clusters. It is advisable to perform shoot thinning on spur-pruned vines when shoot length reaches 10 to 12 inches (25 to 30 cm). At the same time, you may also remove sterile shoots from head-trained canes. Shoot positioning on open gable systems is performed in concert.

This operation only concerns the cluster zone. If side shoots are suppressed beyond this area, the severity of the operation might cause an increase in vegetation. For the same reason, it is important not to remove side shoots too early. If it takes place too late, the clusters might be damaged.

SHOOT TOPPING

Topping helps to shorten vegetation before it starts to block the pathways between planting rows. This opera-

9. Mechanized topping.

10. Thinned vines.

tion should take place as late as possible after fruit set so as to allow the vine shoots to develop as much as possible. If this takes place too early (before or during fruit set), it will have several negative effects: increasing the number of grapes set, causing grapes to become too tight on the cluster, and increasing side shoot vigor.

The first topping should occur 12 to 16 inches (30 to 40 cm) above the last wire. It is important to carry out this topping as high and as late as possible, since it induces vigor and may therefore be detrimental to grape quality. A second round of topping may sometimes be necessary toward the end of July when certain later shoots have caught up to or surpassed the earlier shoots. Here as well, it is important to cut as high as possible.

Vigorous cultivars, such as 'Flame Seedless', should not be topped until there are at least 2 feet (61 cm) of vine growth beyond the cordon wire, as the internodes are still elongating within this portion of the vine.

Topping merely serves to unblock vegetation from the pathways and is not intended for squaring the vine (photo 9).

For the best 'Muscat' (muscadine varieties) coloration, topping should be done as lightly as possible.

PLACING CLUSTERS AND STRIPPING
LEAVES FOR AERATION
In France, this is commonly called "hanging the clusters": it refers to the manual placing of clusters in order

to verify the quality of the harvest. Clusters often stand up (are vertically oriented upright) before flowering and then fall after fruit set as the grapes develop and become heavier. During this period of development, the clusters may overlap with leaves, wires, or other clusters; such overlap will compromise the harvest, potentially induce botrytis, and reduce coloration.

Placing the clusters happens after fruit set, in July, before the cluster "closes," so as not to wound them and before the bloom forms on the grape surfaces. It is essential to handle the clusters with care since the rachis breaks easily and any damage may lead to botrytis infection.

At the same time, lightly stripping off leaves will aerate the area around clusters, with the goal of removing overlapping leaves or the one or two leaves that might be touching the cluster. However, this light stripping should not expose the grapes to sunlight, lest they risk damage from sunburn.

THINNING THE CLUSTERS

Keeping a fair number of buds will also mean thinning the cluster load. This is an important time in the season, for thinning will help to determine the level of the harvest's quality. Thinning should take place from the end of July until the middle of August. If it occurs any earlier, there will be a risk of slowing maturity by reinvigorating the vegetation. You can thin more or less intensely depending on how hardy your vines are. Research with 'Flame Seedless' in California has shown best results for coloration and berry size when cluster thinning took place between pre-bloom and berry set + 4 days. At berry set + 6 days (berry softening), cluster thinning reduced packable yields and fruit quality.

Cluster thinning enables you to:
• limit any excess load after fertilization;
• eliminate half-clusters and the third and fourth clusters on a vine shoot, any clusters that will be too tight (often found on spurs), and malformed clusters;
• promote aeration, since there will be fewer clusters;
• relieve over-loaded vine shoots in the middle of the cane;
• help to ward off botrytis.

The amount of thinning done in the first few years may only concern 40 to 50% of clusters (photo 10). And thinning should occur earlier (mid-July) when a vine is weaker, allowing it to nourish its remaining clusters and promoting berry development. Climate plays a role in the amount of thinning, as does irrigation.

Thinning should occur later (early to mid-August) when the vine is vigorous or if the clusters are compact or tend to remain green.

How should you thin the clusters? It is important to practice on a few trunks, first removing half-clusters and tighter clusters and verifying the count to compare it with the expected harvest. It is simplest to decide on a number of clusters to keep per trunk and stick to it. From time to time, verify the count on a few trunks.

ADDITIONAL MANAGEMENT PRACTICES IN CALIFORNIA FOR SOME TABLE GRAPE VARIETIES

Bloom thinning of berries is practiced in some varieties (such as 'Crimson Seedless') by the use of gibberellic acid (GA). A typical application of 1 gram GA per acre applied at 80 to 90% bloom increases berry length and berry weight without reducing total or packable yields or return bloom. Not all varieties respond to GA.

Nearly all 'Crimson Seedless' (and many other red varieties) vineyards in California require Ethrel (ethephon) for optimum color development. Ethrel is a commercial product that releases ethylene gas, the naturally produced fruit-ripening growth regulator.

Typical application rates of 3/4 to 1 pint Ethrel per acre in mid-July at berry softening or veraison, and again in mid-August (three to four weeks after veraison), are most effective for fruit coloration. Ethrel use softens the berries, but this effect can be minimized by making applications only at berry softening + 3 to 4 weeks. Color development may be slightly delayed.

Autumn

HARVESTING

Fruit quality is the ultimate goal of all of the summer work. Harvest can take place when grapes have reached a certain level of maturity. For example, 'Chasselas' reaches maturity at 17° Brix. U.S. standards for table grapes include a variety of quality measures; however, Brix is not included, whereas color is very important. Perhaps, in the case of California, this is because Brix development is not a problem under normal cultural practices.

Now harvest can begin. This means cutting off ripe clusters (photo 11), which generally requires two or three passes: the first time yields 20% of the clusters, the second time yields 50%, and the third yields 30%. This is sequential harvesting.

The advantages to sequential harvesting include:
- accelerated maturity in the clusters that weren't removed in a previous round;
- better cluster homogeneity.

11. Cutting the cluster.

For harvesting, you can use:
- a pair of pruning scissors;
- slotted wood or plastic crates.

Grapes should be harvested in dry weather to prevent the risk of fruit rotting.

PRUNING

After harvest, you can prune your clusters in the field or the workshop. This operation consists of removing unwanted grapes from the cluster, in preparation for consumption.

STORING GRAPES

Certain conservation methods will allow you to keep grapes for up to three months. Storing grapes successfully requires that you have satisfied several conditions:
- the grapes are healthy as a result of good irrigation and fertilizers;
- the grapes must be whole and undamaged at maturity;
- various cryptogamic diseases (botrytis, blight, powdery mildew) have been kept at bay;
- at harvest, you have been careful not to mix in dried grape stalks or fruits that are rotten, damaged, or ruptured;
- you have harvested the grapes at optimal maturity and placed them in cool conditions as quickly as possible.

It is possible to keep clustered or wrapped grapes in good conditions for up to two weeks as long as the temperature in the cooler doesn't get too low (between 44° and 50° F or 7° and 10°C). For longer storage, lower temperatures around 32° F (0° C) will be necessary, as will a sulfur dioxide (SO_2) spray on each of the crates.

POSSIBLE PROBLEMS DURING VINE TRANING

If there is too much vegetation or if clusters are of low quality, you can take the following measures:
- reduce or discontinue the use of nitrogen fertilizers and limit phosphorous and potassium;
- manage irrigation, watering only after July 14 and making sure not to over-water;
- make pruning cuts further up on branches;
- top the vine later;
- do not remove buds, but do thin clusters;
- do not till the soil.

If the vine is weak or there is a low number of clusters, you can:
- use a fertilizer in the spring 3.7 lb/acre (20 kg/hectare) of nitrogen, 9.2 lb/acre (50 kg/hectare of potassium and phosphorous, (each) around the base of the vine trunk (see Appendix C: U.S. Standard Equivalents for Nitrogen);
- prune shorter, leaving only seven or eight eyes;
- remove buds more selectively;
- till the soil to reinvigorate it.

HAZELNUT

Author	Jean-Paul SARRAQUIGNE
Collaborator	Éric GERMAIN

GENERAL OVERVIEW

History and Phytogeographical Origins

The origin of the hazelnut tree (also called "filbert") dates back to a distant time. Two species, the ancestors of our current hazelnut trees, date to the Tertiary period (Miocene epoch): *Corylus insignis* Herr with narrow leaves, and *Corylus mac-quarry* with broad leaves—the precursor to the common hazelnut tree, *Corylus avellana*. The fruit of the wild hazelnut tree served as food during antiquity, and people were already aware of its nutritional value.

Known since nearly 3000 BCE, hazelnut trees held an important place in Greek mythology and in the ancient cultures of Turkey, where the hazel branch was a symbol of peace. Its cultivation is quite ancient. It is believed that the hazelnut tree grew in China twenty-nine centuries before Christ. In Europe, cultivated hazelnut trees were imported from the Black Sea region to Greece and Italy, where the Romans called them *avellana*. Arab populations improved the trees' cultivation in Sicily and Spain.

Even though native species (*C. americana* and *C. cornuta*) exist in North America, the tree's cultivation only goes back two centuries on this continent, with domestic varieties derived from the European hazel, *C. avellana (photo 1)*.

The common hazelnut, *C. avellana*, originated in Europe and Anatolia. It grows as a shrub or small tree and is particularly abundant in temperate climates, from Portugal and Ireland in the west to the southern

1. A tree of the Tonda di Giffoni variety.

Urals in the east (Ukraine and Kazakhstan). Its **planting zone** reaches latitude 68° on the western coast of Norway, in Sweden, and in Russia. In southern Europe, *C. avellana* grows in Spain, Sicily, and Greece. In Asia, it reaches from Turkey across the Caucasus into eastern Iran and toward Syria and Lebanon in the south.

Botanical Classification

Depending on the author, one can distinguish between twelve and twenty-five species or subspecies of hazelnut tree, among which only a few are of interest for cultivation. Together, these species constitute the *Corylus* genus, which belongs to the order Fagales and the Betulaceae family, in the Coryleae tribe. Recently,

Veli Erdogan and Shawn Mehlenbacher regrouped the hazelnut species into the three types outlined in *table 1*.

C. pontica Koch, which includes most Turkish varieties, is now considered a subspecies of *C. avellana* (*photo 2–3*).

Currently, breeding for improved characteristics centers in Oregon in the United States. The hazelnut breeding program at Oregon State University uses the genetic diversity in the genus *Corylus* to create new **cultivars** via interspecific crosses for the Oregon industry. The major objectives of the breeding program are suitability to the blanched kernel market and resistance to eastern filbert blight (EFB), the most significant pest of the genus. Three recent cultivar releases ('Lewis', 'Clark', and 'Sacajawea') have partial resistance, while 'Santiam' is the first cultivar (released in 2005) to have complete resistance

GROUP	SPECIES	AREA OF DISTRIBUTION
Avellana group (shrub)	*Corylus avellana* L. *Corylus maxima* Mill. *Corylus Americana* Marsh. *Corylus heterophylla* Fish.	Europe, Anatolia, Caucasus, Urals Anatolia, Eastern Europe North America Manchuria, Korea, Japan
Cornuta group (shrub)	*Corylus cornuta* Marsh. *Corylus californica* Rose *Corylus sieboldiana* Blume	North America North America Mongolia, Manchuria, Korea, Japan
Colurna group (tree)	*Corylus colurna* L. *Corylus chinensis* Franchet *Corylus jacquemontii* Decaisne *Corylus papyracea* Hickel *Corylus ferox* Wallich	Eastern Europe, Anatolia, Caucasus to the Himalayas Central China Afghanistan, northern India China Intermediate zone of the Himalayas central China, Nepal, Sikkim

Table 1. Species in the genus *Corylus*, shrubs and trees.

from its parent cultivar, 'Gasaway'. Trees of 'Santiam' are slightly smaller than 'Barcelona', the dominant commercial cultivar in the United States, and produce small nuts that have fewer defects and a higher percentage with kernels. ("Blank" nuts without kernels are considered a defect.) 'Santiam' nuts mature and fall free of the husk two to three weeks before those of 'Barcelona', a real advantage in avoiding fall rains that damage the crop.

Soil and Climate Limitations

THE HIGH-PRODUCING COUNTRIES
Worldwide commercial production of hazelnuts, based exclusively on the *C. avellana* species, is mainly concentrated in four countries in the Northern Hemisphere. Turkey is by far the most important, with an annual production estimated between 700,000 and 750,000 tons *(photo 4)*. Italy is in second place with a production of 130,000 to 140,000 tons from four regions: in decreasing order, Campania (Naples), Lazio

2-3. *C. pontica* hazelnut tree and *C. avellana* var. *purpurea* hazelnut tree.

4. Growing area in the Akçakoca region, Turkey.

(Viterbo), Piedmont (Turin), and Sicily (Messina). In North America, the state of Oregon alone posts significant hazelnut production, placing it third in the world with an average of 45,000 tons from approximately 25,000 acres (10,117 ha)—ahead of Spain's orchards, which produce 26,000 to 28,000 tons.

A few other countries obtain modest production levels of hazelnuts that don't end up on the world market. These include Greece, Iran, Azerbaijan, Georgia, and China. France currently produces 5,300 tons, with a moderate growth that may increase its yield to about 6,700 tons within five or six years.

TECHNICAL AND ECONOMIC LIMITATIONS

Production systems for hazelnuts are above all dependent on the economic context of the given country. That is why we find highly mechanized growing in Oregon and France, intermediary systems in Italy and Spain, and a fully manual method focused on cheap manual labor in Turkey. In France, producers have opted for 74-acre (30 ha) plots that are owned individually or collectively with neighbors.

SOIL REQUIREMENTS

The root system of the hazelnut tree displays a high density of roots in an area that roughly matches the tree's **canopy** size. There are not many anchoring roots. Most of the root system grows in the first 50 to 60 yards (46 to 55 m) of growing area, regardless of the soil type.

In order to develop well, the tree needs a depth of at least 20 inches (50 cm) in level, even ground. The most favorable soil types are silty clay, clay loam, a small area of silty soil (less than 65% silt), or in rare cases, silty sand.

Moreover, hazelnut trees love aerated soil and hate excess water. Thus, locations should be chosen for their ability to drain well. The hazelnut also needs regular watering starting from June until the last ten days of August.

The rate of active calcium must remain lower than 10%. Beyond 8%, there is a great risk of iron **chlorosis** *(photo 5)*, which reflects competition between iron and calcium cation uptake, resulting in iron inadequacy and chlorosis (leaf yellowing). The hazelnut tree is rather flexible in terms of soil pH, producing satisfactorily in a range from 6.2 to 7.8. The ideal pH range should be from 6.5 to 6.8.

LIMITING CLIMATIC FACTORS

In general, hazelnut species are cultivated in temperate climates. Numerous climatic factors must be considered in relation to the hazelnut's cultivation.

Cold requirements and breaking dormancy: Research in this area expresses the cold requirement in terms of number of hours below 45°F (7°C). The chilling requirement, expressed as "chill hours" or hours $\leq$ 45°F, varies according to the hazelnut **variety**'s origins. It is

5. Symptoms of iron **chlorosis**.

Type of organ	Catkin	Inflorescences (female)	Vegetative buds
Number of hours at T < 45° F	< 100 to 365-480	480-600 to 1170-1255	600-680 to 1170-1255

Table 2. Scale of cold requirements for 13 varieties. (Source: S. A. Mehlenbacher, 1991.)

on average the highest among vegetative buds, mid-range for pistillate flowers, and lower for catkins (male inflorescences). In varieties studied at the University of Oregon, the spread of cold requirements is defined by the values shown in *table 2*.

Sensitivity to low winter temperatures: Freeze damage on old wood is rare on hazelnut trees. Only temperatures that go below -13°F or -25°C (in the -18 to -22°F or -29 to -30°C range) cause damage on old wood. Vegetative buds and pre-blossoming pisillate flowers resist temperatures as low as -4°F (-20°C).

Closed catkins, with their tightly overlapping scales, are unaffected by temperatures from 3 to 4°F (-16 to -15°C).

Sensitivity to late-winter and spring frost: This phenomenon affects young leafy shoots, some of which grow from pistillate flowers bearing future hazelnuts at their tips. The young leafy shoot is the most sensitive organ to cold, since **lethal temperatures** vary from 26°F (-3°C) during the later part of the first year after planting to 28°F (-2°C) during the third year after planting *(photo 6)*. Several factors may slightly alter these thresholds, such as the progressive arrival of cold temperatures or the tree's hydration, which is itself a function of the soil's water content.

Heat requirements and fruit set: One peculiarity of the hazelnut's floral biology is that fertilization and the resulting **fruit set** only happen around two and a half months after **budbreak**, at a stage toward the end of May or the beginning of June when the young fruit measures about one-third of an inch (roughly 10

6. Frost damage on a shoot.

mm), although flowering and **pollination** occur in mid-winter. Normal embryo development requires that daily high temperatures not drop below 70°F (21°C) for three consecutive days.

Rainfall: It is remarkable that the major growing areas for the hazelnut (with the exception of

Tarragon in Catalonia, Spain) have an annual rainfall between 40 and100 inches (102 and 254 cm), which means the hazelnut tree needs to be well irrigated in order to develop and produce consistent and abundant fruit. In September and early October, however, higher rainfalls are undesirable since they prevent the **involucres** (the "husks" formed by **bracts**) from drying out, thereby diminishing fruit **dehiscence**. Soggy ground also impedes mechanical harvesting. At the moment of flowering, from December to the latter third of March, prolonged rainy spells are unfavorable to pollination.

Relative humidity and wind: Hazelnut trees do not do well in arid areas, particularly if there is too much wind. Relative humidity should not drop below 70%, except infrequently. Finally, persistent winter winds are likely to hamper pollination.

In terms of recent research in France, a national meteorological study conducted in 1986 at the request of the National Association of Hazelnut Growers determined the favorable areas for hazelnut cultivation in France. This zone consists primarily of central Aquitaine and central Midi-Pyrénées, reaching slightly to the northwest into Charente and Charente-Maritime (as long as frosts and limestone can be avoided) and to the southeast in the Lauragais region (if trees can be sheltered from wind).

In the United States, production in Oregon centers in the Willamette Valley, which has ideal climatic

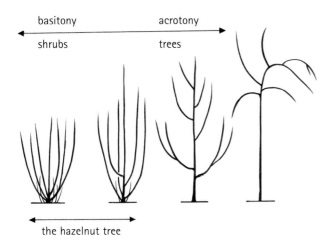

Fig. 1. The hazelnut tree is a shrub.

conditions. The only limiting factors to production in this area are blight resistance and overlap of flowering of cultivars, as **cross-pollination** is a requirement. As new cultivars become available, grafting onto existing rootstocks or propagation of new trees by budding onto selected new rootstocks is ongoing in U.S. (Oregon) production. The use of grafted trees is an option for producing a large number of trees in a short period or for converting trees from one cultivar to another (called "top-working"). Rootstocks may be used to vary the range of suitable production areas for a particular cultivar, but they need to be selected for their influence on **precocity**, vigor, yield, and nut quality of the grafted tree. As interspecific hybrids are developed, not all may have **grafting compatibility** with all rootstocks.

TREE MORPHOLGY

Tree Type and Branch Organization

BASITONY OF THE ENTIRE PLANT AND ACROTONY OF THE YEARLY GROWTH

Coryllus avellana is a bushy shrub by nature, capable of emitting numerous root suckers and shoots. But due to the constraints of mechanical harvest, commercial production requires a single trunk to which shake-harvesters can attach. This shape does not prevent shoots from appearing. These shoots, called **epicormic branches** or even **reiterations**, are the expression of the plant's strong natural **basitony**. This will happen in autumn, during a short period after the leafy shoots have stopped growing and preceding the start of the tree's **dormancy**. Basitonic organization arises when **apical dominance** disappears from the growing cycle *(photo 7)*. It allows short, stiff shoots to form along the lower portions of the tree that, in the following spring, will become hardy epicormic branches *(figs. 1 and 2)*.

In young hazelnut trees, another expression of basitony is evident in the fact that secondary axes (lateral branches) *(see fig. 10)* inserted in the lower trunk strengthen and grow more quickly over the years than the two axes above them. This behavior results very quickly in a shrub-type tree (demonstrating pluri-axial form).

7. Basitonic growth throughout the tree (Pauetet, 2 years).

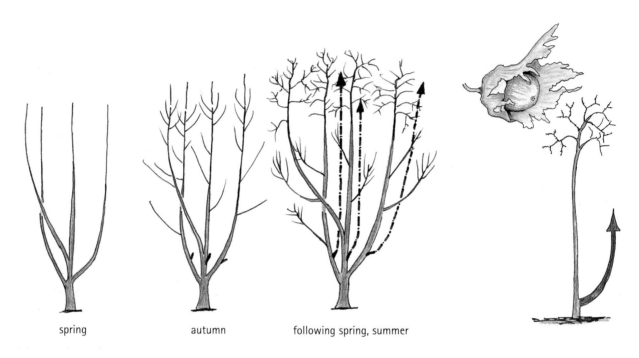

spring   autumn   following spring, summer

Fig. 2. The process of epicormic branch formation on hazelnut trees: basitonic reiterations often arise when there is abundant fruiting.

For current-year branches, the organization is quite opposite and of an **acrotonic** type: it begins as dormancy ends, with growth slowing over the year from **distal** section to **proximal** section. The buds on the upper third or fourth of the branch will produce stronger lateral shoots. This acrotony, which differs by variety, does not fully inhibit buds in the branch's middle section and ends up creating a kind of "fish-bone" branching habit *(photo 8)*.

DISTINCT MALE AND FEMALE INFLORESCENCES
Hazelnut flowers (in all *Corylus* species) are unisex and grouped by inflorescence *(fig. 3)*. Male flowers, which have no petals, are inserted at the catkin's **rachis** in a helical arrangement. Each catkin has 130 to 280 male flowers.

The female flowers are located in pistillate inflorescences, recognizable during blossoming when the red **stigmata** emerge from the top. These are in fact

8. Acrotony of the annual branches (Butler, 5 years).

166

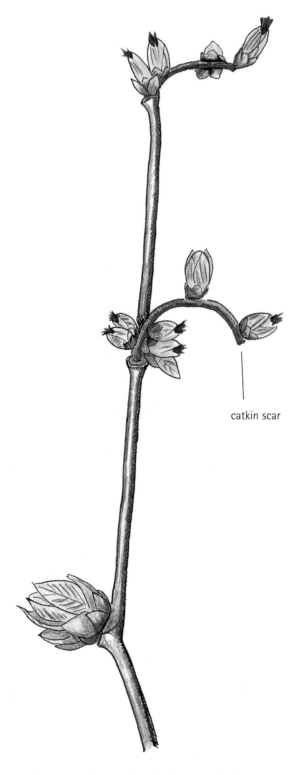

catkin scar

Fig. 3. A Fertile de Coutard branch with several inflorescences.

mixed buds, containing both a **preformed** branch of five to seven **nodes** and an **apex**, a fertile part made up of bracts. The **bracts** (a leaf associated with the reproductive components of a flower) yield two flowers at their axil, each one enveloped in three tightly joined bracteoles. The bracteoles (small bracts) will produce the **involucre**, a sort of leafy cup in which the hazelnut is encased while it reaches maturity. Each pistillate flower contains an average of eight flowers.

All the inflorescences are located on shoots from the prior year, yielding a sort of "mixed branch." At each of the different nodes on these branches, one may find vegetative buds, pistillate flowers, and catkin peduncles, the latter also bearing buds and female flowers.

The *Corylus* genus is **monoecious**, meaning that each tree yields both male and female inflorescences *(photos 9 and 10)*.

9. Fruiting branch on the Fertile de Coutard variety.

10. Annual branch.

CROSSING THE PRINCIPAL VARIETY
WITH SEVERAL POLLINATING VARIETIES

Pollination is an important factor in attaining abundant hazelnut production, since without exception this species is **self-incompatible**.

Hazelnut pollination is strictly **anemophilious**—that is, it requires wind to spread the pollen. The tiny pollen grains (25 to 40μm in diameter) are easily transported by the wind over a distance of hundreds of yards. In commercial growing sites, plots are designed so that pollinators are within 25 to 30 yards (23 to 27 m) of the varieties to be pollinated. Pollination occurs primarily when stigma receptivity on the base variety is simultaneous with pollen emission from at least one of the pollinator varieties. But pollination is also tied to certain rules of pollen incompatibility among different varieties. Choosing the pollinator will require integrating these two criteria.

The desired proportion of pollinator trees within a hazelnut orchard ranges from 8 to 12%. Their position within the orchard has to be based on maintaining light within the population of trees, which is not as common with other fruiting species. It is hard to avoid with the hazelnut tree. The best compromise consists of alternating every third row with all of the pollinators and the principal variety.

VARIED GROWTH DEPENDING ON THE TREE'S AGE
AND THE BUD'S LOCATION

Young springtime shoots are preformed in the vegetative and flowering buds. Prior to budbreak the buds contain the future stem, which may or may not terminate in an inflorescence. This preformed stem includes either five to seven nodes or nine to ten, depending on whether it will yield a fruiting shoot or a vegetative shoot.

The first phase is quite rapid: during April, the young shoot elongates exponentially. At the end of May or in early June, growth stalls on fruiting shoots terminated by a cluster of young hazelnuts as well on the weaker vegetative shoots located in a **basal** or medial position on the support branch. Their vegetative apex drops, placing the **subterminal** bud in an **apical** position, and spurring growth in the buds below them. Subsequently, these shoots will demonstrate **sympodial growth** *(fig. 4).*

The more vigorous shoots, most of which will be terminal or subterminal on the previous year's branches, continue to grow until the beginning of July. In turn, they will lose their terminal bud.

Sprouts and epicormic branches develop in one single growth cycle until all of the leaves have dropped. This behavior can be observed in young trees.

Primary growth, therefore, does not take place uniformly throughout the hazelnut tree: it is sympodial on short and fruiting shoots, yet may remain **monopodial** on more vigorous branches.

Species Variability

Even though, at first sight, intraspecies variability of the hazelnut tree may seem unimportant, there are

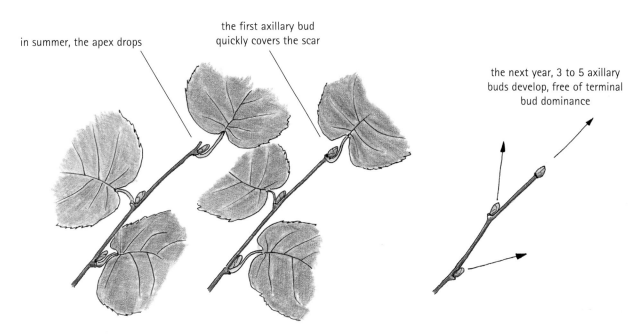

in summer, the apex drops

the first axillary bud quickly covers the scar

the next year, 3 to 5 axillary buds develop, free of terminal bud dominance

Fig. 4. Early in its development, hazelnut trees exhibit sympodial growth.

notable **phenotype** differences in terms of both veg-etation and fruit.

TREE VARIABILITY

The hazelnut displays wide variability in terms of numerous characteristics.

Vigor: In France, even at nurseries—particularly when trees are produced by layering—there is a notice-able difference in vigor among varieties *(fig. 5)*. Among cultivated varieties, for example, one can distinguish three levels of vigor:

- extremely vigorous: 'Fertile de Coutard' (syn. 'Barcelona'), 'Pauetet', 'Segorbe', 'Corabel®';
- average vigor: 'Ennis';
- less vigorous: 'Negret', 'Tonda Romana', 'Du Chilly'.

Vigor is less variable among U.S. varieties.

Branch density: Certain varieties, such as 'Butler' and 'Tonda Romana', do not branch much. In contrast, 'Ennis' produces thick «fish bones» by combining short **internodes** and weak acrotony on the current year's

axis. Examples of intermediate cases are 'Merveille de Vollwiller', 'Corabel', and 'Jemtegaard 5', all of which branch well owing to weak acrotony combined with low basitony.

The length of internodes and bud phyllotaxy: The length of internodes may vary according to variety, but this aspect does not seem to be related to the plant's other behaviors, such as vigor. With the common hazel-nut tree, *C. avellana*, the **phyllotaxy,** or bud placement along the leafy shoot, varies *(photo 11)*. Generally, this species' phyllotaxy is multidirectional. However, under certain growing conditions bud arrangement is distinct, meaning that buds are located 180° from one another in a fish-bone pattern. This type of positioning reflects **amphitony.**

Wood flexibility: For the moment, 'Corabel®' offers a unique case within France's cultivated varieties. It has supple wood that allows the branches to bow under the weight of their normal hazelnut production load, which is relatively low. The American native 'Beaked

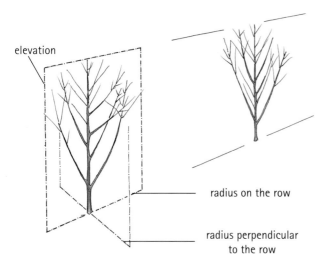

elevation

radius on the row

radius perpendicular to the row

Fig. 5. Different tree dimensions, allowing growers to determine proper planting distances.

Hazelnut' (Corylus cornuta Marsh.) also has long, flexible shoots that were used by the native Americans to make twisted rope.

Angle of insertion of branches on their axis: Grown varieties and hybrids have notable distinctions in terms of **insertion angle**. On 'Daviana', OSU. 55-129 (N 626), and to a lesser degree 'Ennis', 'Segorbe', and 'Tonda Romana', primary branches grow at narrow angles to the trunk. 'Fertile de Coutard, 'Corabel', H. 295-28, and N 593 present more open angles.

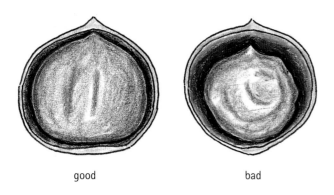

good   bad

Fig. 6. Yield at breaking (kernel either fills the shell or does not).

11. Phyllotaxy at different levels (types 2-5) on a Corabel®.

Tree habit: The tree's habit results on some level from the various aspects we have just covered *(photos 12-15)*. Among the examples mentioned above, 'Daviana' and OSU. 55-129 are fairly erect varieties. In contrast, H. 295-28 as well as several Turkish cultivars ('Palaz', 'Sivri', 'Tombul') tend to hang more.

FRUIT VARIABILITY

Hazelnut characteristics relate to either the fruit in its shell (shape, size, evenness, color, shell thickness) or the nut itself (shape, size, smoothness, skin color, amount of corky residue, **trimming** ability, size of internal cavity, lipid content). The nut yield, also called the "kernel yield" *(fig. 6)*, is another important criterion for selection, applicable both to commercial hazelnuts and to the hazelnuts people eat from trees growing at home. Depending on the cultivar, the nut yield may vary from 35 to 52%.

Annual Hazelnut Cycle, Phenology, and Floral Induction

ANNUAL CYCLE

Figure 7 outlines the annual cycle for a hazelnut tree in growing conditions typical of southwestern France. In fact, this cycle is probably not significantly different from that of hazelnuts grown in Oregon in the United States.

PHENOLOGY

In terms of the hazelnut's **phenology**, the identifiable stages have been defined and codified. *Figures 8 and 9* show female and male stages, respectively, that are optimal for pollination.

FLORAL INDUCTION AND ALTERNATE BEARING

Male floral induction: The first signs of catkin differentiation within the buds are visible in the latter third of May for 'Fertile de Coutard' (syn. 'Barcelona'). Inflorescence density is maximal on short shoots (less than 6 inches or 15 cm long), with the distal part of the branch still exhibiting a vegetative tendency.

12-15. Two-year tree types. From left to right and top to bottom: Ennis, N 731 hybrid, N 722 hybrid, N 687 hybrid.

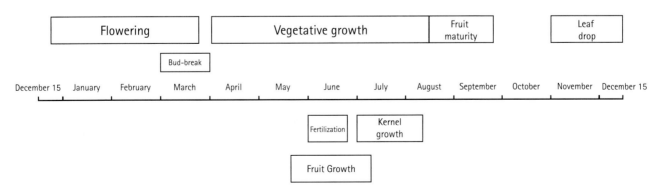

Fig. 7. Annual cycle of hazelnut trees.

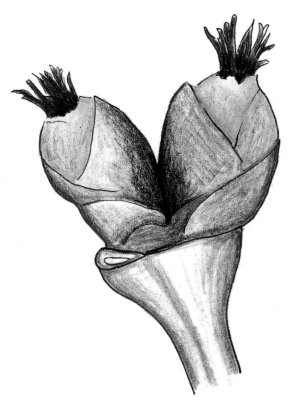

Fig. 8. Inflorescences as blossoming starts, stage Ff1.

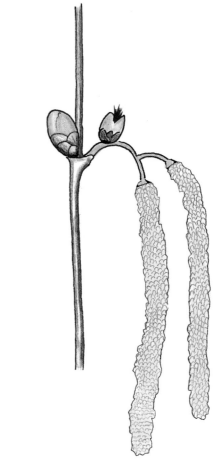

Fig. 9. Full catkin blossoms, stage Fm2.

Female floral induction: The first hint of flowers appears just after the start of female **floral induction,** which occurs around the end of June or during the first ten days of July. Three factors play a role in the number of female flowers initiated:

- *the health of the "mixed branches":* regardless of the tree's age, the amount of female flowers tends to increase with the length of growing shoots (6 to 18 inches, or 15 to 45 cm).
- *their origin:* short fruiting shoots that grow from pistillate flowers alternate systematically in almost all varieties. The presence of fruits strongly inhibits flower production for the following year in this type of shoot. Fortunately, the tree creates new shoots from vegetative branches to compensate for the inhibition that floral induction causes. In this way, **alternate bearing** in well-maintained and balanced trees becomes much more restricted.
- *sunlight:* light is paramount for hazelnuts, as with other species, affecting both floral induction and the average number of hazelnuts per inflorescence.

Description of the Fruit

The hazelnut is a dry fruit in a shell, with a single seed (with some exceptions). It can be **indehiscent** or dehiscent depending on the variety. In botany, the

172

term **achene** denotes this type of fruit when it is inde-hiscent *(photo 16)*.

In terms of nutritional value, the hazelnut contains an oleaginous seed whose lipid content ranges from 52% to more than 70%, depending on the variety. The make-up of hazelnut oil, combined with its high content of the antioxidant vitamin E, makes the hazelnut useful for preventing cardiovascular disease and certain cancers.

The shelled hazelnut contains about 0.2 ounce of fiber for every 3.5 ounces (7 to 8 g per 100 g).

BASICS AND PRINCIPLES OF TRAINING

Brief Historical Overview

In France, professional hazelnut orchards currently maintain open-wind forms, related to the lower-branch vase structure, on three or four **scaffold branches**. (In contrast, hazelnut tree shape in the United States is rounded, not vase-shaped, with mechanical topping and hedging serving as the main types of pruning.) Productive orchards tend toward thinning instead of full pruning. The aim is to create "chimneys" or light wells by removing excessive branches, scaffolds, or lower laterals; flattening trees out; using mechanical cropping; and in certain cases, removing every other tree.

In a fair number of plots more than twenty years old, the tops of the hazelnut trees start to age rapidly, even if they are well lit. This slows vegetative growth and fruiting, while the wood, trunk, and root system appear preserve their potential.

Current Thinking on Hazelnut Training

The reasons for pruning should follow the natural behavior of a given species as well as its requirements

16. Fresh Ennis hazelnuts cracked half open.

for producing quality fruits that are abundant and consistent year after year. Current understanding on hazelnut growth can be described in the following manner.

Hazelnut fruiting presents no real difficulty. As the juvenile evolves into an adult tree (demonstrating **ontogeny**), its first flowers appear on third-order axes—meaning during the second year from planting for layers that have not been cut back at the time of planting, and during the third year from planting for the opposite case *(fig. 10)*. Fruiting starts during the third and fourth years from planting.

At latitude 45° N, the rule allowing for light to reach the base of the trees is based on balancing the tree height with the width between planting rows. Hazelnuts can tolerate a 3 to 5 foot (1 to 1.5 m) differential on this rule, meaning that tree height may be 3 to 5 feet higher than the width of the space separating rows, without causing any problems for fruiting. Moreover, fruit weight, unlike with many other fruiting species, does not tend to bend the branches, except in certain cases.

This species therefore needs to develop a sufficient number of new shoots each year in order to fruit regularly (see "Floral Induction and Alternate Bearing" earlier). This presupposes that branches on axes I and II will grow about 16 inches (40 cm) per year. Not pruning will promote higher fruit production than the shape of the tree itself. Individuals that are not pruned will start producing earlier. In these conditions, there is an excellent balance of growth and fruiting throughout the tree. These numbers will be higher than on individuals that are structured or excessively pruned.

Light is essential for the tree to be able to spread its new shoots and bear annually. Given 5-1/2 yards (5 m) of space between rows, an abundance of sunlight will continue to shine on the population for seven to ten years after planting, depending on how hardy the variety is and how fertile the soil (most often until the eighth year after planting for more vigorous varieties).

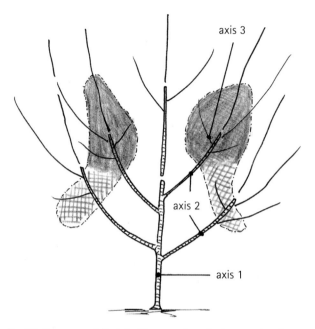

Fig. 10. The areas of first fruiting on a tree that was not cut back at planting.

PRACTICAL CONCERNS

The ideas described above should guide practitioners in choosing their planting system. The tree's natural basitony, the lack of bowing caused by fruiting, and the need for sufficient annual growth are some of the factors that combine to quickly yield tall, well-shaped tree forms over the years.

Planting distance is a determining factor in training hazelnut growth. This should be decided on the basis of tree vigor and soil fertility.

The idea of shaping the tree has waned, in favor of progressive thinning of branches that are too low—especially when they inhibit cultivation work or when insufficient light reaches the tree's lateral branches. Moreover, mechanical hedging along a row of adult trees will produce quite different results from thinning. The hedging will allow current shoots to be renewed on the sunniest sections of the tree if fruiting has become insufficient.

Pruning and thinning of limbs are recommended only when sunlight can no longer reach into and among the trees. At that point, light wells should be created to revive annual shoots and regularize fruit production.

PROPOSED GROWING METHODS

Free Vertical Axis

Results from growing experiments indicate that a free vertical axis is the best compromise between the species' natural behavior and the industry's production constraints.

PLANTING AND THE START OF PRODUCTION

We recommend the free vertical axis to both the professional grower and the amateur, replacing the lightly structured vase method that is currently used in most French hazelnut orchards.

The free vertical axis method consists of the following steps:

- leaving the vertical layer intact *(photos 17 and 18)*.
- using bamboo and wires to prop the tree *(photo 19)*.
- clearing the first 28 to 31 inches (70 to 80 cm) above the soil after the first year from planting, depending on the tree's vigor. If the first-year

17-18. Evolution of a layer in 1st leaf. 17: Butler in early spring; 18: Vertical Axis Ennis in summer.

19. A young transplant at 2 years.

20. Bending secondary branches on a Corabel® hazelnut at 3 years, cut back at the end of the 1st year.

shoots are strong, growers should undertake pruning in the spring and summer.

• treating **sylleptic** shoots in the nursery: bending rather than cropping around the base. A sylleptic shoot that is left to grow vertically will quickly become "a tree within the tree," accelerating the tree's evolution to a pluri-axial form. Even though they are rare in the hazelnut tree, the few sylleptic branches emitted by layers in the nursery should be bent during the summer of the first year, as well as the second when necessary. Bending should be combined with slight twisting by holding the branch with two hands protected by leather gloves. The goal is to "crease" the libero-ligneous vessels (the subcortical tissue that conducts sap flow). The preferable time for this is in the latter half of June

before

after

Fig. 11. Bending technique.

to late July *(fig. 11; photos 20–23). [Note that this step relates primarily to nursery personnel.]*

- suppressing branches that are too low and in the way.
- consistently controlling root suckers starting in the second year from planting, in order to maintain well-lit and well-aerated leafing at the center and to aid with harvest. The best results come from a combination of manual pruning (assisted or not, preferably combined) and chemical treatment.
- maintaining proper planting distances: this is one of the keys to a successful hazelnut orchard, which we will discuss later in this chapter.

The Multi-Branch Tree or Shrub

This is the most natural way to shape a hazelnut tree and probably the simplest to apply. It is particularly useful for the amateur grower. This type of planting works well with smaller cuttings (16 to 18 inches tall,

or 40 to 45 cm) as long as their base diameter is at least roughly 0.8 inch (20 to 22 mm) and they are well rooted. It is neither necessary nor desirable to cut back the layering at the time of planting.

The tree will consist of several principal axes (order-I axes) growing at erect angles, often around 25° to 30° from vertical. In order to create healthy secondary axes (order-II axes) and proper aeration within the shrub, the number of limbs should not exceed four. This can be reduced to three and sometimes even two, in order to eventually flatten out the tree.

As we saw with the free vertical axis method, branching will vary from one tree to another within the same variety. This may produce two types of behavior in the young hazelnut tree:

During the first two to three years, the order-II axes will grow along a gradient from bottom to top, which will reverse in the third or fourth years.

Alternatively, in the first or second year from planting, the order-II axes along the bottom of the trunk will clearly dominate those in the distal part,

21–23. Evolution of a Corabel® hazelnut tree over 3 years (years 3, 4 and 5).

177

expressing the tree's clear basitony—which the tree will maintain *(fig. 12)*.

Lateral branches that are too low, situated along the first 31 inches (80 cm), will have to be suppressed in the second or third year, preferably during summer pruning around mid-July. This intervention is justified based on the competition found between order-I axes. Removal may facilitate both manual and mechanical upkeep in the orchard.

Visitors to gardens and orchards in traditional production areas (such as Spain and Italy) can readily see that hazelnut shrubs naturally generate root suckers *(photos 24–25)*. When the tree is maintained with a single trunk as the base, root suckers become more common. Thus, with the multi-branch method of growing, root suckers should be pruned or killed off regularly.

PLANTING AND THE START OF PRODUCTION
The bushy seedling should planted vertically and left intact. The plant should not be pruned at the end of the first year.

Any plants that appear to show a preference for distal zones (acrotonic development) should be left alone the following year. On plants with basitonic growth, the number of limbs should be selected for in the second

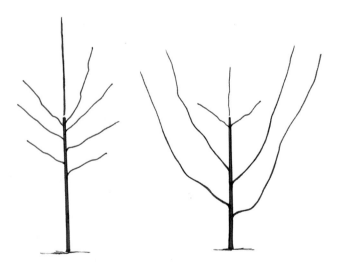

Fig. 12. Two behaviors of first-year hazelnut trees.

year whenever their number exceeds four. Pruning may take place in the summer or winter depending on how vigorous the tree is.

Root suckers should be suppressed.

UPKEEP DURING FULL PRODUCTION

For vertical axis and shrub methods, we ask the same questions, and for the same reasons. However, it is probable that hazelnut trees grown as shrubs will acquire volume more quickly than those grown with the free vertical axis method, and that flattening and reduction of the number of principal axes will occur sooner.

Four Questions to Ask Before Pruning

In reality, pruning for upkeep consists of thinning entire branches. The type of intervention should be based on the answers to four essential questions that the practitioner should ask.

*Is natural **extinction** excessive (fig. 13)?* If this is not the case, the pruning goal will be to create light wells by suppressing lateral branches from among pairs that are too close to each other.

Are the rows spaced adequately for light to reach lateral branches or for growers to maintain the tree practically? If the answer is negative, lower lateral branches can be suppressed or pruned (prune only the side branches), but these interventions must be executed with the tree's height and volume in mind.

Are the current year's shoots more than 6 to 7 inches (15 to 18 cm) long on average, and are there enough of them? A shoot that is shorter than 6 inches means that the hazelnut tree is not regenerating itself correctly. It will be necessary to revitalize terminal shoots throughout the tree. Thinning the population may help.

*How tall are the trees, and how tall have twelve- to

24-25. Shrubby hazelnut trees.

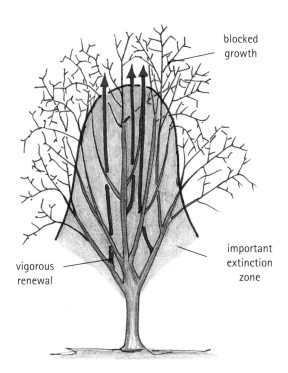

blocked growth

vigorous renewal

important extinction zone

Fig. 13. Excessive naturally-occurring extinction.

fifteen-year-old hazelnut trees grown? It may not be easy to establish an answer to this question, especially if the trees are growing on a hillside. But this is the question that will decide if you should preserve all the trees or not. If the answer is negative, you should suppress every other tree *(photo 26)* or every other row *(photo 27)*. From there, you should decide if the tree's structure needs to be simplified, particularly in terms of flattening temporary trees *(fig. 14)*.

Flattening Trees: The Preliminary Phase for Thinning a Population

Flattening trees that are slated for elimination is one way of creating a light well within a population, for the time being. This is a temporary stage before progressively cutting down half the trees with the goal of restructuring the orchard. On a free vertical axis, this will primarily occur with second-order axes. This method of restructuring is a good solution in orchards where the space

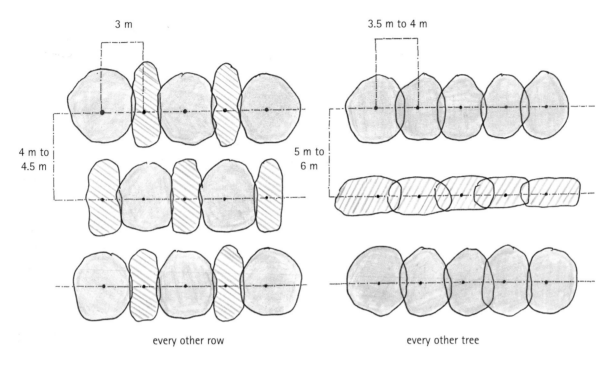

3 m

3.5 m to 4 m

4 m to 4.5 m

5 m to 6 m

every other row

every other tree

Fig. 14. Two strategies for thinning a hazelnut orchard and technique for flattening the trees.

26. An orchard thinned by removing every other tree: the sun reaches the ground.

27. Suppressing every other row of trees.

between rows is closing down, when tree height is more than 1.5 yards (1.4 m) as wide as the spaces between. As a reminder, growing hazelnut trees at the 45th parallel requires a 1-to-1 relationship between tree height and row spacing to allow enough light to reach the plants.

- *If the tree won't grow more than 7.5 yards (7 m) high:* The restructuring option here is to suppress every other tree and flatten temporary trees perpendicularly to the planting line.
- *If the tree grows more than 8.5 yards (8 m) high:* In this case, you should eliminate every other row. Flatten trees parallel to the planting line within rows that are to be suppressed, and perpendicular in rows to be kept.

Renewing Old Trees

THE PROBLEM

The question of renewal, sometimes called "regeneration," commonly arises in orchards more than twenty years old where hydro-mineral alimentation is judged to be sufficient. The trees' tops will start to age in spite of abundant sunlight and will no longer grow or produce fruit as they once did *(photo 28).*

Our first thought on this problem is that growers should give hazelnut trees the opportunity to regenerate early enough, particularly while maintaining enough space around them (based on their potential growth) and thereby privileging light around the fruiting areas. With this in mind, the reasonable chronology is: first, thinning the population; then, undertaking tree renewal.

Renewing Unstructured Vase Trees

In France, we only have limited experience with hazelnut renewal in terms of unstructured vase trees. There are three possibilities:

28. A Segorbe hazelnut tree reacts to renewal pruning.

- progressively cutting back on the tree's structure, which is the most commonly recommended technique;
- cutting back the whole tree all at once, which is not commonly practiced;
- regenerating from a tree that has been completely cut back to its base, an approach that is still under evaluation.

Each time an epicormic branch grows spontaneously at a spot in the canopy that is considered appropriate for renewing the mother branch, it must be preserved. It will quickly gain strength.

Renewing Vertical Axes

Trials and commercial plots that are involved in renewing vertical-axis trees are too recent to provide conclusive results.

The use of spontaneous reiterations may be handled in the same way as outlined above for the unstructured vase tree.

Renewing Shrubs

The shrub structure is probably the best adapted for renewal. Of the shrub's three or four primary axes, it is fine to drastically cut one of them back to about 10 to 12 inches (25 to 30 cm) from the ground. As with the free axes, the practitioner should envision utilizing spontaneous reiterations wherever possible, whether these are good-quality epicormic branches or root suckers that are well situated within the shrub.

29. The fungus *Pellinus* sp. growing on a pruning wound.

30. Protecting a pruning wound.

31. Scarring on a protected pruning wound.

Healing Pruning Scars

Wherever renewal efforts involve big cuts (often done with a chainsaw), the wood may rot from rain or become colonized by **carpophore** fungi (capped), most often saprophytes. Certain fungi, such as *Phellinus* sp., may become parasitic and cause major branches to die (*photo 29*).

Wood affected by parasites will soften and may be hollowed out by large birds (green woodpeckers, grey-spotted woodpeckers, magpies, and jays), which then break the hazelnuts in these cracks and cause further damage.

To prevent these problems, it is advisable to make cuts on secondary axes as vertically as possible and as flat to the mother branch as possible. There are special cells located within that joint to help with healing. When cutting branches that are nearly vertical, be sure to make the cuts at a slight angle. In any case, wounds more than 3 to 4 inches (8 to 10 cm) in diameter should be protected from water while they heal, either with putty or with bitumen (*photos 30 and 31*).

PLANTING DISTANCES

Planting distances based on varietal vigor and soil fertility will determine which options to choose for restructuring a hazelnut orchard and at what moment. They will also help in deciding on pruning routines for upkeep or renovation.

Today, we estimate that 'Corabel®' requires more space than other varieties grown in commercial orchards, based on its vigor and branch flexibility. In contrast, certain weaker varieties (such as 'Tonda Romana') may be planted closer together.

Table 3 may help in deciding how densely to plant.

With less vigorous varieties, it seems unlikely that a grower would choose to suppress every other row. Depending on soil fertility, either all of the trees or every other tree should be preserved.

Soil fertility \ Variety	Corabel® variety	Other varieties with moderate to high hardiness	Other varieties with low hardiness
Average to good, with the possibility of suppressing every other tree	6 x 3m, or 555 trees per hectare	6 x 2.5m, or 666 trees per hectare	
High, with the possibility of suppressing every other row	5 x 3.5m or 5 x 4m, or 500 to 571 trees per hectare	4 x 3.5m or 4.5 x 3.5m, or 635 to 714 trees per hectare	
Average to good, without thinning			5 x 3.5m, or 571 trees per hectare
High, with the possibility of suppressing every other tree			5 x 2.5m, or 800 trees per hectare

Table 3. Recommended planting distances.

KIWI

| Author | Michel RAMONGUILHEM |
| Collaborator | Jean-Louis TAILLEUR |

GENERAL OVERVIEW

History and Phytogeographical Origins

The kiwifruit originally grew in Southeast Asia and was first commercially cultivated in New Zealand, having been introduced to both New Zealand and the United States (California) in 1906. "This large egg, with a coat of brown fur and emerald green flesh" (a phrase quoted from a New Zealand professional magazine) inspired many different efforts in the marketing world—including New Zealand's national bird, the kiwi.

Originating in the wooded mountain regions along the Yangtze River, it was the natural food preference of monkeys. The *yang-tao* (its Chinese name) was also called the "macaque peach" in a collection of poetry dating from the tenth century BCE.

In its self-sown state, a few species of this fruit also grow in countries adjacent to China, from the 50th parallel north down to the equator: Korea, Japan, Thailand, India, Malaysia, Vietnam, Siberia, and the Himalayas. Of course, its preferred climate is nonetheless one of natural warmth and humidity. Between 1925 and 1940, a few New Zealand pioneers (such as Jim Mac Laughlin, Denzil Forester, Hayward Wright, Graham Turner, Bruno Jus, Arthur Stoddart, and Graham Bay Liss) planted a few stems and, starting in 1950, began exporting the plants—Stan Conway especially. At that time, the fruit was commonly called a "Chinese gooseberry."

Today, the kiwifruit is a recognized and sought-after exotic fruit. Present in all areas of trade, it has slowly entered the European diet. What's more, since the time of the earliest Chinese dynasties this fruit has been credited with numerous medicinal benefits: as protection against hepatitis, as a digestive aid, for curing hemorrhoids, and for preventing kidney stones, hypertension, and dyspepsia as well as prematurely graying hair! For the past few years, in certain European countries medical professions have recommended it as a preventative food against flu (due to the fruit's high levels of vitamin C) and certain cancers.

Dry kiwifruit wines, liqueurs, fruit paste, sorbets, and pastries are a few of the specialties that bear witness to this fruit's culinary flexibility.

Commercial planting in California began in the late 1960s. From 50 acres (20 ha) in 1970, the industry in California had grown to more than 8,000 acres (3,237 ha) by 1988; however, U.S. kiwifruit production has been declining since the 1990s. Acreage in 2006 was reported to be 4,300 (11,740 ha) by the California Kiwifruit Commission. In noncommercial settings, kiwifruit has been grown in Virginia, South Carolina, Alabama, Georgia, and Florida, although no commercial plantings are present in these states. Freeze damage is a significant risk in locations other than California, Florida, and the Southwest, where intense heat, low humidity, and infrequent rain tend to be more problematic (in California and the Southwest).

Family—Genus—Species—Varieties

- Family: from the family Actinidiaceae, the kiwifruit is a creeper that can reach dozens of feet high in the wild.
- Genus (generic name): Actinidia.
- Species (specific names): there are more than sixty. We will focus on two: *A. chinensis*, a smooth-skinned **variety** exhibiting wide variability; and *A. deliciosa*, a species with hairy fruits. Hardy (less frost-susceptible) kiwifruit (*A. arguta, A.*

kolomikta) are much smaller than *A. deliciosa*, which is grape-size or slightly larger. *A. arguta* has a smooth, edible skin *(photo 1)*. In all varieties, the fruit is best when soft-ripe at harvest and will only ripen during storage if harvested after the fruit reaches physiological maturity (after seeds turn black and sugar content is 8 to 14%). The fruit's storage life is short, and the fruit are susceptible to ripening by ethylene. Hardy kiwifruit are occasionally grown and marketed in Oregon and British Columbia, where the primary **cultivar** is 'Ananasnaya', sometimes shortened to 'Anna'. 'Issai', a less hardy *A. arguta* cultivar, was introduced from Japan in 1986. *A. arguta* reportedly can tolerate winter temperatures as low as -25°F (-32°C), but freeze damage to new growth in the spring is similar to the damage described for *A. deliciosa*; thus, actual frost tolerance is not clear.

1. *A. arguta* W20

Since this plant is **dioecious**, meaning unisex, the presence of male plants is necessary in the vicinity of fruit-producing female plants. Male **canes** are usually spaced every third cane in every third row. They represent 10% of the planting in California, where three or four hives of honeybees are provided per acre.

The number of commercial cultivars is quite limited. In the *deliciosa* species, we can distinguish female varieties introduced in the 1950s until the early 1990s such as 'Abbot', 'Allison', 'Bruno', 'Hayward', and 'Monty' *(photo 2)*, which are still the dominant varieties grown in New Zealand. Today, 'Hayward' remains the most commercially produced variety worldwide, thanks to its size and long shelf life. Yet, in terms of private vineyards, 'Bruno', 'Abbot', and 'Monty' may also be good choices for planting, since they often have higher-quality taste. They can still be found in

2. *A. deliciosa*, Monty variety.

specialized nurseries. New varieties selected at the end of the twentieth century include 'Tomua4', a precocious variety (a month earlier than 'Hayward'); 'Moncap', from La Capou and Montauban in southwestern France (one month before 'Hayward'); 'Summer 33734', an Italian variety that has been commercialized through a club (Summer Kiwifruit France), is sold only to professionals, displays **precocious** maturity (50 days before 'Hayward'), and is sweeter and less acidic but also small; and 'Summer 46054', of the same origin and sold under the same conditions, with later maturity (35 to 40 days after 'Hayward') and similar size but sweeter and less acidic.

New male varieties include 'Matua' ("father" in Maori), which is hardy, highly productive of flowers and pollen, and has a long flowering period; 'Tomuri '("late" in Maori), which is less hardy with late and abundant flowering, simultaneous to 'Hayward'; and 'Autari4', an Italian variety that flowers at the same time as 'Hayward'. Male varieties in the "M" series have also been selected: M51, M54, M55, M57 and M58 for early to mid-season flowering; M52 and M56 for mid-season flowering; and M53 for late flowering. The most recent selection in the "M" series, 'Chieftain', has abundant flowers that coincide with those of 'Hayward'. With 'Hayward', flowering seems to be most simultaneous to 'Chieftain', 'Autari', and M52 and M56 males.

The 'Chico' or 'Chico Hayward' (selected in California) plants available from nurseries in the United States are similar or almost identical to the New Zealand 'Hayward'. In California, it is possible to successfully pollinate 'Hayward' females with 'Chico' (male), 'Matua', or 'Tomori'. For earlier-flowering female varieties such as 'Abbott', 'Allison', and 'Bruno', the male variety 'Matua' is a better choice.

Two new varieties (*A. chinensis* Planch.) were released by the University of California–Davis in 2008: 'Eldorado' and 'Nugget', as well as an early-blooming male pollenizer, 'Early Bird' (Ryugo and Stover, 2008). Both fruiting varieties are relatively hairless and thus don't require peeling. 'Eldorado' bears one or two fruits on the **basal nodes**, similar to 'Hayward', while 'Nugget' bears clusters of cordate (borne on the cordon) fruits on basal nodes. Both mature around September 10 in Davis, California (latitude 38.55 N, longitude 121.74 W). These new varieties have yellow flesh when mature (changing from green), with typical flavor and sugar content (13.5–15.0° Brix). Reported fruit weights for 'Eldorado' and 'Nugget' are approximately 4 and 2 ounces (106 and 60 g), respectively, on non-thinned canes. The new cultivars will not be patented, but **scions** will be available through the National Clonal Germplasm Repository at the University of California, Davis. In the *chinensis* species, available female cultivars are not very numerous today. 'Hort 16A–Zespri Gold 4', a New Zealand variety with yellow flesh, is distributed through a club that is open only to professionals. Its smooth, sweet fruit has a tendency to bruise and tear. It is harvested slightly later than 'Hayward'.

'Chinabelle 4' is a French variety from the Capou agricultural high school in Montauban. Its smooth, yellow fruit is of average size.

Male varieties are more numerous. These include 'Meteor', a New Zealand variety with precocious flowers, recommended for pollinating 'Hort 16A–Zespri Gold 4'; 'Sparkler', a New Zealand variety that flowers later than 'Meteor' and is recommended for pollinating 'Hort 16A–Zespri Gold 4'; and 'Pollichina', a La Capou-Montauban variety that should be avoided as it does not flower in time for 'Chinabelle'. Other selections are in process.

Cultivars from the *A. melandra* and *A. purpurea* species show interesting prospects, including future commercial varieties with red flesh.

To summarize, for enthusiasts, only 'Hayward', 'Abbot', 'Bruno', and 'Monty' are readily available today.

Main Growing Areas

In the Northern Hemisphere, kiwifruit cultivation occurs in Asia, North America, and Europe. Among European countries, Italy is the top producer, followed by France, Spain, and Greece. In the Southern Hemisphere, New Zealand is the leading country, followed by Chile and South Africa. In France, the southwest (Pyrénées-Atlantiques, Landes, Tarn-et-Garonne, and Lot-et-Garonne regions) produces two-thirds of the national harvest. The rest comes from the eastern plains of Corsica and the Rhône-Méditerranée basin.

Soil and Climate Limitations

SOIL
Kiwifruit plants need to be in soils that thaw rapidly in the spring. Alluvial soils are the best. Growers should avoid soils that are rich in clay, for they will lead to insufficient growth and become a factor in deficiency. Highly calcareous soils should also be avoided. The pH level should remain lower than 7.7 and/or the **active limestone** content below 5%.

Climatic elements that have the most impact on kiwifruit development are water, wind, frost, and sunshine.

WATER
It is important to avoid asphyxiating areas. Because kiwifruit roots need a lot of air, the ideal soil is one that dries rapidly, such as permeable alluvial soil.

In more complicated areas, growers should provide an organic substratum in a sufficiently large planting hole, and always on a hill. But even on slopes it is advisable to avoid making any type of trough around the roots. In these cases, you should work with cuttings with bare roots and plant during the winter, rather than working with cuttings in a container (see

"Choice of Plant Material" later in this chapter). Excess water can promote not only root asphyxiation but also the appearance of *Phytophtora cactorum*—a fungus that attacks the stem and roots, causing the plant to die.

The kiwi's water requirements are rather high. It is advisable to water regularly in the ground area under the **canopy** (the area of the plant's leafing). An important rule of thumb is to imagine the root system as mirroring the dimensions of the foliage. All the roots must get water; if they do not, the leaves' stomata will remain closed wherever there is low moisture, leading to a reduction or even a complete halt of photosynthesis, which would in turn cause poor plant health.

In ideal soil situations, and keeping rainfall in mind (use a rain gauge), as a general rule the plants should receive at least 5 to 6 inches (120 to 150 mm) of water per month—roughly one-tenth of an inch per day, or 3.5 to 5 l/m² in the months of June, July, August and September. If the soil is dense, you can lower those rations by 20 to 25%.

WIND

Wind is one of the worst enemies of the kiwi. Windy areas are absolutely to be avoided. Plant growth will come to a standstill, and leaves will show considerable wilting (necrosis and leaf drying). In addition, lateral stems and/or renewal sprouts may tear off (see "Choice of Plant Material" later in this chapter).

Because the kiwifruit loves "subtropical" climates, humidity levels are a primary factor in the development of its leaf system.

Kiwifruit should be planted with as much protection from the wind as possible or positioned near a natural windbreak (an appropriately dense forest species) or an artificial windbreak (a screen with the right density mesh). Planting in this way will permit proper light

3. Frost-protecting ice on fruits in November prior to harvest.

4. Frost-protecting ice sprayed as water from above in the spring.

porosity and sufficient ambient ventilation (growers should plan for 50% porosity).

Paradoxically, wind is both an aid and a hindrance in terms of kiwifruit **pollination**. Studies differ as to whether pollination should be considered **anemophilous** or **entomophilous**. Kiwifruit pollen is dried by the wind and does not stick to the flower, thus allowing insects to carry it from flower to flower. Even though these two actions (pollination via wind and insects) appear to complement each other, numerous trials have shown that bees seem essential for obtaining a sufficient number of seeds (pips) in the fruit, leading to better fruit development.

In the absence of any natural population of honeybees or bumblebees, growers should bring in beehives. It is now possible to buy sets of three bumblebee hives; bumblebees are busier pollinators than honeybees and can work in lower temperatures (as low as 50°F or 10°C).

FROST RISKS
The risk of frost is the third factor that growers should not neglect. Avoid any frost-prone area *(photos 3 and 4)*. Frost will affect the kiwifruit plant according to the following parameters:
- complete destruction of the wood between -0.4°F and 5°F (-15° and -18°C);
- frost on open buds, in the spring, between 26°F and 29°F (-1.5° and -3°C);
- frost on flowers at 32°F (0°C);
- frost on blossomed flowers between 30°F and 33°F (0.5° and -1°C);
- frost on fruits at 30°F (-1°C).

In terms of home planting, it is difficult to fight off spring frosts since most solutions are costly (heating candles, wax molds, sprinkling the foliage).

Note: until the age of four, it is strongly recommended that trunks be protected during the winter with hay bales stacked together. That protection may be removed at the beginning of April.

SUNSHINE
Shaded areas hinder photosynthesis, affecting kiwifruit development and taste. Also, bees tend to gather less nectar in shaded areas.

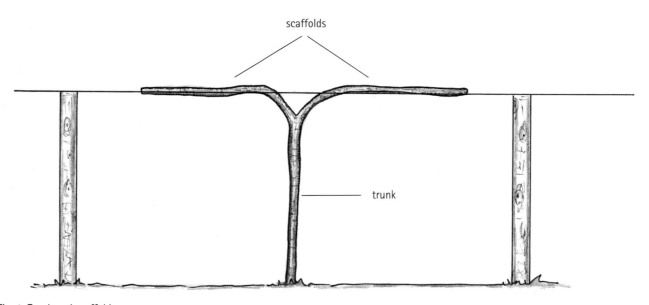

Fig. 1. Trunk and scaffolds.

TREE MORPHOLOGY

In productive plantings, the kiwifruit climber comprises a trunk, cordons, lateral canes called "canes", fruiting canes, and renewal and epicormic canes—not to mention leaves, flowers, and fruits.

The Trunk

On a vine/cane-growth species, a trunk is almost nonexistent: the main cane of a young plant will soon wrap around its support (another plant, stakes, etc.). In terms of cultivated vines (which are artificially supported), similar to other fruiting species, the trunk *(fig. 1)* constitutes the primary branch system; as its diameter increases, so will each **apex** in the aerial system. In

the early stages, the single apex must be hardy; as the future trunk evolves, it must remain absolutely straight and unimpeded by its stakes in order to form correctly and produce healthy stems.

Cordons

Cordons are analogous to **scaffolds** in trees. These form when the trunk splits into two arms that will grow along a horizontal wire crossing the trunk.

When working with the well-recognized "T" or "tunnel" configuration *(fig. 1)*, which is simpler on a practical level for both professionals and enthusiasts, the scaffolds constitute logical prolongations of the trunk. These will become the definitive support structure for future lateral canes.

The Laterals or Canes

Like fruit-tree branches, canes are branches that grow directly from the cordons and bear fruit. These primary structures for production must be renewed each year *(fig. 2)*. Given that these laterals produce "hanging" harvests and future renewals, the goal should be to obtain a maximum number of sufficiently hardy laterals in order to guarantee continued production.

During the first year after planting (the year that the leaves appear), canes may produce a few fruits along the first 8 to 12 inches (20 to 30 cm; at the axils of the first seven or eight leaves) starting at their point of insertion on the cordon *(fig. 2)*. These sites will only produce once. In the following year, only the next buds will generate fruiting canes.

During the second year after planting, the laterals produce fruiting canes that will become the privileged support structure—in terms of both quantity and quality—for production *(fig. 2; photo 5)*. After picking, in

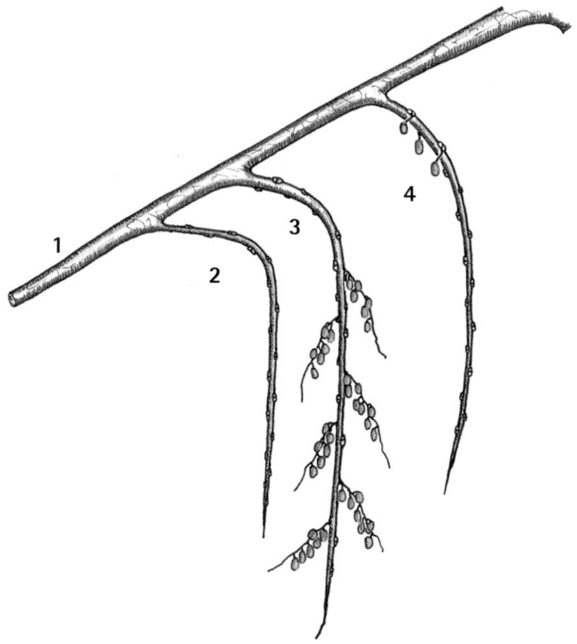

Fig. 2. Laterals.
1: scaffold; 2: annual lateral, no fruit;
3: lateral with flowering shoots (2nd year);
4: annual shoot in first-year production.

the winter of the second year, it will be necessary to replace them by using lateral wires to bow the renewal canes, which will have appeared over the year on the laterals themselves *(fig. 3)*. These renewal canes will become laterals depending on their position on the wires and their production capacity.

New laterals may also break through directly on the cordons.

To summarize, the kiwifruit produces canes throughout the year from branches that developed during the prior year—the laterals. In these agronomical conditions, each lateral has a life expectancy of two years before being replaced.

5. Laterals with their fruiting shoots in 2nd year.

Fruiting Canes

There are two types of fruiting canes: determinate and indeterminate.

Determinate canes: The so-called "determinate" canes are compact and relatively short due to their brief growing cycle. They terminate in tightly clustered buds *(fig. 3; photo 6)*. These are the best fruiting structures since they are fertile and numerous. They naturally grow in a fish-bone form along the **median** of the laterals. The more fruiting canes there are, the greater the production will be.

These determinate canes may be present on the cordons, generally producing excellent-quality fruit and allowing "gaps" to be filled in where laterals may be lacking.

Nevertheless, when the number of laterals seems sufficient, growers should remove the determinate canes inserted along the trunk to allow more light to

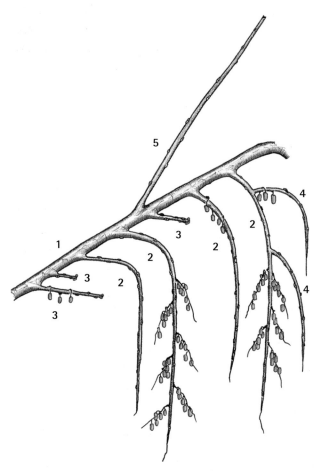

Fig. 3. Various kiwifruit shoots.
1: scaffold; 2: lateral; 3: determinate fructiferous shoot; 4: renewal shoot (indeterminate shoot); 5: epicormic branch.

6. Determinate flowering shoot.

inches (60 to 80 cm), their buds are often vegetative and do not yield fruiting canes.

Epicormic canes are generally suppressed. However, if no or few laterals exist in that spot, their presence may be useful: short growths with two buds around late May or early June will induce less hardy branches that will fruit. They can thus be used as renewal laterals.

Leaves

The kiwifruit leaf is simple, rather sizeable, slightly dentate, and "egg-shaped," appearing in an alternating arrangement with somewhat hairy stalks. The lower face of the leaf, which is also pubescent, is light green, while the upper face on currently cultivated varieties is deeper green and appears smooth and waxy.

Most cultivated species are deciduous.

Flowers

Flowers start at the leaf axil, either singly or as an **inflorescence** *(photo 7)*. Primarily dioecious, male and female flowers do not grow on the same canes, but this characteristic is not an absolute. Whether male or female, the flower is cupuliform (cup-shaped) with five petals (five to eight in 'Hayward') and can be white, yellow, or pink depending on the species *(photo 8)*.

The flowers display numerous **hypogynous stamens** (**perianth** and **androecium** inserted below the ovary) with long, thin filaments attached dorsally and in the middle of oscillating **anthers** that are yellow, brown, or deep violet.

The male flower is identifiable by its small rudimentary ovary and small styles. Its pollen is quite abundant. The female flower is recognizable by its numerous styles and developed **stigmata** *(fig. 4)*. It is usually larger than the male flower. Its pollen is not

access the upper portions of the climber's tunnel. In general, on 'Hayward', 50% to 70% of buds will produce fruiting canes, with each cane yielding two to six fruits (often, four or five).

Indeterminate canes: Canes that grow continually are called "indeterminate." They develop on the laterals *(fig. 3)*. In terms of their hardiness, each lateral may produce many of these canes or none. If they are too hardy, summer pruning will be necessary.

When several canes develop on a single lateral, only one should be kept—the one closest to the cordon—to ensure lateral replacement.

Epicormic Canes or "Reiterations"

These canes are quite hardy and grow directly from the cordon, often vertically *(fig. 3)*. Thickening quickly, they are too hardy to serve as laterals. On the first 24 to 32

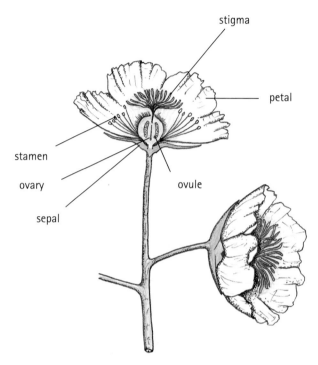

Fig. 4. Female inflorescence.

7-8. Floral buds and flowers.

viable. The stamens often have shorter filaments and smaller anthers.

Fruits

The fruit of *Actinidia deliciosa* is a brown-colored (the color of the hairs) **berry** with a green epidermis containing hundreds of small black seeds, lined up and spread throughout the light green flesh caused by presence of chlorophyll *(photo 9; fig. 5)*. While the flesh is light green in the *deliciosa* species, it can range from yellow to dark green in the *chinensis* species. Depend-

ing on the variety, the shape, size, and hairiness may also vary considerably.

Each fruit of *Actinidia deliciosa* may contain up to 1,400 seeds. A minimum of 800 seeds (optimally, 1,100 seeds) is required for achieving an ideal fruit weighing 3.5 ounces (100 g). That is the average weight considered respectable for enthusiasts and minimal for professional growers.

The kiwi, like the pear and the avocado, is harvested when hard. It should be allowed to ripen until it is soft to the touch before being eaten. The fruit is picked without its peduncle, which is left on the bud at harvest.

For harvesting, a minimum refractometric index (RI; soluble solids, which include sugars) of 6.2 should be reached before picking. Of course, amateur growers (as well as professionals) may wait until November to harvest, especially in areas unaffected by frost, in order to obtain a better-tasting fruit, making sure that the fruits remain quite firm.

9. Fruit set.

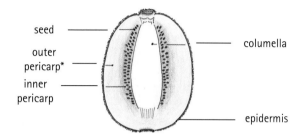

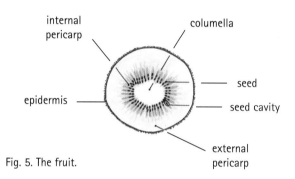

Fig. 5. The fruit.

To eat them at their best, place kiwifruit in a fruit bowl or plastic sack with a few apples. In little time, the ethylene produced by the apples will accelerate the kiwifruits' ripening. If there is no refrigeration available to maintain a temperature of 32°F to 34°F (0° to 1°C), kiwifruit may be kept in a cool, aerated area free of other fruits.

Kiwifruit pulp surrounds a central column lying lengthwise (the "columella") that is whitish-green or cream-colored. The seeds surround the columella in two rows (fig. 5). The edible fruit includes the pulp, the columella, and the seeds.

Annual Plant Cycle

Below is a calendar of main stages (see also table 1 and fig. 6):

- Winter **dormancy**.
- **Budbreak**: end of February through March.
- Cane growth: April–May.

Stages		Benchmark stages in flowering buds	Dates (for southwestern France and California)
1		Dormant bud	Winter
2	A	Bud swelling. Start of growth	End of February / beginning of March
3	B	Visible burr	
4		Full bud-break	
4-5	C	Rolled leaves	March 8
5		Leaves open	March 20
6	D	Leaves spread	March 30
	E	Floral buds appear	
	F1	Flowers start to open	
	F2	Full blossom	End of May, beginning of June

Table 1. Phenology. Phenological stages were placed into 6 categories by Brundell in 1975: 1, 2, 3, 4-5, 5, 6. Today in France, these have been replaced with stages A, B, C, D, E, F1, and F2.

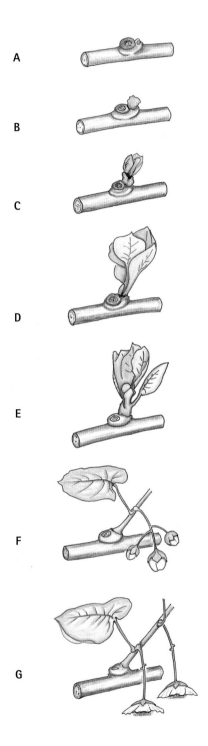

- A
- B
- C
- D
- E
- F
- G

Fig. 6: Phenological stages. A: bud swelling; B: visible burr; C: leaf veins appear; D: first leaf spreads, floral buds not visible; E: floral buds appear; F: start of blossoming; G: full blossom.

- Male blossoms: May 25–30.
- Female blossoms: end of May–beginning of June.
- **Fruit set**: first ten days of June.
- First cell thickening: June–July.
- Second cell thickening: August 15 until harvest.
- Harvest: October 25 to November 10.
- Leaf dropping, end of activity: first autumn frost.

Note the rather long period of eighty days between budbreak and blossoming. Blossoming lasts for about nine days on 'Hayward' varieties.

FLORAL INDUCTION

Contrary to other fruit species in latitudes where **floral induction** occurs in the summer prior to blossoming, even though the **meristem** has been initiated during the preceding summer (July–August), floral induction on the kiwifruit only occurs in the weeks prior to blossoming. (This is similar to the olive tree, the avocado tree, and certain citrus trees.) Thus, the kiwifruit bud must not encounter any stress—or as little as possible— in terms of nutrition, watering, or climate between the fifteen to sixty days prior to blossoming (meaning April and May).

BASICS AND PRINCIPLES OF TRANING

Choice of Plant Material

Growers should select cuttings that are at least eighteen months old, sold with bare roots and planted during the winter period *(figs. 12-1 and 12-2)*, instead of younger cuttings sold in containers for planting after the risk of springtime frost has subsided. The latter are fragile and require more work and time in order to start growing. In this case, it is essential to avoid breaking the soil around the roots, provide water, protect the plants against pests, and then follow up on water needs and weed control *(fig. 11-1)*. In certain

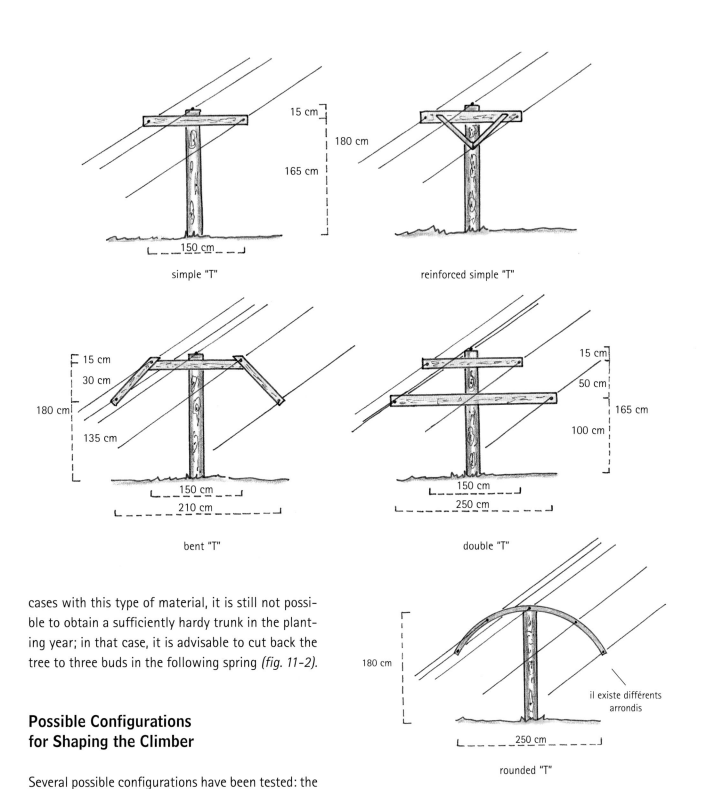

simple "T"

reinforced simple "T"

bent "T"

double "T"

cases with this type of material, it is still not possible to obtain a sufficiently hardy trunk in the planting year; in that case, it is advisable to cut back the tree to three buds in the following spring *(fig. 11-2)*.

Possible Configurations for Shaping the Climber

Several possible configurations have been tested: the "T" shape, the pergola, and variations on both.

il existe différents arrondis

rounded "T"

Fig. 7. "T" configuration. The height of the trellis may vary.

10. An older transplant on a "T" trellis.

11. A trellis designed to help bend canes.

The "T," or "tunnel," configuration *(fig. 7)* is the one that professionals most commonly use today. It is equally recommended to novices since it is a simple way of making production perennial. Several "T" shapes are possible *(photos 10 and 11)*.

Professionals in Mediterranean climates sometimes use the pergola configuration *(fig. 8)*, but it is mostly a method for amateur growers who wish

Fig. 8. Pergola.

to combine the useful with the aesthetic—in order to relax under a fruited vault. To do this, you can shape a few kiwis planted against a pergola, which you can buy at a nursery. With this configuration, laterals will grow horizontally and not "hang" as they would in a "T" configuration. It is important to train the plant correctly to allow light in, which is indispensable to photosynthesis. What's more, in this situation, pruning and care of the climber will be more tiring since you will always be doing it "with arms raised"!

Possible variations of "T" and pergola configurations are options for amateur growers who only have one wall to plant against. You can extend a wire between two bolts in the wall as a support for the cordons. The laterals will only grow on the one side, either "hanging" or horizontally. For this to happen, the overall infrastructure will require either two lateral wires or a pergola section with dimensions corresponding to the configuration *(fig. 9)*.

Planting distances should be 16 feet (5 m) between rows and 13 to 16 feet (4 to 5 m) between stems (canes) in each row.

You can ensure pollination by planting a male cane for every five female canes maximum, staggered along each row. For enthusiasts planting a single female,

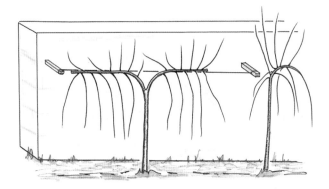

Fig. 9. Possible variations: against a wall with the male cordon left free.

remember that a male is indispensable in order to obtain fruit.

Different Areas of the Canopy

There are three distinct areas on a kiwifruit plant *(fig. 10)*. Understanding the distinctions is important since it will help you in forming and maintaining the kiwifruit according to the desired shape. These zones are easily identifiable on-site. Each year, when new laterals are chosen and bowed, they are redefined.

- *Zone A: The Sunlight Zone*—This is the upper area of the cordons, forming a 30° angle from the vertical. It is also the zone for cordon renewal.
- *Zone B: The Production Zone*—This is the medial zone of the cordons. It forms a 90° angle starting 30° from the perpendicular (the edge of zone A) and extending 30° below horizontal *(photo 12)*. It is the best production zone because it is where "hanging" production occurs *(photo 13)*. It is also a zone for renewal, at least in its upper sections.
- *Zone C: The Walking Zone*—This is the area below the cordons. It forms a 60° angle starting from zone B. It is essentially a walking zone, especially with "T" bar configurations.

12. Under the canopy.

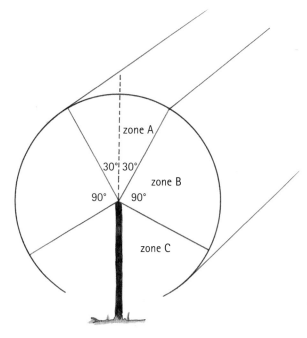

Fig. 10. The three zones on the cordon.

13. Production on canes.

14. Cordons.

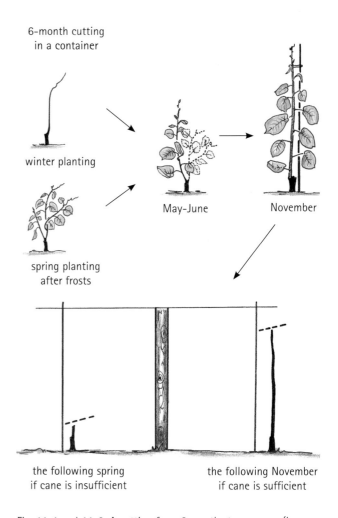

6-month cutting in a container

winter planting

spring planting after frosts

May-June

November

the following spring if cane is insufficient

the following November if cane is sufficient

Fig. 11-1 and 11-2. A cutting from 6 months to one year (in a container).

Shaping the Trunk and Cordons

TRUNK FORMATION
See figs. 11-1, 11-2, 12-1, and 12-2.

CORDON FORMATION
Cordon formation occurs through annual progression, and it involves successive controlled cutting. *Figures 11 and 12* show how to control cordon development though pruning in order to obtain laterals and fill in space around the two arms. It is important to be able

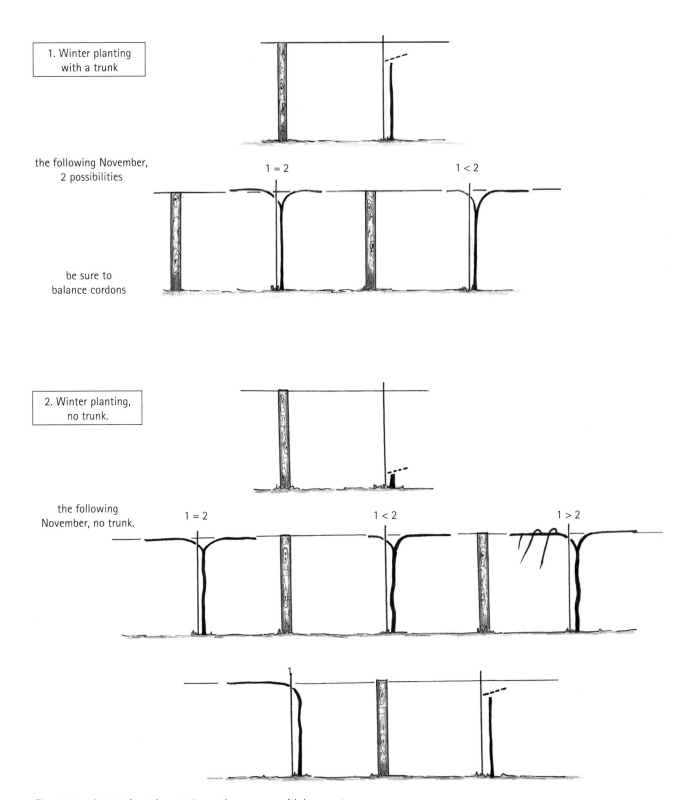

1. Winter planting
with a trunk

the following November,
2 possibilities

1 = 2   1 < 2

be sure to
balance cordons

2. Winter planting,
no trunk.

the following
November, no trunk.

1 = 2   1 < 2   1 > 2

Fig. 12.1 and 12.2. A cutting at 18 months or more, with bare roots.

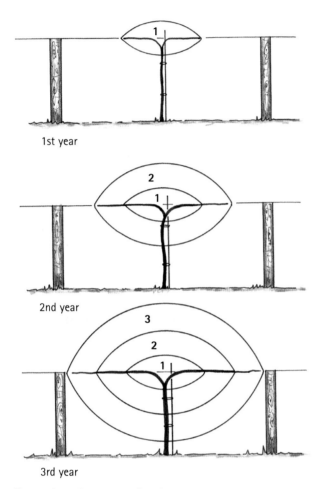

1st year

2nd year

3rd year

Fig. 13. Annual sequence of cordons.

to stall new laterals so that cordons fill in the interval between two stems regularly *(fig. 13)*. It generally requires three years to fill in this interval *(photo 14)*. Cutting back is "controlled," meaning that only a portion of the cordon stays on the wire. The length of this portion will vary depending on how hardy the cordon is and when the cutting or **pinching** takes place *(figs. 14-1, 14-2, 14-3)*. In fact, it is necessary to have potential vegetation capable of developing from the cordon prolongations while also creating sufficient laterals.

The length of the preserved cordon portions is generally around 3 feet (1 m).

CORDON EXTREMITIES

In order to achieve the best "tunnel" possible, the cordons' extremities should be as hardy as the medial and beginning portions. It is not always easy to obtain sufficient hardiness toward the cordons' ends to create beautiful laterals; sometimes "holes" form that are difficult to fill in later. To avoid this problem, cut the cordon back about 24 inches (60 cm) from the extremity *(fig. 15)*. Doing this will allow laterals to grow sufficiently so that you can shape them into a V. On these laterals, the fruiting canes and the renewal canes will fill in the space between the bifurcations.

Positioning the Laterals

Laterals, which are perpendicular to the cordons, rest on metal wires. They may be bent starting at the end of January when sap starts to flow but should be maintained on wires in order to remain parallel to one another. On a distance of 16 feet (5 m) between stems in a row, each plant will produce about twenty-five laterals.

However, if no means are in place to prevent damage from spring frost, it is advisable to wait out the frost season before beginning to bend the laterals. (Remember, it is not as cold at the top as it is at the bottom!)

Thinning Female Stems

Rather than use the word "pruning," it is better to use the term "thinning." It is true that renewing fruiting structures consists solely of practicing resection (of the whole or part) on the laterals, replacing those that have already produced with new ones *(fig. 16)*. Given the simplicity of this technique, thinning is generally

KIWI

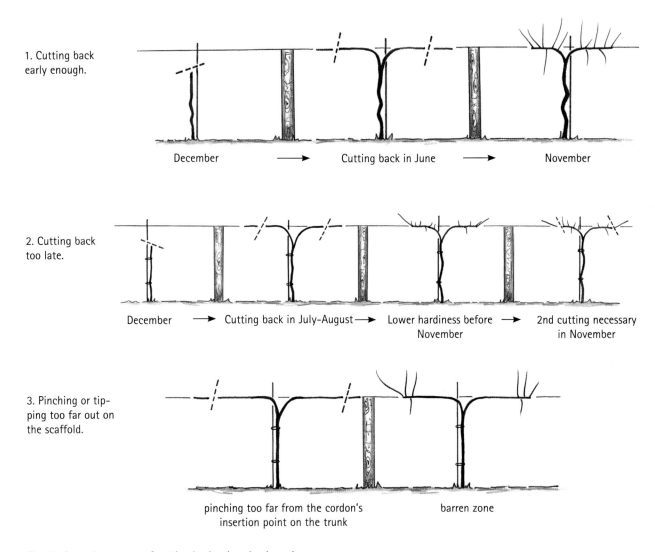

1. Cutting back early enough.

December ⟶ Cutting back in June ⟶ November

2. Cutting back too late.

December ⟶ Cutting back in July-August ⟶ Lower hardiness before November ⟶ 2nd cutting necessary in November

3. Pinching or tipping too far out on the scaffold.

pinching too far from the cordon's insertion point on the trunk

barren zone

Fig. 14. Annual sequence of cutting back using shaping wires.

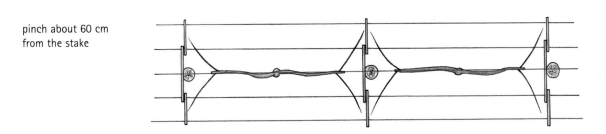

pinch about 60 cm from the stake

Fig. 15. Cordon terminations, viewed from below.

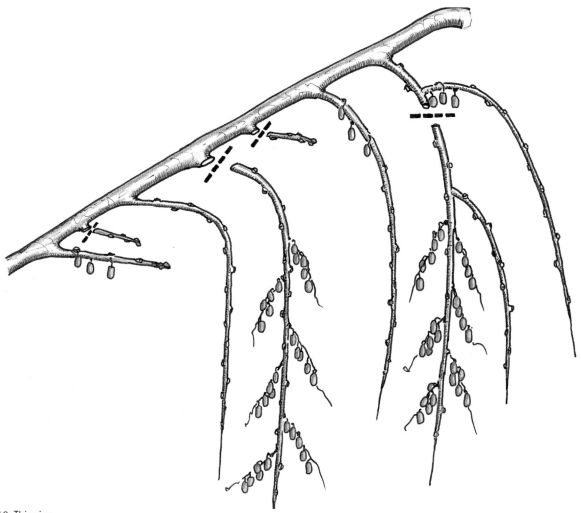

Fig. 16. Thinning.

enough. So, during the vegetative cycle, we may see two simultaneous productions that are easy to identify:

- current-year growth, "hanging" and forming the tunnel;
- growth for the following year, formed of young canes for renewal or new laterals, situated above the tunnel, where future harvests will occur.

Renewing laterals: In order to renew, it is important to choose laterals during the winter. You should select those growing from upper buds rather than lower buds. In fact, during bending, as the branches growing from

lower buds get twisted, a longitudinal crack might appear on the first inch or so (the first few centimeters) that will compromise the branch's future.

Pruning epicormic canes: Suppression of epicormic canes may begin when they reach 20 inches (50 cm). It is best to handle this as early as possible to avoid any competition that may arise.

Summer cutbacks: Shortening branches in the summer will provide clearer passage between the rows, optimizing light and aerating the fruits. One or more summer prunings are strongly recommended; sometimes three are necessary. The process will mostly involve branches and/or indeterminate fruiting canes. You can make these cutbacks from mid-June until September. Shorten the structures four to six nodes beyond the last fruit.

Thinning Male Stems

Once blossoming has ended, male stems, like their female counterparts, need to be thinned—but be careful not to bow their laterals. Leave them free until winter, when you will position them on lateral metal wires at the same time as the female stems.

Thinning the Fruit

Thinning fruits means creating an even balance between the plant's potential and the number of fruits it can yield. This requires suppressing flowers and/or excess fruit, with the goal being to control load density in order to have better fruit size at harvest that year and better **floral induction** the following year. There are two periods when thinning the kiwifruit is necessary: pre-floral thinning, from late April to early May, until May 15; and post-floral thinning, from June 10 to approximately July 10.

Suppressing the floral buds is more quantitative than qualitative. Depending on the year, the number of inflorescences will vary. When they are numerous, you should remove lateral buds and keep only the central, dominant buds. You should also remove deformed (double or flat) buds from the base of a branch or a fruiting cane. The occurrence of fused flowers—a common phenomenon in kiwifruit—gives rise to large, flattened fruits called "fans," which are considered defective for commercial purposes. In California, canes generally provide their first commercial crop in the fourth season. Full production is reached within eight to twelve years.

15. Fruit cane with four fruits.

A. deliciosa fruits reach almost full size in August but are not mature enough for harvest until late October or early November (after the seeds turn black and sugar content is >6.5%, which is optimal for further ripening after harvest). Starch in the fruit is converted to sugar following harvest when appropriate maturity has been achieved. When the fruit is ready to eat, it should contain 12 to 15% sugar. It should be enough to keep about four fruits per fruiting cane (trying to calculate for optimal production from the specific stem) *(photo 15)*.

Thinning small fruits is more qualitative than quantitative and allows for "adjusting" load density. You should remove the "forgotten" fruit from pre-blossoming, deformed fruits (double or flat), poorly pollinated fruit (round fruit), and any fruit with surface abrasions.

Calculating an Optimal Load Density

This calculation is based on the following factors:
- 23 laterals per kiwifruit plant;
- 15 buds on average per lateral branch;

- budbreak of 60% of the buds (or 9 per lateral branch);
- production of 3.5 fruits per fruiting cane;
- an average fruit weight of 3.5 ounces (100 g).

These conditions will create a load of 725 fruits per kiwifruit plant (23 X 9 X 3.5) or 72.5 kilos—roughly 160 pounds—per kiwifruit plant (725 X 0.1).

PROBLEMS DURING TREE GROWTH

Problems result primarily from excess or diminished vigor.

Excessive Growth

Excessive growth, to the detriment of fruit regulation, may generally result from:
- soil that is overly rich in organic matter;
- overuse of nitrogen fertilizer;
- over-watering.

Vegetation becomes overabundant, causing problems with shade, aeration, and potential evaporation. The proposed solutions are either preventive at the soil level or corrective at the plant level.

PREVENTIVE ACTION
Avoid planting in overly fertile soil. The ideal soil has between 2 and 3% organic matter.

Limit nitrogen nutrients. Apply a maximum of 1 pound (0.5 to 0.6 kg) of nitrogen for every 220 pounds (100 kg) of anticipated fruit based on the budbreak sequences until the end of June, as a nitric form (NO^{3-}) for the final applications. (Units of nitrogen are calculated as actual lb or kg of N per unit area = acre or hectare; this calculation depends on the form of nitrogen, such as $CaNO_3$ or KNO_3. (See Appendix C: U.S. Standard Fertilizer Equivalents for Nitrogen.) In California, 150 lb (68 kg) of actual nitrogen per acre is recommended on mature canes, while recommended usage in New Zealand is up to 200 lb (91 kg) N per acre due to much more vigorous growth there. Only nitrogen is generally applied in California, but a complete fertilizer with a ratio of about 3-1-2 (NPK) is acceptable. Smaller amounts of N are recommended on sandy soils to avoid tissue burning.

Fertilizer applications should be completed by mid-summer to avoid late, succulent growth that winter frosts might easily damage. Avoid using any fertilizer containing chloride.

In California, canes are generally irrigated weekly during the growing season. Growers should control watering according to load density and vegetative growth.

CORRECTIVE ACTION
Summer intervention, partial thinning, removal of epicormic canes, and the shortening of indeterminate structures are highly recommended. In fact, the goal is to reduce the potential areas of growth. Ironically, when faced with excessive growth, it is best to remove some wood!

Weak Stem

The solutions for this problem are never simple, whether they are preventive or corrective.

PREVENTIVE ACTION
Prevention involves promoting a hardy formation of the stem during the first years and then managing the load density through thinning of branches and fruits.

CORRECTIVE ACTION
When vigor wanes, it is necessary to create a better balance between foliage surface and root potential:

reducing the canopy is a must. Intervention consists of two processes:

- suppressing a number of laterals or canes during the winter (stick to about fifteen, with an even distribution along the two cordons);
- allowing only two or three fruits per fruiting cane.

Adding nutrients will help jump-start the root system. Spread organic matter and slow-release nitrogen into two cylindrical cavities that are 24 inches (60 cm) deep, with a 6-inch (150 mm) borer, 20 to 24 inches (50 to 60 cm) on either side of the trunk.

RENEWING THE KIWIFRUIT TRUNK

Partially or totally renewing a trunk or cordon is sometimes necessary. In this case, quite often vegetative growths will appear at several spots on the kiwifruit plant (on the trunk and/or the initial bowing of the cordons, in the trunk axis). As it grows, the starting sprout should be progressively directed onto the central wire above the cordon to be replaced. You will remove the old cordon during the next winter.

You can also suppress the cordon to be removed before creating the new one. This intervention may privilege the growth of new canes that will be easier to manage.

The choice of replacement structures is important. A cane should be vigorous without being epicormic. The latter, which tends to be too vigorous, prefers **reiterating** on the bow that will be created when it is attached to the wire, rather than creating a balanced and sufficient production of future laterals. Bare areas also arise on epicormic canes. Even in the case of progressive formation, it is wise to avoid this choice.

To heal any wounds that result from pruning, apply copper sulfate, making sure the paste remains somewhat fluid. In exceptional cases such as strong winter frost or wood disease, ratooning the stem is possible as long as there are new and useable canes along the trunk.

OLIVE

Authors	Pierre CHOI
	Pierre-Éric LAURI
	Nathalie MOUTIER

GENERAL OVERVIEW

History, Phytogeographic Origins, and Distribution

The olive tree is characteristic of the Mediterranean basin. The wild olive tree (oleaster) is common among shrubby vegetation around the Mediterranean. This is probably the origin for cultivated olive trees. Archeological studies of olive tree cultivation date back to 4000 BCE. The Phoenicians and Greeks contributed significantly to the expansion of olive cultivation around the Mediterranean perimeter in the last millennium before Christ.

More recently, Spaniards introduced olive tree cultivation into America (Argentina and the United States) in the sixteenth to eighteenth centuries; Italian and Greek immigrants introduced it into Australia and South Africa in the nineteenth century; and the French brought it to China in the twentieth century. Still, about 97% of the 800 million olive trees grown worldwide are found in the Mediterranean basin *(fig. 1)*.

FAMILY—GENUS
- Family: Oleaceae
- Genus: *Olea*
- Species: *europaea*
- The olive tree: *Olea europaea* L.
- The cultivated olive tree: *Olea europaea* L., subspecies *sativa* Arcang.

Fig. 1. Map of olive production worldwide.

The genus *Olea* includes about thirty-five species, but only *Olea europaea* L. is found in Mediterranean regions.

Throughout the world, about 2,500 **varieties** can be distinguished. These are generally grouped according to their use:

- varieties for oil production: 'Picual' and 'Arbequina' in Spain; 'Frantoio' and 'Leccino' in Italy; 'Koroneiki' in Greece; 'Aglandau', 'Bouteillan', and 'Olivière' in France;
- varieties for table olives: 'Gordal' and 'Manzanilla 'in Spain; 'Conservolia', 'Kalamata', and 'Chaldiki' in Greece; 'Mission' in the United States; 'Bella di Spagna' and 'Bella di Cerignola' in Italy; 'Picholine du Languedoc' and 'Lucques' in France;
- varieties with multiple purposes: 'Hojiblanca' in Spain; 'Picholine Marocaine' in Morocco; 'Dan' in

Syria; 'Arauco' in Argentina; 'Tanche', 'Cailletier', 'Grossane', and 'Salonenque' in France.

Comparative Production Yields

Production in the United States is exclusive to California's Mediterranean climate. Originally, the industry centered on oil production; however, when canning technology was developed in the early 1900s, higher prices for canned olives changed the industry's focus. Until the early twenty-first century, 90% or more of production has been for canned product (the California "black" olive); but with changing consumer tastes and the current high demand for olive oil, acreage for oil olives in California has increased rapidly. Much of the change has also been driven by the high cost of hand labor, which is involved in many aspects of the production of table olives. High-density and super-high-density oil olive trees, which tend to be much smaller than the varieties traditionally grown in California for canning, allow for mechanization of pruning and harvest; these technologies are also under development for table olive trees in California (2006–2010, University of California–Davis). In Spain and other Mediterranean countries, the majority of olive production has always been for oil, with a small percentage of the crop being used for curing table olives.

Although olives are an important California crop, with growing importance for oil production, the acreage in California compared to Spain's (the largest world producer of olive oil by far) is quite small. In 2009, total world production of olive oil was 26,785,000 metric tons, of which Spain produced nearly half (International Olive Oil Council; IOOC). In 2002, California had 39,591 acres (16,022 ha) of olives grown on 1,549 farms, while Spain had 5,662,139 acres (2,291,396 ha) of olives grown by 571,150 producers (U.S. Census of Agriculture). California produces the majority of olives that Americans consume as fruit, but only a small percentage of the oil that is consumed in the United States—estimated at 50 million gallons (187 million liters) annually and $1 billion in import value (2,600,000 metric tons of oil imported in 2009; IOOC).

Although the U.S. population is large, per capita consumption accounts for only 7% of the entire world production of olive oil. Thus, the United States represents a vast potential market far beyond its current domestic level of consumption. California oil production is approximately 300,000 gallons or 1,135,624 liters (30,000 metric tons; IOOC), and the increasing U.S. demand for high-quality oil (growth of demand is estimated at 88% in the last decade) far outstrips both current production and probable future production. Indeed, future production could potentially require 350,000 acres (141,640 ha) to offset what is currently imported. The change in olive planting in California is

unlikely at any time in the future to reach that level. Much of the imported oil comes from Spain, although the oil's origin is not always Spanish (Spain imports oil from other producing countries for repackaging).

The International Olive Oil Council (www.internationaloliveoil.org) oversees olive oil quality in most of the producing countries. In 2010, standards of the IOOC were adopted by the industry in California under California State law, ensuring excellence of product.

Olive production in most of the Mediterranean region (including Spain) is "dryland," or non-irrigated, in most acreage. Many olive groves throughout the Mediterranean are planted where little else will grow: on rolling hills with rocky soil. In contrast, California's olive production is typically on level and productive irrigated land in the Central Valley, where deep alluvial soils promote optimal tree size and production. Even the small percentage of irrigated olive acreage in Spain is many times larger. The largest producer of olive oil in California as of 2010, the California Olive Ranch in Oroville, is Spanish-owned; but acreage for oil olives is expanding rapidly throughout the state, often in place of other crops that were not as readily mechanized or not as high value. Acreage for table olive varieties that are not "California black olive"–processed is also expanding. However, due to the high manual labor involved and the more limited demand, this is occurring on a much smaller scale.

Olive Varieties Grown in California

The four main varieties of olives grown in California used to be 'Mission', originally cultivated by the Franciscan missions; 'Manzanillo', the most commonly planted; and 'Sevillano' and 'Ascolano', which are large olives. For decades, these were almost the only olives grown commercially in California. All four varieties were used almost entirely for table olives.

There is now a very wide diversity of olives grown in

California. The selection of olive varieties for planting depends on the intended use of the fruit and the density, or planting spacing, of the trees in the orchard. As of 2005, the five most important California varieties, in descending order of crop size, were 'Manzanillo', 'Sevillano', 'Mission', 'Ascolano', and 'Barouni'. Of these, 'Mission' is the best for oil extraction, with an oil content of 20 to 24%. Next is 'Manzanillo', with an oil content of 18 to 20%. Oil content varies both by variety and by fruit maturity. When a squeezed fruit exudes a milky liquid, oil production has begun.

Since 2000, while table olive acreage has decreased in California, oil olive plantings have steadily increased. The main varieties being planted are as follows: 'Arbequina', 'Arbosana', 'Koroneiki', 'Frantoio', 'Leccino', 'Pendolino', 'Taggiasca', and 'Coratina'. Common choices for high-density orchards (250 to 300 trees per acre) include 'Arbequina', 'Arbosana', 'Frantoio', 'Leccino', 'Pendolino', 'Taggiasca', and 'Coratina'. 'Koroneiki' is suitable for super-high-density planting (650 to 900 trees per acre). High- and super-high density orchards can accommodate over-the-row mechanical harvesters.

VARIETAL CHARACTERISTICS

- 'Arbequina'—an oil variety from northern Spain with small fruits that yield aromatic and fruity oil with very little pungency or bitterness; the oil has a short shelf life of about one year.
- 'Ascolano'—a traditional California large-fruited variety, mainly used for table olives. It is the most cold-hardy of all table varieties grown in California. The oil is very aromatic, but the oil yield is very low. 'Ascolano' olives bruise easily and suffer damage even when cured if not harvested with care. **Fruit set** is somewhat low. The fruits do not turn black at maturity.
- 'Coratina'—from Puglia, Tuscany. A fast-growing, erect olive variety that does well in hot climates and produces a strong-tasting, peppery oil.

- 'Frantoio'—the most common variety for Italian oil. The yield is quite high. The flavor is strong, with some pungency.
- 'Kalamata'—the most common Greek variety grown for cured fruit consumption.
- 'Koroneiki'—a high-quality, Greek oil variety.
- 'Leccino'—oil from this tree is more delicate than 'Frantoio', and the small to medium-size fruits are also used for table olives. The olives ripen all at once. A vigorous grower.
- 'Maurino —an excellent choice for coastal areas, producing a peppery and fruity oil. A compact grower, slightly weeping.
- 'Manzanillo'—the main variety used for the black "California-style" olive (canned). The fruit matures early and has a medium oil content with mild flavor. The trees are susceptible to cold injury, peacock spot, and olive knot.
- 'Maurino'—an Italian variety used in olive oil blends. The oil is very flavorful and spicy.
- 'Mission'—the traditional California dual-purpose (table and oil) variety with high oil content that can vary in flavor from very bitter to mild, depending on fruit maturity at harvest. The fruit is of medium size and matures late. Trees are very cold tolerant and grow quite tall; thus, it is difficult to maintain small size for higher-density plantings and mechanical harvest.
- 'Pendolino'—an Italian variety that is often used as a pollenizer but that is also **self-fertile**. Used for oil and both green and black table olives.
- 'Sevillano'—a California variety with a very large fruit, generally used as a table olive. It has several minor problems. The oil yield is very low, although the oil is highly sought after, with a mild but very fruity flavor.
- 'Taggiasca'—a self-fertile **cultivar** from Liguria. The small to medium-size olives yield a light, fine oil and are also cured black. The mature tree

has average size and vigor, with a semi-weeping habit. Very late ripening.

Limitations

COLD AND HEAT REQUIREMENTS

Studies that model olive tree flowering patterns suggest that its **precocious** flowering is primarily based on (1) relatively hot temperatures at the beginning of the year, and (2) to a lesser degree, satisfaction of its cold requirements prior to that of its heat requirements.

LETHAL TEMPERATURES

In France, olive trees are located in southern growing areas. Cold winters limit the production zone. The cold may damage young shoots and floral buds early in the year and fruits later on. The trees themselves may show extensive damage when extremely cold temperatures set in after mild temperatures have caused growth to start back up (for example, the great frosts of February 1956). Killing frosts that destroy trees (16°F or -9°C) or major portions of the **canopy** are not problematic in California, although these conditions may occur in some other olive-growing countries; fruits are damaged at 26°F (-3°C). Just such an unusually hard freeze destroyed most of the (small) acreage in Slovenia in the early 1990s. Those trees that survived provided germplasm for selective propagation to rebuild the industry.

Optimal growth temperatures for flowering and fruiting range from around 64° to 72°F (18 to 22°C). Temperatures higher than 86°F (30°C) in the spring may cause flowers to die, but olive trees can tolerate even higher temperatures in the summer. *Table 1* provides a temperature guide for olive trees.

In California, the two regions traditionally used for table olive production are Tehama and Glenn counties in the North State, and Tulare, Madera, and Fresno counties in the South State. Oil varieties are being planted far

Developmental Stages	Temperatures
Winter dormancy (frost risk)	14–53 °F
Spring awakening (frost risk)	23–44 °F
No vegetation	48–50 °F
Bud development	57–59 °F
Flowering	64–66 °F
Fertilization	70–71 °F
End of vegetation	95–100 °F
Risk of burn	> 104 °F

Table 1. Thermal guidelines for the olive tree.

more widely, from Sonoma County in the western North State throughout San Joaquin County just south of Sacramento County (seat of the state capitol), and almost anywhere olives can be grown. The major climatic limitations in these areas are warm winters when buds may expand early and be susceptible to late frost, and adverse conditions during bloom in late April and early May. Both conditions existed in 2006, reducing the table olive crop statewide to about 35% of normal. In the North State, warm temperatures in January were followed by late frost in February, killing the expanding buds and much of the new growth on these evergreen trees. In the South State, storms washed blossoms off the trees, thereby preventing **pollination**. In other years, high temperatures (which can often exceed 90°F or 32°C during bloom in California) and dry winds during bloom can obliterate the crop, as this is a wind-pollinated species with ephemeral flowers. Nonetheless, in most years overset of fruit is much more common. In fact, overset results in extreme **alternate bearing**, as a fruit set of 1 to 2% of the tens of thousands of flowers borne on vigorous California olive trees is sufficient to deplete the trees' reserves.

WATER REQUIREMENTS

The olive tree can handle long periods of dry conditions. But for better economic yield, low or infrequent rainfall (less than 12 inches or 300 mm per year) should be complemented with irrigation during the summer, which is the period when transpiration is higher and when groundwater reserves become insufficient. In France, an average density of 300 to 400 trees per hectare requires an additional 6 to 8 inches (150 to 250 mm) of water per year, spread out from May to September, based on groundwater reserves and rainfall. Olive culture in California is entirely irrigated, mostly by micro-sprinkler or drip, and is monitored and scheduled by evapo-transpiration estimates that maintain orchards at "field capacity." Essentially, the soil is not allowed to dry out between irrigations. Mature orchards may require more than 3 acre feet of water per year.

SOIL TYPES

The olive tree adapts well to relatively poor soil types. However, soils should be light (less than 20% clay), well drained, and at least 5 feet (1.5 m) deep. Growers should avoid hydromorphous soils, which will cause root asphyxiation, as well as soils that are high in salt or overly alkaline (pH greater than 8.5)

CROSS-POLLINATION

The olive flowers are "perfect," having both male reproductive organs (which provide pollen) and female reproductive organs (which collect the pollen and produce fruit after **fertilization**). This is an important attribute for fertilization. In many olive tree varieties, however, pollen will not fertilize ovules in the same variety (in these cases, the varieties are self-infertile). Some olive varieties are partially self-infertile, while others are completely self-fertile. It is essential to use compatible pollinating varieties with self-infertile varieties in order to guarantee fertilization and fruit production. However, even when a variety is self-fertile, it will generally set better when planted with another compatible pollenizer. The orchard should blend different varieties of trees with concurrent flowering periods,

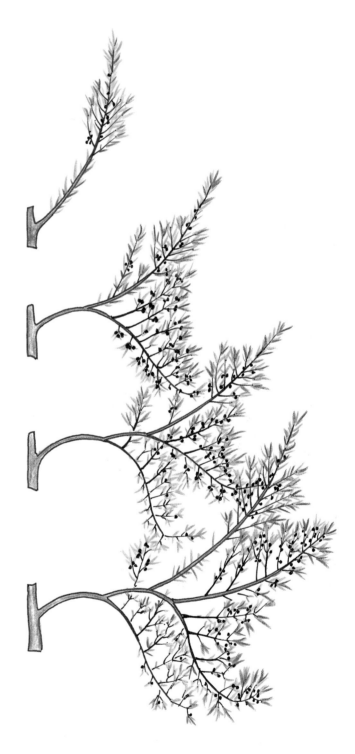

Fig. 2. Evolution from a growth unit to a production unit. Note the progressive hanging of the branches and the sprouting of upright renewal shoots.

through planting or top grafting. Olive pollen is transported by the wind (via **anemophilious** pollination) and does not require bees to guarantee **cross-pollination**, although bees do visit olive flowers.

The following list identifies compatibility characteristics for popular olive varieties:

- 'Ascolono'—not self-fertile; compatible pollenizers include 'Frantoio', 'Leccino', and 'Pendolino'.
- 'Coratina'—compatible pollenizers include 'Frantoio' and 'Leccino'.
- 'Frantoio'—self-fertile.
- 'Leccino'—compatible pollenizers include 'Pendolino', 'Maurino', and 'Frantoio'.
- 'Maurino'—self-infertile; compatible pollenizers include 'Pendolino', 'Leccino', and 'Frantoio'.
- 'Pendolino'—partially self-fertile, but sets best with pollenizers, including 'Leccino' and 'Maurino'.
- 'Taggiasca'—self-fertile.

TREE MORPHOLOGY

Vegetative Characteristics

The olive tree grows up to 16 to 32 feet (5 to 10 m) high and can live for hundreds of years. It exhibits juvenile characteristics during its first years of growth after starting as a seedling. As semi-herbaceous cuttings, faster-producing varieties bear fruit starting in the third year, or around the fifth year for those varieties with later production.

At first, the olive branch is erect. After the second year, growing branches may bend under their own weight or the weight of laterals. This phenomenon increases as the fruit appears *(fig. 2)*. The crown of an adult olive tree is formed with branches that are more curved the older they become. Renewal branches (or renewal units) appear along the curve of fruiting

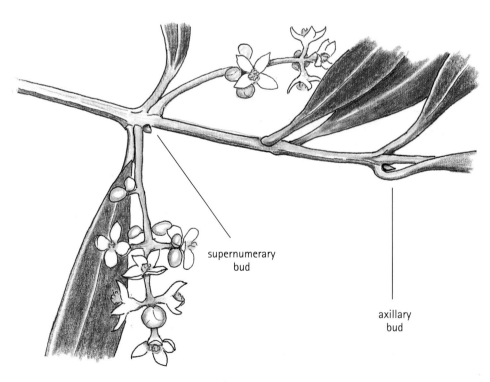

supernumerary bud

axillary bud

Fig. 3. Axillary (gives rise to either a shoot or an inflorescence) and supernumerary buds.

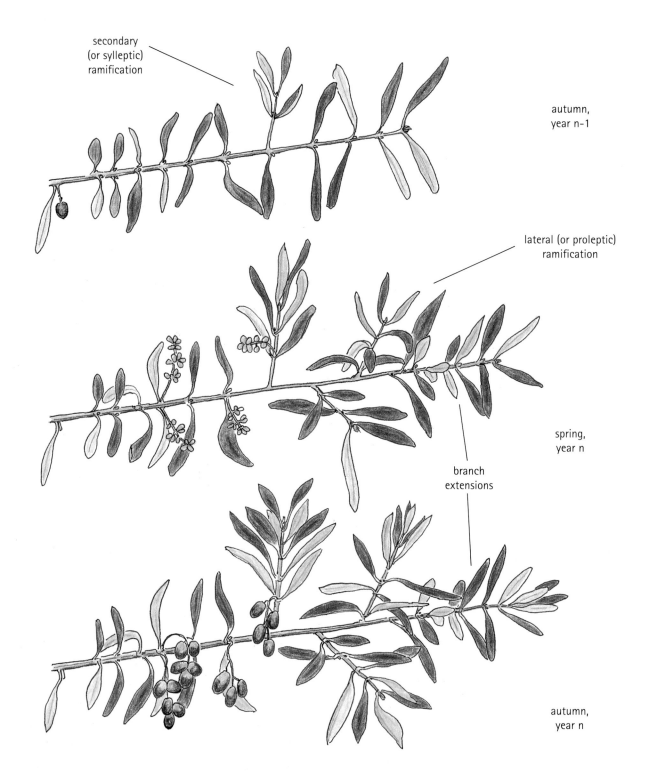

secondary
(or sylleptic)
ramification

autumn,
year n–1

lateral (or proleptic)
ramification

spring,
year n

branch
extensions

autumn,
year n

Fig. 4. Branch evolution (growth, flowering, fruiting) over two consecutive years.

branches (production units). The degree to which a particular tree "weeps," or is pendulous, depends on the variety as well as the training habit.

Growth starts in terminal buds that are preserved from year to year, except when they have been damaged (by frost, fruitworms, etc.). Growth does not fully stop in the winter, so there are no scales by which to mark the passage from one growth year to the next. The only morphological indicators in this area are shorter **internodes**, foliage dimorphism (seasonal variation in leaf size), and a difference in bud tint in the spring.

The silvery leaves of olive trees are easily recognizable. Leaves grow in pairs on the branch with a 90° angle between each pair (an example of crossed opposite **phyllotaxy**). Leaves are persistent and live for two to three years. Each leaf bears a bud component at its axil (a principal **axillary bud** and a supernumerary bud; *fig. 3*). The principal bud may:

- remain **latent** its whole life;
- produce a **secondary shoot** in the same year it forms;
- produce an **inflorescence** or a branch in the following year.

The number of buds on an annual shoot will determine the number of flowers on this shoot for the following year *(fig. 4)*, although in most cases annual shoots will be "flowering" shoots only every other year (thus displaying biennial, or alternate, bearing).

Flowers and Flowering

The olive flower *(photo 1)* is composed of four joined sepals, four petals, two **stamens** with two sizeable **anthers** (male organs), and an ovary containing two ovules (female organs). After fertilization and the withering of one of the ovules, the ovary tissues will form the flesh of the fruit and the ovule will become the pit. This

1. Flowers at various stages of opening.

2. An inflorescence in a leaf axil (Cailletier variety).

process characterizes the olive as a drupaceous fruit (a **drupe**), as are the stone fruits and the date palm.

The existence of **staminate** flowers (aborted ovaries), which is an important characteristic in floral biology, arises in all olive varieties. Ovarian abortion rates depend on the variety, the tree's developmental conditions, and the weather; moreover, the position in which a flower arises on the inflorescence is a strongly determining factor in whether the **pistil** will abort (forming a staminate flower) or not. The formation of a large number of flowers guarantees that the tree will release enough pollen for cross-pollination as the flowers blossom, but it also means that the tree will likely be alternate bearing.

In certain varieties, the anthers do not release functional pollen at **anthesis**. These varieties, known as sterile males (examples: 'Lucques' and 'Olivière' in France and Swan Hill), will require the presence of pollinators in order to produce. Such varieties are favorites of landscape designers, as the trees do not produce "messy" fruits.

The olive inflorescence is a **panicle** yielding an average of eighteen to twenty-five flowers *(photo 2)*. Most often, flowering occurs laterally. It may also occur at the terminal position depending on the variety and its location on the tree (example: 'Bouteillan').

As mentioned above, cross-pollination is almost essential for most olive tree varieties and indispensable for sterile males.

Fruit and Fruiting

The olive is an elongated, spherical drupe *(fig. 5)* with a fleshy pulp that is rich in oil. It starts out green, then becomes purplish-blue during **veraison** (color change), then turns blacker at maturity *(photo 3)*.

The endocarp is a hard pit that generally houses a single seed. The shape of fruits and pits may differ among varieties.

Annual Cycle

The development cycle for olive branches takes place over two years:
- The first year is characterized by the growth of vegetative branches in one or two pronounced

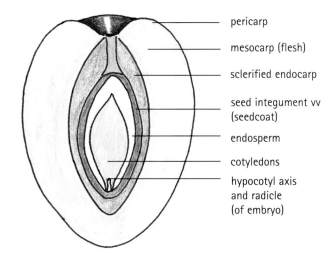

- pericarp
- mesocarp (flesh)
- sclerified endocarp
- seed integument vv (seedcoat)
- endosperm
- cotyledons
- hypocotyl axis and radicle (of embryo)

Fig. 5. Cross-section of fruit (drupe).

waves: the first wave occurs in the spring (March to June in southern France, February to May in California); the second, in autumn, is generally not as strong. The reproductive cycle begins during this first year, with **floral induction** in July and the start of **floral initiation** in November.
- In the second year, floral initiation continues into February, when **floral differentiation** begins. Flowering occurs in May (in California) and May–June (in colder climates such as France). **Fruit set** (June–July) is followed by the growth and maturation of fruits until December.

Olive trees fruit only on wood from the previous year.

During any given year (n), the olive tree is the site of two consecutive biological cycles *(fig. 6)*. In the spring, floral differentiation and the flowering cycle n - 1 take place at the same time as vegetative growth for cycle n (the current year). At the beginning of summer, floral induction for cycle n occurs during fruit set and young fruit growth for year n - 1. In autumn and winter, the end of growth and fruit maturation from cycle n - 1 takes place during the second wave of vegetative growth and floral initiation for cycle n.

Vegetative growth and reproductive development

3. Fruits during color change (Cailletier variety).

sometimes play out on two consecutive portions of an axis at the same time.

A balanced tree fulfills three functions over the course of the vegetative season:

- it produces young leafy shoots from February/March to October;
- it develops fruit from May to December on shoots from the previous year;
- it initiates flowering for the following year from December to February.

The period when the olive tree accumulates nourishment via photosynthesis and forms its reserves is late and short. The leaf reserves of this species will contribute to growth and fruit maturation until October–November. The use of reserves for floral initiation begins in November. This means there is a significant degree of competition for nutrition that plays a non-negligible role in establishing production; it also explains the species' characteristic alternate bearing. The nutritional needs for fruiting are always higher than what the tree can provide.

The Relationship between Vegetative and Reproductive Growth

COMPETITION

There are competitive relationships within the production units (antagonism between fruiting and vegetative growth in the same year), as well as between the production units and the renewals that sprout on the **basal** section of limbs. Removal of inflorescences and young fruits during a high-production year will stimulate branch growth and stronger flowering in the following

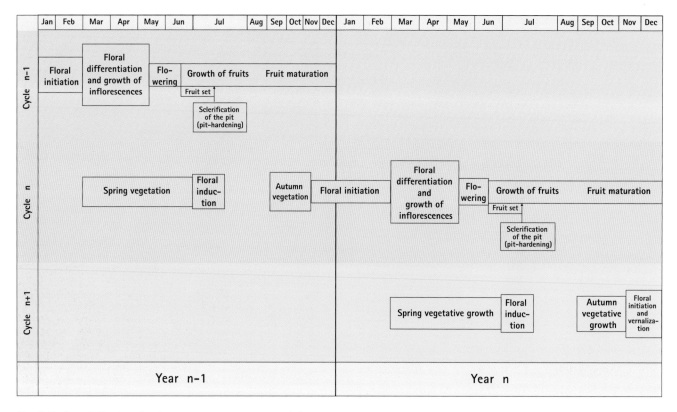

| | | Jan | Feb | Mar | Apr | May | Jun | Jul | Aug | Sep | Oct | Nov | Dec | Jan | Feb | Mar | Apr | May | Jun | Jul | Aug | Sep | Oct | Nov | Dec |

Cycle n−1

Floral initiation · Floral differentiation and growth of inflorescences · Flowering · Growth of fruits · Fruit maturation

Fruit set

Sclerification of the pit (pit-hardening)

Cycle n

Spring vegetation · Floral induction · Autumn vegetation · Floral initiation · Floral differentiation and growth of inflorescences · Flowering · Growth of fruits · Fruit maturation

Fruit set

Sclerification of the pit (pit-hardening)

Cycle n+1

Spring vegetative growth · Floral induction · Autumn vegetative growth · Floral initiation and vernalization

Year n−1 · Year n

Fig. 6. Cycles of olive tree development over a two-year period.

year. Inversely, for certain varieties, a later harvest may cause a reduction in flowers in the following year.

DIAMETER AT THE BRANCH BASE

For any given variety, there is a correlation between (1) the number of inflorescences and fruits that a branch yields, and (2) the diameter of its cross-section. The thicker the branch, the more fruit it will bear.

BRANCH ORIENTATION

The extent of an olive tree's production depends on the following four factors:

- the number of production units per tree;
- the number of fruits per production unit;
- fruit weight;
- for oil, the fat content (the weight percentage of oil in relation to the weight of the fresh fruit).

4. A vase-shaped tree (Picholine variety).

In certain varieties, branch orientation to the vertical plays a major role in the quality of fruiting. Hanging branches bear more fruit than erect branches do. But the weight and oil content of individual fruits are lower on hanging branches. Horizontal branches exhibit an intermediary situation, with the same amount of fruit as hanging branches and the characteristics of fruit and oil content of erect branches. Also, oil yield on horizontal branches is generally higher than on the other two branch types.

PRINCIPLES OF TRAINING

Planting

PLANTING DENSITY

Growers should determine the density for planting on the basis of the chosen variety's vigor and the given orchard's conditions. In poor, shallow, or dry soils (where there is a lack of irrigation), planting density should be low—around 200 trees per hectare (23 feet or 7 m between rows, 23 feet or 7 m between trees). In agronomically favorable situations (deeper soil, availability of irrigation, good fertilizer content, good phyto-sanitary control), population density can reach up to 500 trees per hectare (5 x 4) when using the traditional open vase method of training *(photo 4)* and more than 1,000 trees per hectare (4 x 2.5) when using intensive vertical axis methods *(photo 5).* In France, the planting density required for Appellation d'Origine Contrôlée (Protected Designation of Origin) is 416 trees per hectare (6 x 4) maximum.

Typical planting density for olive varieties grown in California for "black processed olives" has reflected 12-foot by 24-foot spacing (3.5 m by 7 m), yielding 151 trees per acre. In the seventh or eighth year, half of the trees would be removed so as to yield an orchard density of 75 trees per acre. Typical orchard life would be sixty years or more. However, this planting scheme is

5. A tree with vertical axis training (Arquebine variety).

not the current practice, as growers are moving toward mechanization of oil olive varieties. California high-density oil olive orchards are typically planted at 250 to 300 trees per acre, while super-high-density orchards can reach 650 to 900 trees per acre.

CUTTINGS OR GRAFTED TRANSPLANTS?

Currently, in France, most transplanted trees are grown from cuttings. These are solid from the start. The use of rootstocks, however, may prove helpful for controlling vigor and aiding in resistance to soil fungi. Olive trees in California are not grafted onto rootstocks but are propagated from cuttings.

WATERING

After planting, young trees must be watered at their base in order to pack down the soil and avoid the risk

6. Irrigation bowl.

7. A grassy orchard.

of air pockets near the roots. It is important to form a bowl around the base of the plant that will hold 5 to 10 gallons (20 to 40 l) of water *(photo 6)*.

WEEDS

Allowing managed weed growth in the orchard during the autumn after planting will ultimately facilitate the harvest and help to prevent erosion *(photo 7)*.

The First Years After Planting: Let the Tree Establish Itself

The less you prune a young olive tree, the more quickly it will grow and set fruit. Indeed, pruning a young olive tree weakens it and slows the start of production. Pruning to shape the tree must be done as lightly as possible. However, if you want the tree to establish a single trunk, it is advisable to suppress shoots growing along the axis chosen as the trunk to a height of 28 inches (70 cm). You will select **scaffolds** later when the tree enters into production. The speed of fruit set for a single tree will vary according to the variety (starting in the second year for 'Bouteillan', for example, and in the fifth year for 'Lucques'). Most varieties that are grown in California tend to fruit in the third to fifth year.

Despite their diversity in size and strength, most traditionally cultivated varieties (with a planting density of fewer than 500 trees/hectare) are shaped in the same way: via the vase method. However, other

8. Production unit (fruit branch) before and after pruning (Lucques variety).

methods (such as vertical axis) allow denser planting and are well adapted to certain varieties (for example, 'Arbequina') *(photos 4 and 5)*.

Pruning for Fruiting: Allow for Sunlight and Limit Alternate Bearing

Regular pruning for fruiting has two primary objectives: spreading light throughout the tree, and regularizing production. "Suckering" (removing shoots that arise from roots or the trunk) and "skirting" (pruning up pendulous branches to allow mechanical harvest) are common forms of pruning.

SPREADING LIGHT
Light is the energy that makes plants grow. A branch's flower or fruit quality depends on the amount of light received by leaves on the branch that bears them. Equalizing and redistributing light throughout the tree will provide enough light to the leaves and will guarantee the growth of new shoots for fruiting in the following year.

Pruning for fruiting in the olive tree focuses on the progressive sagging of productive fruit branches. This sagging, which is caused by a natural bowing phenomenon, occurs in young, initially upright branches that bend under the weight of their leaves and fruits. Over the years the branches thicken, elongate, and bow. Without proper care, these branches will get in one another's way, block the light, become bare, and only produce at their tips. Pruning these branches involves making large cuts (the principle of "all or nothing"). This helps to prevent an excess of large fruiting branches from piling on top of one another. Eliminating the most disadvantaged bowed branches (below the pile-up) *(fig. 7)* and any overly vigorous **epicormic branches** will simplify the production zone and allow light to better penetrate the entire tree. The large branches should be completely cut off at the base whenever higher branches block them or if they are unproductive or aging. Epicormic branches (watersprouts) should also be eliminated from within the tree since they will create shade and compete with productive branches below them *(photo 8)*.

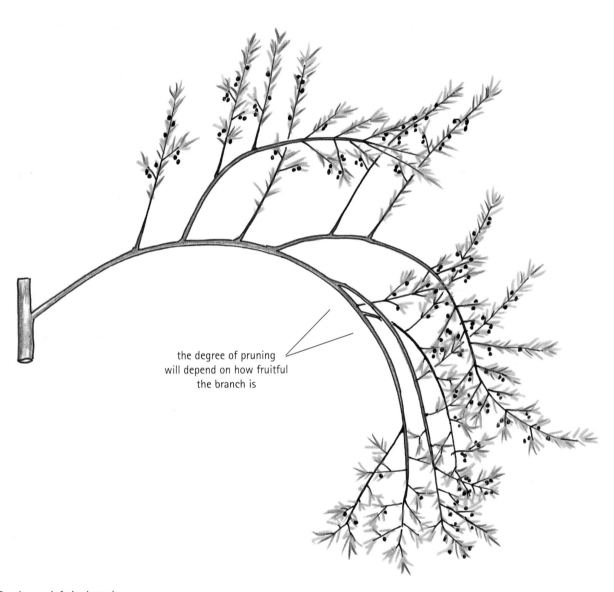

the degree of pruning
will depend on how fruitful
the branch is

Fig. 7. Pruning an inferior branch.

Eventually, as the tree ages, the center will become less productive because light won't penetrate, new buds won't form, and the area of production will become progressively peripheral, increasing the problem of bowed (pendulous) branches. Periodic large cuts will re-stimulate growth, enable productivity to return, and maintain an orchard's production for decades.

REGULARIZING PRODUCTION

As mentioned above, the olive tree's cycle spans two consecutive years. Production from year n - 1 competes for nutrition with branches bearing fruit in year n. An overly high production in a given year (+ year) will greatly diminish branch growth and cause lower production in the following year (- year). Inversely, low production (- year) causes greater branch growth and leads to higher production in the following year (+ year).

Pruning for fruiting targets the limiting of production in a + year in order to stimulate sufficient growth and satisfactory production in the following year. (In other words, a shoot must absolutely be present in one year for production in the following year.) The tree must be able to create shoots while it is yielding fruit, all the while stocking up on reserves that will be sufficient for flower production in the following year.

To limit alternate bearing, pruning should be proportional to the current year's production. Pruning should be light after high production, since excessive fruit production will slow branch growth and lower the reserves for flower formation in the following year. Inversely, pruning should be heavier after a low-production year, since the olive tree will have been able to develop new branches that will produce excess numbers of fruits and flowers in the following year. Wherever there is strong alternate bearing, you can even prune every other year: this will involve pruning a lot the year following low production, and not pruning the year following high production. In this way, you can progressively reduce the alternate bearing of production.

Alternate bearing is primarily caused by an imbalance in the production of shoots, flowers, and fruits. It may also occur during regular growth when flowers are numerous. Yet when the percentage of ovarian abortion is elevated or when good-quality flowers are numerous, then the fruit set is low, in that only 1 to 5% of the flowers present will produce fruit. Nonetheless, in the olive, this can still result in a very heavy crop.

Sometimes, external causes may bring about alternate bearing in a tree's production:

- summer droughts may block current branch growth, in which case flower production for the following year will be insufficient and of lower quality (the flowers are sterile or nonresistant to poor weather conditions); winter frost can seriously damage young shoots and reduce or cancel out production in the coming year;
- disease and pests may destroy terminal shoots, diminish possible production zones, or attack the leaves, thereby weakening the tree and causing it to produce fewer shoots, leaves, flowers, and fruits.

In these situations, the amount of pruning will allow alternant trees to re-balance themselves.

In certain cases, with multi-purpose varieties, growers prefer to allow alternate bearing instead of suppressing it. In fact, in a - year, though fruits are less numerous, they are quite big and may be used as table olives. In a + year, the tree will bear numerous small fruits that can be used to produce oil.

Thinning Fruits

Thinning fruits, in the strictest sense, is not practiced on olive trees. However, green-crop harvest in September–October allows the remaining fruits to thicken up. Growers can then harvest them as black olives or for oil production.

Renewing Old Trees

The same advice that applies to young trees also applies when renewing older olive trees cleared from wild land or when transplanting adult olive trees: before pruning them, let them grow. This may take several years. When the shoot is vigorous and the tree has started to produce again, you can apply the principles for pruning for fruiting.

PEACH

| Authors | Éric NAVARRO |
| | Daniel PLÉNET |

GENERAL OVERVIEW

History and Phytogeographic Origins

The cultivated peach tree, *Prunus persicae* (L.) Batsch, belongs to the genus *Prunus* and the family Rosaceae (see Appendix A: *Prunus* Botany). Like the apricot tree, peach trees originated in China, where they grew naturally from the 23rd to the 41st parallel. From this original cradle, the peach tree has undergone a wide geographic dispersion. **Cultivars** from northern China were introduced into ancient Persia (now Iran), where the peach tree took on its botanical name, and then into the rest of the Mediterranean basin. These cultivars adapted well to the temperate and continental cold-winter climates. Cultivars from southern China were better adapted to subtropical climates and have developed in Florida, Israel, and North Africa.

The nectarine (*Prunus persica var. nectarina*) is of unknown origin and differs from peach at a single gene locus, exchanging fuzzy skin for smooth, glabrous skin. Nectarine also has a flavor that is distinct from that of peaches. It is never used commercially for canning in the United States. California is a major producer and shipper of nectarines in the United States. In recent years, a number of white-fleshed nectarine cultivars have been developed for the fresh market. Nectarine export shipments from the United States are on the order of 2.5 million tons annually, from more than 130 cultivars. Most are produced commercially

1. A blossoming peach orchard: rosaceous (showy) flowers and grouped blossoms.

in California's San Joaquin Valley, where the harvest of early cultivars starts in mid-May and the last nectarines are harvested in mid-September. Nectarines are exported mainly to Canada, Taiwan, Hong Kong, Mexico, and Brazil.

THE TREE

Fruit, Floral, and Vegetative Characteristics

FLOWERS
During the springtime before leaves come out, the peach tree covers itself in flowers on the previous year's shoots *(photo 1)*. These flowers are either solitary or grouped in twos and threes. They are composed of five petals that are larger or smaller depending on the cultivar (showy or non-showy type flowers). Bell-shaped flowers yield smaller, dark pink petals that maintain a funnel shape throughout blossoming. Rose-shaped flowers are larger with large, light pink petals.

Peach flowers are **hermaphrodites** (they are "perfect," containing both male and female parts) and fully pollen compatible (**self-fertile**, in most cases). Generally quite fertile, they bear fruit in 70 to 95% of cases. Blossoming is rather short-lived, occurring over a period of about ten days for any given **variety**.

Across varieties, blossoming extends over a month (end of February to end of March) depending on weather conditions. In the spring, trees are generally covered in small fruits and require extensive thinning, unless climatic conditions have damaged the tree.

LEAVES

Leaves are deciduous, simple, and lanceolate. The leaves grow on a petiole that is most often surrounded by a **nectary**, a small protuberance that secrets a sweet liquid. Since nectaries vary in size, shape, and position on the petiole, they are useful for pomological classification.

BRANCHES

For peach trees, a typology of the different types of branches is traditionally used:

- During bloom in May, **spurs** are short branches less than 2 inches (5 cm) long that bear a vegetative bud at the tip and a few floral buds in lateral positions *(fig. 1)*. Most peaches are not spur-bearing but bear on one-year old wood (flowering shoots).

- Flowering shoots are longer branches ranging from 4 to 10 inches (10 to 25 cm) that bear the majority of floral buds. The buds may be clustered in pairs or triplets. Besides a terminal vegetative bud, certain **axillary buds** may also be vegetative *(fig. 2–3)*.

- Mixed branches are branches reaching 12 to 40 inches (30 to 100 cm) in length. They yield both floral and vegetative buds in lateral positions, which allows them to play a double role in fruit production and wood renewal: for this reason, they are considered mixed *(fig. 2–3)*. This is the fruit production unit for peach trees.

- **Epicormic branches** (watersprouts, suckers) are very hardy branches whose length reaches up to 6.5 feet (2 m). They are characterized by the

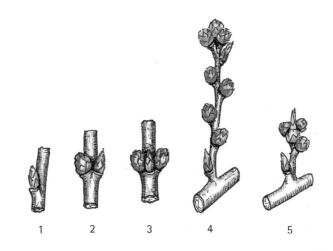

Fig. 1. Lateral buds on branches (1, 2 and 3) and spurs (4 and 5).

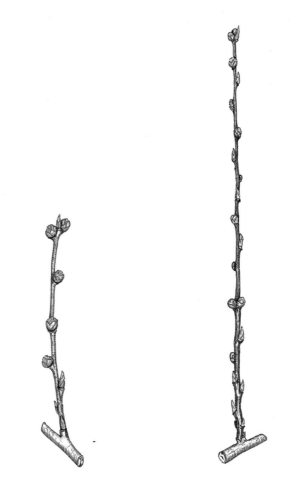

Fig. 2-3. Flowering shoot (left) and mixed branch (right).

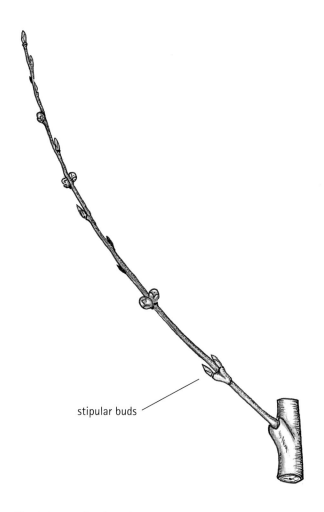

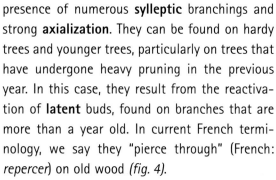

stipular buds

Fig. 4. An epicormic branch: very hardy, longer than 1 yard, yielding secondary branches.

Fig. 5. A secondary branch.

presence of numerous **sylleptic** branchings and strong **axialization**. They can be found on hardy trees and younger trees, particularly on trees that have undergone heavy pruning in the previous year. In this case, they result from the reactivation of **latent** buds, found on branches that are more than a year old. In current French terminology, we say they "pierce through" (French: *repercer*) on old wood *(fig. 4)*.

• Sylleptic branches grow from buds and also grow laterally on vigorous shoots from the same year.

Sylleptic shoots appear frequently on peach trees. These branches may bear fruit in the following year; but since the fruits will generally be of lower quality than those on a mixed branch, these sylleptic branches should be suppressed during winter pruning *(fig. 5)*.

FRUITS

The peach fruit is a **drupe**, like the apricot and other stone fruits. It consists of the following parts, from exterior to interior: the epicarp, or skin; the **mesocarp**,

Epidermis	Pit	Texture of the flesh	Group
soft	free	tender	peach
	adherent	firm	clingstone peach
smooth (nectarines)	free	tender	nectarine
	adherent (freestone vs clingstone, or "cling")	firm (melting or non-melting flesh)	nectarine

or flesh; and the endocarp, or inner layer—which all together constitute the **pericarp**; and the kernel. Cultivated varieties are classed into four groups based on the fruit:

Freestone peaches and nectarines are table fruit. Clingstone peaches are used commercially for canned peaches, fruit cocktail (compote), fruit paste, and syrup. In each of these groups, the fruit may have white flesh, red flesh (genetically close to white), or yellow flesh.

This species exhibits strong variability, particularly as it is the second most widely planted deciduous fruit tree worldwide, after the apple. The spread of maturation dates is equally quite broad: the most **precocious** varieties (extra-early varieties) are harvested at the end of May in southern France (May–June to the beginning of July in the southern United States and California, as one progresses northward); the varieties called "in season" reach maturity in July, and later varieties mature from early August to the end of September. The range of maturity dates can help to spread out the harvest so that peaches may be produced all summer. Note that early flowering during spring is independent of the dates of fruit maturity for the different varieties of peach and nectarine.

The length of the fruit's growth phase (from flowering to maturity) is mostly dependent on the date of maturity. In varieties with early and extra-early maturity, this growth phase is quite short (75 to 90 days). The hardening period for the stone (pit-hardening) occurs simultaneously with the rapid growth phase of the flesh. This explains why many of these varieties are susceptible to cracked stones ("split pits"). In contrast, with "in season" and later varieties, fruit growth takes longer (from three to six months), allowing the stone to harden while the fruit growth slows. Due to the duration of fruit growth, these varieties are less sensitive to cracked stones and have a better potential for larger fruit than precocious varieties do.

Fig. 6 illustrates the different phases of fruit enlargement. Phase I, from flowering to the start of stone hardening, marks an important period of cell differentiation. Phase II corresponds to the period when stones harden and, thus, when fruit growth slows. Phase III is the period in which the flesh grows.

Annual Vegetative Cycle

Let's look at vegetative buds located on branches. During the spring and summer, these buds develop and give rise to vegetative shoots constituting relatively long stems bearing leaves. In July or August, each stem hardens through **lignification** (in French, the shoot is considered *aoûté*, or "August-ed," meaning lignified). At the leaf axils, buds form that are covered in budscales; these will remain in a latent state. Some of the buds will evolve and begin forming the start of flowers. This is **floral induction**, which takes place in summer and is followed by **floral differentiation**. The first flowers to be fully started in the buds are visible with a magnifying glass toward the end of September, but it is not until mid-October that all of the tree's flowers will be completely started. They are not yet functional. The meiosis, or cell division, that will create future pollen grains does not commence until the end of December,

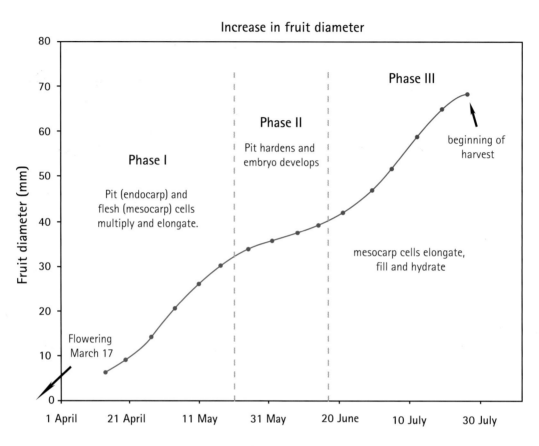

Fig. 6. Rate of diameter increase in yellow peaches, from 2004 (Summer Rich[cov] cultivar).

as it is a sign of completed chill requirement for breaking **dormancy**. Ovule formation begins in early January and ends a few days prior to flowering.

Vegetative and floral buds only develop after a period of dormancy that slowly sets in over the course of the summer in the same year. The end of dormancy occurs when temperatures rise at the end of winter. The species' cold requirement (chilling requirement) is traditionally measured from November 1 until the plant's **budbreak**, totaling the number of hours in which temperatures drop below 45°F (7°C). Certain varieties have less need of cold (these are low-chilling or "low-chill" varieties)—fewer than 650 chill hours—and are primarily cultivated in

Florida, Israel, and North Africa. In more continental zones (France, for example), cultivation induces very precocious budbreak as early as January, which increases the risk of frost damage and makes fruit harvests unpredictable.

In contrast, certain varieties that are better adapted to cold-winter regions may need as many as 950 chill hours. As with the apricot tree, these varieties exhibit some strong anomalies (malformations) in flowers and buds if they are grown in mild-winter regions, causing their fruit yield to be little to nil. This decisive factor should be kept in mind when choosing a variety.

After meeting the chill requirements, the beginning flowers continue to develop. From the end of December (the period of reactivation connected to pollen meiosis) until the flower opens in March, the visual progress of floral buds generally occurs through a series of "reference stages." The resumption of floral bud development occurs earlier than for leaf and shoot buds, except in species with pips (pome fruits), in which both reproductive and vegetative buds break simultaneously.

At the end of winter, the shoots from the prior year become branches (one-year wood) that yield both floral and wood buds: this is the mixed branch, which is the classic production unit for peach trees. The following winter, after yielding fruit and initiating new shoots, this mixed branch becomes two-year wood.

If the two-year wood is not suppressed with pruning, in the following year it will become three-year wood bearing fruiting branches (one-year wood) either directly on the three-year wood (as more recent shoots) or on the two-year wood. Wood that is three years old or older, whose complexity (branching) and elongations have been preserved, constitutes fruiting branches. Depending on the variety, production will occur either on these elongated fruit branches or on shortened, simplified fruit branches, especially on newer mixed branches close to the **scaffolds**. Professional growers call these latter branches "spurs" (French: *coursonnes*). This term does not have the same definition as apple tree spurs, but reflects instead the early notion of *coursonnage*, a French term designating the shortening of production branches with clippers (via pruning).

Annual shoot vigor is a function of its branch position on the tree. Zones that are well exposed to light will generate vigorous shoots. The branch's **insertion angle** also plays an important role: a horizontal position diminishes the terminal bud's vigor. The strongest shoots appear on the bowed sections of branches. In

2. A peach tree seedling in 2nd leaf without pruning, home garden.

practice, growers bend branches in order to diminish shoot vigor, induce new shoots at the base, and promote flower production.

Morphological Types

There is a wide range of habits in different peach tree cultivars. The peach tree is generally **basitonic** and grows as a shrubby tree during the first few years *(photo 2)*. Certain cultivars, however, have a completely weeping habit. When pruning is kept to a minimum, the tree may express a "natural" habit that varies by cultivar *(fig. 7)*.

It is important to differentiate between the dif-

Fig. 7. Different types of tree habit: closed and more open.

ferent distribution types of fruiting branches (mixed branches, flowering shoots, and spurs) according to the cultivar and the tree's growing conditions. In practice, we group varieties into three broad types:

- varieties that produce mainly on mixed branches *(fig. 8)*: these tend to have a precocious maturity (until the end of June), and fruits exhibit limited size. Good-quality fruit production can be obtained on the healthiest mixed branches being renewed closer to the scaffolds or directly on them. Short branches (under 12 inches or 30 cm) are generally located at the extremities of two-year wood and in lower, poorly lit sections of the tree. Whenever possible, they may be removed since they will only bear small, mediocre fruits.

The long, weeping nature of the mixed branches of one-year-old wood that bears fruit is characteristic of clingstone peaches grown in California (where the majority of canning peach production occurs in the United States) and gave rise to their name as "hangers." varieties that produce on all branch types (mixed branches, flowering shoots, and spurs) *(fig. 9)*: certain varieties produce an insufficient amount of flowers on the mixed branches. Others have weaker **fruit set** on shortened two-year-old wood. But most cultivars are capable of producing sizeable, quality fruit on shorter organs (flowering shoots or spurs) inserted on two-year-old wood and fruiting branches. These are usually varieties with later maturity (starting in early August in southern France).

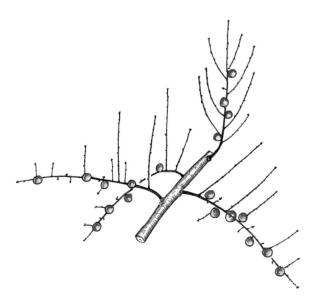

Fig. 8. Varieties producing primarily on mixed branches.

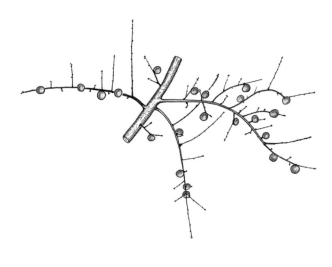

Fig. 9. Varieties producing on all branch types.

- varieties that produce on mixed branches growing from two-year-old wood *(fig. 10)*: varieties in this group exhibit behaviors somewhere between the other two groups. They create mixed branches, but there may be too few for sufficient production. The quality of the fruiting branches will also be better when they are inserted on wood that is two or three years old (two-year-old wood and fruiting branches). Thus, growers should preserve mixed branches that are inserted directly on scaffolds and smaller branches that are located on two- or three-year-old wood. Attention should be paid, however, to issues with small fruits on weak or poorly nourished wood.

Pruning methods will differ between the first group of varieties and the two other groups. In the first group, pruning for the systematic renewal of mixed branches bearing fruit should focus on removing shorter production sections: this type of pruning is similar to what is practiced in vineyards. In the second and third group, pruning should focus on preserving

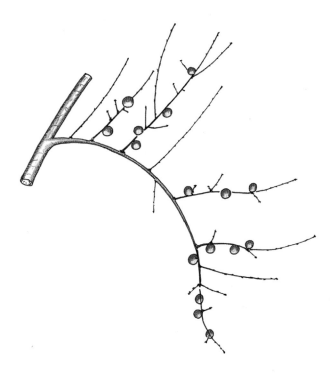

Fig. 10. Varieties producing on mixed branches on 2-year wood.

the best-placed branches and allowing them to grow for two to three years (as you would with plum trees) in order to obtain fruiting branches on which flowering shoots and spurs, in some cases, can develop. These are the trees that produce freestone peaches for the fresh market.

Soil and Climate Limitations and Varietal Adaptation

During the winter, the peach tree is in vegetative repose. Under normal conditions, it may be able to withstand temperatures as low as -4°F (-20°C). After budbreak, floral buds will appear and then young fruits. This is a critical period since peach trees are quite sensitive to spring frosts. For stone fruits with more precocious flowers than those for fruits with pips (pome fruits), the ovary is protected by floral elements. Full harvests may be jeopardized if temperatures drop below 26°F (-3°C) during the pink-bud stage, 28°F (-2°C) in blossom, or 31°F (-1°C) for young fruits. (For more on freezes and frosts, see Appendix B: Freeze/Frost Damage in *Prunus* Species.)

Peach trees prefer deep, permeable, and aerated soils with low limestone levels. The choice of rootstock can help to attenuate these requirements. This choice, in fact, may be more important than with other species (such as the apple) in terms of the orchard's ultimate success.

The traditional rootstock is the peach seedling. It will impart proper affinity and balance out vigor with fruit set. For commercial growing in France, the primary rootstock is the GF 305, selected by the INRA's Grande Ferrade station in Bordeaux from 'Pêche de Montreuil'. Another rootstock that is widely used is 'Montclar® Chanturge', which was also selected at the Bordeaux station using varieties from the Clermont-

Ferrand region. In the United States, peach seedling rootstocks include 'Halford', 'Lovell', 'Hiawatha', 'Ishtara', 'Bailey', 'Siberian C', GF 305, and 'Guardian', which is "short life" resistant. All peach rootstocks are sensitive to wet, poorly drained soils, and peach should not be used as a rootstock when an orchard that was previously planted to peach is once again planted for peach production.

In heavy soils that are less permeable or that drain less in winter, it is preferable to choose a plum rootstock. Several selections are available, including the various Saint-Julien **clones**, based on the 'Saint-Julien' variety from Orléans (GF0655.2, St-Julien hybrid 1 and 2), GF 43, a plum selection from 'Ente' or even 'Brompton', which was developed in England.

In calcareous soils, the chosen rootstock should be a hybrid between peach and almond trees such as GF 677. That rootstock, which is 20% more vigorous than a seedling, is resistant to **active limestone** rates of 7 to 12%. It is also recommended when replanting an earlier-bearing peach tree. Besides the GF 677 ('Amandier'), in the United States other hybrid rootstocks include GF 655 and 'Nemaguard'. Another choice for France would be the recent hybrid selected in Hungary called 'Cadaman® Avimag'.

PRINCIPLES OF TRAINING

Choosing Plants and Training Young Trees

THE CHOICE OF TREES
For commercial planting, three main types of trees are available from the nursery:
- one-year **scions**: the most common, these generally offer a better balance among growth re-initiation after transplanting, price, and the tree's ability to adapt to its future form.

- medium or high stem trees: these trees are available through nurseries and are age two or older. They are pre-shaped at the nursery, generally following a vase pattern, using higher stems (high-budded onto the rootstock). These trees are more expensive and are often slow to grow after being transplanted.
- **dormant-eye** tree grafts: this type of seedling is currently being developed in production orchards. This tree comprises a rootstock onto which one or two dormant buds are grafted, hence the term "dormant eye." After transplanting dormant-eye tree grafts, growers must nip off buds, select the best stems, and protect them from breakage and pests, including rabbits and snails.

Before buying seedlings, a close visual examination will help you choose the best and judge their state of health. A quality peach scion measures 4 to 5 feet (1.2 to 1.6 m) in height and will bear well-developed sylleptic branches. Avoid plants that have no branching on the first 20 inches (50 cm) above the grafting point. They will generally need substantial cutting back in order to form properly; this will weaken them and render their upkeep more difficult in the first year, compared to the dormant-eye seedling.

VARIETAL CHOICE

With several hundred varieties grown by professional arboriculturists in France and several hundred more traditional varieties, some of which are quite ancient, it may be difficult to choose which varieties to plant. Ask for advice at the nursery, and plant cultivars that have been tested and proven productive in your region.

Varieties grown in the United States. Varieties for canning and baby food production are clingstones that are firm-fleshed and suitable for machine harvest,

although most are still hand-harvested. California is virtually the sole producer of canning peaches in the United States. These include, in order of maturity, 'Loadel', 'Fortuna', 'Carson', and 'Dixon' (all extra-early varieties maturing in mid-July); 'Andross', 'Dr. Davis', 'Paloro', 'Peak', and 'Andora' (these mature two to three weeks after the extra-earlies, with the latter three being planted less often); and 'Halford', Starn', 'Sullivan', and a few other mid-season to late-season canning varieties. Several new canning selections are advancing through testing from the breeding program at the University of California–Davis. They display several significantly improved traits: retention of quality on the tree despite extended harvest season (peach x almond hybrids), and compact tree shape with spur production, thus requiring much less pruning.

Varieties of freestone (fresh market) peach are numerous and may be grown in California, Georgia, Arkansas, Texas, and many other locations where not limited by a short growing season. These include, in order of maturity through the summer, 'Earlired', 'Early Redhaven', 'Dixired', 'Redcap', 'Sunhaven', 'Merrill Gemfree', 'Dixigem', 'Redhaven', 'Triogem', 'Fairhaven', 'Western Pride', 'July Elberta', 'Southland', 'Redglobe', 'Elegant Lady', 'Veteran', 'Belle', 'Redelberta', 'Suncrest', 'Sullivans Early Elberta', 'Flavorcrest', 'Fay Elberta', 'Elberta', 'Redskin', 'Dixiland', 'Madison', 'J.H. Hale', 'Gold Medal', 'Afterglow', 'Rio Oso Gem', 'Autumn', and 'Late Elberta'. Virtually all freestone peaches grown in the United States have yellow flesh. Exceptions include 'Early-Red-Fre', 'Arctic Gem', 'Spring Snow', 'Ivory Princess', 'Manon', 'Babcock', and 'Belle'. White-fleshed peaches (and nectarines) are subacid and are favorites of the Asian market.

Following are descriptions of some freestone varieties, including those not listed above:
- 'Arctic Gem'—a white-fleshed peach with subacid flavor; good red skin color, shape, and size (Zaiger Genetics)

- 'Delight'—blushed skin and firm, yellow flesh; subject to split pits
- 'Elegant Lady'—mid-season harvest with heavy production; large and round with very firm flesh and good flavor; skin color is red-yellow and highly colored
- 'Fay Elberta'—an industry standard for fresh, drying, canning, and freezing uses; a large fruit with yellow, juicy flesh and premium flavor; skin is highly blushed
- 'Flavorcrest'—a large to medium, firm-fleshed fruit with good flavor and heavy red blush; sets a heavy crop
- 'Galaxy'—a "flat" or "satellite" peach, 'Galaxy' is an example of a new shape of peach that was first popularized in France as easier to eat out-of-hand due to its shape; the fruit is white-fleshed, highly blushed, subacid, and sweet, ripening in late July
- 'Gene Elberta'—large with very good flavor; highly blushed, heavily productive, and suitable for canning and freezing in addition to fresh eating
- 'June Pride'—a Zaiger variety that is firm and large with good color and exceptional flavor
- 'Manon'—white-fleshed and subacid, with excellent color and flavor; early ripening
- 'Nectar'—white-fleshed and delicate with excellent flavor and color; skin is strawberry pink-red
- 'O'Henry'—an industry standard that is large, with good firmness and flavor; skin is highly colored; a late, heavy producer
- 'Pretty Lady'—a firm fruit with good flavor and non-melting flesh; skin is highly colored; tree growth is highly vigorous, producing a heavy crop of large fruits that ripen uniformly; ripens slightly later than 'O'Henry'
- 'Red Haven'—an industry standard that is firm,

	Voluminous trees with sturdy scaffolds	Less voluminous trees with weaker scaffolds
A lot of long branches (> 16 in / 40 cm)	AI	BI
Predominance of small branches (< 8 in / 20 cm)	AII	BII

with very good, low-acid (not subacid) flavor and richly red skin color overlying a yellow background

- 'Springcrest'—a large to medium fruit with firm yellow flesh, highly colored red skin, and very good flavor
- 'Spring Rose'—white flesh, very early and highly aromatic with sweet flavor; skin is highly colored red; needs heavy thinning
- 'Sugar Lady'—a large to medium fruit with subacid, white flesh that has exceptional flavor; freestone and heavily blushed (Zaiger Genetics)
- 'Zee Lady' and 'Zee Red'—Zaiger varieties that are large and firm with yellow flesh and exceptional flavor; both are highly productive

Nectarines grown in the United States include, in order of maturity, 'Armking', 'Sunfree', 'Desert Dawn', 'Sunlite', 'Sunred', 'Sunripe', 'Independence', 'Harko', 'Sun Grand', 'Stark Sunglo', 'Flavortop', 'Fantasia', 'Firebrite', 'LeGrand', 'Red Jim', 'Garden Delight', and Fairlane'. All have yellow flesh.

- Nectarine varieties for California are listed below. All have well-blushed skin and are highly flavorful when grown with adequate light and summer warmth:
- 'Garden Delight Miniature' nectarine—self-fertile, large, yellow freestone; matures in mid-August in California; the heavy-bearing, small tree can be covered for frost protection; 500 chill hours (Zaiger Genetics)

- 'Nectar Babe Miniature' nectarine—mid-season, yellow freestone; heavy-bearing, small tree; pollenize with 'Honey Babe', other peaches, or nectarines (Zaiger Genetics)
- 'Necta Zee Miniature' nectarine—self-fertile; matures in mid-June to early July in Central California; vigorous growth to 6 feet (1.8 m); 500 chill hours (Zaiger Genetics)
- 'Arctic Blaze'—self-fertile, white, low-acid nectarines; early-season harvest with firm flesh and rich flavor; very sweet when allowed to mature until soft-ripe; large size with red and white skin; harvest mid to late August in Central California, after 'Arctic Queen' white nectarine; 700 to 800 chill hours (Zaiger Genetics)
- 'Arctic Glo' and 'Arctic Rose'—self-fertile, sweet and subacid, white nectarines; mature in late June–early July in Central California; 600 to 700 chill hours (Zaiger Genetics)
- 'Arctic Queen'—self-fertile, super-sweet and subacid, white nectarine; similar to 'Arctic Rose' but maturing in early August in Central California; 600 to 700 chill hours (Zaiger Genetics)
- 'Arctic Star'—self-fertile, early-season, white-fleshed nectarine that is super-sweet and subacid; semi-freestone with dark red skin; harvest mid to late June in Central California; chilling requirement possibly fewer than 600 chill hours (Zaiger Genetics)
- 'August Glo'—self-fertile, late yellow nectarine with tangy, rich flavor; large fruits mature in late August–early September in Central California, about one month after 'Fantasia'; chilling requirement probably 600 to 700 hours (Zaiger Genetics)
- 'Cavalier'—self-fertile, orange-yellow blushed skin with yellow freestone flesh; resistant to brown rot; ripens mid to late July in Central California,

one week before 'Elberta' peach; hardy, developed in Virginia; 700 to 800 chill hours
- 'Desert Dawn'—self-fertile, yellow semi-freestone nectarine adapted for warm winter climates (low chill, 250 chill hours); matures mid to late May in Central California (Zaiger Genetics)
- 'Desert Delight'—self-fertile, low chill variety (100 to 200 chill hours); large red-skinned fruit with yellow flesh; matures mid-June in Central California (Zaiger Genetics)
- 'Double Delight'—self-fertile, heavy-bearing, yellow nectarine with exceptional flavor and large, double pink flowers; matures mid-July in Central California; 650 chill hours (Zaiger Genetics)
- 'Fantasia'—a commercial standard that is self-fertile; large and yellow-fleshed freestone; matures late July–early August in Central California; 500 chill hours
- 'Flamekist'—a commercial standard that is richly flavored; large and firm with red over yellow skin; self-fruitful; matures late August–early September in Central California; 700 chill hours
- 'Flavortop'—self-fertile, firm, yellow freestone with excellent quality; ripens in mid-July in Central California, between 'Independence' and 'Fantasia'; susceptible to bacterial spot and tender to winter cold; 650 chill hours
- 'Goldmine'—self-fertile, white freestone; small to medium size; juicy and sweet; a well-established variety for California and western Oregon; ripens in August; 400 chill hours
- 'Harko'—self-fertile, sweet, firm, yellow, semi-freestone; cold-hardy Canadian variety that ripens with 'Redhaven' peach in early July in Central California; tolerant of bacterial spot and brown rot; 800 chill hours
- 'Independence'—self-fertile, firm yellow freestone with bright red skin; rich flavor, tangy and sweet;

winter and frost hardy; matures in early July in Central California; 700 chill hours

- 'Jolly Red Giant'—one of the largest nectarines if properly thinned; self-fertile; freestone with yellow flesh; matures in mid-July in Central California; 600 chill hours (Zaiger Genetics)
- 'Juneglo'—self-fertile, early-season nectarine with yellow flesh; ripens in late June in Central California, seven to ten days before 'Independence'; semi-freestone when soft-ripe; winter and frost hardy; 700 chill hours (Zaiger Genetics)
- 'Late LeGrand'—a traditional, yellow-fleshed nectarine that is self-fertile, with red and yellow skin; matures in mid to late August in Central California; 600 chill hours.
- 'Mericrest'—a self-fertile, yellow freestone that is very cold hardy, frost hardy, late blooming; even crops after sub-zero winters; fruits are large with rich tangy flavor; matures mid-July in Central California; 800 chill hours
- 'Panamint'—self-fertile, red-skinned yellow freestone; aromatic, intensely flavored, with a nice acid–sugar balance; dependable producer and a long-time favorite in warm-winter Southern California climates; late July–early August maturing; requires only 250 chill hours
- 'Redgold'—self-fertile, maturing in July in California, early August in Oregon; yellow, freestone flesh with very red skin; fruit set is moderate and fruit are large; the tree is overly vigorous and requires a lot of pruning
- 'Sauzee King'—"satellite" (flat) nectarine; early season, white flesh, red-yellow skin; the tree is precocious and produces heavily; thinning is required to size the large fruit; chilling requirement estimated at 500 hours (Zaiger Genetics)
- 'Silver Lode'—self-fertile, early-season, white-fleshed freestone with rich, sweet flavor; creamy

yellow skin, blushed and dotted with red; matures about late June in Central California; old favorite for Southern California, first introduced in 1951; relatively low chilling requirement of about 400 hours

- 'Snow Queen'—self-fertile, early-season white freestone; matures late June in Central California, about two to three weeks before 'Babcock' peach; estimated chilling requirement is 250 to 300 hours

Three varieties of nectarines are grown in Oregon's Willamette Valley:

- 'Juneglo' (mid-July)
- 'Harko' (late July)
- 'Fantasia' (mid-August)

Varieties for the eastern United States. Characteristics that are most important for consideration include: resistance to brown rot and bacterial spot, low cracking incidence (due to rain and humidity), and winter hardiness. Most locations are not well tested, so recommendations for a given location are not guarantees.

Recommendations for Virginia might provide some guidance:

- 'Sunglo'—developed in Merced, California, and introduced in 1962; freestone, yellow-fleshed with good size; harvest at the beginning of August; flesh is firm and somewhat dry; flavor is fairly good, but the variety is susceptible to bacterial spot
- 'Redgold'—developed in Alabama and introduced in 1956; trees are very productive; fruit is large and yellow-fleshed, firm with excellent flavor; matures in mid-August
- 'Fantasia'—in Virginia, it is moderately susceptible to bacterial spot and the fruit usually has a poor finish with russeting

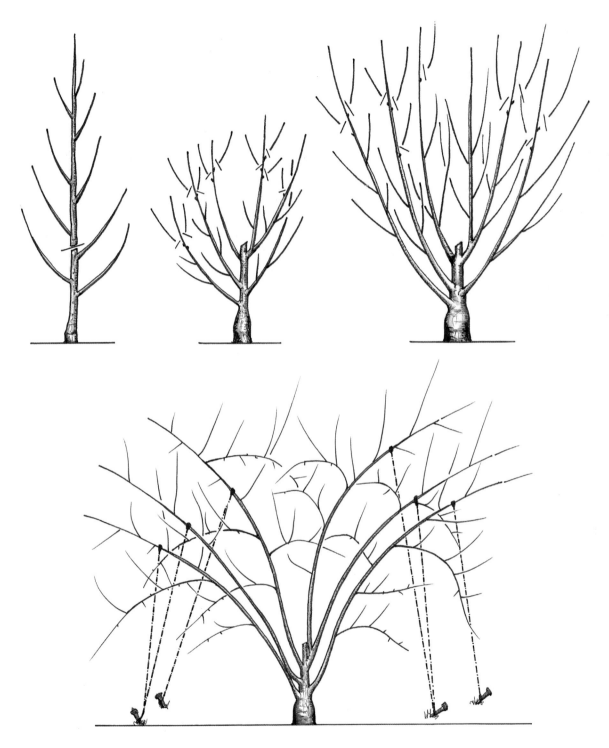

Fig. 11 (top). Shaping trees into Dôme Leydier during the first two years.
Fig. 12 (bottom). Shaping trees into Dôme Leydier in 3rd leaf.

241

3. Six-year-old Dôme Leydier trees in a home garden.

4. A Dôme Leydier orchard at harvest. The stakes hold up scaffolds weighed down by fruit load.

- 'Royal Giant'—released in 1977 by Floyd Zaiger; harvest season begins August 28 to September 4; flesh is clingstone and fibrous; average size with fair to good flavor, on the acid side; quite susceptible to brown rot

CHOOSING THE SHAPE FOR YOUNG TREES

With peach trees, there is currently no single dominant shape in France as one finds with other species. Obtaining a consistent, quality harvest will be possible regardless of whether the tree is shaped as a palmette, axis, or vase. In the United States, most peach and nectarine trees are grown in a vase shape, with larger size for processing (canning, clingstone) peaches due to vigor and smaller size for fresh market peaches and nectarines. Peach trees in California tend to be more vigorous than elsewhere, due to the climate and soils. Newer pruning strategies include the quad and the vertical (or Kearney) V, both developed for California peach and nectarine at the University of California-Davis. The quad is similar to the vertical V, but with four axes instead of two.

Prior to transplanting, it is important to consider two parameters that will determine the state of the future fruit tree: (1) planting distances, and (2) the **architecture** of the tree's permanent scaffolds, or its shape. These two parameters should be adapted to the size of the orchard as well as the anticipated vigor of the trees (combination of rootstock, variety, and soil fertility).

Shaping for volume: Dôme Leydier (figs. 11 and 12). Two techniques can be used for shaping a young tree and determining its future scaffolds: pruning with shears and bending. Bending of limbs is not practiced to any great extent in peach and nectarine grown in the United States.

Shaping a tree with shears is a highly technical and artificial undertaking. Furthermore, the necessary summer pruning will traumatize young peach trees. We prefer a more natural shape inspired by a form that professionals have used since the 1980s: the Dôme

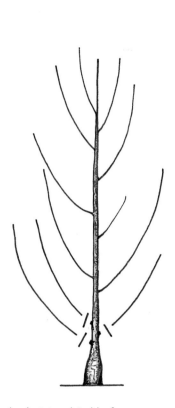
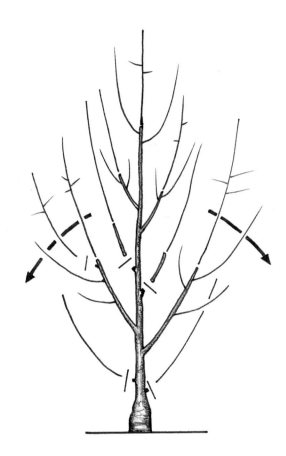

Fig. 13. Palmette shaping in 1st and 2nd leaf.

Leydier, named after the man who conceived it, Raoul Leydier, an arboriculturist from Grans in Provence *(photos 3 and 4)*.

This shape, which is very easy to create, promotes rapid entry into abundant production starting in the third year from planting. The scion is cut back at the moment of transplanting to 16 to 20 inches (40 to 50 cm) above the ground in order to promote future scaffolds (four to six per tree, depending on available space). After this first cutting, the grower must select the best shoots. You should promote their growth by **pinching** back excess or lower shoots as well as sylleptic shoots in the upper third of the tree. This way, you favor the peach tree's natural growth in the first year. Shoots may

reach more than 5 feet (1.5 m) tall. Over the course of the summer, install stakes to support the young trees and prevent them from breaking. Continue pinching and propping into the second year in order to reinforce the scaffolds. In France, when the scaffolds reach a height of 8 to 10 feet (2.5 to 3 m) in autumn, they are tied down from their tips with string or strands of tarp in order to make them as horizontal as possible. This creates a vault (French: *dôme*) in the orchard on which new branches and future fruiting branches can position themselves.

Natural palmette-type shaping on a wire structure (fig. 13). During the first year after planting, pinch to pro-

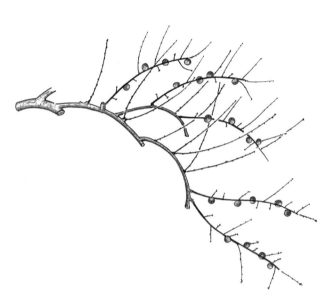

Fig. 14. A 4-year mixed branch variety.

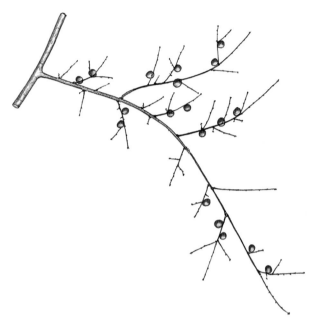

Fig. 15. A 3-year fruit branch on a variety producing primarily on 2-year wood.

mote growth on three branches that will become the tree's future scaffolds. Over the course of the summer, based on these branches' length, you should attach the branches to a wire structure: one in the center positioned vertically, and the two other to the center on either side and slightly angled. The angle will vary depending on their vigor, with the hardiest branches being angled further down.

TRAINING THE ADULT TREE

As with other species, you can observe tree behavior and develop future production zones using fruiting branches that are more than three years old *(figs. 14 and 15)*. For the peach tree, branches (mixed branches, fruiting shoots, etc.) can also fruit using old wood (scaffolds or sylleptic branches). For certain varieties, this type of production may be desirable—notably, for precocious varieties.

Evaluating the Training Method and Fruit Load in the Tree

Before pruning, it is essential to take stock of the tree's vigor and to understand what type of branches predominate. For this, we propose two criteria that will determine the training method to use. These observations should take place as winter is ending, starting in the fourth year after planting and continuing each year thereafter.

The first criterion involves evaluating the volume of vegetation and the scaffolds' vigor:
- A: trees have strong scaffolds and a good volume of vegetation, with thick trunks and scaffolds;
- B: trees have weaker scaffolds and less vegetation, with thinner trunks and scaffolds.

The second criterion involves evaluating the length and vigor of shoots from the prior year:

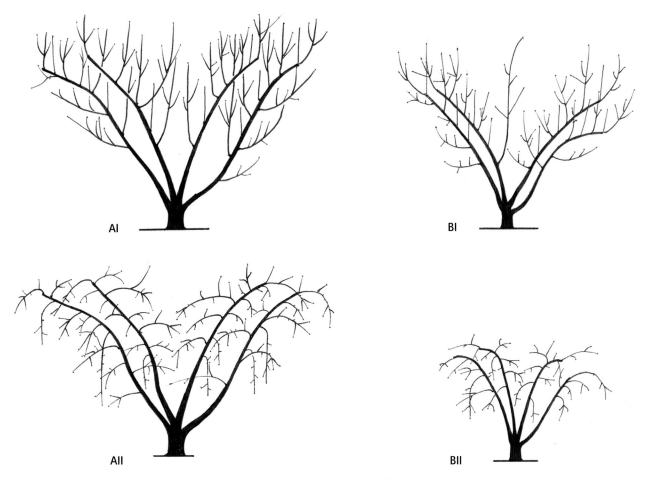

Fig. 16. Watch the trees to determine their hardiness and a balance of growth – fruit.

- I: shoots from the prior year are long (sometimes more than 16 inches or 40 cm) and relatively abundant (over a hundred shoots for trees more than four years old);
- II: shoots are shorter (often less than 8 inches or 20 cm) and not as abundant; there are very few shoots longer than 16 inches (40 cm).

Combining these two criteria allows us to classify four broad types of trees:

We will now explain these differences and offer a training method adapted to each type of tree for fruit pruning and fruit load. You can adapt this advice according to the experience that you gain as you observe how your trees react *(fig. 16)*.

TYPE AI

This is a vigorous tree with a good volume of foliage. Regardless of its age, this tree is in good health and capable of bearing many good-quality fruits (several hundred). This is the ideal situation, since peach trees need to be vigorous in order to adequately nourish all the fruit and at the same time ensure good vegetative growth that will allow branches to renew in the following year.

With a precocious variety, the healthiest mixed branches should be preferred. It is advisable to prune down the number of these branches so as not to overload the tree. Use shears for this cutting, with the aim of preserving the healthiest and best-placed branches—if possible, on two-year-old wood. The preserved branches will have been bent the year before (in France). For a tree in the fourth or fifth year after planting, a proper load is around 80 to 120 branches longer than 16 inches (40 cm), or 20 to 30 branches per scaffold. All of the others will have to be suppressed.

With a later variety or one with the potential for sizeable fruit, it will also be necessary to limit the number of productive organs. In this case you should preserve the fruiting shoots, but make sure the selected branches are well spaced on the fruiting branches. The branch load should not be more than 160 productive organs.

Clear the base of these branches of all production in order to aerate the tree and limit the fruit's sensitivity to disease. The resulting light well will also allow optimal sun on leaves and shoots, improving branch quality for the following year.

The trees in type AI will need to have their vegetation pruned in order to regulate vigor and maintain or develop their production potential. Badly placed young shoots (in the light well), as well as epicormic branches, should be removed by hand or with shears.

TYPE AII

This type of tree has sufficient volume and sturdy scaffolds but weaker annual shoots, perhaps due to excessive loads in the prior year. It is characterized by numerous productive organs but of limited dimension (flowering shoots; spurs occasionally). With a precocious variety, it may be risky to prune fruits in this situation. With later varieties, the production of smaller branches isn't a problem because it will not necessarily prevent fruit from being pruned. However, as the fruits are often susceptible to disease, aerating the tree is a must.

For all varieties, the goal is to control fruit branch load, on fruiting shoots and spurs, by selecting the longest branches as well as the best-placed smaller limbs. This operation can be done with a gloved hand or with shears. Maintain a small mixed branch on fruit branches, with a fruiting shoot or spur (rarely) every 6 to 8 inches (15 to 20 cm). Suppress any branches that tend to hang, and clear the base of the branches completely in order to create a light well around the scaffolds and within the foliage.

You must also think about watering and adding nutritive elements in order to sustain vegetative shoot growth.

TYPE BI

Here we encounter trees whose growing conditions have not been favorable in the first years. This type of tree, whether it is late or precocious, can only handle a limited load of branches (and therefore fruit) in order to guarantee a quality harvest and reactivate scaffold growth. You should aim to keep forty to eighty mixed branches per tree (vary this depending on the tree's hardiness and the variety's maturity period). If scaffolds don't have fruit branches yet, the goal will be to spread branches along the scaffolds, organizing them in a spiral.

It is important to obtain satisfactory growth, which requires proper watering and the addition of fertilizer.

TYPE BII

This tree seems to have a major problem in terms of vigor. This is related to a lack of roots or a repeated excess of fruit load. For one or two years, the priority will be to renovate vegetative growth. In order to do that, it is advisable to leave a lower yield of fruits on the tree (only a few dozen fruits), and only prune lightly. Remove poorly placed branches in terms of lighting or those that are in excess or blocking one another. Additionally, it will be necessary to start using techniques that promote good vegetative growth: adding and tilling organic materials (compost and/or manure) around the base of the tree at the end of winter, and then complementing them by applying nitrogen fertilizers in mid-spring and early summer (end of April and mid-June, for example). (See Appendix C: U.S. Standard Fertilizer Equivalents for Nitrogen.)

Watering should occur regularly (from May to the end of July), and over-watering should be avoided, which would cause the roots to asphyxiate. In August and September, space out waterings in order to promote branch lignification and prevent excessive growth on shoots that would turn into epicormic branches and develop sylleptic branches. Only after this type of training, which regenerates the tree's vegetative growth and consolidates its branches, will it be possible to return to AI- or AII-type training.

Chronology of Interventions

Training a tree requires several interventions spread out over the course of the year *(fig. 17)*.

WINTER
Winter is reserved, as we've seen, for observing the tree and selecting the fruiting organs by pruning for fruiting. This intervention takes place with shears in January or February and privileges the longest and best-placed branches on a tree or fruit branch. You should adapt the number and choice of branches to the tree's fruiting type and to its vigor as described above. It is also important during this period to eradicate peach leaf curl (a fungus), which is highly damaging to branch growth in sensitive varieties.

SPRING
In the spring, during and after blossoming, it is possible to readjust the tree's branch load by removing excess branches that may have been left to handle weather damage (spring frost, for example).

Next, the longer and more important work will

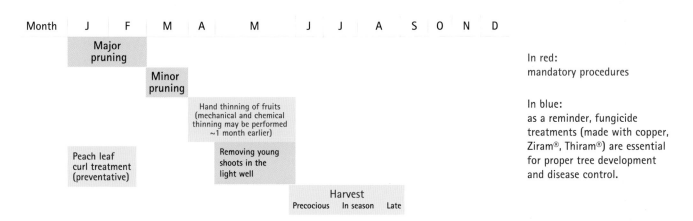

Fig. 17. A chronology of interventions in southeast France; similar in California.

Removing vegetative shoots:

5. On scaffolds.

6. In a zone that will promote epicormic branches (where pruning has occurred).

7. Branch base prior to removal.

8. Base of the same branch, cleared to allow light to penetrate.

begin on small (walnut-sized) fruits: hand thinning. This intervention aims at suppressing excess fruits after fruit set. You will have determined the fruit load ahead of time based on observing the tree and using different training methods. The number of fruits to leave on a given branch will depend on its length. The general rule is to leave one fruit for every 6 inches (15 cm) along the branch (approximately a hand's length, breaking up clustered fruits). Thus, three to five fruits will be preserved on mixed branches based on their length. On short branches, such as spurs and fruiting shoots, you should preserve a single fruit.

It is preferable to remove fruits located too close to the tree's base, as they will become damaged as they grow. Fruits at the tips of branches should be removed as well, since their weight will bend the branches and stop proper alimentation. Once hand thinning has been completed, it is worth counting the fruit to verify that the tree's total load does not exceed pre-determined numbers.

Finally, you should take advantage of the spring for regulating the growth of vigorous trees: this means manually removing vegetative shoots that may grow during manual thinning. This technique helps to control tree vigor by spreading energy throughout all of the tree's shoots. It also improves the tree's aeration and guarantees better light reception on leaves, branches, and fruits; and it reduces fruit sensitivity to disease. The technique, however, should be used with caution on young or slow-growing trees since it may too strongly affect vigor. The removal can be done with a bare hand or with leather gloves from late April to mid-June, based on the production zones and the maturity dates of the trees involved *(photos 5 and 6)*. The goal is to intervene and suppress any vegetative shoots that are already excessively vigorous and that may become epicormic branches. These shoots are generally found near older cuts on the scaffolds, at scaffold tips (erect shoots), or at the bowing summit on vigorous branches that were bent or that have fallen under the weight of their own fruit. Intervention should also include clearing the base of fruit branches and the insertion points of branches *(photos 7 and 8)* in order to remove excessive vegetation and aerate foliage. In many situations, this operation will make traditional summer pruning optional.

SUMMER

In summer, harvest dominates over a period of time based on the maturity periods of the varieties. The sensory quality of the fruits will be at a maximum when they are approaching their physical maturity.

The constraints of modern marketing distribution and the distances between areas of production and consumption do not allow for fruit to be harvested at full maturity, as would be the case in home gardens. Regardless of commercial constraints, you should select the fruit to be picked according to the following criteria: the fruit must be colored, evenly shaped, plump, and soft to the touch *(photo*

9. Fruit ready for harvest (Roussane de Monein).

9). This stage of maturity does not occur simultaneously for all fruit on a given tree, which means that picking will take place three to eight times over a period of days. Keep in mind that the best-quality, sweetest, and most aromatic fruits are generally the largest and best positioned on the tree (in terms of light exposure and good-quality support branch). Progressively, fruit quality will diminish in a tree as picking continues: the last-fruit picked may be better used for cooking.

In summer, pruning is an intervention that can serve to manage excessive vigor by using shears to cut down epicormic branches (erect shoots longer than 3 feet or 1 m that are highly lignified), as these may hinder future mixed branches *(photo 10).* For precocious varieties harvested in June and early July, intervention occurs after harvest and is often necessary since this early release of fruit alimentation and weight usually promotes strong summer growth. In the case of "in season" and later varieties, summer pruning can happen once or twice. The first time occurs a month prior to harvest, though it may be more advantageous to replace this by removing precocious vegetative shoots following the methods described above. The second intervention occurs after harvest, with the goal of promoting the lignification of shoots.

During summer interventions, it is possible to reduce hardiness on certain shoots and certain wood by using the bowing method. Do this with string or wires. You can bend stronger mixed branches and two-year wood located in vigorous zones when they are not busy with production. Bending can also happen during winter pruning.

CONCLUSION

The peach tree is a species that only produces on one-year-old wood, which must be renewed each year.

10. Competition from epicormic branches weakens branch extensions.

This implies guaranteeing sufficient tree growth for a quality fruit harvest and the formation of young shoots that are able to become healthy mixed branches in the following year. It is therefore essential with this species to privilege all of the techniques that we've outlined in this chapter that play a determining role in growth (irrigation, fertilization, and phyto-sanitary protection).

Apart from describing pruning techniques that may appear somewhat complex, we hope to have imparted a fundamental idea: training a tree results from observing it and understanding how it functions. Techniques such as pruning, removing, and bending are meant to help the tree express its own potential and not to restrict it to shapes or training methods that are poorly adapted to the species or cultivars included in an orchard. Observation also allows us to take stock of this species' genetic diversity and to adjust accordingly.

As with many fruit tree species, the shape of the tree has little importance. It is, however, necessary to construct a solid structure within the tree so that it may yield quality production consistently and sufficiently.

Rather than speak in terms of traditional forms, it is indispensable that training methods and intervention techniques improve the distribution of light within the tree's foliage. As this is the site of carbon assimilation, it must be present in every zone of vegetative and fruiting growth. The peach tree species has a strong ability to set fruits, so it is essential to maintain a good balance between vegetative growth and the number of fruits. Controlling fruit load through hand thinning is indispensable and must be done with the greatest care so that you obtain excellent-quality fruits that fully meet your expectations.

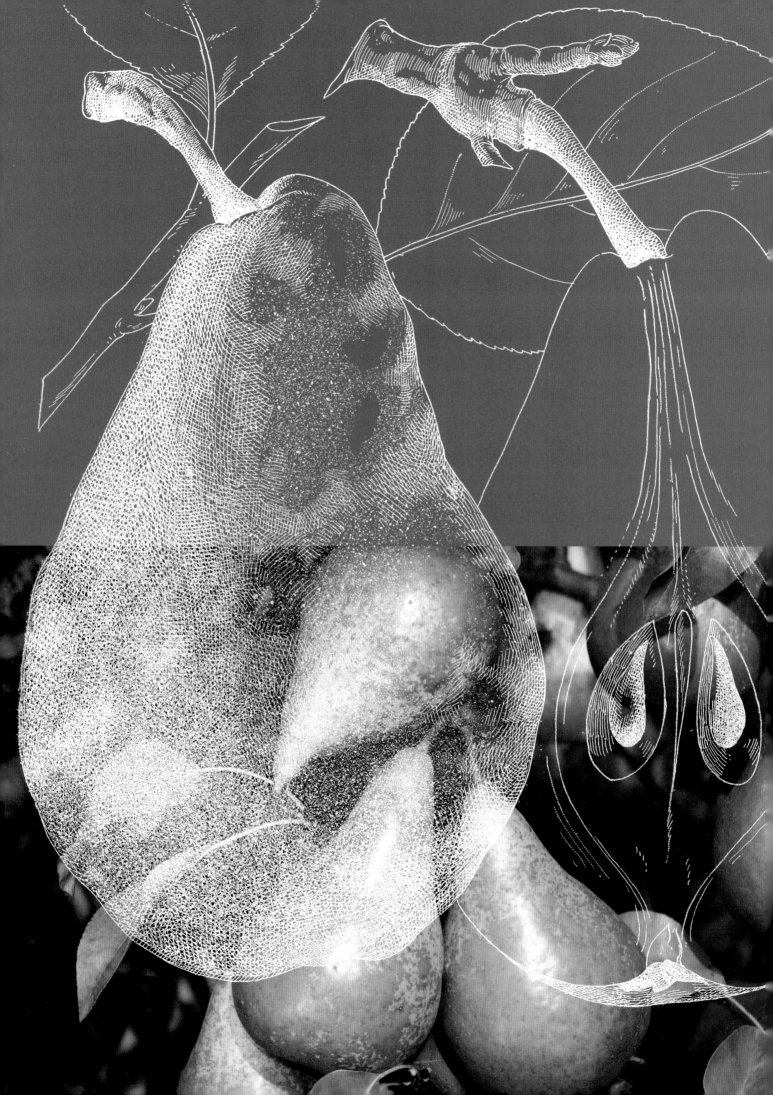

PEAR

Authors	Bernard FLORENS
	Pierre-Éric LAURI
	Marcel LE LEZEC
Collaborator	André BELQUIN

GENERAL OVERVIEW

History and Phytogeographic Origins

The first traces of pear tree cultivation date back to 4000 BC in China. The Romans practiced systematic grafting and developed about sixty varieties, thereby playing a major role in domesticating the pear tree in Europe. Pear trees were probably introduced into France as the Roman Empire expanded. In the Middle Ages, France's cultivated varieties, such as 'Caillou Rosat' and 'Poire d'Angoisse', had such little flavor that people only ate them when cooked. It was not until the Renaissance that varieties with better-quality fruits appeared. During the reign of Louis XIV, more than 500 pear varieties, including 'Frangipane' and 'Cuisse Madame', were grown. Most of today's cultivated varieties are the result of selections made in the nineteenth century.

Worldwide Production

Worldwide production of pears is dominated by Argentina and China as exporters, and by Russia and the European Union as importers. A total of 12.6 million tons are grown in China and slightly more in Argentina. In 2008, the U.S. production was about 8,000,000 metric tons (USDA World Market and Trades Report, Jan. 2008); over 90% of the country's production is in the Pacific Northwest (Washington and Oregon) and California. Some production also occurs in New York, Pennsylvania, Michigan, Idaho, Utah, Colorado,

1. William's/Bartlett pear (synonymous).

2. Conférence pears.

and Connecticut. Three varieties dominate the world market: 'Williams' *(photo 1)*, known as 'Bartlett' in the United States and 'Williams Bon Chretien' elsewhere), grown in all of the producing countries; 'Packham's Triumph', mostly grown in the Southern Hemisphere; and 'Conférence' *(photo 2)*, primarily grown in Europe.

U.S. production for fresh market is about 60% of the total pears grown domestically; the remainder is processed, mostly as canned fruit. Fresh market pears in the United States are primarily 'Green Anjou', 'Red Anjou', and 'Bartlett', with smaller amounts of 'Bosc', 'Starkcrimson' ('Red Clapps Favorite'), 'Comice', 'Seckel', 'Red Bartlett', and others. 'Bartlett' dominates California's crop, which sets parthenocarpically under California's climatic conditions, as does 'Bosc'; most growers don't place beehives in their orchards as a result. 'Bartlett' is becoming gradually displaced by other varieties, especially red pears, due to customer demand. Washington State grows most of the 'Green Anjou' fruit (the most exported variety) and is the top U.S. producer, followed by Oregon and then California.

The predominant summer variety of pear grown in California is 'Bartlett'. Other varieties of European summer pears grown in the United States are 'Red Bartlett', 'Red Sensation', and 'Starkcrimson'. The predominant fall pear in California is 'Bosc', followed by 'Comice', 'Seckel', 'Beurré Hardy' ('French Butter Pear'), and 'Forelle'.

Europe produces about 2.5 tons per year. The volume of 'Conférence' pears has increased over the past several years. Production of 'Abbé Fétel' and 'Rocha' has also increased significantly. Production of the other varieties has either leveled out or started to decline.

With about 250,000 tons per year, pear production in France comes in third behind that of Italy and Spain, among European producers. The Rhône-Méditerranée basin is the primary production zone, accounting for about 60% of France's total production. The Loire Valley and southwestern France are also two major areas in terms of national production. The range of varieties in France is relatively extensive compared to other countries in the European Union. Yet two summer varieties, 'Jules Guyot' and 'Williams', account for about 60% of over-

3. Alexandrine Douillard pears.

methods, it is possible to eat fresh pears from mid-July until the end of March. The fruits are also used for various preparations: syrup, sorbet, nectar, perry, and liqueur (made with 'Williams').

Botanical Classification

The pear tree, like other species of fruit trees with pips (Maloideae tribe), is probably the result of allopolyploidization (the fusion of genomes from two or more species; see also ploidy) between fruit tree species with pits (Prunoideae tribe) and spirea species (Spiraeoideae tribe).

The pear tree belongs to the Rosaceae family, the Pomoideae subfamily (fruit trees with pips), and the genus Pyrus communis L. The genus Pyrus includes about twenty species from Europe, Asia Minor, and North Africa, as well as over 2,000 varieties. Its fruit is a drupe with a fleshy mesocarp. Pyrus communis L. is the basis for European and American varieties. Chinese (Li) and Japanese

all production. The range of autumnal varieties is even greater—with 'Doyenné du Comice', 'Conférence', 'Alexandrine Douillard' *(photo 3)*, 'Beurré Hardy', and 'Louise Bonne d'Avranches'—yet their production volumes are considerably smaller. Cultivation of winter pear varieties has dropped considerably, for fireblight has caused the decline of the principal variety, 'Passe Crassane'. Recent plantings of 'Angélys cov' (a new variety created by the INRA) should help expand the offerings for winter pears.*

The pear is a fruit that is eaten either fresh or cooked. Due to the pear's adaptation to different climatic conditions as well as progress in conservation

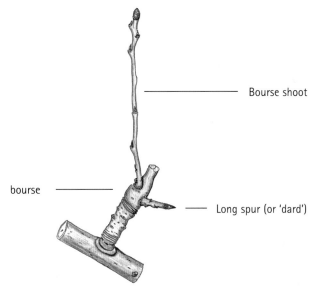

Bourse shoot

bourse

Long spur (or 'dard')

Fig. 1. Flowering shoot on a pear tree.

* The cov superscript stands for certification d'obtention végétale, a legally registered trademark for plants in France.

(Nashi) species, in contrast, derive from the oriental species Pyrus serotina and Pyrus bretschneideri Redh.

Soil and Climate Limitations

The growing area for pear trees is more limited than that for apple trees, and it is less present in southern zones. It is generally found in temperate zones at altitudes of up to 2,625 feet (800 m).

Satisfying the plant's cold requirements in winter helps to synchronize the start of springtime vegetation. This varies according to variety: from 660 to 1,100 hours (temperature lower than 19°F or -7°C). The use of various rootstocks helps the plant adapt to different conditions. Pear trees are best suited for silty or sandy-clay soils. Pyrus types are better adapted to calcareous soils, dryness, and winter cold. Quince types are less susceptible to root asphyxiation. (See *table 1* for a range of damaging frost temperatures.)

4. A fruiting William's branch.

THE TREE

Vegetative and Floral Characteristics

BRANCHES

The pear tree displays strong apical dominance, which more or less inhibits the evolution of lateral buds. Branches develop from vegetative buds. Based on the variety's genetic characteristics and the individual tree's growing conditions, these buds will evolve into vegetative or fruiting organs. Annual shoots are primarily vegetative. Bud growth, which is related to climatic conditions, occurs over two periods: from April to the end of June; and then after an interruption during the summer, it starts back up at the end of August. In very favorable conditions, growth is continual and produces epicormic shoots, which are a sign of excessive vigor or imbalance between growth and fruiting.

	Swelling bud		Visible petals	First flower	Full bloom	Thickening fruit
	C	C_1	E_2	F_1	F_2	J
Temperature	18°F	21°F	27°F	28°F	29°F	30°F

Table 1. Range of spring frost risk. Source: Fleckinger (INRA).

5. Fruiting on crowned brindles.

Certain branches are capable of floral induction during the year they form. Depending on the variety and the buds' level of nourishment, several types of fruiting branches can be identified: fruit spurs, crowned brindles, and flower buds in a lateral position on one- or two-year-old wood *(fig. 1)*:

- fruit spurs consist of short vegetative growth (less than 2 inches or 5 cm) terminated by the formation of a flower bud;
- crowned brindles have the same physiological structure, but on a longer shoot (from 2 to 8 inches or 5 to 20 cm; *photo 5*).

These two types of organs are of particular interest since they are capable of producing large fruit.

- Flower buds form in a lateral position along one-year wood on certain varieties. For very fertile varieties such as 'Harrow Sweet ᶜᵒᵛ' and to a lesser degree 'Williams' *(photo 4)*, the setting of these lateral flowers will induce smaller fruits of lesser quality.

Two-year branches generally have a better potential for flowering and fruiting. On this type of wood, lateral vegetative buds become fruiting organs during the second year. On varieties with limited size potential ('Harrow Sweet ᶜᵒᵛ', 'Louise Bonne d'Avranches', and 'Docteur Jules Guyot)', the presence of several fruits in a lateral position on two-year wood may limit the fruits' size.

On certain varieties, such as 'Doyenné du Comice', 'Beurre Hardy', and 'Louise Bonne d'Avranches', sprouts are essentially vegetative. Depending on their length, they are called "spurs" (shorter than 2 inches or 5 cm) or "shoots" (longer than 2 inches). Depending on the variety, vegetative branches will only become fruiting organs in the following year (or years).

As the wood ages, the number of active buds (function points) decreases in most varieties. Yet certain varieties such as 'Doyenné du Comice' preserve a higher number of function points on old wood.

THE EVOLUTION OF FLOWERING BUDS

Flowering buds can be distinguished from wood buds because they are larger and rounder. Floral induction takes place from the end of May until the end of July

8

6

9

7

10

6-10. Various floral stages in a group of pear trees on the same day.

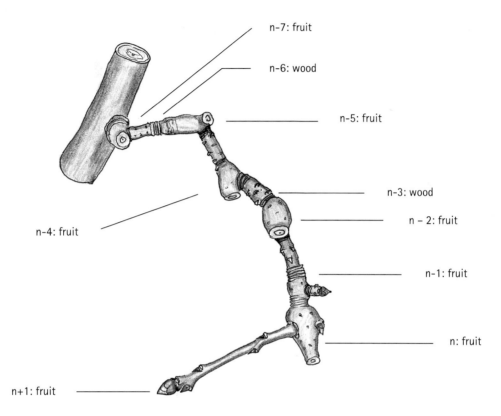

n-7: fruit

n-6: wood

n-5: fruit

n-3: wood

n − 2: fruit

n-4: fruit

n-1: fruit

n: fruit

n+1: fruit

Fig. 2. Chronology of bearing and branching on fruiting shoots.

in the year preceding the buds' effective flowering. Any stress that occurs during this period may hinder blossoming in the following year. As vegetative growth starts back up in the spring, these buds will evolve into inflorescences composed of a rosette with five to seven leaves at its base, and then a corymb consisting of five to seven flowers (photos 6–10). At the leaf axils, buds may develop and produce bourse shoots.

The production capacity for corymbs may vary from one fruit ('Doyenné du Comice', 'Passe Crassane', 'Cascade® Lombacad') to two or three ('Conférence', 'Harrow Sweet[cov]', 'Docteur Jules Guyot'). This is very much related to pollination conditions and flower density. A tree with fewer flowers will have more fruits per corymb than will a tree with more flowers. The inflorescences therefore seem to regulate fruit

set based on the quality of their nutrition. As the fruit develops, these corymbs evolve into bourses. The latter have a certain functional autonomy and play an important role in regulating vegetative growth and fruiting (fig. 2). On well-nourished inflorescences and fertile varieties, bourse shoots may form at the tip of floral buds that will blossom in the following year (crowned brindles or fruit spurs). This type of growth helps to establish the tree in its fruiting cycle and promotes better control of vigor.

On varieties that have more difficult fruiting, such as 'Doyenné du Comice', this phenomenon occurs less frequently; bourse shoots are more often shoots or spurs with no terminal blossom.

Poorly nourished corymbs will form vegetative buds in the following year that may remain latent or die off

POLLINATION AND FRUITING

Pear flowers are hermaphrodites: they contain both male organs (which provide pollen) and female organs (which receive pollen and bear fruit after fertilization). For most varieties, flowers bloom before the leaves come out. As most varieties are self-incompatible, it is necessary to provide cross-pollination with a compatible variety that flowers simultaneously. Certain varieties, such as 'Docteur Jules Guyot' and 'Conférence', are capable of producing parthenocarpic fruits when cross-pollination does not occur, but their fruits are of lower quality.

The blossoming period is short, occurring from the end of March to mid-April depending on the region. The pollen from pear flowers is not easily dispersed by the wind. During this period, because weather conditions are often quite unpredictable, the role of entomophilious insects such as bees is important. After petals fall and depending on the weather conditions during flowering, fruit set on corymbs may be relatively high, yielding up to four to six fruits.

The period from May to June is characterized by successive waves of physiological drop. This results from competition playing out in vegetative growth and then fruit thickening. Only the best-pollinated and best-nourished fruits will remain on the tree.

Development and Varietal Behaviors

For most pear varieties, the trunk dominates. 'Conférence' is one of the few varieties that is an exception, naturally adopting a bushier habit. However, there is a wide range of habits related to the wood's characteristics, particularly in terms of its flexibility and the position of inflorescences:

- Varieties such as 'Williams', 'Harrow Sweet^{cov}', 'Elliot ^{cov}', and 'Packham's Triumph' have more flexible wood and a strong capacity for flowering on one-year wood, resulting in a weeping habit.

This characteristic means that fewer interventions are necessary during the period of tree formation.

- Varieties such as 'Docteur Jules Guyot' and 'Alexandre Drouillard' also reach fruit set rapidly but have more rigid wood, creating a semi-erect habit.
- 'Doyenné du Comice', 'Beurré Hardy', and 'Conférence' have slower fruit sets and rigid wood, resulting in a more erect habit. Training these three varieties requires several major interventions.

Pear varieties may be classified into four groups according to three factors: how quickly the fruit sets, the variety's susceptibility for alternate bearing, and potential fruit size:

- a group with more difficult entrance into fruit production and higher tendency toward alternate bearing: 'Cascade®', 'Doyenné du Comice', 'Beurré Hardy';
- a group with high tendency toward alternate bearing and smaller fruits during a high production year: 'Louise Bonne d'Avranches' (a variety yielding small fruits), 'Alexandrine Douillard', 'Conférence', 'Docteur Jules Guyot';
- a group with limited size potential but no alternate bearing: 'Harrow Sweet^{cov}'; a group with low alternate bearing and small fruits: 'Williams', 'Packham's Triumph'.

Rootstocks

Pear tree growth is strongly affected by the rootstock. This choice is the essential element for a transplanted tree's success. Primarily, two species are available on the market: quince trees and pear trees. Rootstock selection is based on cultivar compatibility, susceptibility to pests (primarily fireblight, oak root fungus, and pear decline), soil texture and drainage, and weather conditions in the planting zone (the orchard site). The more common European rootstocks used in the United States are 'Winter Nelis' (*P. communis*), Pyrus betulifolia, and 'Old Home' x 'Farmingdale' crosses (*P. communis*). Less common are P. calleryana and 'Bartlett' (*P. communis*).

QUINCE TREES AS ROOTSTOCKS

The quince tree (genus Cydonia) is often used as a rootstock in Europe but rarely in the United States or Canada.

Problems with quince rootstocks include winterkill (lack of hardiness), reluctance to develop bearing surface, and low production per acre. It is estimated that 70% of pear plantings in North America are on seedling rootstocks grown from open-pollinated 'Bartlett'. Many rootstocks are from the clonal 'Old Home' x 'Farmingdale' (OH x F) series, with OH x F 97 being the most popular, but OH x F 87, 69, and 40 are also being grown. The OH x F series has the advantage of rapid fruit set, larger fruit sizes, and medium hardiness. Quince, on the other hand, tends to reduce tree size by controlling

11. Grafting ridge on a Louise Bonne d'Avranches variety on a BA 29 rootstock, age 9.

vigor, but it does not produce a well-cropped tree in the United States; moreover, in terms of grafting compatibility, quince appears to be incompatible with commercial pear varieties grown in the US. In the climatic conditions of southeastern France, the rootstock affinity between quince trees and most varieties ('Williams', 'Docteur Jules Guyot', etc.) is often unsatisfactory.

Several factors signal an incompatibility between the quince rootstock and the scion: a heavy contour ridge at the graft union *(photo 11)*, weak vegetative growth, and early reddening of the leaves. Such incompatibility will strongly hinder the tree's development of a healthy structure, and it may lead to the tree's death in extreme cases.

The quince tree's hardiness may vary in terms of the chosen rootstock. In France, the 'Provence BA 29' quince tree is the most vigorous. Rootstocks from the 'Angers' quince, the 'EMA' quince tree, 'Sydo', and 'Adams 332' are considerably less vigorous. The 'EMC 'quince tree is the least vigorous of the lot. 'Angers' and 'EMC' quince trees are less well adapted to the climate in southeastern France and are not recommended for that region.

PEAR TREES AS ROOTSTOCKS

The pear tree (*Pyrus domestica*) is the other species used for rootstocks. This group of rootstocks is more commonly called "Franc" in France. When grown from non-selected seedlings, these rootstocks lend more vigor than quince trees do, and they show good affinity with pear varieties. Their vegetative behavior is heterogeneous, and fruiting occurs later than it would with quince rootstocks. They can induce smaller fruits and should therefore be avoided.

Recent work with Pyrus has allowed two cloned selections to spread in French pear production: 'Farold® 87 Daytor' and 'Pyriam[cov]'. These two rootstocks exhibit a level of vigor somewhere between that of the "Francs" and the quince trees. They improve vegetative behavior as well as rapidness of fruit set. Size and quality of fruits are equivalent to those grown on a

12. Smooth grafting point on Pyrus types.

quince rootstock. The affinity between pear varieties is excellent, as indicated by an unblemished grafting point *(photo 12)*. These two new selections help avoid any failures resulting from the lack of affinity between quince trees and most pear varieties, offering new growing possibilities in southern France.

PRINCIPLES OF TRAINING

Planting

Recommendations are identical to those for other species:

- Planting should take place sufficiently early (November–December) to promote root growth.
- Root tips should be refreshed with cutting and, if necessary, a mud bath (pralinage).
- The grafting point should be about 4 to 6 inches (10 to 15 cm) above the ground. In regions of southern France where we've observed problems with quince tree affinity (mainly with 'Williams' and 'Docteur Jules Guyot'), the grafting point may be buried 4 to 6 inches (10 to 15 cm) below the soil surface to promote rooting of the stock.

Depending on the chosen training method, the scion may or may not need to be cut back. Growers often use a wire trellis or stakes for the axis; these must be put in place at planting. This procedure will help most of the existing shoots to recuperate and position themselves in order to optimize and more rapidly establish the tree's structure and the start of production (should the existing shoot be left). In the United States, growers typically head back the newly planted tree to an unbranched trunk about 30 inches (76 cm) high.

It is important to water the scion abundantly at planting and afterward if conditions are dry. Pyrus rootstocks have a less developed root system when the tree is young than quince rootstocks do, as well as a more delicate recovery.

Scions that are not cut back will require more consistent watering. In the springtime following planting, their root systems will be less developed and their leaf

This technique is widely used to allow the quince tree to send out new roots at the grafting point while also promoting the pear variety's roots. In this way, both types of roots nourish the tree.

In certain cases, roots produced from the scion variety will develop to the detriment of the rootstock, which will end up dying. Maintaining fresh soil (with frequent, but not excessive, irrigation) is the primary condition for succeeding with this technique.

This rooting of the variety will generally cause excessive vigor.

surface will be greater than on scions that have been cut back.

Training the Tree

On traditional support-structure forms (palmette, flag) and those without support (vase), the process of establishing and shaping the tree's structure occurs progressively. Pruning for shape is highly structured. Selection of three to four well-spaced scaffolds when they grow out starts the training system in the first year after planting. The heading back at planting and the later selection of newly produced scaffolds will avoid a delay in moving from the juvenile stage to fruit production, thereby encouraging fruit production by the third or fourth year after planting.

13. Vase shaping stimulates and concentrates vegetation.

These new training methods are based on observing vegetative growth and limiting the number of highly targeted interventions that help to quickly establish a balance between vigor and fruit set. In some cases, it is advisable to encourage precocity (early bearing), depending on growing conditions, scion and rootstock varieties, and cultural practices associated with training.

This objective can be reached with different training systems. Axis and palmette seem to be the most appropriate forms for many locations, although an open vase structure is quite successful where light interception is high, vigor is high, and soils are very productive (photo 13).

Tree Evolution in the First Four Years

AXIS TRAINING (fig. 3)
In general, during the planting year the pear tree will exhibit weak vegetative growth. This growth will become stronger in the second and third years after planting, when the rootstock's root system has taken hold. In subsequent years, vegetative growth is much greater (the phase of tree establishment). The goal for training the tree is to use this growth potential to establish the tree's structure while controlling its vigor to accelerate flower production. Training the pear tree along an axis is similar to that used for apple trees (photo 14).

At planting, the scion may or may not be cut back to remove all branching, but it is important to suppress all lateral branches located at a height of 3 feet (1 m) or less. These low branches have no future and may get in the way of future branches on the axis. Operations during the first year consist of attaching the scion to a stake or wire trellis and suppressing low branches. At the end of the first year after planting, use string or metal wire, limb spreaders, or weights on well-developed branches to bend them to the horizontal (90°) or to roughly 45–60° in a somewhat less horizontal position. Pear

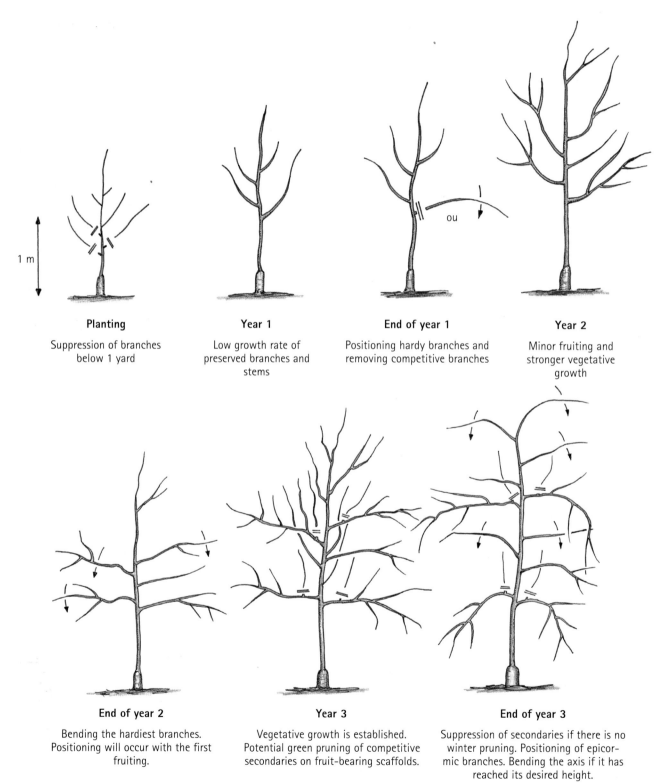

1 m

Planting

Suppression of branches
below 1 yard

Year 1

Low growth rate of
preserved branches and
stems

End of year 1

Positioning hardy branches and
removing competitive branches

ou

Year 2

Minor fruiting and
stronger vegetative
growth

End of year 2

Bending the hardiest branches.
Positioning will occur with the first
fruiting.

Year 3

Vegetative growth is established.
Potential green pruning of competitive
secondaries on fruit-bearing scaffolds.

End of year 3

Suppression of secondaries if there is no
winter pruning. Positioning of epicormic branches. Bending the axis if it has
reached its desired height.

Fig. 3. Training the transplant axis to 3rd leaf.

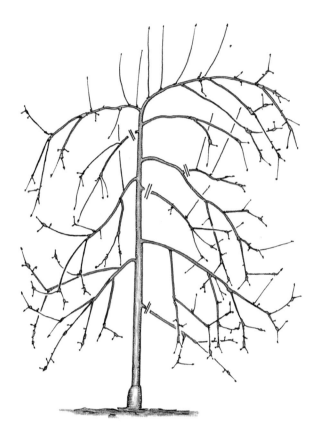

Years 4 to 6

Continue the same techniques. In the following years, shape
a light well (40 to 60 cm), based on the tree's foliage.

Years 6 to 7

Suppression of one or more scaffolds. Maintain the light well.
Possible removal of a few branches.

Fig. 3. Training the axis, adult tree.

naturally assumes a very vertical growth form without
bending, and vertical branches become strongly vegetative. If potential scaffold branches are in competition
with the axis (having an equivalent diameter to the axis)
or are fairly vertical, it is advisable to remove them.

In general, this work begins in the second or third
year when tree growth has become established. Unlike
with the apple tree, it is important to not bend branches

below the horizontal. That would prevent terminal buds
from developing and would promote reiteration along
the bowed limbs.

For most varieties, positioning the branch horizontally or slightly higher promotes a new distribution of
vegetative growth. It slows terminal bud shoots and
favors development in lateral branches. Vigor is better
controlled, and floral induction becomes more rapid and
consistent. As fruits form, branches will hang progressively downward due to the fruits' weight, continuing
vegetative growth at nodes that will form future fruiting branches *(photos 15 and 16)*. All fruiting branches
should be established according to this technique.

For certain varieties with relatively flexible wood,
such as 'Williams', 'Harrow Sweet[cov]', and 'Packham's
Triumph', the majority of branches will position themselves naturally. Only the most vigorous branches (epicormic branches, or watersprouts) will require bending
or removing (unless you plan to use them to regenerate
scaffolds that have been removed in older trees).

14. Vertical axis in 9th leaf "Madame Bonnefond" variety

15. Fruiting causes the branch to bend without stopping terminal acrotonic growth, thereby preventing branching.

16. Red mutants on a 4-year William's axis: branches.

On more rigid varieties, such as 'Docteur Jules Guyot', 'Doyenné du Comice', and 'Conférence', bending the future fruiting branches is necessary.

The vigor of the axis can be controlled either naturally with fruiting or artificially with bending at a height between 8 and 10 feet (2.5 and 3 m)—to be determined by the strength of the rootstock and the variety. Avoiding excessive nitrogen fertilization will also help to control pear tree vigor. (See Appendix C: U.S. Standard Fertilizer Equivalents for Nitrogen.)

Palmette Training *(fig. 4)*

Palmette and vase shaping differ from the axis method in that they involve cutting back the scion to a height of 24 to 28 inches (60 to 70 cm) at planting. The goal of this cut is to promote several homogeneous shoots (ideally, three to five) that will become the future scaffolds. During the first year, these shoots should be tied, maintaining the terminal bud as vertically as possible so that vegetative growth continues in the terminal section of the branch.

At the end of the first year, it is advisable to angle the two most vigorous shoots (45° maximum). Preserve the terminal bud in a close-to-vertical position to promote growth at the tips of future scaffolds. Angle the other branches according to their vigor (the more you angle them, the less vigorous they will be). Continue to apply this principle in the following years until the tree has acquired the desired volume and height (8 to 10 feet or 2.5 to 3 m). The terminal sections of the two dominant scaffolds should be placed flat on the last wire. Establishing the scaffolds can be compared to slowly opening a fan as the tree's structure grows.

At the end of the second or third year, tie a branch vertically between the two scaffolds in order to fill in the middle space. Its vigor will not compete with the already well-established scaffolds. The lateral branches that will be initiated on the scaffolds starting in the second year, and continuing into subsequent years, should be positioned according to the same principles described above for the axis method. Competing epicormic shoots must be suppressed.

Palmette training is more technical than axis training, but it permits better control of vigor for the more vigorous varieties, such as 'Doyenné du Comice'. Cutting

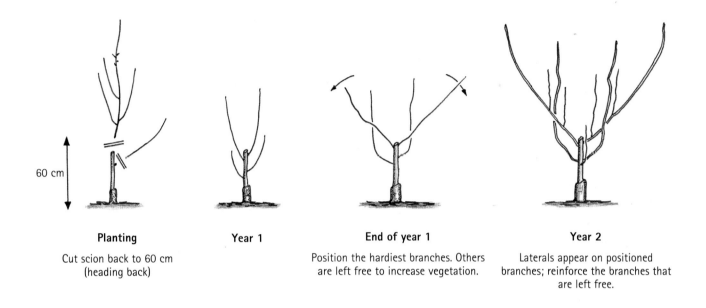

60 cm

Planting

Cut scion back to 60 cm
(heading back)

Year 1

End of year 1

Position the hardiest branches. Others
are left free to increase vegetation.

Year 2

Laterals appear on positioned
branches; reinforce the branches that
are left free.

End of year 2

Continue angling the tips of scaffolds. Eliminate
competitive epicormic shoots and bend the others
in order to establish fruit branches.

End of year 3

First fruiting as fruit branches take position.

Fig. 4. Palmette training from planting to 3rd leaf.

End of year 4

Continue selecting lateral fruit branches and suppressing competitive epicormic branches. Position branches on the central axis.

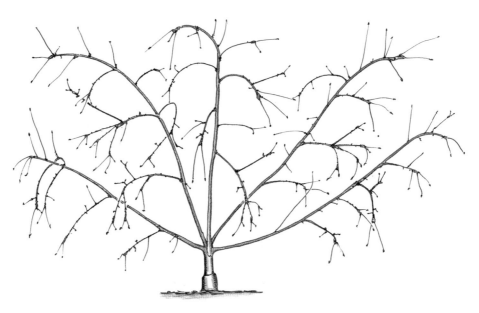

Year 5 and 6

The tree structure becomes established as the two scaffolds flatten out and the central axis has been bent.
Create a light well 40 to 60 cm wide. In coming years, suppress any excess fruit branches.

Fig. 4. Palmette training, as the tree becomes adult.

back the scion at planting slows the start of production by one year. However, this deferral of production becomes negligible by the third or fourth year.

From our observations, it seems that clippers are rarely used for structuring the tree. They should be used initially only to cut back the scion during palmette planting or to suppress low branches on the axis.

In the following year, you may use clippers to suppress unrecoverable epicormic branches that develop on the bows of the axis or fruiting branches.

Thus, the tree's structure is established with wiring, and its vigor is regulated by bending or angling branches according to palmette or similar systems. These training methods allow optimal use of vegetative growth. They are particularly well adapted for the potentially extreme hardiness of two new rootstocks, 'Farold® 87 Daytor' and 'Pyriam^{cov}'.

Light Penetration and Fruiting Branch Selection

While the tree's structure is taking shape, the high number of fruiting branches that develop (fifteen to twenty per tree) helps the space fill in quickly, regulating vigor and reducing any delays in the start of production.

But as the tree ages, it will be necessary to maintain the proper amount of vegetative growth on these future fruiting branches. This can be accomplished by systematically eliminating all epicormic branches and any branches that develop on the axis or on fruiting branches (along the first 16 to 24 inches or 40 to 60 cm). This intervention can take place starting in mid-June (via green pruning by hand) or during the winter (via suppression with clippers).

Be careful. If summer pruning occurs too early, the tree might form new shoots that will not be frost-tolerant.

During the winter, it will also be important to intervene on fruiting branches by suppressing any spindly shoots or poorly nourished fruit spurs. The latter are often located underneath the branch. When flowering is high, you may also suppress excess fruit spurs. Use an equilifruit gauge to evaluate the level of flowering and the amount of intervention needed. On pear trees, a load level of five to six fruiting points per cm^2 (1 per in^2) is a good compromise (see the discussion of the equilifruit in the "Apple Trees" chapter).

All these operations help to improve light penetration within the fruiting branches, promoting nourishment and better-quality fruiting organs. Starting in the sixth or seventh year, the trees begin to balance out: fruit production increases, and the tree's structure is established. The selected fruiting branches are well branched out and more voluminous.

At this stage, it is important to think about completely suppressing weaker fruiting branches or those that are poorly lit. The latter are often located in the lower section of the tree, as flower buds will not form where light is inadequate.

This intervention should continue in subsequent years based on the tree's growth, eliminating any competition between productive structures and ensuring optimal development of the fruiting branches.

On more balanced trees, these suppressions will affect neither vigor nor production, but will contribute to maintaining proper light and nutrition for the different function points.

Regulating Fruit Load

While the tree is developing its structure and then during adulthood, it is necessary to prevent an overabundant fruit load based on the tree's capacity for fruiting branch production (photo 17). During the

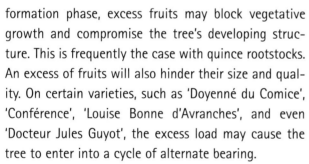

17. In need of thinning.

18. Vase: poor distribution of vegetation on the tree.

formation phase, excess fruits may block vegetative growth and compromise the tree's developing structure. This is frequently the case with quince rootstocks. An excess of fruits will also hinder their size and quality. On certain varieties, such as 'Doyenné du Comice', 'Conférence', 'Louise Bonne d'Avranches', and even 'Docteur Jules Guyot', the excess load may cause the tree to enter into a cycle of alternate bearing.

Currently, manual thinning is the only method for pear trees that is known to preserve fruit size and quality. This intervention should take place at the end of fruit drop (end of May–early June). It consists of eliminating all smaller or poorly formed fruits, and then excess fruit. The first studies done with an equilifruit show that a load index of between three and four fruits per cm^2 (1 fruit per 2 in^2) will yield larger fruits. Hand thinning is only profitable with high-value varieties or where manual labor is inexpensive.

RENEWING OLD TREES

The Primary Problems Encountered

Any imbalances found in old trees are often the result of pruning or shaping methods. In general, these trees have an excess number of structures. As the tree ages, these scaffolds and secondary branches start to compete and receive diminishing amounts of light and food.

On trees that haven't been pruned, you may find structures that have no vegetative growth at all. The number of functioning points (bourses, twigs, spurs) is generally quite high, but they are of very low quality. Production is lower in general, and the fruits are small.

If older pruning techniques (pruning to shorten) were poorly handled, this will lead to imbalances (photo 18). The systematic halting of the tree at a certain height (often with mechanical topping) based on palmette or vase training systems will stimulate more vegetative growth at the tips, causing epicormic branches to form. Concentrating growth in the upper area of the tree will create a veritable screen that blocks light penetration, causing the lower sections to wither and perish. In some cases this is difficult to avoid—for example, when pruning out fireblight-infected shoots or when renewing very old pear trees that were shaped decades ago, such as the 60- to 100-year-old orchards in California's Sacramento Delta.

Proposed Solutions

Managing light penetration is essential for reinvigorating and rebalancing vegetative growth on these types of trees. Progressively suppressing weaker or poorly lit scaffolds and secondary branches will help to reactivate growth in the lower sections of the trees.

On pruned mature trees, you can control the upper section by selecting a single epicormic branch (watersprout) per elongated scaffold *(photo 19)*. These epicormic branches will absorb and direct part of the hardiness while suppressing other watersprouts, thereby limiting the number of other branches that develop. On overly vigorous trees, green pruning will be required: this consists of suppressing all the upper epicormic branches. Each watersprout selected to direct vigor during the growing year may be cut back partially or completely during dormancy. Then the cycle starts again annually.

A similar strategy can serve during the early years of the tree's development. If allowed to grow during the tree's formative period, by the third or fourth year after planting these watersprouts will branch out and

19. Axis: wait for end of bloom and bearing to halt growth before shortening the tree to a more reasonable height.

enter into production. Only at that moment may you may think about scaling back the tree's height. Do the pruning during winter, preferably above any lateral fruiting branches with more open angles. Fruiting on these extensions will limit any untimely vegetative growth. Suppression of excess scaffolds and secondary branches may continue for several years. This progressive restructuring will promote the formation of numerous branches on the lower section of the tree, will help to restart growth, and will balance out the entire tree.

As we've mentioned, these branches can be used to help initiate fruiting branches and to suppress the vigor of older structures.

PLUM

Author	Michel RAMONGUILHEM
Collaborators	Gilles ADGIÉ
	Henri AZZOPARDI
	Pascal JARGAUD

GENERAL OVERVIEW

History and Phytogeographical Origins

The origins of the plum tree are highly unclear. It is commonly believed that wild plum trees (blackthorn trees), which were abundant in France's forests and hedges, are the ancestors of cultivated prune trees, yet there is also reason to believe that other types of trees originating in Greece and Asia Minor may have been introduced and hybridized. Among Prunus, the plum group is the most diverse, including perhaps as many as twenty species. P. domestica is most likely native to western Asia, from the Caucasus Mountains.

Plum trees are a very rustic species. Cultivation first started in northern and northeastern France, then moved toward the south and particularly the southwest within Europe. P. domestica was first introduced to North America by Spanish missionaries (West Coast) and English colonists (East Coast). Louis Pellier, a Frenchman, introduced dried plums to the United States in 1856 after he was unsuccessful in gold mining during California's gold rush. Pellier established an orchard in the Santa Clara Valley; his success gave rise to the dried plum industry. Thereafter, the "French" prune of California (an offshoot of 'Le Petite d'Agen') spread across the country once the transcontinental railroad was constructed.

'Reine-Claude', created by Pierre Belon (a botanist under the reign of François I in the early sixteenth century), was likely named for the king's first wife, Queen (French: reine) Claude. It has been renamed

1. An orchard of Prune d'Ente (Lot Valley, France).

several times and became part of the multitude of known European plums in the eighteenth century, of which there were more than 270 varieties. Starting in the nineteenth century, outdoor seedlings gave rise to highly differentiated 'Reine-Claude' varieties such as 'Reine-Claude de Vars' and 'Reine-Claude de Moissac'. In the 1950s, the INRA in Bordeaux carried out clonal selections on 'Reine-Claude Dorée', among which three INFEL clones were distributed: 'INFEL® clone 119', 'INFEL® clone 1330' *(photo 13)*, and INFEL® clone 1380'. Several other 'Reine-Claude' types still exist today: 'd'Althan', 'd'Oullins', 'Tardive de Chambourcy', 'de Moissac', 'Précoce Léon Hisse', 'Gabrielle Combes', 'd'Écully', 'Diaphane', 'Hâtive Diaphane', 'Vio-lette', 'Souffriau', 'Maffre', 'Davion', 'Mespoulet', 'de Crest', 'de Juillet'.

According to thirteenth-century literature, the Duke of Anjou first introduced 'Mirabelle'. But tests conducted on plum stones found during excavations showed that they were already being eaten during the Roman occupation. The name Mirabelle started spreading in the seventeenth century and was recognized in the eighteenth century. It is a variety that is primarily planted in eastern France, in Lorraine and Alsace *(photo 3)*. It is produced as a table fruit, for pastries, and for eau-de-vie.

Plums will always delight as a table fruit, as prunes (including baked or stuffed prunes), as jelly, as eau-de-vie. In gardens and commercial orchards, whether used as fresh fruit or for pastries, the plum tree is today one of the most highly cultivated fruit trees in the world, with orchards now spreading into Eastern Europe.

Worldwide Production of Plums and Prunes

The production of table plums in France is on the order of 38,500 tons (of which 20,000 tons come from the southwest). Production of 'Prune d'Ente' (for prunes) reaches 100,000 tons, primarily in Lot-et-Garonne and surrounding areas (photo 1).

We should note that prune production in other countries—notably in California, Chile, China, and Argentina—is much higher than in France. Italy recently established a breeding program for Japanese plum that is adapted for northern Italian growing regions and that uses California varieties as a starting point.

Today, most dried and fresh market plum production is in the western United States (California, Oregon, Washington, and Idaho), with the vast majority in California's Central Valley (Sacramento and San Joaquin valleys, combined). In these areas, the Mediterranean climate discourages disease and rain cracking, and chilling is adequate (800 to 100 hours at or below 45°F or 7°C). The Japanese plum, Prunus salicina (actually from China, introduced to Japan only about 200 years ago), was introduced in the 1880s and accounts for most of the fresh market production worldwide. Japanese plums bloom later than European plums and thus may be better choices where spring frosts occur. (See Appendix B: Freeze/Frost Damage in Prunus Species.)

Meanwhile, P. domestica is most often produced for the dried fruit market, particularly in France and California, where it is called "prune" and "dried plum" interchangeably. The word "prune" was adopted from the French word for "plum" (pruneau). It applies to certain plums that are less juicy and firmer than fresh market plums (although Italian and French prunes are sold fresh), have high sugar content at maturity, and dry well without fermentation due to the sugar content.

VARIETAL RANGE

A considerable number of varieties among the plum species are produced in France and California. Two regions in France stand out today for their varietal assortment: Lorraine, with 'Mirabelle' and 'Quetsche';

2. T.C. Sun.

3. Mirabelle de Nancy.

and the southwest, with 'Reine-Claude', Japanese-American varieties, and 'Prune d'Ente'. (The latter is also the major dried plum produced in California, where it is known as 'd'Agen', 'French', or 'Improved French'). In California, the French prune is produced throughout the Central Valley. Japanese plums and their hybrids (*P. salicina* x *P. domestica* and plum–apricot hybrids) are largely produced in the San Joaquin Valley (southern Central Valley). As with European plums, many flesh and skin colors occur in Japanese plum cultivars.

The European plum varieties come from the species *Prunus instititia* and *Prunus domestica*. They have a wide range histories and situations (see Appendix A: *Prunus* Botany). Many varieties have completely disappeared or have become extremely exclusive. In terms of table plums, these include (for France): 'Prune de Briançon', 'Saint-Pierre', 'Prune-Pêche', 'Précoce de Tours', 'Mirabelle Précoce', 'Monsieur', 'Royale de Tours', 'Bleue de Belgique', 'Kirke', 'Diaprée Rouge', 'Impériale de Milan Musquée', and 'Goutte d'Or de Coë'.

Burbank developed the modern California "Japanese"–style plum by intercrossing Chinese plums (*P. salicina* and *P. simonii*) with native plums of various origins (*P. americana*, *P. munsoniana*) and plums of Eurasian origin (*P. cerasifera*). Burbank's cultivars became the foundation for the Japanese-type plums produced in the U.S. Ongoing breeding programs, particularly those of the U.S. Department of Agriculture, have resulted in high-quality plum cultivars that are better adapted to various locations. Interspecific hybrids of plum and apricot were initially produced with a 50–50% contribution from each species through Burbank's pioneering work, but most recent breeding programs have concentrated on hybrids with more or less of each species (called "pluots" and "apriums"). Pluots predominantly are the result of work by several California breeders—most notably, by Floyd Zaiger and his family of Zaiger Genetics in Modesto ('Black Cat', 'Dapple Dandy', 'Flavor Fall', 'Flavor Giant', 'Flavor

Queen', 'Flavor Supreme', 'Flavor Grenade', 'Flavorich', 'Flavorosa', 'Flavorella'). Elsewhere in North America, both *P. domestica* and *P. salicina* are grown (in Oregon, Washington, Michigan, and Idaho in the United States; in Ontario and British Columbia in Canada). Cultivation of these in California is not as widespread due to several factors: winter temperatures severe enough to cause cold injury to shoots, fruiting spurs, trunks, and roots; spring frost potential during bloom (especially for Japanese plums); rain-cracking incidence; and humid conditions during bloom and fruiting that create high disease potential. In areas where these conditions prevail, it is best to locate plantings near large bodies of water (like the Great Lakes) where there is a moderating climatic effect, or on sunny slopes that allow good air drainage.

California's predominant commercial varieties of fresh market plums (Japanese type) constitute approximately 70% of the total U.S. plum production. Approximately 250 varieties of plums are produced in California for the fresh market on 38,000 acres; about

ten varieties make up over 70% of the volume shipped domestically and for export. New varieties are planted to existing acreage annually at the rate of 6–8% to satisfy changing consumer tastes, thus, 'niche' varieties may be chosen for their maturity window, better quality, or improved attributes.

Attributes that have driven recent varietal choices include: better flavor, larger sizing potential (ability to increase size with more thinning), earlier and later harvest, better or more consistent yield, and skin or flesh color "appeal." Almost 70% of both old and new plum varieties grown in California have been bred by private breeders, with most of the germplasm resulting from hybridization of *P. salicina*, the Japanese plum with various diploid plum species, not the hexaploid European plum, *P. domestica*.

'Red Beauty' (or 'Red Beaut') and 'Black Beauty' ('Black Beaut') are two of the earliest varieties, with

'Santa Rosa' (not widely grown commercially today) maturing soon after. 'Blackamber', 'Queen Rosa', 'La Roda', and 'El Dorado' follow 'Santa Rosa'. Mid-season varieties include 'Friar', 'Duarte', and 'Simka'. Late varieties are 'Kelsey', 'Casselman', and 'Angeleno'. The varieties of highest volume, as reported by the 2010 California Tree Fruit Agreement (CTFA) are 'Blackamber', 'Friar', 'Fortune' and 'Angeleno'.

While 'Santa Rosa' plum and 'French' prune are self-fertile, requiring only bees (but not other plum varieties) for fruit set, many Japanese-type plums are self-sterile or only partially self-fertile. 'Royal Diamond' is self-sterile, while 'Autumn Giant' is partially fertile. 'Black Amber', 'Black Star', 'Golden Japan', 'Royal Diamond', 'Songold', and 'T.C. Sun' (photo 2) are compatible with 'Autumn Giant'. 'Autumn Giant', 'Black Star', 'Golden Japan', 'Larry Ann', 'Songold', and 'T.C. Sun' are compatible with 'Royal Diamond'. For home orchards, it is often possible to satisfy pollination requirements by planting multiple-grafted trees, with up to four varieties on a single trunk. Most varieties grown in the United States are self-fertile. Pluots, however, generally require pollenizers, which can be either plum or apricot.

The following varieties constitute the majority of the fresh plum market in the United States:

- 'Red Beauty' ('Red Beaut')—when fully ripe, has dark red-purple skin and is slightly soft to the touch; taste is sweet and very juicy with a slightly tart skin.
- 'Black Beauty'—resembles 'Red Beauty' in shape and size; however, the skin is a darker, purplish black.
- 'Santa Rosa'—an older variety that Burbank originated, commonly produced in California's coastal Santa Clara Valley before heavy urbanization; nowadays 'Santa Rosa' is mostly a "backyard" variety, good for both eating and making preserves due to its smaller size, softer flesh, and skin with a tangy, juicy, flavorful taste; reddish-

purple skin and amber flesh with a slight-to-pronounced red color.
- 'Queen Rosa'—very similar to 'Santa Rosa' on the outside except for its greenish-yellow top, near the stem; the mild and very juicy amber flesh becomes tangy when cooked.
- 'Cassleman'—the best-tasting late-season plum; skin color is bright red; flesh is a deep amber color, giving the plum a very sweet, meaty taste.
- 'Black Amber'—a super-large, beautiful black plum primarily used for puddings, pies, and sauces.
- 'Angeleno'—a huge purple plum with a very sweet, meaty, yellow flesh; a very versatile plum that is excellent for pies, jams, and sauces; also delicious when eaten fresh.
- 'Simka'—a very large, heart-shaped, purple plum with a firm, pleasantly sweet, golden flesh.
- 'Laroda'—a dark purple plum similar to 'Santa Rosa', but larger and harvested approximately five to six weeks later; one of the best fresh plums with an excellent, juicy flavor.
- 'El Dorado'—bright red to reddish skin with purple highlights; amber flesh with a mellow, sweet flavor; stays firm during cooking, making it a great plum for canning.
- 'Friar'—has an either a deep blue or purplish-black skin color with amber flesh; provides a sweet taste when ripe.
- 'Kelsey'—a green-skinned plum that yellows at maturity; has a pointed stylar end with a heart-like shape; the large, firm, aromatic plum offers a rich flavor when ripe.
- 'Wickson'—similar in appearance to 'Kelsey' but lacking the pointed stylar end; a Luther Burbank-bred plum.

Growing prunes for fresh market. Some prunes are also grown for fresh market (not dried) in California. Their cultivation and handling are different than that for drying.

Improved 'French' and 'Moyer' are the only two varieties of prunes that are packed and shipped fresh in large quantities in California (4,000–5,000 tons for 'French' and half that for 'Moyer', annually). Minor production of 'Sugar Prune' and '707 Prune' varieties accounts for the balance of approximately 3% of the total fresh market plum crop grown in California.

In general, 'French' is preferred for its superior sugar content, but it is also significantly smaller than 'Moyer'. 'French' sets heavily and must be thinned heavily as well via pruning, for best fresh market size. 'Moyer' comes into production best as trees mature, setting very lightly when trees are young. Thus, 'Moyer' should be minimally pruned to encourage precocity, avoiding dormant-season heading cuts especially, and concentrating on thinning cuts for better light penetration. Unlike other prunes, 'Moyer' prunes are sometimes hand-thinned to break up clustered fruit, as any other hand thinning is too costly.

U.S. standards for fresh market prune-plums require the fruit surface to be at least 50% mottled red and no more than the rest of the surface light green. 'Moyer' prunes must average a minimum of 16% soluble solids (sugars); 'French' and all other varieties must average 19% sugars for fresh market. Most prunes grown for the fresh market are exported to Asian markets, where very high sugars are preferred in stone fruits; thus, these prunes are called "sugar plums."

THE FRUIT

The plum is a drupe with an edible, fleshy pericarp. It can have a round or elongated shape. Its delicate skin is smooth and waxy, offering an extraordinary range of colors and hues: yellow, green, golden, purplish-blue, blue, reddish-purple, pinkish, and stained.

THE TREE AND ITS TRAINING

Training techniques for plum trees have changed considerably in France lately. Until recently, most texts recommended rather severe pruning, with consecutive cuts made early in the season. These recommendations often lacked any well-established physiological or agronomical basis and generally led to serious imbalances that favored irregular vegetative growth and slowed the start of fruiting. Today, this practice has come into question because trees were becoming too vigorous, and eventually uncontrollable, not only for novice growers but also for professionals! Recent developments with other species (particularly with the apple tree) have helped to alter the pruning techniques used on plum species, which is one of the most vigorous.

The shape and profile of a tree are not definitively important. Training the fruiting branch is all that needs to be considered, as it is the one site for intervention to regulate fruiting. The training of plum trees recently has focused on a more natural branching, more akin to the species' natural habits.

The art of training lies in finding a balance between growth and production.

In the United States, some commercial growers are modifying the traditional methods for hand pruning on the most common form used for dried plum—the vase, or open center, shape. Instead, these commercial growers are now using mechanical pruning (topping, hedging, and making various angled cuts in the middle for light penetration).

The Influence of the Rootstock

In France, for Japanese-American varieties, the primary rootstocks are the 'Myrobolan B INFEL® 18' clone (virus-resistant) and the 'Myrobolan' seedling (partially infected). These materials display adequate behavior in terms of low root asphyxiation and low susceptibility to ferric chlorosis. For European varieties, the most common rootstocks are 'Myrobolan'. They are grafted on 'Mariana GF 8-1 clone INFEL® 8', which shows good resistance to root asphyxiation. These rootstocks require soils with active limestone rates below 10%.

With the evolution of the orchard toward a smaller tree profile, rootstocks with low to average vigor are recommended today—for example, 'Jaspi® Fereley' clone INFEL® 2038 and 'Wangenheim Quetsche'.

The main rootstock clones for domestic plum trees are as follows:
- extremely high vigor: 'Mariana GF 8-1'; 'Myrobolan B'; 'Myran® Yumir'; 'Myrocal® Fercino';
- average vigor: GF 43; 'Ishtara® Ferciana'; 'Jaspi® Fereley'; pentaploid Marian hybrids P 10-2 and P 8-13; 'Brompton';
- less vigor: 'Pixy';
- very low vigor: 'Plumina® Ferlenain' (P2038).

The less vigorous trees allow manual harvesting for table fruit varieties, with no need for a ladder. Moreover, certain rootstock selections improve varietal productivity (measured as yield efficiency, kilo produced per cm^2, or pound per in^2,) of the trunk's cross-section): this is the case with 'Ishtara®' and pentaploid 'Mariana' hybrids.

In California, in terms of cultivation of prunes, 'French' prune is produced primarily on four rootstocks: 'Myrobalan' seedling, 'Myrobalan 29C' (P. cerasifera; propagated by hardwood cuttings), 'Marianna 2624' (P. cerasifera x P. munsoniana; hardwood cuttings), and, less frequently, peach seedling (P. persica L. 'Lovell' and 'Nemaguard').

Prune is commonly grown on flood-irrigated, fine-textured, poorly drained soils and often on bacterial canker (Pseudomonas spp.) replant sites in California, although much acreage is also no-till turf and either micro-sprinkler or drip irrigated. The rootstocks used for prune in California are those best adapted to these conditions, in that they tolerate heavy soils with poor drainage (peach rootstock, however, does not). These rootstocks vary in terms of several factors: size of the tree that is produced, disease resistance, nutrient uptake, and cropping.

The following list describes characteristics of rootstocks used for plum and prune:
- 'Nemaguard'—peach rootstock; produces a vigorous, larger tree; resistant to root-knot nematode and excellent for well-drained soils.
- 'Lovell'—peach rootstock; more tolerant of wet soils and more cold-hardy than 'Nemaguard'; susceptible to nematodes in sandy soils.
- 'Marianna 2624'—plum rootstock; the shallow root system produces a smaller tree; much more tolerant of wet soils than 'Lovell' or 'Nemaguard'; resistant to oak-root fungus and root-knot nematodes.
- 'Myrobalan 29C'—plum rootstock; the shallow but vigorous root system produces a tree intermediate in size between those grown on 'Marianna' and peach; tolerates wet soils and is immune to root-knot nematodes with some resistance to oak-root fungus.
- 'St. Julien A'—plum rootstock; a semi-dwarfing rootstock good for cold areas with fluctuating spring temperatures due to inconsistent spring weather conditions; preferred over 'Citation' in north coastal mountains of California and in Oregon.

Proposed Techniques for Training Prune and Plum

TRAINING SYSTEMS USED IN THE UNITED STATES
Throughout the United States, prune and plum trees are generally trained as open center or vase shape, maintaining several main scaffolds and secondary laterals. Plum trees grow fairly vigorously until dormancy, particularly under mild conditions, and must be pruned annually to regulate crop load and to encourage light penetration

into the canopy. Most pruning takes place in the dormant season, although some may occur in summer.

Because plums tend to grow fairly upright with dense branching, it is advisable to choose no more than four or five scaffolds during tree establishment for main scaffolds. The resulting shape will be a roughly conical form with a "light well" in the center. Vertical V and modified central leader training systems may also be used; however, summer pruning in all systems must keep the canopy relatively open for light penetration, which will increase fruit production. Flower buds form on lateral twigs and spurs that are at least two years old, as well as on one-year-old shoots to a lesser degree. Winter pruning should remove 60 to 80% of the spurs, primarily those that are older, to regulate crop load. The modified central leader system, which promotes a main trunk with whorls of scaffolds spaced well apart, allows good light penetration, as do the vase and vertical V systems.

Planting distances depend, in part, on the need for moving equipment through the orchard and also on the growth habit imposed through the chosen training system. Prunes are mechanically thinned and harvested by "trunk shakers." This management practice and the trees' vase shape call for planting distances greater than those used for fresh market plums, which are hand-thinned and hand-harvested.

Thus, the training of dried and fresh plum trees differs largely according to management practices (mechanical or hand labor) and considerations for light penetration. The latter are more important for "coloring" the mature plum in fresh market production. Also, because fruit size is so important, fresh market prune trees are pruned significantly more than those whose fruits are used for drying.

General principles of pruning are similar for both fresh market "domestic" or European plum and Japanese plums (and pluots), for purposes of reducing flower number and crop load. Hand thinning of fruits in either dried or fresh market plums is prohibitively expensive. Thus, the following pruning practices will improve fruit size, color, and sugar content:

- opening the center of the tree to allow light penetration for improved fruit coloration;
- reducing tree height to permit easier harvest;
- removing long "whips" (or excessively vigorous branches);
- heading back spur-bearing laterals to preferentially improve their vigor.

It is important not to remove too much "wood" from the center of the trees, lest the remaining limbs become sunburned. Also, because fruits from the trees' interior are generally of poorer color and quality, it is important to eliminate them by removing fruiting wood (short laterals with and without spurs) from the trees' center. Removing some of the secondary and tertiary laterals from the center will also keep the light well open.

Tree height for fresh market plums and prunes is usually limited to 12 to 13 feet (4 m), allowing for hand harvest with conventional 10- to 11-foot (3 m) ladders that are necessary to reach the highest-quality fruits at the treetops. Maintaining that tree height in dried plum culture, as in fresh market plums, is traditionally accomplished by hand, but dried plum growers who need to save on high labor costs increasingly are employing mechanical hedging and topping. However, this approach has the unwanted side effect of encouraging excessive shoot growth at the top of the tree, which can increase shading problems. Summer pruning generally only involves the removal of vigorous interior and exterior shoots that are not needed for fruit production in subsequent years. It is advisable to remove these suckers or water sprouts entirely, leaving no "stubs," or to head them back to 4 to 8 inches (10 to 20 cm) in length where needed to prevent sunburn.

The open center/vase-shaped tree is most commonly used for both Japanese and European plum varieties, including all prunes. The resulting tree is the largest of the different forms used for plums; without appropriate pruning, heavy top growth causes over-shading of lower limbs and the tree center. Trees are planted 16 to 20 feet (5 to 6 m) apart for European plums, 10 to 20 feet (3 to 6 m) for Japanese plums. Row spacing is 18 to 20 feet (5.5 to 6 m) apart for prunes, allowing for typical orchard equipment, especially trunk shakers, as these trees are generally mechanically thinned and harvested. Japanese plums may be planted in rows similarly spaced, or somewhat closer together.

The vase shape is established in the following sequence from planting, when trees are headed back to a single leader that is 2 to 3 feet (approximately 1 m) tall, removing all side branches. In the first year, select three to five limbs distributed evenly around trunk. Leave small branches on these limbs for early fruiting and sunburn protection. Head limbs back to half their length (24 to 30 inches or 61 to 76 cm). These will become the primary, or main, scaffolds. In the second year, select one or two lateral limbs on each primary. Head these back to half their length (24 to 30 inches or 61 to 76 cm). Remove other limbs.

The modified central leader system makes a smaller tree, about half the size of a vase type. This form is useful for Japanese plums and pluots when a smaller tree is desired. After the first year of growth without heading back, select three to five lateral branches, with the lowest being about 12 to 15 inches (30 to 38 cm) above the ground, spaced evenly around tree 2 to 3 feet (approximately 1 m) apart vertically. Head the leader to its desired final height, and head back any laterals that may compete with the leader (those growing very vigorously and of large caliper, or diameter). In following years, develop another series of laterals every 2 to 3 feet higher up on the central leader. It will likely be necessary to physically spread the laterals when they are 5 to 6 feet (1.5 to 2 m) long in order to form a proper angle (about 45°) with the trunk.

The vertical V (or Y) system produces a small tree that is mostly used for peaches and nectarines, but sometimes for plums as well. Start by heading back to 2 to 3 feet (roughly 1 m) at planting. With this system, trees may be spaced 7 to 10 feet (2 to 3 m) apart within the row and 15 to 17 feet (4.5 to 5 m) between rows, depending on the need for moving heavy equipment. Lateral branches are spaced along each of the two scaffolds.

Young trees in any of the training systems should always be "long pruned" for early production. Summer pruning and light heading on young trees will encourage spur development on exterior fruiting shoots. Bending will reduce vigor and promote flower bud production, but care should be taken to avoid bending branches so flat as to cause sunburn *(photo 8)*.

TRAINING SYSTEMS USED IN FRANCE

We propose two tree configurations. Although visually distinct in shape (a single axis in one case and several in the other), the two training methods discussed here, solaxe and multi-axis, can be developed and handled in the same way on any of the axes *(photos 4, 5, 6)*.

4. Solaxe in bloom.

5. Young solaxe orchard taking shape.

6. A path along multi-axis Vase trees.

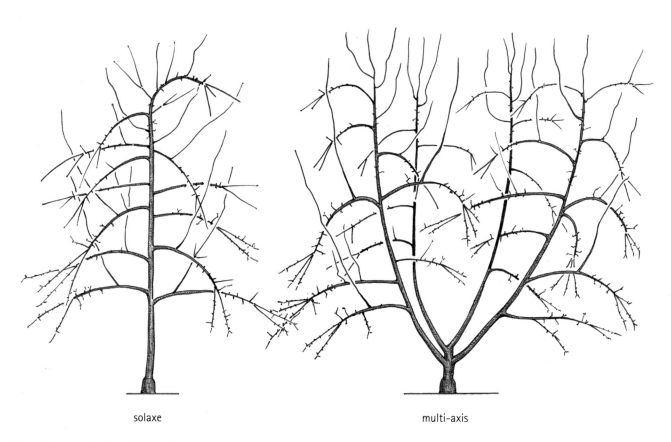

solaxe

multi-axis

Fig. 1. Solaxe and multi-axis (Vase).

Solaxe. Fruiting branches are trained around a single axis (the trunk). Balance and continuity come from respecting the branching and fruiting modes for each variety, as this species is polymorphous *(fig. 1).*

Multi-axis. The multi-axis is a replacement for the vase. The trunk is shorter (20 to 24 inches or 50 to 60 cm) and splits into five or six axes that will support the future fruiting branches. Each of these axes is trained according to the solaxe method *(fig. 1).*

These trunk divisions (axes) should remain as erect as possible so that they won't be "sunburned," suffering burns on the bark or the wood itself. In plum trees, this is the primary reason for a tree's structures partially dying off.

CHARACTERISTICS OF THE CONCEPT

Fruiting branches will establish themselves freely and progressively around the trunk. Left alone, they will produce fruit for short periods and naturally find their balance. When fruit production at the top of the tree stops its growth, the tree will be uniformly vigorous. Since production occurs in a "centrifugal" fashion (heading away from the center), the tree is forced to open up at the center. Thus, trees trained according to the Solaxe and modified central leader styles are cylindrical, with a central light well.

Fruiting zones evolve as short production cycles are renewed through the removal of poorly placed fruiting organs (within the tree's center or under branches). Similar to practices for other species (especially the apple, but also the cherry), we speak of extinction. For plum trees, extinction does not mean suppressing just buds, but entire fruiting spurs. It could be considered a "mini-thinning." Extinction helps regulate the load density and redistribute vigor along the fruiting branches throughout the tree. If there is too much extinction, however, unwanted vigor may increase.

7. A Prune d'Ente fruit branch.

The Tree's Structures

There is a range of terminology to describe the types of branches on a fruit tree. Primary sap flow results from apical activities—those in the terminal bud on each shoot (A3). In lower sections of the tree, the fruiting branches (A2) and trunk (A1) serve merely as connectors and will only evolve in their growth when there is intense A3 activity. Keeping in mind the centrifugal force governing sap distribution, let's outline the tree's structures and their names:

- A1: the trunk;
- A2: fruiting branches (lateral shoots);
- A3: spurs;
- AC: epicormic branches, also known as water sprouts or suckers. The French abbreviation AC comes from the expression aspiration concurrentielle, which refers to competitive sap flow because water sprouts are present only when there is an inherent imbalance in A3 aspiration (or sap flow).

In short, the tree develops in a hierarchical fashion: A1–A2–A3. Once there is an established physiological balance, acrotony takes over and A3 becomes the focus for the rest of the tree's life.

The Trunk

The trunk is the tree's primary structure. Good vegetative growth in the first two years will be necessary for obtaining the hardiness that the trunk requires. It should be as cylindrical as possible.

With multi-axis and vase training, the trunk constitutes a short section 20 to 24 inches (50 to 60 cm) above the ground that will yield four to six subdivisions (the future axes).

Fruiting Branches

Distributed along the Solaxe trunk or the multi-axis subdivisions, fruiting branches are the ones that bear fruits, which grow directly on the branch for the first

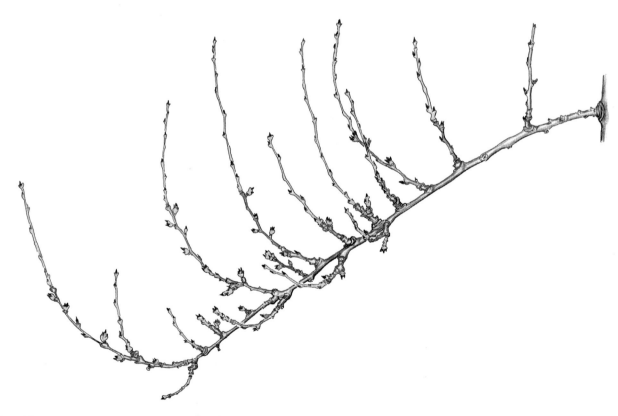

Fig. 2. The fruit branch, regardless of its training (solaxe or multi-axis).

few years. Later on, these branches will be the support for all shorter fruiting spurs *(fig. 2)*. They remain the site where fruiting ebbs and flows throughout the tree's life, as growth occurs and short branches are renewed.

There is no ideal theoretical number of fruiting branches to maintain on a plum tree. Each variety has its own mode of branching *(photo 7)*.

Short Branches

Spurs. These bear the most fruit. They are branches shorter than 1 inch (3 cm), with floral buds in lateral positions and a vegetative bud at the tip *(fig. 3)*.

Fruiting shoots. These are branches with several vegetative and floral buds. Floral buds develop at the base of the fruiting shoot, and vegetative buds at the tips *(fig. 3)*. Keep in mind that longer fruiting shoots (longer than 12 inches or 30 cm) will develop at the ends of fruiting branches and will participate in the latter's evolution, creating bifurcations.

Vegetative shoots. These branches bear only vegetative buds *(fig. 3)*.

Epicormic Branches
(Suckers or Water Sprouts)

These are vertical branches with a thick diameter and vigorous growth *(fig. 4)*, usually found near the base of a fruiting branch. They tend to cause an imbalance in tree growth. By keeping them, you will be creating a "tree within the tree"!

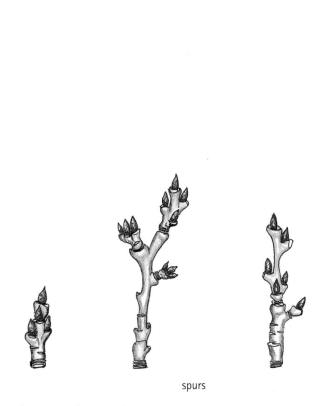

spurs

spur   vegetative shoot

Fig. 3. Spurs and other branches

Planting the Tree

Recommended planting distances for solaxe and multi-axis trees are determined by their ultimate profile (mature size and shape).

For solaxe, modified central leader, and vertical V:

- 16 feet (5 m) between rows and 7 feet (2 m) within each row for European varieties ('Reine-Claude', 'Quetsche', 'Mirabelle').
- 15 feet (4.5 m) and 5 feet (1.5 m) for Japanese-American varieties ('T.C. Sun', 'Golden Japan', 'Fortune', and others, including pluots).

For multi-axis or vase:

- 16 to 18 feet (5 to 5.5 m) between rows and 13 to 15 feet (4 to 4.5 m) within each row for European varieties ('Reine-Claude', 'Quetsche', 'Mirabelle').

Note that multi-axis is not recommended for Japanese-American varieties because they are susceptible to apricot leaf roll. To better handle any incidence of this, when trees have started dying off it is preferable to grow smaller trees in greater number.

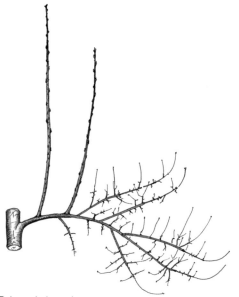

Fig. 4. Epicormic branches.

PRECAUTIONS AT PLANTING

For solaxe training, overly hardy and/or overly erect secondary branches should be suppressed.

For multi-axis training, the scion should be cut back to a height of 20 inches (50 cm) above the ground. This will cause several axes to form *(fig. 1)*.

Particular cases: in order to obtain sufficient axes, certain varieties such as 'Reine-Claude de Bavay' often require additional cutting at the end of the second year.

For all of these cases, the grafting point should be located 8 inches (20 cm) above the ground.

PUTTING TRAINING INTO PRACTICE

Chronology of Interventions

YEAR 1

A1: With both solaxe and multi-axis systems, the tree will establish its structure rapidly, either through your cutting back of the axis once (multi-axis) or not cutting back at all (solaxe) *(fig. 5A)*.

YEARS 2 AND 3

A2: It will be important to bend branches below the horizontal *(fig. 5)* since this will help to start fruiting and to slow branch elongation. The angle will help to progressively ramify the branch's terminal zone. This acrotony will promote a centrifugal evolution of fruiting around the tree *(fig. 5B)*.

Bending should occur on branches that have already attained sufficient length (about 3 feet or 1 m). Depending on when the branches reach that length, you can create the angle during the winter after vegetative shoots grow, or during the summer of the second year, or during the winter after two years of growth. The bending may cause water sprouts to occur near the branch's insertion point on the trunk.

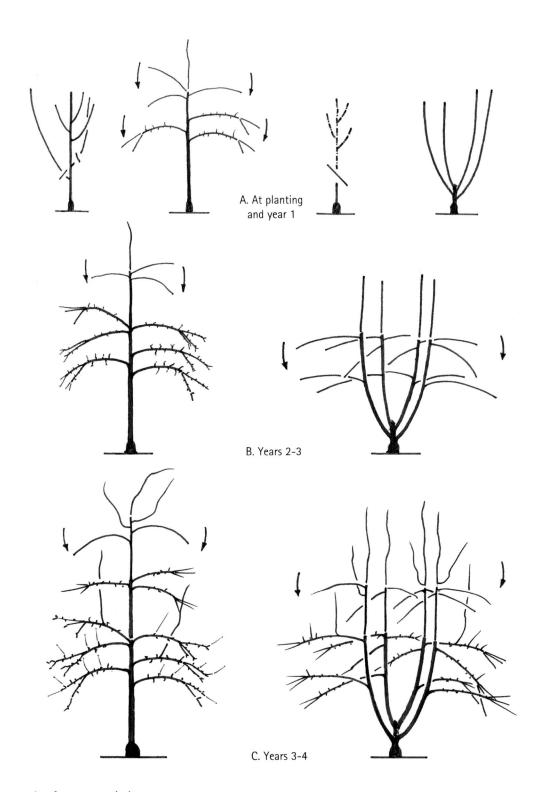

A. At planting
and year 1

B. Years 2-3

C. Years 3-4

Fig. 5. The tree takes form progressively.

8. Optimized bending.

9. Bifurcations (branching).

Systematic suppression of these water sprouts is an absolute necessity. It is advisable to perform this operation in the summer to limit their tendency to sprout back up in the same spot. On angled branches, spurs will appear in greater number and will have a higher tendency to bear fruit.

As these structures appear on the tree and continue to grow (from the first year to the end of the third), no shortening (tipping) should be done. Any current or anticipated bifurcations should be left intact (photo 9). This will be proof of the tree's natural distribution of vigor (on the way to a balanced state) and will be the sites of the future fruiting branches (A1).

As we've mentioned, there is no specific number of fruiting branches to aim for. As the tree takes shape, you should preserve all the branches. Thereafter, you can progressively suppress certain branches for any of the following reasons: lack of light, excessive hardiness, or poor placement (too low, overlapping, etc.).

With the two fruiting structures in place—spurs and lateral shoots—production is guaranteed since they bear fruit simultaneously (photo 10). Yet this guarantee depends on climatic conditions (cold, humidity) during the previous year, at floral induction, as well as during the current year.

You may need to suppress a few short branches that are poorly lit or that develop in lower positions on the fruiting branch. Consider this suppression as an anticipated cleaning of a zone that will eventually yield less vigorous or less fertile structures.

A3: Keep all short branches at first, since these will ensure well-distributed vegetative growth.

AC: Systematically remove epicormic branches (water sprouts) at the beginning of summer (end of June–early July) to avoid competition, especially as the tree continues to take shape.

AFTER YEAR 3

The tree's growth will be progressive for A2 and A3 (and highly so in years 2 and 3), filling in a volume that will become nearly definitive around the eighth year (fig. 5C). For the whole period of increasing volume,

10. Starting in the third year, fruit will colonize the top of the axis (Reine-Claude).

11. Reine-Claude de Moissac.

you should leave branch bifurcations intact in order to promote the best possible distribution of vigor.

For A2, a great many short branches will appear; therefore, extinction will be necessary. This means removing the weaker fruiting shoots, which are often "hanging," as well as any surplus spurs. Any production occurring in a badly located spot or in excess will throw off the tree's balance and yield smaller fruit. Keep the best-placed branches in order to reinforce the tree's architecture.

The Importance of Light Penetration

It is important to create a light well within the tree, proportional to its volume, so that sunlight can penetrate. You can accomplish this by clearing the bases of fruiting branches and encouraging a centrifugal development.

In fact, the light well helps to suppress any shoots in the first 16 to 20 inches (40 to 50 cm) of fruiting spurs, measured from their point of insertion on the trunk.

Bowing (bending or spreading) the fruiting branches (A2) will help in creating the light well, will facilitate the penetration of light to the center, and will optimize photosynthesis within the canopy. Spurs will remain active all along each branch. It is important to clear the bifurcation joints on A2 branches, up to about 4 inches (10 cm), practicing extinction on buds and short branches (photo 9). The goal is to allow light to penetrate both vertically and horizontally into the canopy.

Varietal Behaviors

VARIETIES THAT PRODUCE REGULARLY
These include most of the Japanese varieties: 'Allo', 'Obilnaya', Golden Japan', 'Blackamber', 'Friar', 'T.C. Sun' (photo 12), and blue plums in the domestica species such as 'Président', 'Stanley', and 'Prune d'Agen'.

Their production levels may quickly become excessive. In these conditions, later varieties like 'T.C. Sun', 'Président', or 'Prune d'Agen' may break along their axes or at the axis joints (along branches or at the bases

12. Variety T. C. Sun.

of branches) on multi-axis, vase, and vertical V trees. Certain fruiting branches may even break off the trunk under the weight of their own fruit.

With these varieties, you will need to handle all winter thinning by pruning, suppressing spurs and fruiting laterals, and doing any subsequent fruit thinning earlier in the tree's life and more intensively.

VARIETIES THAT NEED HELP

The best example here, for France, is 'Reine-Claude de Bavay', but this is also the case for 'Reine-Claude de Moissac' (or 'Gauthier') *(photo 11)* and 'Reine-Claude d'Althan'. Their fruit set is generally heavy, but they have a natural tendency to self-thin via late physiological drop of "set" fruit ("June drop"), which prevents them from becoming overloaded. Winter interventions will have to be regular but moderate; suppressing spurs and fruiting laterals will not be necessary, and thinning will rarely be needed.

UNPREDICTABLE VARIETIES

The main variety in this group is the famous 'Reine-Claude Dorée', as well as its preferred pollinator, 'Royale de Montauban'.

Very often, and despite abundant flowering, 'Reine-Claude Dorée' may end up with very few fruits. People often blame bad weather during flowering, a lack of bee activity, poor affinity with pollinating varieties, and so on. Yet sometimes the tree may be overly generous, and with practically no physiological drop the excessive load might hurt its quality. In this case, early and intense hand thinning can save the harvest.

To complicate things even more, an excessive fruit load sometimes causes a drop in flowering in the following year (alternate bearing), which will heighten the impression of the tree's unpredictability.

To address these issues, be sure to have the best possible situations in place for pollination, planting near the 'Royale' pollinator or even 'Stanley' or 'Prune d'Ente'.

Bees are indispensable, since 'Reine-Claude' is self-sterile (totally incapable of self-pollinating). If production is better ensured in this way, it is advisable to begin winter interventions after the first large harvests.

'Mirabelle' presents another case. Its unpredictability primarily arises from its tendency toward alternate bearing. When there is abundant flowering, production will generally follow. In this case, during a year of strong flowering, you will need to thin fruiting branches and/or short, hanging branches.

These few examples demonstrate how important it is to find a proper balance between growth and fruiting. Each variety, each orchard, and even each tree may have its own rhythms for finding balance. Professional arboriculturists and novices alike have to practice their skills of observing tree behavior and its reactions to interventions, rather than merely applying strict rules defined ahead of time.

THE RECOMMENDED STRATEGY

Cutting Back, Extinction, Thinning, Epicormic Pruning

This four-part harmony should become the directing motif or the beat to follow in terms of making interventions to guide the adult tree's natural evolution after it has begun producing. Let's begin with some definitions:
- cutting back: overall suppression of the structure.
- extinction: definitive removal of spurs or fruiting shoots.
- thinning: partial or total suppression of flowers or fruits.
- epicormic pruning: removal of epicormic branches (water sprouts).

The goals are to:
- avoid favoring basitonic zones that are too vigorous. For this reason, any fruiting branch with a thick diameter located in the lower portion of the tree should be removed, especially if it has not been bent or spread sufficiently.
- prevent competition with the trunk, which occurs with thicker fruiting branches inserted at any point on the tree: low, medium, or high.
- be mindful that when two trees stand next to each other, it is important not to keep the branches between them (in the direction of the row). Those branches would quickly die from a lack of sun, and the quality of their production would suffer. When you are pruning and bending or spreading limbs, it is recommended that the branches alternate along the entire height of the tree; similarly, in all training systems, you should remove limbs that cross over each other.
- regulate fruit load in order to diminish or completely avoid alternate bearing, by cutting branches back and/or extinguishing the short branches mentioned above. You can complete this opera-

13. Reine-Claude 1330.

tion later by thinning the fruits on short branches where hand thinning is sufficiently economical.
- remember that the prune tree species tends to reiterate (display frequent growth of epicormic branches); thus, you must do epicormic pruning, or suckering. It is more efficient to carry out this procedure in the summer (summer pruning) than the winter. Summer interventions help "put the brakes on" vegetation, whereas winter intervention "accelerates" the take-off of springtime vegetation.

Nutritional and Water Needs for Maintaining Balance

NITROGEN AND POTASSIUM NUTRITION
It is best to address nitrogen (N) needs in March. Do not exceed:
- for solaxe: 2 ounces (60 g) (N units) per tree;
- for multi-axis: 4 ounces (120 g) (N units) per tree.

Dried plum in California requires 100 pounds (45 kg) actual N (N units) per acre annually. Less vigorous trees (whether due to training system, rootstock, or scion cultivar) require somewhat less N, depending on planting density and crop load. Fresh market prunes and plums that receive too much N will not develop the intense color needed for quality. (See Appendix C: U.S. Standard Fertilizer Equivalents for Nitrogen.)

Prune is an especially heavy user of potassium, and other plum trees are to a lesser extent. Potassium deficiency results in sunburn, shoot dieback, increased incidence of bacterial canker, and reduced cropping. You can avoid deficiency by making four to six foliar treatments of potassium nitrate during the preharvest growing season and large soil applications of potassium sulfate every three to five years, lower-level annual soil applications, or fertigation with potassium through the drip system. July leaf sampling for deficiencies is a normal commercial practice.

WATER

Water is also essential for maintaining balanced growth:
- for solaxe: 8 gallons (30 l) of water every ten days, from fruit set to harvest (keeping in mind rainfall and compensating for the difference);
- for multi-axis: 16 gallons (60 l) of water every ten days, from fruit set to harvest (keeping rainfall in mind and compensating for the difference).

Irrigation needs in U.S. plums depend on where they are grown, the size of the tree, and the planting density. In California, where irrigation is most needed, "field capacity"—the amount of water needed to maintain even soil moisture without deficit irrigation—is essential for fruit sizing and preventing fruit cracking. The latter becomes a problem when the orchard is allowed to dry out and then is heavily irrigated.

Restructuring or Renewing a Tree

Progressive overgrowth, a failure to suppress of epicormic branches, overly strong basitony, or lack of light in the canopy are all factors that may cause a tree to become over-abundant and require restructuring (photo 14).

You will have to help rebalance the tree. This goal sometimes follows defined stages with interventions adapted to each individual case. There is, nonetheless, a hierarchy for handling these interventions:
- cut back any overly vigorous fruiting branches with a thick diameter, regardless of their location in the tree;

14. An example of restructuring.

15. Restructuring a vigorous orchard.

- cut off epicormic branches, if any remain;
- perform extinction of short, useless branches (excess or overly vigorous brindles and/or flowering shoots);
- establish a central light well that is sufficiently broad;
- clear the joints of fruiting branch bifurcations.

These interventions will promote consistent fruiting.

If cutting back large branches causes new shoots to sprout at the cuts, you can use them to initiate new fruiting branches (C2) that should be bent.

Cutting back the axis or axes in the summer (end of June to end of August) is certainly possible for any tree that has taken on too much height, as long as the tree is established and well balanced. When performed during the summer, this operation may not prevent water sprouts from growing on the cut *(photos 15 and 16)*.

Challenges

EXCESSIVE GROWTH

Any excess vigor may lead to reduced production. Yet, paradoxically, in order to combat this vigor, wood must

16. With solaxe, the top of the tree is more easily handled (Prune d'Ente, 10 years).

be removed! In fact, each vegetative point—especially the most vigorous—only serves to amplify overall vigor. The numerous apices carry out photosynthesis and stimulate the development of the root system. In this case, the recommended interventions in summer are as follows:

- cut back thick branches for better redistribution of vigor;
- systematically suppress epicormic branches;
- angle the branches deeper so that their vegetative production slows.

On overly hardy trees, or if you wish to restructure trees, be careful to avoid over-watering. Also, use nitrogen sparingly.

EXCESSIVE WEAKNESS

This is rarely the case with plum trees. Nonetheless, if you are faced with a weak tree, extinction (suppression) of any shaded or useless short branches will be the primary intervention. This includes branches found in the light well or those that hang. In this way, you will revitalize the remaining branches with no detriment to the tree's structure or volume.

Cutting back the lowest branch on the trunk will help to increase sap flow to the middle and upper zones.

You can remove some of the spurs on the fruiting branches that remain, usually those located on the bottom of the branches. This intervention can be done by hand or by scraping with clippers. Carry out these interventions in winter.

Finally, if winter interventions do not prevent fruit production from becoming excessive in relation to the tree's vigor, you will simply need to thin the fruits by hand. This will be beneficial to fruit size and quality if you complete it before the stone hardens. You can either pick the fruits by hand or strike the fruiting branches with a light stick, such as bamboo.

At this point, you can increase nitrogen supplements (+ 20%) and should absolutely be aware of any water shortages.

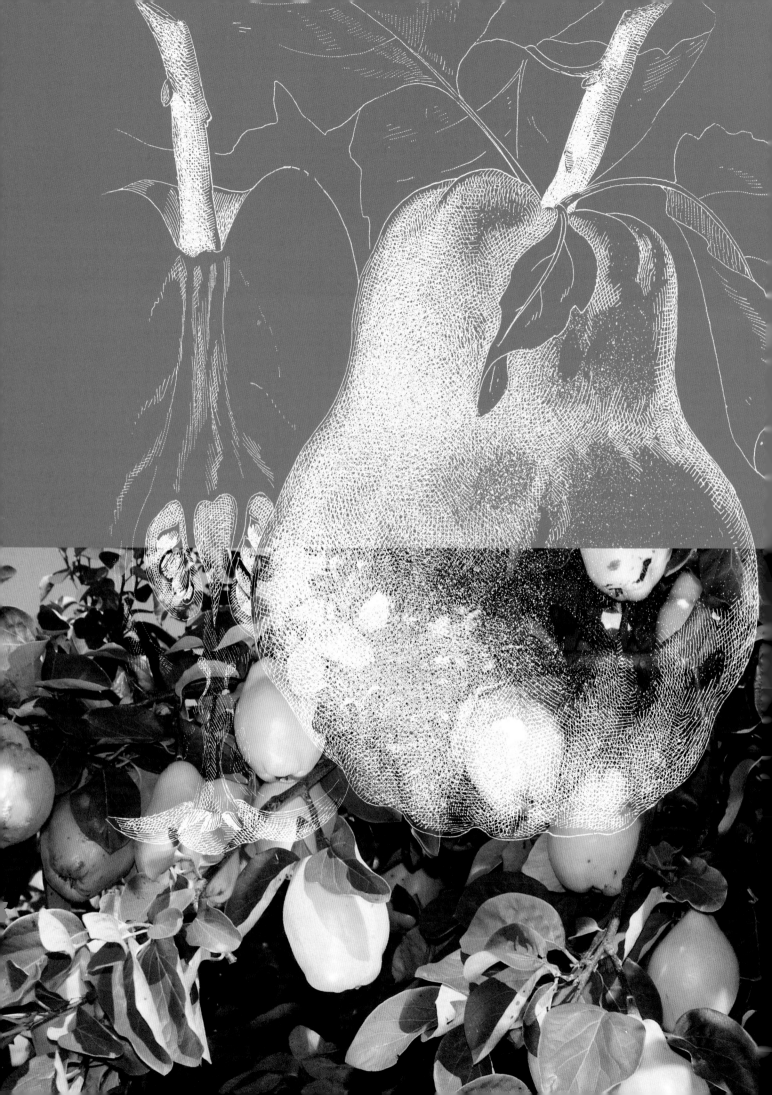

QUINCE

| Authors | Jean-Marie LESPINASSE |
| | Évelyne LETERME |

PHYTOGEOGRAPHICAL ORIGINS

The quince tree, *Cydonia oblonga* Mill, belongs to the Rosaceae family, in the Pyreae or Pomaceae tribe. This species originated in the Balkans and along the Caspian Sea and became sub-spontaneous throughout southern European countries, in North Africa, and in temperate America. It is one of the oldest cultivated trees in European gardens. Yet, although the tree can handle rather Nordic situations, it is difficult for its fruits to ripen there.

Due to elevated heat requirements in autumn in order for its fruits to mature, the quince tree is primarily cultivated in southern Europe, Portugal, the countries of the former Yugoslavia, and France—particularly in the central, southeastern, and southwestern regions. In the United States during colonial times, the quince was widely cultivated for use in jams, jellies, various preserves, and baked goods. However, with the widespread production of apples and pears, as well as the year-round availability of those fruits, quince cultivation in the United States became rare, except for pear rootstocks.

In 1996, orchards in France covered only 361 acres (146 ha), producing 2,200 tons. Two Luther Burbank **cultivars**, 'Van Deman' and 'Pineapple', are commercially grown in California today. However, overall quince production in the United States is too low to be tracked by the USDA National Agricultural Statistics Service. Worldwide, about 106,000 acres (42,897 ha) of quince produce a total crop of 335,000 metric tons, with Turkey being the largest producer at 25%. China, Iran,

1. Quince orchard.

Argentina, and Morocco each produce less than 10%. Production in the United States represents only about 250 acres (101 ha), mostly in California's San Joaquin Valley and primarily with the cultivar 'Pineapple'.

THE TREE

The quince tree is a rustic species that is very resistant to soil humidity and winter cold. It flowers quite late (May), affording protection from springtime frosts. However, poorer and drier soils, compact clays, and too much limestone are unfavorable to its growth. The maximal rate of **active limestone** in the soil is 8%, beyond which there is an increased risk of iron **chlorosis**.

It is a bushy tree *(photo 1)*, closer to a large shrub, rarely surpassing a height of 16 to 20 feet (5 to 6 m).

This species is also used as a primary rootstock for grafting pear trees. In England, France, and the United States, quince is primarily grown as a dwarfing pear rootstock. This use was developed in France more than five hundred years ago. Common **clonal** rootstocks grown in the United States include 'Quince A' and 'Quince B' (from England) and 'Provence Quince' from France. Two groups of quince rootstocks have been selected in France: the Angers quince tree and the Provence quince tree. As mentioned, quince rootstocks are used to dwarf pear trees, reducing tree size by up to one half and creating a tree that is **precocious** with a larger fruit. However, in terms of **grafting compatibility,** many pear trees are not compatible with quince rootstock. If the dwarfing habit of quince rootstock is desired, these must be grafted with an interstock such as pear varieties 'Comice', 'Old Home', or 'Beurre Hardy'. In California, no commercial European pear has been successfully productive with quince rootstocks.

THE FLOWER

Flowers are solitary, ranging from white to pinkish, and are found on the ends of one-year branches or short shoots *(photos 2 to 4)*. The different varieties are self-compatible, but cross-fertilization improves the number of seeds within the fruit.

THE FRUIT

The quince's fruit, which varies in both size and shape, is pulpy, hard-skinned, and not very juicy or sweet, but it is very rich in perfume and tannins and astringent. It is used as a commercial fruit, particularly in preparing jams, preserves, syrups, liquor, cider, and quince paste. Due to its sharp and bitter flavor, it is not eaten in its raw state. Its traditional medical usage primarily related to its astringent and anti-diarrheic properties.

Selected quince trees are not very numerous. They are propagated through grafting, using common quince trees. Their fruits are quite large and the color of yellow straw. The best-known varieties are 'Du Portugal', a shrubby **variety** with average hardiness that matures at the end of September; 'Géant de Vranja', with very large fruits (sometimes weighing more than 35 ounces or 1 kg), maturing in mid-October; and 'Champion',

2-3-4. Flowering stages.

7. Champion quince (*Les Meilleurs fruits du XXe siècle*, Paris, SNHF, 1928).

hardy with precocious fruiting and an erect habit, maturing in late October. *(See photos 5–7.)*

Local quince shrubs often have small but aromatic fruits. It was from those shrubs that the INRA in Angers, France, selected the BA29 rootstock, which is less susceptible to iron chlorosis and more resistant to highly acidic soils. The BA29 rootstock belongs to the group of Provence quince trees.

TRAINING THE QUINCE TREE

At First Glance, the Quince Tree Is Startling!

There are few quince tree orchards, yet it is easy to find quince trees along roadsides in France. In the Garonne region, they used to demarcate property lines. Their ability to regenerate created a perpetual barrier or boundary.

This use in delineating property lines was so wide-

5-6. Vranja quince (top) and Portugal quince (bottom).

8-9. Shoot blocked by fruiting.

spread that another, old French word for quince tree, *lo codonhièr*, means "property line." It is easy to recognize quince trees in August and September from the roadside. Bending from the weight of their fruit, they form a "ball."

In fact, this species has a rather spectacular shape and fruiting pattern:

- strong, **orthotropic** first growth;
- consistent and efficient **acrotony**;
- heavy natural bud **extinction**;
- a single fruit per floral bud.

Quince trees combine all of the characteristics of a well-performing species with autonomous and regular fruiting. Let's take a look at how they have blended growth and **fruit set**.

The first shoot or shoots that establish the tree in its natural habit are vigorous; but extremely strong acrotonic development quickly stops their growth, as does subsequent significant fruiting *(fig. 3)*. This liberating of the **axillary** eyes in the **distal** sections of vigorous branches is caused by a blockage in the **apex**, either

by a terminal flower and its fruiting or by the death of that apex. With **apical dominance** thus suppressed, a dozen shorter branches will develop and begin to fruit rapidly *(photos 8 and 9)*. This is a typical example of **sympodial growth**.

This type of fruiting favors a ball-shaped tree. Though certain branches don't bend (with growth impeded by setting fruit), most hang over under the weight of their heavy fruits. This bending of the branches causes hardy **reiterations** to grow, which will in turn be impeded *(fig. 3)*.

Quince fruiting resembles that of the apple tree (the acrotonic types), but the way it functions displays three characteristics that are specific to quince: the bourse shoots are long and thin; they seem to have priority in the fruit branch's evolution *(fig.1)*; return bloom—or bourse-on-bourse—is common, and there is only one flower per floral bud; and most varieties exhibit considerable extinction of fruiting structures. As a result, without pruning or thinning it is possible to notice a

Fig. 1. A bourse on bourse fruiting habit.

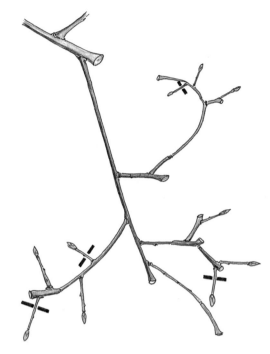

Fig. 2. Control the number of spurs by eradicating some: remove surplus floral buds and keep the healthiest.

fair balance between the tree's vegetative growth and its fruiting.

Combining these behaviors (acrotony, priority to the bourse and return bloom, and natural extinction), we can understand how most varieties continue to produce without extensive intervention from growers.

However, *fig. 2* shows how certain varieties can develop a crop overset. In these cases, growers should undertake artificial extinction (see the chapter on apple trees).

A Few Recomendations For Training

At planting, it is preferable to privilege the axis. A structure created by a trunk bearing branches around itself is often more productive: it affords better use of light, and it permits easier fruit-branch control under the best conditions.

However, keeping in mind the overall flexibility of the quince's wood, you must stake the trunk to keep it upright until it reaches a certain height (8 to 10 feet or 2.5 to 3 m). Lateral branches on the axis, which are future fruiting branches, may be relatively erect since this species' strong acrotony imposes a terminal fruiting that stops and bends the branch. Artificial bending will only be necessary if a branch starts to compete with the axis. At three or four years, fruiting takes over. It will then be necessary to pay attention to the three levels of evolution from vegetative shoot to fruit before intervening:

- control overly hardy reiterations in the summer *(fig. 3)*;
- keep an eye on the development of new fruiting branches;

10. Fruit branch.

11. A well balanced tree.

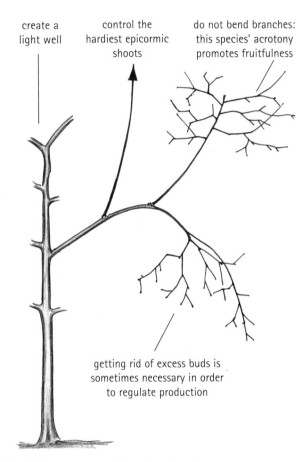

create a
light well

control the
hardiest epicormic
shoots

do not bend branches:
this species' acrotony
promotes fruitfulness

getting rid of excess buds is
sometimes necessary in order
to regulate production

Fig. 3. Four recommendations for quince trees.

• if these are already producing and sagging, you can practice springtime extinction of badly placed or excessive floral buds to help lighten the load *(fig. 2)*.

Direct light remains an essential requirement for fruiting. Thus, it is advisable to maintain a well of light within the tree's center in order to bring light within the productive crown when the sun reaches its zenith.

This species, being quite bushy, can easily thrive in more voluminous shapes (multi-axis, etc.). The advantage of vertical axis or solaxe derives from the facility for controlling fruit branch evolution in species that are slowed by overlapping *(photo 11)*.

The quince adapts well to the model we have described here, yet it still requires a fair amount of phyto-sanitary attention since its foliage is quite sensitive to entomosporiosis *(Febraea maculata)* and its fruit is susceptible to monilia *(Monilia fructigena)*, carpocapsa *(Cydia pomonella)*, and the Oriental peach moth *(Cydia molesta)*. Furthermore, quince, like its relatives the apple and the pear, it is highly susceptible to a severe a disease called "fire blight"; if untreated, this bacterial infection will eventually kill the tree. Prevention requires spraying with copper and/or antibiotics as well as pruning out any affected tissues that show black and dying parts.

WALNUT

Authors   Francis DELORT
Éric GERMAIN

GENERAL OVERVIEW

Botanical Classification

The common walnut tree, Juglans regia L., belongs to the genus Juglans L. in the family Juglandaceae. This genus consists of about twenty species categorized into four groups (table 1).

All species in the Juglans L. genus are **diploids** with $2n = 2x = 32$ chromosomes. Trees in the Juglans nigra species are deciduous with large, pinnate leaves with seven to nine leaflets. The **monoecious** species bears separate male and female flowers on the same tree: the male **inflorescence** is a "catkin," and the female inflorescence is a **pistillate** spike with two to three or more flowers. The pistillate flowers are pollinated by the wind. J. regia is **self-fertile**, but it is heterogamous, either **protandrous** (male flowers

Group	Species
Common walnut trees (Persian or English walnut)	Juglans regia
Black walnut trees	Juglans nigra, Juglans major, Juglans hindsii (Jeps.) Jeps. ex R.E. Sm.
White walnut trees	Juglans cinerea
Butternut trees	Juglans sieboldiana, Juglans mandchurica, etc.

Table 1. Botanical classification for the Juglans genus.

emerging first, the usual condition) or **protogynous** (female flowers emerging first) depending on **cultivar**. Thus, **cross-pollination** is necessary between cultivars with overlapping bloom of the appropriately sexed flowers.

Catkins are borne laterally on one-year wood, and pistillate flowers are borne terminally or laterally (in newer cultivars) on the current season's wood. The fruit-bearing habit is terminal or lateral, with bearing beginning two to seven years after planting. Fruits have an irregularly **dehiscent** husk in that it does not split into four even sections like its relatives, the pecan (*Carya illinoisensis*) and the hickory (*Carya sp.*). Cultivars of the "common" walnut (English or Persian walnut are synonyms) derived originally from either the Carpathian Mountains or Persia; they can be characterized by cold-hardiness, based on the origin of the original germplasm. Carpathian cultivars are more cold-hardy than those originating in Persia.

Origin of the Species

The common walnut tree, *Juglans regia* L., originated in central Asia. It appeared in its current form tens of thousands of years ago in the western mountain regions of the Himalayas, including Kashmir, Tajikistan, and Kyrgyzstan. It first moved westward into the semi-mountainous zones of Uzbekistan, Afghanistan, northern Iran, the Caucasus, and eastern Turkey. It then spread east into northern India and Nepal, and northwest to Xinjiang province in western China.

In all these areas, the common walnut tree still exists in its wild form in layered forests. In Uzbekistan, Kyrgyzstan, Tajikistan, and Xinjiang province, there is still quite a range of genetic variability, particularly with those **varieties** that gave us the trees we cultivate today.

Extension of the Species

Prior to the first ice age, the common walnut tree spread eastward into Manchuria, Korea, and Japan, and westward to Portugal and Morocco, passing through the Balkans. Because this species exhibits a natural antagonism between fruiting and vegetative vigor, as the tree spread it progressively changed via natural selection from a highly flowering one to a very vigorous one that primarily flowers at the terminal position of one-year branches.

Due to this natural vigor, it has been able to survive competition in forests from other vigorous species such as the oak.

Since Neanderthal times, walnuts have been associated with prehistoric diets when humans still picked their food. From that time on, the spread and evolution of the walnut tree have been intimately connected to human history.

Alexander the Great introduced the highly productive ancestral walnut trees from central Asia into Macedonia (in northern Greece) in the fourth century BCE while leading his armies through Persia to Samarqand. Walnuts were also spread during the Middle Ages, especially by merchants in southern Turkey using the Silk Road. These Asiatic trees **hybridized** naturally with native species that fruited terminally, serving as the basis for the laterally fruiting walnut trees that exist on the northern Mediterranean coast and the Moroccan Rif.

These trees are highly productive because they yield fruit all along the one-year shoots. They were widely multiplied as seedlings throughout the Roman Empire. The common walnut tree was introduced into South America during the Spanish and Portuguese conquests in the sixteenth century.

The English walnut's introduction into North America dates from the seventeenth century in the eastern United States and from the second half of the nineteenth century on the West Coast. In the West, there

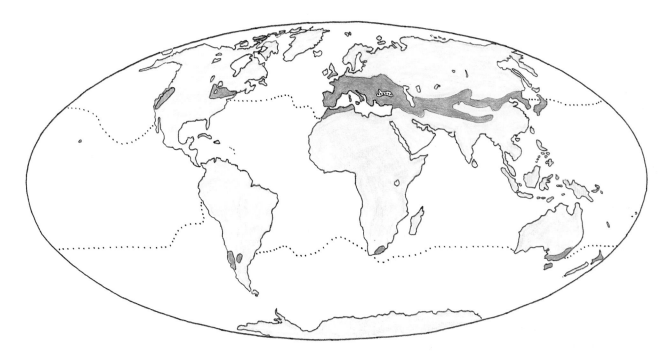

Fig. 1. Walnut cultivation areas throughout the world.

were two waves of importation: in the north, in Oregon, the trees were French varieties introduced by a grower from the Isère region who immigrated to that area in 1870; in the south, around Los Angeles, the trees were seedlings planted by a community of monks who came in 1850 from Santiago, Chile, to preach to the first settlers in the "Far West".

In the Southern Hemisphere, with the exception of Chile and Argentina, significant walnut cultivation in South Africa, Australia, and New Zealand began only at the beginning of the twentieth century. In those countries, production still remains quite low.

Growing Areas and Worldwide Production *(fig. 1)*

Juglans regia L. is currently grown for its fruit and wood in the Northern Hemisphere between latitudes 30° and 50° and in the Southern Hemisphere between latitudes 30° and 40°. California is the principal production area for English walnut in the United States, with 218,000 bearing acres (88,222 ha) in 2008 valued at $754 million.

The export forecast for 2009–2010 of U.S. walnuts was 230,000 metric tons in-shell: this represents 60% of the total estimated exported tonnage worldwide of 385,000 metric tons (USDA statistics), with decreasing shipment to the European Union and increasing shipment to Mexico, Turkey, and China. Worldwide production for the same period is expected to reach 1.2 million metric tons. Turkey has become a large market for in-shell walnuts, ultimately re-exporting a shelled product. China consumes virtually all the walnuts it produces. Europe lacks sufficient production and imports about 100,000 tons per year, primarily to Germany and Spain, and mostly from the United States.

California's English walnut-growing areas are

located throughout the Central Valley. Its soils are deep and fertile, and the temperate climate affords a long growing season with hot summers and cold winters with infrequent freezes. Lack of rain during the growing season reduces the incidence of walnut blight. Intensive breeding (USDA-funded) for improved varieties has been based at the University of California–Davis since the early 1980s. These efforts emphasize size, thin shells, high yield, disease and pest resistance, light-colored kernels and seedcoat (pellicle) kernels, and novel coloration of seedcoat (including red).

In France, the common walnut tree is present in every region, but it primarily grows in the Dauphiné region: Isère and Drôme (19,768 acres or 8,000 ha; 13,000 tons), and in Périgord: Dordogne *(photo 1)*, Lot, Corrèze, and Charente (18,533 acres or 7,500 ha; 12,000 tons). More recently, cultivation has spread into the Garonne Valley. There are two protected designations of origin: Noix de Grenoble and Noix et Cerneaux de Périgord.

Limiting Factors

TEMPERATURES

Walnut trees are very sensitive to late fall or early spring frosts beginning with **budbreak**. When fully **dormant**, most varieties are fairly hardy. Hardiness, as well as chilling requirements, differ widely among cultivars; thus, choice of cultivars should suit local conditions. Male inflorescences (catkins) and female flowers are easily damaged or destroyed when temperatures fall below 28°F or 29°F (roughly -2°C). Cultivated varieties in France have budbreak that occurs after April 15. Most of the varieties originating out of California, as well as eastern and southern Europe, cannot be planted

1. An older walnut tree in Dordogne, France.

in France because their blossoms are too **precocious**, emerging more than a month earlier in spring. In California, varieties have been chosen for this characteristic, as well as for good overlap in bloom with male flowering (in pollenizers).

Any autumn frosts (end of October–early November) while leaves are falling can also be quite harmful to walnut trees, especially in young plants when temperatures drop rapidly below 17°F to 19°F (-8° to -7°C), and particularly after a warm period. Trees will show serious signs of damage: necrosis on the trunk or at **scaffold** bases, and death of one-year shoots. Those varieties that drop their leaves later—notably, the California varieties—are particularly sensitive to autumn frosts, which are atypical in California.

In the winter, temperatures dropping below -4°F (-20°C) may cause the bark to rupture, which can cause the tree to die. This damage (known as frost cracks) is even more severe if temperatures jump back up during the day, such that south- and west-facing surfaces are particularly vulnerable. Temperatures in the Central Valley, California's walnut-growing region, rarely drop below the mid-20's F (around -4°C); more commonly, winter lows are around freezing. California's walnuts are cold-hardy to 12° to 15°F (-11° to -9°C). Chilling requirement is 400 to 1,600 hours.

With the need for late leafing characteristics to avoid walnut blight, cultivars with higher chill requirements have been produced. Carpathian cultivars of *J. regia* are more cold-hardy and can be grown in the Pacific Northwest, the mid-Atlantic, and the southeastern United States. One such cultivar is 'Cascade', which has large nuts with up to 56% kernel "fill" of the shell and is highly rated in quality. In France, cold requirements for ending bud dormancy are usually met as early as January. After that date, satisfaction of heat requirements—which differs according to each variety's place of origin—determines the period of budbreak.

Current research (from 2008 onward) at the University of California–Davis models chilling accumulation for walnut in the state using data from the last forty years. Decreasing chill accumulation trends predict that reduced levels of chill accumulation will threaten walnut production in the future (Luedeling et al., 2009). This research, which is ongoing, is illustrative of a problem for all but the lowest chill–requiring temperate tree crops in California.

RAINFALL
Walnut trees require 28 to 31 inches (700 to 800 mm) of rainfall annually, spread out over the summer season. This is a relatively high water demand (4 inches or 100 mm per month) during the summer, at the moment of fruit ovary growth (June–July) and as the kernel grows (August–September). Any deficit during these periods will affect **floral induction** and, therefore, the volume of production for the following year. In addition, heavy springtime rain may induce bacterial and fungal infections, particularly walnut blight.

Heavy rainfall in October during harvest can damage fruit quality. Also, high humidity during this period can cause husks to burst and blacken. Adherent, blackened husks increase cullage. In the winter, where soils are dense or poorly drained, excess water causes the roots to asphyxiate, often leading to the tree's death. Walnut trees are particularly sensitive to this problem.

WIND
Strong winds during blossoming are bad for proper **pollination**. Walnut pollen is quite light and can easily be swept beyond the orchard. Furthermore, the distance over which walnut pollen can travel and remain viable is very short. In France, the Mistral and Tramontane winds are therefore harmful factors for walnut cultivation. High winds can cause blow-over wherever trees are shallowly rooted or waterlogged

SUN AND TEMPERATURE

Excessive sun irradiation can cause sunburning of the kernel, particularly in thin-husked, thin-shelled English walnut varieties. Growing conditions in California have dictated the selection of varieties that are less prone to sunburn, which increases cullage of nutmeats. High temperatures (100°F or 38°C and above) result in dark kernels or black-spotted kernels ("pepper spotting"), whereas lower-than-optimal temperatures during nut development (for both English and some black walnuts) typically cause kernel shrivel. Summer temperatures of 80° to 90°F (27° to 32°C) are ideal for kernel development during the one to two months prior to harvest for adequate kernel size and oil content.

SOIL

Deep soils that are rich in limestone and clay are the most favorable to walnut cultivation. The best range for pH level is from 6 to 7.

Ground that is too loose, sandy, or shallow tends to induce bacterial infections. Soils that are too alkaline, with more than 5% of **active limestone**, increase the risk of ferric **chlorosis**. The following levels in other nutrients signal deficiencies: nitrogen, below 2.3%; potassium, below 0.9%; zinc, below 15 ppm. Toxicities occur at the following levels: boron, above 300 ppm; sodium, over 0.1%; chlorine, over 0.3%. (See Appendix C: U.S. Standard Fertilizer Equivalents for Nitrogen.)

TREE MORPHOLOGY

The vegetative cycle of walnut trees differs slightly from that of most other fruit trees. In France, budbreak occurs in late April, flowering in May, and ripening between the end of September and the end of October. Leaf drop starts at the end of October, or later where frosts do not occur until November or December (as in California).

Growth of Annual Shoots

Springtime shoots are completely **preformed** in the vegetative and flowering buds that have differentiated at the leaf axils during the previous growing season. Already before budbreak, these enclose a very short, thin stem with twelve or thirteen foliage points, and they may or may not be tipped by an inflorescence. After budbreak, leaves develop quickly. Stem elongation is nonetheless slow at first. It speeds up when leaf development has ended, then slows again before it finally halts about four to five weeks after budbreak—toward the end of May or early June in colder regions; a month or so earlier in lower latitudes.

Certain vegetative shoots and most flowering shoots end their annual development at the same time as determinate shoots. Others, after an apparent resting period of about twenty-four to thirty-five days, start to grow again at the end of June or beginning of July: in the United States, these are called "lammas shoots" (in France, they are called "Saint-Jean shoots"; *photo 2).* These lammas shoots can comprise one to three growth units that elongate during periodic extension "flushes" of growth that are separated by either slowed or interrupted growth. The first growth unit (phytomer) is preformed in the bud and induced to growth at the break of dormancy. Subsequent phytomers are **neoformed**, arising after the dormant period and without a resting bud, in response to optimal growing conditions.

Two types of late-season, semi-indeterminate shoots can be found in woody plants: the lammas shoots that elongate from current-year terminal buds (as in walnut), and **proleptic** shoots that develop from

2. Fruiting branch with bi-cyclical growth. The "necked eye" under the walnut yields a summer shoot (2nd cycle).

current-year lateral buds at the base of a terminal bud. Both types may occur alone or in combinations. In contrast, **sylleptic** shoots develop from **axillary buds** on an elongating shoot, which then grow out into branches before they fully form as dormant buds. Sylleptic shoots develop early in the season.

Lammas shoots are numerous in young trees and can be quite vigorous. This phase of new growth exhibits itself first as a rapid production of new **internodes**, which then elongate. The process lasts about four weeks on average. Certain of these **bicyclical** shoots stop growing as early as mid-July.

In the case of fruiting branches with summer shoots, growth starts out as **monopodial** and then becomes **sympodial** once slender buds take over; these are usually located immediately below the walnut *(photo 2)*. They bear new shoots that lengthen and produce **cataphylls** along the base (which fall rapidly); then they produce leaves as small leaflets, and finally leaves of normal size. This summer shoot is entirely preformed in the springtime "necked eye" that yields it. As soon as growth restarts at the end of June, the relay bud encloses about seventeen well-defined leaf points on average.

In the case of bicyclical vegetative branches, the new summer shoots continue to grow monopodially from the terminal buds of spring shoots. As with the "necked eye" on flowering shoots, the terminal bud is completely formed by the beginning of summer before it initiates, containing an average of twenty leaf appendages. The intra-annual interruption in the growth process of bicyclical vegetative shoots is distinguished by the presence of a second growth stage in the medial zone characterized by tight cataphylls and by leaves with shorter leaf blades.

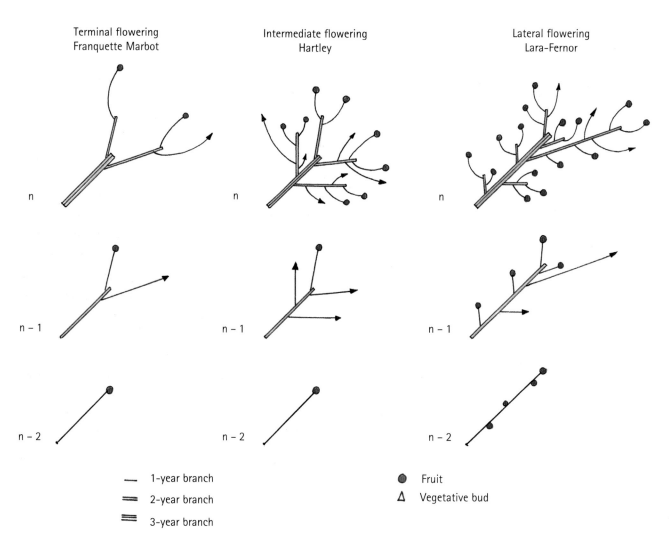

Terminal flowering
Franquette Marbot

Intermediate flowering
Hartley

Lateral flowering
Lara-Fernor

n

n

n

n – 1

n – 1

n – 1

n – 2

n – 2

n – 2

— 1-year branch

= 2-year branch

≡ 3-year branch

● Fruit

Δ Vegetative bud

Fig. 2. The principle types of walnut flowering.

Fruiting Types

For the common walnut tree, *Juglans regia* L., there are three primary fruiting types: terminal, intermediate, and lateral, with a range of variations among these types *(fig. 2)*.

FRUITING AT THE TERMINAL POSITION
On one-year branches, fruiting buds are located only in a terminal or **subterminal** position. Due to a strong **acro-** tonic tendency in these branches, only buds situated at the terminal part of the shoots will break; those in medial and **basal** positions remain **latent**. There will be few secondary branches as a result, as well as large barren spots along the branches. Fruiting is primarily localized in the tree's periphery *(photo 3)*. Fruiting is slow, as is potential production. This fruiting type is by far the most common. It is notably representative of walnut populations in France as well as in eastern and northern Europe, such as 'Franquette', 'Marbot', and many others.

3-4. Terminal (top) and lateral (bottom) fruiting.

INTERMEDIATE FRUITING TYPE

As with the preceding case, female floral induction only occurs on buds located in a terminal or subterminal position on one-year branches. However, in the spring, a large number of lateral shoots break through from the vegetative buds not only in **apical** positions but also in medial and even basal positions. These relatively vigorous shoots will produce fruits in their terminal positions in the following year. The tree branches and walnuts grow in relatively long production periods spread out over the length of the branch. This fruiting type displays relatively rapid fruiting and a much higher level of production than trees with terminal fruiting. The California variety 'Hartley' is representative of this fruiting type.

FRUITING ON LATERAL STEMS

In this situation, fruit buds are spread along the one-year shoots. Due to a slight acrotonic tendency, most of these buds break in the spring and produce short flowering stems along the branch, with walnuts at their tip *(photo 4)*. When they receive enough sunlight, these lateral stems continue to produce for several years. Walnut production forms a kind of "sleeve" over the branch.

These varieties reach **fruit set** much more rapidly than those with terminal fruiting, and their production potential is at least double. California varieties and new INRA varieties are representative of this fruiting type.

TREE PHYSIOLOGY

Floral Induction

On the common walnut tree, *Juglans regia* L., inflorescences are unisex. The distinct male and female pistillate flowers are present on a single tree, since the walnut is a monoecious species. These flowering buds

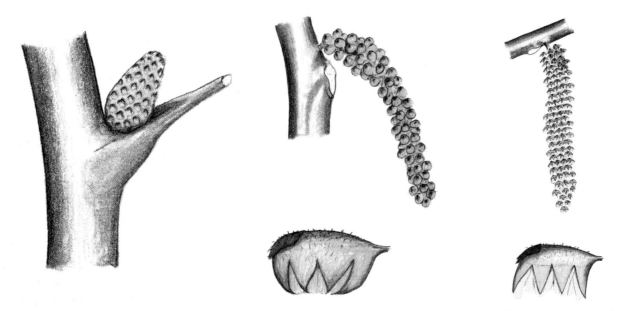

Fig. 3. Three phenological stages of catkin formation flowering at the end of summer. From left to right: Amv (catkin end of summer), Dm2 (male flowers opens) and Fm2 (total dehiscence of anthers).

are inserted at the axil of leaf scars on one-year-old branches. For this species, as with many fruiting species, floral induction strongly correlates with the level of light received by the growing shoot. Vigorous, well-lit branches are the most flowering.

Male pistillate flowers consist of 100 to 160 flowers. These flowers are inserted along the axis of the inflorescence, forming a catkin that is able to produce up to 1,800,000 grains of pollen.

Female flowers emerge at the extremity of stems that are preformed in flowering buds and are most often single or grouped in twos and threes. Quite rarely, they may form a bunch, as with 'Quenouille'. These flowers have no petals and are tipped with two highly developed **stigmata**.

MALE INFLORESCENCES

Floral induction of male flowers begins quite early in the season, immediately after budbreak. It becomes irreversible about twenty to twenty-five days later. In early June, globular, pinkish catkins are clearly visible

at the leaf axils *(fig. 3)*. During the summer, from mid-June to the end of September, the catkins elongate into a conical shape and lose their pink color in favor of a greenish tint. During this summer period, **stamens** form, and then **anthers** with their embryonic pollen sacs. In early October, the catkin reaches a length of 0.2 to 0.3 inch (5 to 8 mm), becomes grey-brown, and stops growing.

After winter, about three weeks before budbreak, the catkin starts to elongate again and reaches a length from 0.5 to 0.8 inch (13 to 20 mm). At this stage, pollen grains start to form. Then growth accelerates, and in one week the catkin goes from being 0.8 to being 1.5 inches (20 to 40 mm) long. A week later, it loses its rigidity and the male flowers separate. Then the evolution becomes more rapid. In about ten days, male flowers space themselves out and begin to open. The anthers spread out and turn yellow. They then begin to open starting from the base of the catkin; in two or three days the catkin releases all of its pollen, particularly during the warmer hours of the day. Then the empty anthers blacken and dry out, and the catkin falls to the ground. This evolution can be even faster in higher temperatures.

FEMALE INFLORESCENCES

The first sign of differentiation of female flowers within the buds happens around mid-July, about two and a half months after budbreak.

During late July and early August, the **bract**—which along with its two bracteoles will release the outer ovary wall—appears laterally on the already formed floral apex or apices. The evolution of fruit buds stops during the entire season of vegetative dormancy and starts back up two to three weeks after budbreak, or about a month and a half prior to flowering. The final hard budscales on top fall off. At this stage, the bud is no longer enveloped (except by other scales that are undifferentiated and semi-membranous). The bud continues to swell, and it is possible to observe the leafy bracts that hang below covered in whitish hairs. This is the white-bud stage. Then the bud elongates and the tips of outer terminal leaflets appear. This is budbreak *(fig. 4)*. Rapidly, the bracts spread out and the first leaves begin to expand. As these first leaves separate, their leaflets become clearly distinct. In the following days, the leaflet blades completely deploy on the first leaves.

The young leaves become more or less angled, allowing the female flowers to appear. Within a few days, stigmata emerge from the **perianth**, elongating and progressively diverging, ready to collect pollen *(fig. 5)*. They continue to elongate and curl up. In the days to come, they become striped with thin brown filaments, dry out, and turn black.

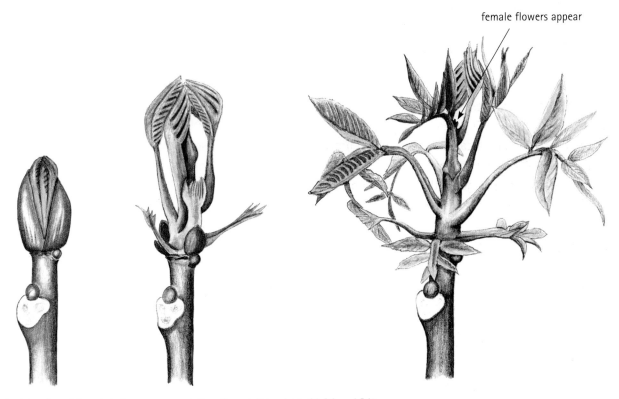

female flowers appear

Fig. 4. Bud-break and female inflorescence evolution. From left to right: Cf, Df, and Df2.

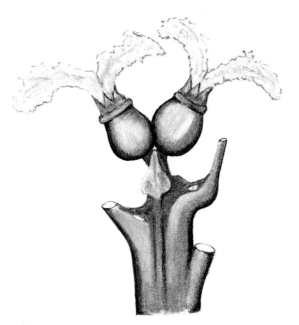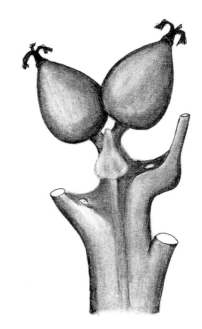

Fig. 5. Full blossoming and walnut formation. From left to right: Ff2 and Gf.

FLOWERING AND DICHOGAMY

The duration of female flowering on a single tree depends on the variety and may even vary for a given cultivar according to the temperatures reached during this period. Precocious varieties also generally take longer to flower than later varieties that flower even when temperatures are high. On average, blossoming occurs within a given variety for fifteen to twenty days, with full blossoming of the tree lasting only eight to ten days. For certain varieties, and especially in certain years, a minor amount of later flowers will produce smallish walnuts when they are fertilized.

Pollen emission from the catkins on a single tree covers a period of eight to fourteen days depending on the variety, but full male blossoming lasts only around five or six days, or less in higher temperatures.

When the trees become adults, one almost always finds a few later catkins that extend the period of pollen emission. In general, male and female blossoming lasts longer on adult trees than it does on younger trees.

For *Juglans regia* L., male and female flowers on a single tree emerge at different times. This phenomenon is called **dichogamy**. Male flowering may be more precocious than female flowering, in which case the variety is considered protandrous. In the reverse situation, the variety is considered protogynous. If the two blossomings coincide, we speak of **homogamy**.

PERIOD OF FLOWERING

Depending on climatic conditions (primarily, heat accumulation), flowering dates within a variety can vary considerably from one year to the next. At higher latitudes such as the Garonne Valley and Périgord in France, or in Oregon, except for trees with later bud-break, full male flowering spreads from mid-April (for the most precocious varieties) to the end of May (for later varieties). As for female flowering, this begins around April 15 for the most precocious varieties and ends, with few exceptions, during the first week in June for the later varieties.

Most varieties originating in California, northern and eastern Europe, the Mediterranean basin, and central Asia have a precocious to very precocious blossoming period, occurring fifteen to thirty-five days prior to that of 'Franquette'. These varieties are also quite sensitive to springtime frosts.

Practical Layout for Proper Pollination

Even though the common walnut tree, *Juglans regia* L., is a self-fertile species, the possibility for self-fertilization for most varieties is generally not more than a couple of days. This is due to several factors: the short lifespan of the pollen, the short period of receptivity in stigmata, and the substantial difference in flowering periods for male and female flowers of the same variety.

This dichogamy is characteristic of most varieties, which are protandrous, with male blossoming only overlapping female blossoming for a couple of days. The presence of pollinators on male blossoms that arrive later than the principal variety is therefore quite important.

Female flowers on walnut trees do not attract insects. Pollination is therefore completely **anemophilious:** wind carries the pollen over great distances, although the pollen's viability decreases rapidly with distance.

STRUCTURE, DEVELOPMENT, AND FRUIT MATURITY

Description of the Walnut

The fruit of the walnut tree consists of an envelope (the husk) surrounding a sizeable stone (the walnut). This nut has a **lignified** shell enclosing an edible nut (the kernel).

THE HUSK

This fleshy green envelope starts as the external wall of the ovary. It is relatively thin, measuring about 0.2 inch (4 mm) thick on average. The imprint of its internal vascular network corresponds to the visible furrows in every walnut shell. At maturity, the husk splits open and liberates the walnut, causing it to drop to the ground. Rain or continually high humidity accelerate dehiscence. However, if relative humidity is quite low, which is rather common in California, the husk tends to dry out and maintain the fruit on the tree even after physiological maturity has been reached. The husk is a source of tannins, traditionally used in leather "tanning."

THE SHELL

The shell comprises two symmetrical valves side by side. The joining section is relatively pronounced and most often affects only the top part of the fruit *(fig. 6)*.

For *Juglans regia* L., the shell is furrowed, bumpy,

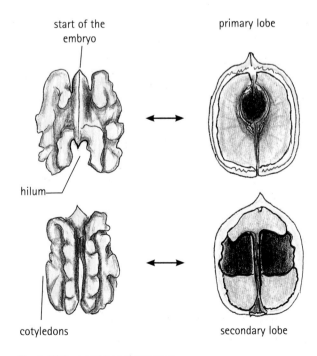

Fig. 6. Walnut and kernel structure.

and generally anfractuous (unsplit) along the joining section. It varies in thickness by variety, ranging from 1 to 2.5 mm. Open sutures of the shell are a defect and are selected against in breeding programs. The general shape of the walnut is also variable by variety: it can be heart-shaped, elliptical, oblong, egg-shaped, conical, or round. Its base and summit have different shapes, and the pistillary point on the tip of the fruit is either nonexistent in certain cases or quite developed in other cultivars.

The inside of the *Juglans regia* L. walnut is incompletely divided into four compartments by two perpendicular walls:

The primary wall is more developed and grows perpendicular to the joining valves. It almost completely splits the shell cavity into two compartments.

The secondary wall lies between the joined valves dividing each of these two cavities. It is more developed at the base of the walnut but still somewhat present at the top of the fruit.

THE KERNEL

The kernel forms as a brain-shaped nucleus with a highly furrowed surface, nearly filling the walnut. The primary wall divides it into two main lobes, each of which is divided near the top and more toward the bottom by the secondary wall *(fig. 6)*. The kernel represents 35% to 60% of the dried walnut's weight.

Fruit Growth

When the stigmata have finished drying out, about ten days after fertilization, the young fruit begins to grow very rapidly. It gains an average of 1 mm in diameter per day over nearly four weeks until the end of the first third of July—or earlier in warm climates, as in California. That is the moment when the first signs of the shell's lignification appear, starting at the top of the fruit and continuing down the joint. Walnut growth slows in the two weeks following lignification. The volume of the walnut in its husk maximizes around mid-July, or about nine weeks after flowering.

Shell lignification is complete about two weeks later, toward the end of July. The size of the nut corresponds to the amount water the tree has received during this rapid period of fruit growth. A lack of water in June or the first part of July causes the walnuts to be smaller.

KERNEL FORMATION

The first divisions in the embryo that will become a seed (the kernel) begin ten to fourteen days after fertilization. Rapid kernel growth begins in the eighth week after flowering, at the same time as the fruit nears its maximum volume. Ten weeks after pollination (at the end of July for 'Franquette'), the embryo nearly fills the entire embryonic cavity. This cavity reaches its definitive volume in mid-August, and until that date the cotyledons have a gelatinous appearance. The cotyledons reach full development, depending on the variety, in the first or second third of September, or about three weeks prior to maturity. At that moment, the internal walls turn brown and the fruits can be harvested and sold as fresh walnuts. During the month before the fruit drops, the kernel continues to accumulate dry matter and undergoes substantial changes in chemical composition. The amount of water that the tree receives during this period affects the kernel's development. A lack of water during that time causes lower kernel yield and, in the worst cases, collapsed kernels.

FRUIT MATURITY

Maturity can be defined as the moment when the kernel completes its evolution, or when the husk splits open *(photo 5)*.

In France, the period for maturity spans more than a month and a half: from mid-September until the final

5. Walnuts at maturity.

ten days in October, or even early November for trees with extremely late budbreak. Full maturity for varieties grown in France generally happens at the end of September or the beginning of October. There is a strong correlation between floral precocity and the timing of maturity. The period separating these two stages for most varieties averages about 145 days, but it may vary by a week depending on summer weather conditions.

VARIETAL CHOICE

Several criteria should be considered when choosing the most appropriate variety. These criteria relate not only to the plant material but also to technical limitations and considerations tied to the production goals. Budbreak of the chosen variety must occur during a period where there is practically no risk of frost. The plant material must also have low sensitivity to bacterial infection and anthracnosis.

Technical Limitations

At this level, it is necessary to distinguish between classical varieties with terminal fruiting and newer varieties that bear fruit on lateral stems. The latter varieties achieve fruit set more quickly and have quite an elevated level of productivity, but they are very demanding in terms of soil quality. For these varieties, it is especially important to pay attention to all of the factors involved in growing: fertilizer, irrigation, method for training the tree, and soil upkeep.

Diseases of Walnut: A Consideration in Varietal Selection

Walnut blight (*Xanthomonas campestris* p.v. *juglandis*) is a bacterial disease that attacks walnuts beginning in early spring, particularly when there is frequent rain or dampness. Early-blooming walnut cultivars are more susceptible than those that bloom later.

Walnut blight causes flower and nut drop, as well as lesions on nuts that persist on the tree, producing shriveled and moldy kernels and predisposing the nuts to NOW infestation. Copper (Bordeaux) applications during April and May are the usual treatment.

Armillaria root and crown rot (*Armillaria mellea*) is a fungal disease that damages walnut trees after wet conditions in the spring or fall, causing a decline in leaf growth and eventual death. Pre-planting fumigation in late summer to early fall can control Armillaria rot. Other management methods include using a resistant rootstock ('Paradox') and removing nearby infected trees.

Crown gall (*Agrobacterium tumefaciens*) is a bacterial disease that may become a problem at any time during the year. It enters through wounds. Younger trees are more prone to the disease, which develops underground as galls and causes stunted growth or wood rot. Cultural controls consist of avoiding injury to roots, planting a less susceptible rootstock ('Paradox)', and practicing good orchard sanitation. A biological control agent, *Agrobacterium radiobacter-84,* can be used before trees are planted to prevent crown gall.

Phytophthora root and crown rot (*Phytophthora* spp.) occurs in cool, wet conditions. Phytophthora penetrates the tree at the roots or at the crown, causing stunted development of leaves and tree decline. Water management and the use of a less susceptible rootstock ('Paradox') are important.

In California, harvest begins in late August and lasts through mid-November, depending on variety, region, and whether plant growth regulators are used for nut removal. Early harvest is preferable to reduce pest infestation; thus, growers may use ethephon (a commercial product that releases ethylene gas, the "ripening" growth regulator) to advance and synchronize harvest among nuts of varying maturity, including the pollenizers. This approach minimizes navel orangeworm (NOW) infestation, risks of mold in nuts under rainy conditions, and multiple harvests. Harvest involves the use of mechanical shakers, after which nuts are swept into windrows in the orchard and removed for drying.

Growers remove "mummy" nuts (those that remain on the tree after harvest) in the winter for navel orangeworm control. Because NOW over-winters in mummies on walnuts, almonds, and other crops, orchard sanitation is important wherever navel orangeworm incidence is high. Mummy nuts are removed by mechanical shaking—often after a heavy fog or light rain, which makes the mummies heavier and easier to remove. Mummies are then either removed or destroyed.

Another important pest of walnut, as well as many other tree crops, is codling moth (*Cydia pomonella).* This pest infests walnuts from mid-April until late September in two to four generations per year, with early-season cultivars being the most affected because the nuts develop early and support the first generation of larvae. The larvae feed on the developing kernel and also leave behind an open nut that is subject to NOW infestation. The first nuts to be infested by codling moth larvae drop to the orchard floor, while subsequent-generation larval infestations result in nuts that do not drop and get shaken with the crop, requiring cullage. Codling moth management has few controls, although growers use pheromones to disrupt mating and also use chemical pesticides (organophosphates and pyrethroids).

Walnut husk fly (*Rhagoletis completa*) causes damage mainly to mid- and late-season walnuts from June through mid-October with a single generation per year. The female fly lays its eggs beneath the husk, where the larvae grow and feed for about a month, causing the husk to decay and blacken. The larvae then drop to the ground and pupate, leaving behind a shell that is stained from the husk decay, reducing nut quality. The damaged nuts may remain on the tree, providing infestation sites for NOW. The best management practice includes removing black walnut trees (and any other non-cultivated walnut trees) from roadsides and other non-managed areas (those that are untreated for pests). Baited attractants that include organophosphate or pyrethroid can be applied in July or August. Usually, application to alternate rows is sufficient.

Walnut aphid (*Chromaphis juglandicold*) and dusky-veined aphid (*Callaphis juglandis*) are additional pests that damage trees during spring and summer by feeding on the leaves and exuding "honeydew," which encourages sooty mold to develop on the growing husks and nuts. Heavy aphid infestations result in **defoliation**, causing sunburn on the nuts. Because female aphids can reproduce asexually, many generations are possible each year. Biological control using a predator wasp (*Trioxys palladus*) is possible; and although some non-specific predators may manage the dusky-veined aphid, sooty mold usually damages the nuts before the dusky-veined aphids come under control. Chemical controls for aphids are best applied post-bloom.

Various mites are also problematic in walnut orchards. However, two practices can reduce their incidence: reducing dust that interferes with mite predators, and maintaining healthy, unstressed trees. Acaracides may be required to control mites.

Californian Varieties

Commonly planted commercial varieties in California are 'Franquette', 'Hartley' (the most common), 'Payne', 'Vina', 'Chico', 'Howard', 'Sunland', 'Serr', and 'Chandler' (most common in new plantings). 'Tulare', 'Sexton', 'Gillet', and 'Forde' are new cultivars recently released from the University of California–Davis. The following discussion describes each variety.

'Chandler', a University of California–Davis release, is one of the most important commercial nuts. It crops heavily, bearing on laterals (80% of lateral buds are female) as well as on terminals. It is self-fertile. Harvest occurs in the middle of the walnut season. The tree is a standard large walnut tree, about 40 feet (12 m) in height, of moderate vigor, and somewhat upright growing with moderate spread. Chilling requirement is 700 hours (the range of chill requirement for walnut is 400 to 1,600), and the tree is late to leaf, leafing out about three weeks after the early-leafing varieties such as 'Payne', 'Serr', 'Ashley', 'Sunland', 'Chico', and 'Vina'. 'Chandler' is somewhat resistant to walnut blight. The nuts are large, smooth, and well sealed, and almost all the kernels have a light-colored skin. 'Chandler' can be pollenized by 'Cisco' and 'Franquette'.

'Chico' is a small, upright tree that produces laterally and heavily; thus, it is well adapted for the home orchard. Although early to leaf and mature, 'Chico' is

6. Franquette.

be pollinated by local varieties unless late-flowering pollenizers are present. Most Californian varieties are suceptible to walnut blight and are therefore poorly suited to wet and humid areas, but 'Franquette' seems to have some degree of blight resistance. It is vigorous and spreading, slow to come into bearing, and a terminal bearer; therefore, the crop load is lower than that of other varieties.

'Gillet' is precocious and bears heavily even on young trees, with an early harvest (ten to twenty days before 'Chandler'). 'Gillet' leafs out early (seven to ten days before 'Chandler'), fruits exclusively on laterals, and is resistant to blight. The tree grows vigorously. Its well-sealed nuts have light kernels that are large and easy to remove.

'Gillet' can be pollenized by 'Payne', 'Vina', 'Serr', and 'Sexton'.

'Hartley' is a medium to large tree that leafs out mid to late season, thus requiring a late-blooming pollenizer such as 'Franquette'. 'Hartley' mostly bears terminally. Because it is late to bloom and mature, it is not well adapted to cool and short growing seasons, although production is good in regions with long, warm seasons. 'Hartley' is susceptible to blight, but only moderately so. 'Hartley' has a well-sealed, large nut with a light-colored kernel.

'Howard' is upright and of small to medium size, moderately vigorous, and adaptable to the home orchard. 'Howard' bears on laterals (approximately 80% of lateral buds are female), leafs out midseason, and is not as susceptible to walnut blight as most other Californian varieties. Yield is good with large, smooth nuts that are well sealed. The kernels are light-colored. 'Howard' can be pollenized by 'Franquette', 'Cisco', and 'Tehama'.

'Payne' is a medium tree that bears laterally (80%). Although its nuts are medium to small in size, the crop load is good. 'Payne' leafs out early and thus

very susceptible to blight. The nuts are small and of good quality. 'Chico' can be pollenized by 'Payne', 'Serr', 'Vina', and 'Sunland'.

'Cisco' is well adapted to the home orchard or garden, as it is both a small tree and upright, not spreading. The nuts are large, but for commercial plantings the kernel quality is not optimal. 'Cisco' is not resistant to walnut blight. 'Cisco' pollenizes another relatively small cultivar, 'Howard', as well as 'Chandler'.

'Forde' produces high early yields on moderately vigorous trees, providing an early harvest "window" (five to ten days before 'Chandler'). 'Forde' leafs out early (five days before 'Chandler'), fruits exclusively on laterals, and is resistant to blight. The nuts are large and well sealed, and the kernels are very light in color. Potential pollenizers are 'Payne', 'Vina', 'Serr', and 'Sexton'.

'Franquette' *(photo 6)* is a late-leafing, old French variety that is best for areas with late spring frosts. However, as it is also late flowering, it will not usually is not good for areas with late frost; nuts are early to mature. Because its susceptibility to blight is high, 'Payne' is not adapted to regions with spring rains or high humidity.

'Serr' is a Californian cultivar that was released in the late 1960s and has subsequently been identified with a pronounced tendency toward "pistillate drop." With heavy pollen load, the pistils in 'Serr' produce ethylene gas, which causes abscission and lack of nut set. Control with the ethylene inhibitor ReTain (Valent BioSciences) has been promising but inconsistent. 'Serr 'grows vigorously, producing large trees that require light, annual pruning. 'Serr' bears large, well-filled, thin but strong-shelled nuts on laterals as well as terminally, producing a moderate crop. The tree leafs out early and thus is unsuitable for areas with late spring frosts, but it is somewhat resistant to blight. On very fertile, well-drained soils, 'Serr' tends to be an excessively strong grower and is difficult to control. It can be pollenized by 'Chico' and 'Tehama'.

'Sexton' is precocious with very high yields and early harvest (one or more weeks before 'Chandler'). 'Sexton' leafs out early (seven days before 'Chandler'), is blight resistant, and bears exclusively on laterals. Both male and female flowers are abundant, with overlap in bloom; moreover, a second bloom period may occur, producing a few small nuts. The nuts are smooth and round with good seals and good shell strength; the light, large kernels shell out easily. 'Sexton' has a densely branching **canopy** and may require substantial training and pruning of young trees to prevent overbearing; thus, it is harder to train than other walnuts. Potential pollenizers are 'Chandler', 'Howard', and 'Tulare'.

'Sunland' is an early-leafing Californian cultivar with good crops of very large, late-maturing nuts borne laterally. 'Sunland' is very susceptible to blight.

'Tehama' is a late-leafing Californian cultivar with large nuts that are easy to crack, but the large and vigorous tree yields a light crop. Although 'Tehama' leafs out late, it is very susceptible to blight.

'Tulare' ('Serr' x 'Tehama') is a newly released Californian walnut, upright and moderately vigorous. It is self-fertile and thus does not require a pollenizer. 'Tulare' blooms late but matures mid-season, bearing mostly on lateral buds; being precocious, it comes into bearing early and heavily. The nuts are large, round, and well sealed.

'Vina' is a Californian cultivar that is slow to establish but that bears high-quality, medium-sized, well-sealed nuts laterally and terminally, resulting in a heavy crop. The tree is of small to medium size. 'Vina' is well adapted to high summer heat, leafs out early, and is highly susceptible to blight. It can be pollenized by 'Chico', 'Chandler', 'Howard', and 'Tehama'.

The Primary French Varieties

'Franquette', originally from the slopes overlooking the right bank in Isère, is by far the most commonly planted variety. It is fairly vigorous with a semi-erect habit. Its late budbreak occurs during the last ten days of April, which allows it to avoid later spring frosts. Its males bloom late, in the first half of May, and the females' flowering is late. This is a variety with terminal fruiting and rapid fruit set that is consistent, and it exhibits a relatively high level of production. It reaches maturity late, in the first half of October. It is not very susceptible to bacterial infections or anthracnosis. Due to its relatively rapid fruit set, its good productivity, and the high quality of its kernels, 'Franquette' is the best of the French varieties with terminal fruiting.

'Lara®' *(photo 7)* is a variety selected by Lalanne

7. Lara®.

8. Fernor®.

nurseries in the Bordeaux region, based on seedlings from the American 'Payne'. The adult tree is of average vigor and displays a semi-erect to semi-spread habit; therefore, it is well adapted to the vertical axis method. With its fruiting occurring on lateral stems, this variety arrives very rapidly at fruit set and offers high productivity. Its precocious budbreak generally occurs a dozen days prior to that of 'Franquette'; thus, the tree's production may be affected by spring frosts in certain years. This is a protandrous variety with precocious male and female flowers. The fruits are susceptible to bacteriosis at times. The walnuts from 'Lara®' trees are round and plump. Since it is a variety that reaches maturity early and produces a kernel that is not very bitter, it is of great interest for marketing fresh walnuts.

'Fernor®' *(photo 8)* was created in 1978 by the INRA in Bordeaux, crossing 'Franquette' with 'Lara®'. This variety displays average vigor and a semi-erect habit. With fruiting occurring on lateral stems, it offers rapid fruit set and high productivity. Budbreak is late, as is male flowering. This variety is not very susceptible

to bacteriosis or anthracnosis. Its maturity is late. The 'Fernor®' walnut is elongated, reminiscent of 'Franquette' but with a bumpier shell. Its fruit ranges from medium size to rather large, and its kernel is of excellent quality.

'Marbot', which originated in Corrèze, is primarily grown in northern Lot and southern Corrèze. Its principal quality is that it reaches maturity eight days earlier than 'Franquette', which makes it of interest to walnut sellers. Its rapid fruit set and productivity are equivalent to those of 'Franquette'; but its male and female flowers are more precocious by about a week, which makes it more susceptible to spring frost. 'Marbot' is relatively resistant to bacteria and anthracnosis.

'Parisienne', originally from Vinay, is mainly cultivated in Isère. Part of its production is sold as fresh walnuts. Yet it is of limited interested due to its slow fruit set and uneven productivity. Its rectangular fruits are of ample size.

The joint between its valves is somewhat small, and its kernel is often veined. Despite these issues, 'Parisienne' is considered a hardy, rustic variety with late budbreak and good resistance to bacteriosis.

Pollinator Varieties

The varieties currently planted in France are all protandrous. Their period for emitting pollen overlaps female flowering only for a couple of days at most. If climatic conditions are poor during this minor overlapping of the two flowerings, self-pollination may be insufficient for satisfactory production. It is therefore necessary to plant pollinators.

The choice of pollinators for varieties with later female flowers, such as 'Franquette' and 'Fernor®', falls into two **genotypes**: 'Ronde de Montignac' and 'Meylannaise'. For 'Marbot', which is more precocious by a week, the primary pollinators should be 'Franquette' or 'Fernette®'. 'Ronde de Montignac' should also be present in order to cover the last part of the flowering. For 'Lara®' and 'Ferjean', which have equally precocious flowers, the main pollinator should be another variety with lateral fruiting, 'Fernette®'. Here again, growers can cover the end of the female flowering period by planting 'Ronde de Montignac'.

'Ronde de Montignac' was first grown in Dordogne. It is a homogamous variety whose later pollen emission in southwestern France coincides perfectly with full receptivity on 'Franquette' stigmata and the end of female flowering on 'Lara®'. Starting in the fourth or fifth year after planting, this variety is covered in catkins, allowing decent pollination as soon as the principal variety has started producing. The abundance of male flowers in adult trees is also quite remarkable. The relatively vigorous tree stands semi-erect. It is not very susceptible to bacteria or anthracnosis. It has rapid fruit set, good productivity, and precocious maturity.

'Fernette®', which was created in 1978 by the INRA in Bordeaux by crossing 'Franquette' with 'Lara®', produces fruits on lateral stems. 'Fernette®' therefore sets fruit rapidly, showing better productivity than 'Franquette'. Its vigor is average. Its semi-erect to semi-spread habit lends itself well to vertical axis training techniques. Budbreak is late, and the trees are resistant to bacteria and anthracnosis. The variety's rapid production of catkins after planting and its exceptional male flowering make it a good pollinator, especially for 'Lara®' and 'Marbot'. 'Fernette®' produces large, round walnuts reminiscent of 'Lara®' walnuts. Its shell is thin yet firmly joined, but often poorly lignified.

J. NIGRA CULTIVARS

More than 400 cultivars of J. nigra, or black walnut, have been identified and/or bred, including cultivars specifically for the production of furniture veneers (Purdue University breeding program). The following lists identify cultivars that are used the most. Their states of origin (given in parentheses) provide good information for the natural range of cultivation.

The list below includes J. nigra cultivars used for nutmeats:

- 'Burns' (Ontario, Canada)—small and thin shelled with high kernel content that shells out on a single crack as halves.
- 'Edras' (Iowa)—large kernels with easy crack-out.
- 'El-Tom' (Ohio)—'Thomas' x 'Elmer Myers' varietal cross with a thin shell, high kernel content, and a light-colored kernel.
- 'Grundy' (Iowa)—high kernel weight, easy crack-out, few "blanks" (nuts that don't fill the shell); does not appear to be well adapted to warmer zones (such as Kentucky southward) in that its yields are reduced and it doesn't establish in new plantings as well as some other varieties.

- 'Hare' (Illinois)—a large, smooth nut with good shell crack-out and high kernel weight; easily propagated by budding onto rootstock; well adapted to Illinois, Missouri, and areas with similar growing conditions.
- 'Mintle' (Iowa)—despite its small size, this nut has a with high kernel weight and very rich flavor; exceptional total kernel percentage; unusual in that the nuts can be stored at room temperature for up to two years without developing rancidity.
- 'Monterey' (Pennsylvania)—large kernels and high kernel content; easily propagated by budding and grafting of budwood.
- 'Myers' (Ohio)—perhaps the industry standard for its very thin shell and ease of crack-out with a large percentage of halves; highly resistant to anthracnose; well adapted to southern states within the black walnut range (north of the "pecan belt"); tends to produce shriveled nut-meats and poor yields in more northern locations (Nebraska northward).
- 'Ohio' (Ohio)—identified in 1915 and a favored cultivar since then for good crack-out and kernel (halves) recovery; moderately resistant to anthracnose, but highly susceptible to walnut husk fly maggot.
- 'Pinecrest' (Pennsylvania)—large kernels with low "blanking" (empty shells); readily propagated by budding and grafting.
- 'Snyder' (New York)—large, medium-color kernels; well adapted to New York State and Ohio.
- 'Sparrow' (Illinois)—easy crack-out; high kernel production (but often small kernels) with excellent flavor and color; highly resistant to anthracnose.
- 'Todd' (Ohio)—a large nut with a smooth shell that cracks well, but not well adapted to northern growing conditions.
- 'Vandersloot' (Pennsylvania)—large kernels; good crack-out; resistant to anthracnose leaf spot.

The following list presents the best *J. nigra* varieties used for timber. They have been selected at Purdue University for form, rapid growth to harvest height, and diameter. (Many also produce good nut crops.)

- 'Fayette 1'—while fast growing, it has only average straightness; abundant, alternate bearing; very highly resistant to anthracnose.
- 'Knox 1'—rapid growth; heavy annual bearing; good anthracnose resistance but below average in straightness; susceptible to late spring frosts due to early leaf-out.
- 'Lawrence 1'—very rapid growth; good straightness; excellent anthracnose resistance; abundant cropping but **alternate bearing.**
- 'Lawrence 2'—moderately fast growing; exceptionally straight and relatively short with large diameter that doesn't taper; firmly rooted, thus not prone to blow-over; very good anthracnose resistance; outstanding annual nut-bearer.
- 'Purdue 1'—yields heavily without alternate-bearing habit; bears abundant crops each year with nuts set on lateral shoots (typical for English walnut but not for black walnuts, which normally bear on terminal shoots); susceptible to anthracnose.
- 'Purdue 3'—rapid growth habit; straight growth for even timber; late to leaf out (desirable to avoid late frost); good anthracnose resistance; nut production is light and erratic.
- 'Tippecano 1'—fastest growing of Purdue's patented timber varieties with good straightness; somewhat susceptible to anthracnose; low nut-meat yield.

Rootstocks

Rootstocks allow varieties to be propagated through grafting and also allow adaptation to specific soil and climatic conditions, which can influence the **scion**'s resistance to disease, flowering behavior, and yielding characteristics. There are two common methods of propagation. The first involves whip grafting, using one-year-old budwood cuttings. The second involves budding on seedling rootstocks in the nursery or on established rootstocks in the orchard to avoid replant decline. Such decline is a problem where orchards are replanted on the same ground or where row crops previously were planted. Budding on seedling rootstocks also promotes precocity of production.

CHOICES IN FRANCE

In France, seedlings from the common walnut, *Juglans regia* L., are currently the best choice for rootstock in most situations: they offer good resistance to ferric chlorosis, good **grafting compatibility (blackline** type), and satisfactory hardiness for most varieties, including those that fruit laterally. These seedlings' use is limited, however, by their susceptibility to root asphyxiation and **root disease,** or root rot. 'Manregian' is the selection most tolerant of blackline (a reaction to cherry leafroll virus that has infected the tree).

In the near future, this limited choice should increase with rootstock **clones** from in vitro cultures that will be vigorous and resistant to cherry leafroll (blackline). These are pre-selections created by the Centre Téchnique Interprofessionnel Des Fruits et Légumes (CTIFL) using *Juglans regia* L. descendants and by the French National Institute for Agricultural Research (INRA) with retro-crossings using *J. regia* L. and first-generation interspecies hybrids between *J. nigra* L. and *J. regia* L. that will allow better balance between growth and fruiting, especially when handling larger fruit loads.

CHOICES IN THE UNITED STATES

English walnut seedling rootstocks are not typically used in California, as the trees lack vigor and produc-tion. Northern California black walnut (*J. hindsii*) is traditionally the most common rootstock, although 'Paradox' (*J. hindsii* x *J. regia*) is recommended. 'Paradox' seedling rootstocks have higher variation than black walnut and are more susceptible to blackline. 'Paradox' is preferable for poor, hilly soils and for improved resistance to crown rot and root lesion nematodes, while *J. hindisii* is recommended only where blackline is epidemic.

Soil Requirements of the Walnut Tree

Before planting a walnut orchard, it is essential to understand soil quality in order to ensure proper installation. The adult walnut tree has a large root system. Contrary to common thought, the root system lacks a taproot. The taproot starts on seedling rootstocks and then disappears rapidly once the tree is transplanted. The highly developed root system is concentrated in superficial layers. Roots extend quite far and deep if the soil consistency allows sufficient water availability.

High levels of limestone content limit a soil's biological activity. If active limestone levels surpass 5%, then ferric chlorosis may set in, especially in dense, poorly drained soils. Walnut trees prefer soils with a more neutral pH balance (between 6 and 7.5). In highly alkaline soils (pH higher than 8.2), certain elements such as phosphorous, iron, boron, and zinc start to become insoluble, preventing roots from assimilating them.

Highly acidic soil (pH lower than 6) is also harmful to walnut trees. Most major elements become less available, and corrective lime washing is necessary to ensure proper calcium assimilation and to raise the pH level.

Irrigation is necessary for walnut trees to survive. In fact, tree load and fruit quality depend on proper water status. Over the vegetative season, the walnut tree goes through different stages of development, and a lack of water during those periods will compromise the potential harvest (in both quantity and quality) for the current year, for the following year, and for the lifetime of the orchard. A lack of water in June and early July will have negative repercussions on fruit size and vegetative growth. In July, drought will cause malformation of flowering buds that produce the subsequent year's harvest. From mid-July to mid-September, low levels of water will lower the kernel's quality.

Planting

PREPARING THE SOIL BEFORE PLANTING
After conducting a soil analysis, it is important to correct mineral levels. Subsequently, tilling is recommended to work fertilizer and organic material into the soil. It is essential to till the soil prior to planting, using some sort of clawed tool.

CHOOSING THE TRANSPLANT AND PLANTING
Planting should take place as early as possible at the end of autumn, promoting good development of the seedling for the following year. The quality of the transplant will affect the tree's growth, so it is essential to carefully determine the scion's health, especially in terms of bacterial cankers. The transplant should be well rooted. It is preferable to select a smaller but better-rooted transplant than a larger transplant with fewer roots. Walnut tree seedlings are sensitive to autumn frost, so be sure to inspect trees for frost damage prior to purchase. Ask for a guarantee from the nursery.

If the soil has been properly prepared, it will not be necessary to dig deep holes. Keep the grafting union 6 inches (15 cm) above the soil. Since the soil will collapse a bit after planting, make sure the surrounding soil is packed down enough to prevent holes where water might collect during the winter or spring.

PLANTING DISTANCES
Because the walnut develops into a broad tree, it is necessary to leave space so that it can develop unhindered. Modified central leader is the most common training system in California walnut production. Varieties that bear laterally and heavily tend to be smaller trees and amenable to higher-density plantings, while varieties that bear terminally require wider spacing. Typical spacings for commercial English walnut orchards are as follows, with central leader–trained trees and irrigation by flood, solid set sprinklers, or microsprinklers:

- standard = 30' x 30' (48 trees/acre); 9m x 9m (19.4 trees/hectare)
- high density = 24' x 24' (76 trees/acre); 7m x 7m (31 trees/hectare)
- hedgerow = 11' x 22' (180 trees/acre); 3m x 6.5m (73 trees/hectare)

Pollinizer cultivars are planted in solid rows (crosswind) at selected intervals among the main crop variety, usually comprising 10% of the orchard or more if the cultivar is desirable. Hedgerow orchards are "hedged and topped" mechanically to maintain tree size in a smaller space. Traditionally spaced trees in wider plantings are trained to a modified central leader, allowing four or five scaffolds to develop on the central leader before removal of the leader. Thus, the tree is planted, headed back to a single "leader," and allowed to develop scaffolds that are later selected for the best spacing and even size, at which time the leader is removed.

Where planted in traditional spacings rather than in hedgerows, trees are hand-pruned in the dormant season. Trees up to three years old are pruned from the ground, while older trees are pruned every two to three years by hand from a hydraulic lift. During the process of shaping the tree, in the first two to three years after planting, pruning takes place in summer. In France, the most common training system is the vertical axis, which was already in use for other species before its adoption for walnuts.

Starting the Vertical Axis *(photo 9)*

PLANTING
The whole scion is planted without being cut back. Its first-year growth is often low, but in this situation the root system develops optimally owing to the considerable presence of foliage. This is the installation phase.

END OF FIRST GROWTH IN ORCHARD
At this stage of growth, we may find one of two configurations:

- If the shoots are healthy, it is not recommended that the tree be cut back. In the following year, the shoots growing from this axis can be used for shaping the tree.
- If the shoots are weak, it is necessary to cut axis back to 8 inches (20 cm) above the grafting point. In the following year, thanks to good development of the root system, a very hardy shoot will develop and quickly catch up on what's been cut back. However, it will be necessary to prop the young tree because of its extremely rapid growth, especially during very hot periods. In the same year, the trunk will fill in and secondary fruiting branches will appear.

SECOND YEAR AFTER PLANTING:
BENDING THE BRANCHES
With vertical axis growth, the **insertion angles** of the fruiting branches are often too narrow *(photo 10)*, as is the case with certain varieties such as 'Fernor®'. It is important to bend them lower than horizontal

9. Vertical axis Franquette (4 years).

(photos 11 and 12). This operation should take place between the end of July and early September, which is the period when the annual shoot length and the amount of foliage will help to position these future fruiting branches. Being that these are young, tender branches, there should be no need to tie them.

For lower branches, bending is done from the ground. For higher branches, it is possible to lower them with a hook on an extending arm, which will allow you to reach them from the ground. It is still possible to use wires or string, being careful not to strangle the shoots (keep in mind that walnut trees thicken very quickly).

With this configuration, narrow angles on varieties like 'Fernor®' will open up and maintain a smaller

10 to 13. Fernor®, from left to right: narrow branch angles; manual bending; after bending; branch angles after bending.

diameter than the trunk *(photo 13),* helping to prevent it from strangling. This technique promotes a dominant trunk, with the knowledge that height is not a handicap for walnut trees.

In the case of 'Fernor®' trees, branches bent to horizontal will rapidly send out lateral fruiting shoots. When growing 'Fernor®' on a free vertical axis, an inverted conical shape will form; this genotype is particularly **basitonic**. Yet when bending of branches takes place, the cone becomes upright.

With terminal fruiting such as on 'Franquette' *(photo 14),* bending helps the growth of precocious lateral branches, which would not otherwise occur spontaneously in this variety *(photo 15).*

If a tree yields fruit early, resulting in many horizontal branches, distances between trees can be decreased.

In researching rapid fruit set and growth control in trees of each variety, we thought it wise to test the most favorable branch angles. For 'Lara®', an angle of 130° quickly and radically modified the variety's branching method. Though this species is generally **hypotonic** (with growth occurring below branches), branching

14. Franquette tree after bending.

328

15. Lateral fruiting on a Franquette.

became more **epitonic** (with growth occurring above the branches). In this way, the branches were able to receive more sunlight, growing directly toward the sun.

Trees left uncut. If trees have been left uncut, a relatively large number of branches will develop. It is important to preserve all these branches. During the period from late July to early September, you should bend them following the techniques described above (and based on their growth).

Trees cut back. Theoretically, it is not necessary to intervene on trees that have been cut back. But in the case of vigorous trees, it is absolutely essential to bend sylleptic branches, which will serve as future fruiting branches. They will be suppressed if bending is not successful, in which case insertion angles will be too narrow and either the branch will tear at fruit set or it will compete too heavily with the trunk.

THIRD YEAR AFTER PLANTING
Trees left uncut. It is not necessary to prune, but bending new branches along the axis should continue in the summer. The first flowering branches will appear on the shoots that you bent during the prior year.

Trees cut back. On these trees, it is recommended to apply the same techniques as for uncut trees at the second year after planting.

THIRD AND FOURTH YEARS AFTER PLANTING
Practically no pruning will be necessary, except for suppressing a few excess branches that might hinder the trunk's dominance.

PRUNING FOR UPKEEP IN SUBSEQUENT YEARS
When fruiting organs develop normally, the older ones start to be suppressed. This natural dying cycle (**extinction**) helps younger fruiting branches to develop. It is important to stimulate natural development by thinning any excess or badly placed short branches. This artificial extinction will also help to control growth and production.

Extinction

HOW IS IT PRACTICED?
It is advisable to suppress excess or weakened fruiting branches. To facilitate this operation, you can snap them off *(photo 16)* either manually (for the lower branches) or with an extendable hook, similar to the technique for bending branches. You can also perform this operation from the ground. There is no harm caused by this type of intervention in terms of healing. When we use clippers, new shoots or **epicormic branches** develop, whereas snapping the branches does not cause this to happen *(photo 17).*

THE PERIOD OF INTERVENTION
A vertical axis organization helps with extinction, which should take place during vegetative dormancy and may begin once leaves have fallen (November). Around February 15, vegetation starts to grow back on

16. Removing branches.

17. Lara® tree after extinction.

walnut trees, and the pith in the branches makes them more flexible and therefore harder to snap.

THE EFFECT ON SIZE

Artificial extinction helps to control and balance tree vigor and production. Studies have shown that branches shorter than 2 inches (6 cm) will produce smaller nuts. Extinction helps eliminate these smaller branches with their smaller fruits. This should occur during the period when the tree begins producing small fruit, generally around the sixth year after planting. At

that age, this type of intervention is less necessary but will stimulate the growth of fruiting branches.

THE SITES OF INTERVENTION

In order to thin the tree, it is important to first create a well of light in the tree's center—in other words, along the trunk and the first third of the fruiting branches *(fig. 7)*. You should suppress any fruiting branches that have been weakened by prior harvests, those that produce small fruit, those that are extremely sensitive to bacteria, those that receive less sunlight, and those that prevent light from reaching the center of the tree.

THE ADVANTAGE OF THIS TECHNIQUE

This type of intervention can be handled from the ground. The removed organs will generally not grow back: on "extinct" sites, no more pruning will be necessary. In trials of trees ages eight to ten years, twenty hours per acre was enough to carry out this operation.

This method is complementary to the tree's natural behavior since it is an anticipation of natural extinction. It prevents smaller-size fruit and allows light to penetrate into the tree in preparation for fruit production. The openness also helps when applying treatments and may lower the risk of bacterial infection because there is better ventilation.

When using this technique, we suppress a rather large number of small fruiting branches but very little timber. Thus, the tree maintains its natural **architecture**.

Fig. 7. Intervention zones: extinction takes place on the first third of branches.

Authors   René BERNHARD

           Jacques CLAVERIE

Collaborator   Jean AYMARD

APPENDIX A
PRUNUS BOTANY: THEIR USES
AS VARIETY AND ROOTSTOCK

The *Prunus* genus includes several diverse species that are cultivated for their fruit, including almond, apricot, cherry, peach, and plum *(table 1)*. The word *Prunus* characterizes about twenty different botanical species belonging to the subgenus *Prunophora (photos 1–3)*. The American botanist Alfred Rehder (1863–1949) classed species from this subgenus into three sections:

- apricot trees and species that are similar to them;
- North American plum trees;
- European and Asian plums, *P. cerasifera* ('Myrobalan'), *P. spinosa*, *P. institutia*, and *P. domestica* (Europe and western Asia), *P. salicina* and *P. simonii* (East Asia).

Other *Prunus* species from North America are equally used as a **variety** or as a rootstock *(photos 4 and 5)*. These include *P. hortulana* (Asian plum), *P. munsoniana* (Myrobalan), *P. besseyi* (spiny plum), and *P. maritime* and *P. subcordata* (European plums).

A wide range of natural **hybridizations** occurs between various *Prunus* species, and even more artificial hybridizations are possible owing to pollen conservation. Examples: peach x almond; apricot x plum; 'Myrobolan' x peach; *P. cerasifera* x *P. besseyi*. Moreover, by crossing *Prunus salicina* with the North American *Prunus*, hybridizers created "Japanese" plums.

Sub-genus	Species originating from Asia and Europe	Common species name	Common fruit name
AMYGDALUS (one flower per bud)	P. amygdalus	Almond tree	Almond
	P. persica	Peach tree	Peach and pavie (fuzzy skin)
		Nectarine tree	Nectarine (smooth skin, flesh doesn't adhere to the pit)
		Brugnon tree	Brugnon (smooth skin, flesh adheres to the pit)
PRUNOPHORA (1–3 flowers per bud)	P. armeniaca	Apricot tree	Apricot
	P. mume	Japanese apricot	Apricot
	P. salicina, P. simonii	Asian plum	Asian plum
	P. cerasifera	Myrobolan	Myrobolan
	P. spinosa	Thorny prune	Sloe (blackthorn)
	P. insititia	European plum	Damson, mirabelle
	P. domestica	European plum	Reine-Claude, Prune d'Ente
CERASUS (more than 3 flowers per bud)	P. avium	Cherry tree and wild cherry tree	Wild cherry and sweet cherry (gean, or guigne)
			Amarelle (clear juice)
	P. cerasus	Sour cherry tree	Griottes (dark juice)
	P. mahaleb	Sainte-Lucie	Used as a cherry tree rootstock

Table 1. Species in the *Prunus* genus.

1. *Prunus cerasus* (Griotte de Montmorency).
2. *Prunus domestica* (Prune d'Ente).
3. *Prunis institia* (Mirabelle).

As for the *Prunus mariana* GF 8-1 rootstock, this is a hybrid between *Prunus cerasifera* and *Prunus mariana*.

The different species in the *Prunus* genus have chromosomal numbers in multiples of 8: most have 2n = 16 chromosomes (**diploids**), with the exception of the following:

- *Prunus spinosa* and *Prunus cerasus*: 2n = 4x = 32 (**tetraploids**);
- *Prunus institia* and *Prunus domestica*: 2n = 6x = 48 (**hexaploids**).

The so-called Japanese or Japanese-American plums, with their plump, heart-shaped fruits, are hybrids between East Asian species and indigenous species from North America. These varieties were initially created in Burbank, California, in 1870 and were introduced into France at the end of the nineteenth century (in 1887). They have since been crossed with *Prunus cerasifera*.

Crossing *Prunus cerasifera* and *Prunus salicina* brought us 'Methley', 'Golden Japan', and others. This group of early-flowering plum trees is also quite susceptible to problems resulting from **phytoplasma** (bacteria lacking a cell wall that are transmitted by carrier insects), such as apricot leaf roll.

Prunus cerasifera (the 'Myrobolan' plum tree) was introduced into western Europe in the early nineteenth century. It was, and still is, commonly used as a rootstock for cultivated plum trees. Following the death of grafted plum trees, the 'Myrobolan' shoots allowed this species to propagate through the southern regions of France. Some varieties with purple leaves and pointy spurs were used for creating protective hedges around fields. The fruits of *Prunus cerasifera* are **precocious** in their maturity, red or yellow, small, and generally of mediocre flavor. It is a species that blossoms precociously and is generally **self-incompatible**, yielding heterogeneous seedlings as a result.

In 1935, J. Souty (INRA Bordeaux) introduced the *Prunus mariana*, a diploid species that originally came

4. A collection of *Prunus* rootstocks: Saint-Julien, left, *P. pucimba* Micronette P3125, right. Ungrafted rootstocks.

from Texas. The 'Mariana GF 8-1' was selected from its descendance in 1946 and proved to be a hardy, triploid rootstock **clone** (2n = 3x = 24). This clone became interesting for its ability to propagate from cuttings. It is also known for its hardiness and resistance to root asphyxiation, which it inherited from the *Prunus mariana* diploid. (This probably resulted from an unreduced ovule of a *Prunus mariana* that was fertilized with pollen from a *Prunus cerasifera*, giving it 8 chromosomes.)

Indigenous spiny plum trees with limited development, also called "blackthorns", belong to the species *Prunus spinosa*. This tetraploid species (2n = 4x = 32) has small black fruits called "sloes", which are used for making a liqueur. It has often been planted as a decorative hedge. There is a purple-leaf **mutation** that is also good for creating decorative hedges with lower height than those made from purple 'Myrobolan' clones.

The most common plum varieties such as 'Reine-Claude', 'Quetsche', and 'Prune d'Ente' belong to the species *Prunus domestica*. This hexaploid species (2n = 6x = 48 chromosomes) is polymorphous. Its origin is uncertain, as with some of the aforementioned species.

The species *Prunus insititia* is also hexaploid and comes from the natural crossing between *Prunus*

5. A collection of *Prunus* rootstocks: Ishtara® Ferciana, left, and Citation P3166, right. Ungrafted rootstocks.

cerasifera and *Prunus curdica*. This species, which easily forms hybrids with the *Prunus domestica* species, includes plum trees with small, round fruits: 'Saint-Julien', 'Petit Damas', 'Mirabelle', and so on. Yet it is unclear if it is truly distinct from the *Prunus domestica* species, which is also hexaploid.

Several species within the *Prunus* genus can easily cross-breed, and often one comes across interesting descriptions of *Prunus* varieties. Their hybrid nature has been demonstrated through controlled hybrid experimentation. This is the case, in particular, for the following hybrids:

- peach x almond;
- peach x diploid plums;
- apricot x diploid plums.

These hybrids are usually fertile males (for pollen) and in certain cases can produce fruits. Among the natural and artificial hybrids, rootstocks have been selected that carry certain important agronomic characteristics, such as adaptation to damp winter soils, resistance to **chlorosis**, resistance to certain ground parasites (such as nematodes, root rot, and galls), and better production yield.

APPENDIX B
FREEZE/FROST DAMAGE IN *PRUNUS* SPECIES
(COMPILED BY KITREN GLOZER)

PRE-BLOOM / DORMANT DAMAGE TO BUDS

As fruit trees begin growth in the spring, the buds not only begin to swell but also lose the ability to withstand cold temperatures (they lose "cold hardiness" or "winter hardiness"). As the buds develop, warmer temperatures (still below freezing) can damage them. The degree of damage is a function of three factors: temperature, length of time of exposure to that temperature, and degree of development of the buds (or flowers and fruits). Buds that are fully **dormant** can withstand freezing temperatures of 32°F (0°C) and lower without damage because there is no free water present to turn to ice crystals, which constitute the main physical source of damage to the buds' tissues.

For each species, there is a temperature limit called the "critical temperature"—the temperature that buds can withstand for a half-hour without dying. However, damage can occur over a range of temperatures, with more buds sustaining damage at lower temperatures. Not all buds on a tree are at the same stage of development; this is true for buds prior to observable physical changes as well as at pre-bloom and during bloom. For that matter, not all parts of the tree (aside from buds) are equally cold-hardy; some differences are tissue-specific, some are due to location (exposure on the tree), and some are due to the state of development at any given time. Floral parts within a bud can withstand temperatures lower than the tissues that "connect" the bud to the shoot (the vascular tissues that carry nutrients and water), leading to bud failure even without clear evidence of tissue death within the bud. In this case, buds dry up, die, and drop off. Often the freeze will only damage some of the buds, such as the most developed ones or athose in the bottom of the tree. (This is usual case, as the coldest air is generally at ground level.) In rarer cases, buds and/or wood may be preferentially damaged at treetops.

Often in milder climates (as in California, Florida, and the Southwest), a warming period occurs in January or early February that tends to increase flower bud respiration and reduce the depth of the dormant state, thereby reducing winter hardiness. Thus, even without swollen buds or open flowers, temperatures can be low enough to reach the critical temperature for a given species.

Critical temperatures for the various tree fruits have been established in areas where spring frosts are common, such as Michigan and Washington (see tables at right). However, in mild climatic areas, such as California, growing conditions are so widely variable that one cannot depend on the critical temperatures established elsewhere. Moreover, no specific equivalents for mild areas such as California are exact or have been published. One can use the critical temperatures from other growing regions as guidelines.

DAMAGE TO THE TREE CANOPY

The tree's **canopy** (not just buds, flowers, and fruits) may also be damaged by freezes, particularly during the transition into dormancy or out of dormancy when tissues are more active and less cold-hardy. Freeze damage to the vegetative parts of the tree can result in dead twigs, shoots, and **spurs;** it can also predispose the living tissues to bacterial canker and fungal dis-

Critical Temperatures for Specific Sweet Cherry Bud Stages in the State of Michigan									
"Critical temp" °F	3p6	Side Green	Green Tip	Tight Cluster	Open Cluster	First White	First Bloom	Full Bloom	Post Bloom
	23	23	25	28	28	29	29	29	30
10% kill	17	22	25	26	27	27	28	28	28
90% kill	5	9	14	17	21	24	25	25	25

Source: Compiled by Mark Longstroth for the Michigan State University Extension (http://www.canr.msu.edu/vanburen/crtmptxt.htm). Note that there are no values for unexpanded, or dormant, buds.

Critical Temperatures for Specific Sweet Cherry Bud Stages in the State of Washington									
"Critical temp" °F	Bud Swellw	Side Green	Green Tip	Tight Cluster	Open Cluster	First White	First Bloom	Full Bloom	Post Bloom
10% kill	12	21.6	25.3	26.4	27.1	27.1	27	27.7	28
90% kill	1	7.9	13.5	17.8	20.8	23.2	24.6	25	25.5

Source: E.L. Proebsting & H.H. Mills (1978). Low temperature resistance of developing flower buds of six deciduous fruit species. *J. Am. Soc. Horti. Sci.* 103, pp. 192–198.

eases. When this occurs, the current year's crop may not be the only loss; even overall productivity for the tree, or for some trees in the orchard, may be reduced for some time. Different trees may be affected within the orchard, or only parts of the trees due to micro-climactic differences within the orchard or within the tree, or the kind of freeze that occurs. Sometimes a single **variety** may be more susceptible, or different root-stocks may predispose the **scion** (the cropping portion of the tree) to greater or lesser cold hardiness—hence, susceptibility. There are no hard-and-fast rules because there are so many variables; each occurrence must be evaluated case-by-case. However, a wet fall and/or a warm period followed by freezing temperatures often cause an increased incidence of bacterial canker. Winter-kill of buds, bark tissues, and shoots commonly occurs in plants that partially lose hardiness due to relatively warm periods.

REDUCING THE RISK OF FREEZE DAMAGE

Passive Measures

Passive measures involve increasing winter hardiness and planting in appropriate areas. Too much nitrogen fertilizer applied late in the season can delay the tree's entry into dormancy, thereby predisposing the tree to freeze injury because it becomes less winter-hardy. (See Appendix C: U.S. Standard Fertilizer Equivalents for Nitrogen.) Moreover, growers should avoid planting in low areas where frost and standing water can be problems.

Active Measures

Although they are not used widely in commercial areas for sweet cherry in the United States, some measures can be considered: over-tree sprinkling or impact sprinkler soaking of trees to produce ice can maintain temperatures at freezing (32°F or 0°C). These measures see more frequent use on almond trees, as they bloom earlier and are subject to greater risk. Wind machines can move air through the orchard, mixing colder air with warmer air. FROSTPRO is a model of overhead irrigation rates for frost/freeze protection (Perry, 1986*). Some varieties of cherry may be more susceptible than others to frost (Cittidini et al., 2006**). These could be selected preferentially for planting,

Freeze damage to tree parts leads to higher susceptibility to invasive diseases, either by providing sites for pathogens to enter or by increasing stress in the trees.

Fungal diseases such as *Phytophthora* and bacterial diseases such as bacterial canker will increase in incidence with physical damage due to freezing.

* Perry, K.B. (1986). FROSTPRO, a microcomputer program to determine overhead irrigation rates for frost/freeze protection of apple orchards. *Hortscience 21*, pp. 1060–1061.

** Cittadini, E.D., de Ridder, N., Peri, P.L, & van Keulen, H. (2006). A method for assessing frost damage risk in sweet cherry orchards of South Patagonia. *Agricultural and Forest Meteorology* 141(2–4), pp. 235–243.

APPENDIX C
U.S. STANDARD FERTILIZER EQUIVALENTS FOR NITROGEN
(COMPILED BY KITREN GLOZER)

Because fertilizer composition varies, and because certain fertilizers may be chosen for a given crop or a given timing of application, it is convenient to have conversion factors for the essential elements obtained in the most commonly used fertilizers.

Nitrogen (N) is the most important nutrient for plant growth. The table below is an example of conversion factors for various rates of nitrogen in different fertilizers. The term "unit" of N is used to mean "actual lb N" as a rate (applied per acre per year, for example), or "lbN/lb" fertilizer (percentage of N by weight). The term "unit," therefore, does not mean "lb of fertilizer," but refers to the *actual* amount of elemental N to be applied, which must be calculated for each fertilizer.

Types of Nitrogenous[1] Fertilizer (not an exhaustive list)		Equivalents in lb fertilizer per acre					
	% nitrogen	10	40	45	50	90	100
calcium nitrate	15.5	65	258	290	323	581	645
urea (NH$_2$)2CO	46	22	87	98	109	196	217
ammonium sulfate	21	48	190	214	238	429	476
ammonium nitrate NH$_4$NO$_3$	34	29	118	132	147	265	294
monoammonium phosphate MAP	11	91	364	409	455	818	909
PGH+N (ammoniacal N)	15	67	267	300	333	600	667
potassium nitrate KNO$_3$	13.7	73	292	328	365	657	730
UAN (urea ammonium nitrate)[2]	32	471	1884	2119	2355	4238	4709
CAN17, (calcium ammonium nitrate) 2.14lb N/ gallon	17 (5.4% ammonia, 11.6% nitrate)	25 gallons/acre = 53.5lb /acre					

[1] "Nitrogenous," meaning "nitrogen-containing," refers to various chemical compounds that include the element nitrogen, essential for plant growth. Various chemical "residues" that are nitrogenous include: amine (-NH$_2$), ammonium (-NH$_4$), and nitrate (-NO$_3$).

[2] Aqueous solution of urea and ammonium nitrate with varying total percentage of nitrogen in solution; UAN 32 is the most commonly used form in agriculture. Other "grades" of UAN include UAN 28 and 30. All forms of UAN have the same ratio of the different N forms (nitrate, ammonium, and urea) = 25% nitrate, 25% ammonium, and 50% urea; however the *actual* amount of N in each grade differs, based on the ratio of N to water, as UAN is an aqueous fertilizer.

GLOSSARY

Achene or **akene**: a dry, one-seeded, indehiscent fruit with a pericarp that separates from the seed.

Acrotony (*adj.* **acrotonic**): growth that is strongest in distal shoots (*see* **Basitony**; *see also fig. 1*).

Active limestone: soluble limestone that plants can easily assimilate.

Allogamy (*adj.* **allogamous**): reproduction through fertilization by gametes that come either from flowers on a different plant or from different flowers on the same plant *(see* **Cross-fertilization**).

Alternate bearing: a term that characterizes varieties that do not produce flowers or fruits every year; instead, such varieties generally bear every other year. Certain conditions of cultivation (excessive production, heavy cropping, etc.) may cause the phenomenon in some species or varieties that are not normally alternate bearing in fruit production.

Ampelography: the field of botany concerned with the identification and classification of grapevines.

Amphitony (*adj.* **amphitonic**): the preferential development of lateral shoots on slanted branches. The branch and its shoots create a plane (*see* **Epitony, Hypotony**; *see also fig. 2*).

Androecium (*pl.* **androecia**): a group of stamens (male organs) on a single flower.

Anemophily (*adj.* **anemophilious**): the carrying of pollen by the wind; refers to wind-pollinated species.

Anther: a small sac attached to the stalk, or filament, containing pollen. Together, the anther and filament form the stamen.

Fig. 1. Longitudinal symmetry of branching (according to J. Crabbé).

Anthesis: the period when a flower is mature and open, coincident with anther maturity and release, pistil receptivity, and pollination.

Apex (*pl.* **apices**): the tip of a branch, where the apical meristem is located.

Apical: relating to the distal (terminal) extremity of a shoot (as opposed to a lateral location).

Apical dominance: on a growing branch, the controlling influence of the apical meristem, which totally or partially inhibits lower lateral buds from "breaking" and growing out.

Architecture of the tree: the area of botany characterizing a tree's growth (ex.: rhythmic, orthotropic), branching (*ex.:* rhythmic, monopodial), and flowering (*ex.:* lateral or terminal on primary branches) at various stages of its life. The different combinations of these characteristics allow growers to plan their growing area and to class trees, or plants in general, into twenty-three architectural models. Each model may be described from germination to flowering with a succession of axial types called "sequential axes" (*see* **Reiteration**). Knowledge of tree-growth form allows manipulation via tree training and pruning to optimize fruit yield and quality. In the case of rhythmic growth, each new period of growth is a "growth flush" that results in the formation of a growth module, such as branches or roots. Orthotropic growth is "upright" growth (such as a tree exhibits); its converse, plagiotropic growth, is that of a lateral branching form.

Astaminate: having no stamens (*see* **Staminate**).

Autogamy (*adj.* **autogamous**): fertilization of a flower by its own pollen (*see* **Allogamy**).

Axialization: on a leafy shoot, the ratio of stem to leaf, sometimes measured as the weight ratio of these two parts. (*Ex:* for cherry and peach trees, long branches are more axialized than short branches.) This relationship can be important in determining the "bearing capacity" for a growth module (such as a spur or branch), as the number of leaves, or total leaf area, represents the photosynthetic ability of that unit to support flower and fruit development.

Axillary: situated in a leaf axil (said of a lateral bud on a branch).

Basal: situated on a proximal area of a branch, or that closest to the point of origin.

Basitony (*adj.* **basitonic**): growth that is strongest on proximal branches (*see* **Acrotony**; *see also fig. 1*).

Benchmark stage: an easily identifiable phonological stage (*ex.*: blossoming).

Berry: a fleshy fruit that develops from a single ovary with seeds or pips embedded in the fruit flesh. Botanically, berry-type fruits include gooseberry, currant, grape, kiwi, tomato, and watermelon, among others.

Bicyclical: having two growth cycles in a year.

Blackline: in walnut trees, a symptom of infection by cherry leafroll virus (CLRV); it manifests in English walnut (*Juglans regia*) grafted onto black walnut (*Juglans nigra*) rootstock when subcortical tissue dies at the grafting point, forming a black line that prevents sap flow. The virus induces symptoms of delayed graft incompatibility. It also manifests in plum trees as plum/prune brownline (plum chlorotic leafroll phytoplasma) and in some pear trees grafted onto quince when infected with pear wilt phytoplasma.

Blastophagus: *Blastophagus psenes*, or fig wasp; an insect that pollinates fig trees (order: Hymenoptera; family: Agaonides).

Brachystaminate: *see* **Staminate**.

Bract: A leaf associated with the reproductive components of a flower.

Brix or % **soluble solids**: the percentage of fruit juice that is composed of fruit sugars (such as fructose, glucose, etc.).

Budbreak: the first emergence of vegetation as buds open at the end of the dormant season in temperate woody crops.

Cane: a long renewal vine. Following the Guyot pruning method, the creation of a single cane or double canes for a single season's production of grapes (and the following season's renewal spurs) is the final operation of the season before budbreak. It consists of bending the vine shoot during pruning and trellising the vine. This shoot will become a cane.

Canopy: the overall volume of branches in a planting (forest vault). By extension, the term also describes the volume of branches for a given tree or vine. Another term is "top".

Capnode: *Capnodis tenebrionis* L., an insect that attacks tree roots (order: Coleoptera; family: Burprestides). Capnode is a pest of fruit trees in the Mediterranean basin and other semi-arid areas.

Caprification: a method of assuring pollination of the Smyrna and other edible figs in which flower clusters of the caprifig are hung from trees of the edible fig, allowing wasps to carry pollen from the flowers of the caprifig to those of the edible varieties.

Carpophores: a hypogynous fungus that may occur on rotting areas or pruning scars of various trees, including hazelnut and other fruit and nut trees (sp.: *Phellinus*).

Cataphyll: a small, often tough leaf that is part of a bud (budscale).

Catkin: a thin, cylindrical inflorescence, without petals and generally wind-pollinated (anemophilous) but sometimes insect pollinated (e.g. Salix). Catkin flowers are typically unisexual and male, although both male and female flowers may be borne in a mixed catkin (both sexes) or in separate catkins (only male or female).

Chlorosis: a leaf deficiency characterized by a lack of chlorophyll, causing a yellowing of leaves, particularly at the branch apex. Chlorosis is often the result of iron deficiency in the plant, generally produced when soil is highly alkaline, as with calcareous soils (induced deficiency). Iron concentration may be adequate in the soil, but "bound" and unavailable for uptake by the plant.

Climacteric peak or **"crisis"**: a condition in certain fruits in which ripening only occurs following the production of a specific gas, ethylene, created by the fruit itself. A climacteric fruit continues to ripen after harvesting (as with apples and pears, but not cherries). Ethylene also plays a role in the senescence of plant organs.

Clone (*adj.* **clonal**): a plant propagated by vegetative means from the same plant and thus possessing the same genetic characteristics.

Colonization: one or more plant species populating an area.

Corymb: an inflorescence, or cluster of flowers, whose peduncles are spread along an axis. Flowers in a corymb are level at the top of the inflorescence, although they arise from various branching points along the central axis of the inflorescence; anthesis occurs such that the outer flowers open first.

Cross-fertilization: the pollination of a pistil on one flower by the pollen from a flower on another individual. This term is generally used when genetically different individuals (species or varieties) are concerned.

Cryptogam: a member of *Cryptogamae* family of plants, which are non-flowering, non-seed bearing, and reproduce by spores. Mosses and lichens are examples.

Cultivar: a combination of the words "cultivated" and "variety," designating a cultivated variety created by humans most often through hybridization or mutation.

Cyme: an inflorescence, or flower cluster, in which each axis terminates in a flower and underneath which another branch or two develops, also terminating in a flower.

Defoliation: the dropping of leaves. In temperate climates, defoliation typically occurs as winter approaches, but it may also occur after summer droughts due to stress.

Dehiscence (adj. **dehiscent**): the phenomenon of fruit opening upon ripening (see **Indehiscence**).

Dichogamy: the maturation of pistils and stamens in succession, not simultaneously. Cross-fertilization is necessary (see **Homogamy**).

Diclinous: descriptive of a unisex flower—either a male with no pistil, or a female with no stamens. Male and female flowers may occur on the same plant (i.e. "monoecious").

Dioecious: having male and female flowers on different individuals (see **Monoecious**). From the Greek *di-oikistes*, meaning "two houses."

Diploid: *see* **Ploidy**.

Distal: situated at the furthest point from the ground or from the area of origin/insertion (see **Proximal**).

Distichous: in terms of phyllotaxy, a term that describes the organization of nodes on a branch. Distichous leaves alternate around the stem, being arranged in two vertical rows on opposite sides of the stem.

Dormancy (*adj.* **dormant**): a period of inactivity. In terms of buds or seeds, a cessation of growth due to either internal causes (endo-dormancy) or external causes. In the case of buds, dormancy may be caused by growth in other areas (such as apical dominance) or by internal inhibitors that are broken down during the dormant period by chill accumulation.

Dormant-eye trees: trees created via the grafting of one or two buds during dormancy, generally in August.

Drupe: a fleshy fruit that develops from a single ovary, generally with one seed enclosed in a woody shell, or stone (*ex.:* peach, cherry, olive, date).

Effective pollination period (EPP): A concept developed by R. R. Williams (in *J. Hort. Sci. 40* (1965), pp. 31–41) to assess flower receptivity. Williams defined it as the number of days during which pollination is effective in producing a fruit, determined by the longevity of the ovules minus the time lag between pollination (transfer of pollen to the stigma) and fertilization.

Endocarp: The inner layer of the pericarp of a fruit (like an apple or orange) when it contains two or more layers of different texture or consistency.

Entomophily (*adj.* **entomophilious**): the phenomenon of pollen being transferred by insects.

Epicormic branch: a new, vigorous shoot breaking from a location other than a leaf axil and growing mainly upright.

Epiphyte (*adj.* **epiphytic**): a plant that grows on another plant without being a parasite.

Epitony (adj. **epitonic**): the preferential development of branches located on the top portion of an angled or horizontal carrier branch (see **Hypotony, Amphitony**; *see also fig. 2*).

Extinction: the physiological dying off of short branches (spur system, spur, etc.), often those that bear fruit. (Not to be confused with shoot shedding, a common occurrence within older trees due to a lack of light.) By extension, this term also designates the removal of fruiting spurs; in this case, one speaks of "artificial extinction."

Exocarp: The outermost layer of the pericarp of the fruit.

Floral differentiation: the process by which an undifferentiated meristem evolves into an inflorescence or a flower, beginning with floral induction.

Floral induction: a process that occurs in leaves and is transmitted to the undifferentiated meristem, causing flower initiation. More generally, the term designates all changes in meristematic activity from its undifferentiated state to blossoming, or from a vegetative state to a floral state.

Floral initiation: the first stages of undifferentiated meristem transformation into a flowering meristem; floral initiation begins after the signal of floral induction has been received.

Floss: a fibrous covering that protects a bud, especially on vines. It falls off at budbreak.

Fruit set: the first stages of fruit growth following pollination and fertilization.

Gamete: a male or female sex cell containing half of a plant's chromosomes. Associated with fertilization, gametes create the embryos for new individuals.

Genotyping: study of the genetic heritage of an individual.

Grafting compatibility: a perfect grafting of tissues between the variety and the rootstock. For example, the 'Doyenne du Comice' pear tree is compatible with the quince tree rootstock. In contrast, several varieties of apricot tree are incompatible with the 'Mariana GF 8-1' plum tree rootstock.

Hermaphrodite: a flower that contains both male and female organs; a "complete" or "perfect" flower.

Hexaploid: *see* **Ploidy**.

Homogamy (*adj.* **homogamous**): the simultaneous maturation of stamens and pistils on a hermaphroditic flower (see **Dichogamy**).

Hybridization: cross-fertilization between genetically different parents (between species within a single genus, or between varieties within a single species), resulting in the creation of hybrids.

Hypogynous: attached under the pistil. (*Ex.:* a hypogynous perianth has petals, sepals, and stamens arising below the pistil.)

Hypotony (*adj.* **hypotonic**): the preferential development of branches located underneath an angled or horizontal carrier branch (see **Amphitony, Epitony**; *see also fig. 2*).

Indehiscence (*adj.* **indehiscent**): the phenomenon of fruits not opening upon ripening (see **Dehiscence**).

Inflorescence: a cluster of flowers. (*Ex.:* in apple trees, the inflorescence consists of five or six flowers.)

Insertion angle: the angle at which a branch develops from the trunk. Acute angles (30° to 45°) are generally more fragile and prone to breakage than more open angles (45° to 90°).

Internode: the portion of a branch between two successive nodes (*syn.* merithal).

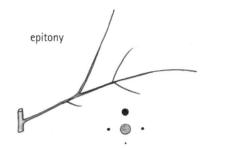

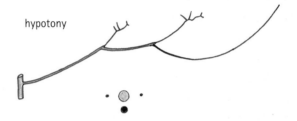

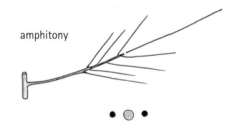

Fig. 2. Lateral symmetry of branching (according to J. Crabbé).

Involucre: a group of bracts (joined or not) at the base of a flower that sometimes envelops the fruit (*syn.* cupule when the bracts are joined). (*Ex.:* the hazelnut fruit is enclosed in an involucre.)

Latent: capable of, but not showing, activity. The term describes a bud that does not grow during the vegetative phase.

Lethal temperature: the temperature above or below which a plant organ or an entire plant dies.

Lignification (*v.* **lignify**): the hardening of wood or a woody seedcoat (as in peach pit) due to lignin deposits in the cell walls of the woody cells.

Longistaminate: *see* **Staminate**.

Median: situated at the middle of a branch.

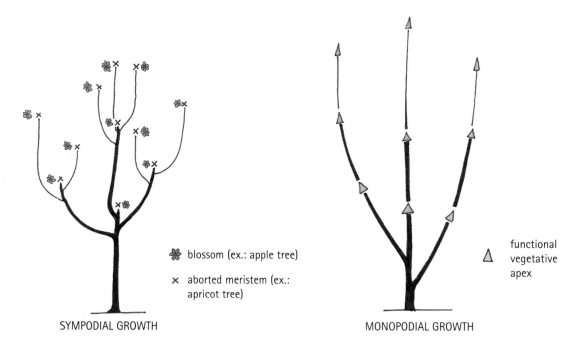

blossom (ex.: apple tree)

x aborted meristem (ex.: apricot tree)

SYMPODIAL GROWTH

MONOPODIAL GROWTH

△ functional vegetative apex

Fig. 3. Monopodial—sympodial growth and branching.

Medullar: located in or related to pith (ex.: medullar deficiency).

Meristem (adj. **meristematic**): undifferentiated cells or cells that have been "induced" to have specific characteristics that are either floral or vegetative. If vegetative, the cells are predetermined to give rise to roots, or shoots with leaves, or various tissues of shoots and roots. Shoot meristems may be terminal or axillary (a lateral shoot arising in a leaf axil) and may eventually give rise to lateral branches, leaves, and flowers. Aerial meristems (floral or shoot) are contained within a bud. "Primary" meristems give rise to epidermis, vascular cambium, and pith; in so doing, they are responsible for primary growth, or an increase in length or height. "Secondary" meristems include the vascular and cork cambia, which produce new vascular tissues (including wood) or cork, respectively, throughout the life of the plant.

Merithal: see **Internode**. Can also be used as a synonym for "leaf blade."

Mesocarp: the fleshy part of a drupe located between the epidermis and the seedcoat (exocarp).

Mesostaminate: see **Staminate**.

Monoecious: bearing male and female flowers on a single individual (see **Dioecious**).

Monopodial growth: growth that displays a single-axis pattern resulting from one meristem. Branching of that axis is called monopodial (see **Sympodial growth**; see also fig. 3).

Mutation: a sudden change either in gametes or in a part of a tree. (Ex.: for a variety of apples, variations in fruit coloration—"uniform" or "streaked"—often result from mutations.)

Nectary: a gland-like organ, located outside or within a flower, that secretes nectar.

Neoformed (n. **neoformation**): characteristic of the part of a shoot that grows out of the section that was preformed in the initial bud, in the same year. Its formation is followed by an immediate elongation of the parts that make up this extension of the branch (see **Preformed**).

Node: the point on a branch where organs (leaf, bud, tendril, inflorescence, catkin, etc.) develop.

Ontogeny (syn. **ontogenesis**): the development of the individual from seed fertilization to adulthood.

Oosphere: the female gamete.

Orthotropic growth: growth directed upward. Orthotropic growth generally exhibits spiraled phyllotaxy.

Panicle: a simple, composite, or branching inflorescence (as on the olive tree).

Parthenocarpic: relating to the fruiting of plants that have not been fertilized. The fruit will either lack seeds or expel them early.

Perianth: in a flower, the set formed by the calyx (the sepals) and the corolla (the petals).

Pericarp: the fruit wall, composed of three layers: endocarp, mesocarp, and exocarp.

Phanerogamous: in terms of flowering plants, having obvious reproductive organs (stamen, pistil)—as opposed to cryptogams (mosses, ferns).

Phenology (*adj.* **phenological**): an area of science related to seasonal biological phenomena (budding, flowering, etc.).

Phenotype: the morphologically visible or invisible characteristics that express the interactions of genes (genotype) and environment.

Phyllotaxy: the arrangement of leaves around a branch (*ex:* spiral, distichous, opposed, alternate, etc.).

Physiological drop: the phenomenon that occurs after fertilization when the tree naturally drops its excess fruits, generally in several waves.

Phytoplasma: bacteria lacking cell walls that colonize honeycombed tubes, transmitted by vector insects (*ex.:* chlorotic leaf curl on an apricot tree or pear decline).

Pinching (*syn.* tipping): the act of pruning the distal tips of a growing axis in order to promote new branches, fruit growth, or floral induction and fruiting in the following year.

Pistil (*adj.* **pistillate**): the female organ of flowers on phanerogamous plants; composed of the following three elements from base to tip: ovary, style, stigma.

Planting zone: the land space in which a species is cultivated.

Ploidy: the set of chromosomes in each cell. In cells responsible for reproduction (pollen, ovule), each chromosome is unique. These are haploid cells. Their number, represented by n, is generally fixed for a given species. In other cells (composing leaves, branches, etc.), the chromosomes are paired (2n; diploid), tripled (3n; triploid), in quadruplet copy (4n; tetraploid), or more. Ploidy designates the degree of replication for this base number.

Pollination: the transfer of pollen from a male plant's anthers (dioecious) or from male organs (monoecious) to the female flower's stigma or to female organs.

Pralinage *(syn.* mud bath): the coating of freshly cut roots, prior to planting, with a mixture of water, clay soil, manure, or any other organic material or growing compound (hormones, etc.) to avoid drying and to promote root development.

Precocity (*adj.* **precocious**): the characteristic of flowering and bearing fruit early in the life of a tree or vine, which may be conferred by genetics (i.e. a cultivar characteristic) or a cultural practice (e.g. rootstock selection, such as a dwarfing rootstock, or pruning/training habit).

Preformed (*n.* **preformation**): characteristic of the growth of a branch section previously contained within a bud. It may or may not be followed by a neoformed section (*see* **Neoformed**).

Proleptic branching (*n.* **prolepsis**): branching that develops in the year after the carrier branch grows. This is also called "deferred branching" (*see* **Sylleptic branching**; *see also fig. 4*).

Protandrous (*n.* **protandry**): related to the stamens maturing before the stigma of the pistil is receptive.

Protogynous (*n.* **protogyny**): related to the stigma being receptive before the stamens are mature.

Proximal: situated closest to the ground, the area of branch insertion, or in relation to the described organ (*see* **Distal**).

Rachis: on a compound leaf, the main leafstalk that supports the leaflets; in an inflorescence, the main peduncle supporting the flowers.

Reiteration: the phenomenon wherein a plant repeats all or part of its base architecture. In fruit arboriculture, a good illustration of reiteration occurs when an epicormic branch develops from a pruning scar. By definition, this epicormic branch, induced by the pruning, is not a sequential example of branching (*see* **Architecture of the tree**). If left to develop freely, it may constitute the equivalent of a new tree within the initial tree (recognizable by an architecture that is identical to that of the carrier tree). This new section is called the "reiterated complex" or, more commonly, a "reiteration."

PROLEPTIC

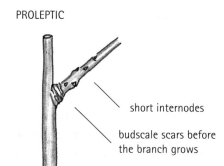

short internodes

budscale scars before
the branch grows

SYLLEPTIC

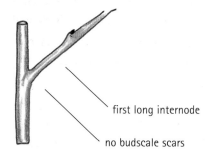

first long internode

no budscale scars

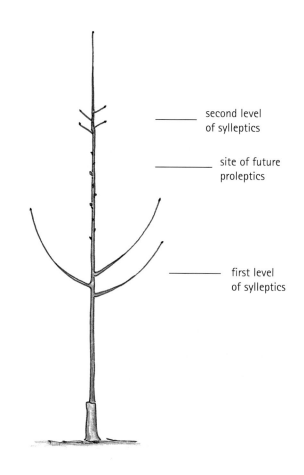

second level
of sylleptics

site of future
proleptics

first level
of sylleptics

Fig. 4. Sylleptic and proleptic branches on a scion.

Rhythmic: having a growth cycle with successive phases, or flushes, of elongation and rest. In climates with strong seasonal contrasts (in temperature or rainfall), the environment imposes rhythmic growth. The term may also describe branching: rhythmic branching is marked by distinct branch stages (ex.: the cherry tree).

Root disease: the rotting of a tree due to attacks by fungal pathogens (such as *Armillaria mellea* and *Rosellinia necatrix*) on the root system that work their way up the base of the trunk.

Row size: a traditional system of measurement used in the U.S. for sweet cherries, derived from the number that fit packed in a row across a standard container (20 lb box) 10.5 inches (26.7 cm) wide. Thus, a 20 lb box of 13-row cherries contains about 1,800 fruit and a 10-row box contains about half as many. The conversion from row size to millimeters is:

Rowsize	Minimum diameter	
	mm	in
9	20.6	75/64
9.5	21.4	71/64
10	22.6	67/64
10.5	24.2	64/64 (1 in)
11	25.4	61/64
11.5	26.6	57/64
12	28.2	54/64

Scaffold branch: a wide-diameter branch growing directly on the trunk (typically in a vase-shaped tree). Scaffold branches constitute the tree's main framework.

Scion: in French arboriculture, the first-year sprout formed by the rootstock and the variety. In English arboriculture, the term applies solely to the variety grafted onto the rootstock.

Secondary shoot: a shoot that develops within the same year as its carrier branch. Also called "sylleptic" (*see* **Sylleptic branching, Proleptic branching**).

Self-compatible: capable of producing seeds following pollination from flowers belonging to the same variety. The term "self-pollination" is also used (*syn.* self-fertile; *see* **Self-incompatible**).

Self-fertile: *see* **Self-compatible**; not requiring another pollinizer to produce fruit.

Self-incompatible: incapable of producing seeds when fertilized by flower pollen from the same variety (*see* **Self-compatible**).

Self-sterile: *see* **Self-incompatible**. Requiring a source of pollen in order to produce fruit.

Side shoot: a healthy sylleptic twig on a vine, growing from an axillary bud (comparable to an anticipated branch on a peach or apple tree).

Spur: a short shoot that bears only a few buds; or a tree with many spurs (as in a "spur type" tree).

Spur system: a short, fruit-bearing branch that grows naturally over several years. Selective pruning, however, can encourage spur production.

Stamen: the male organ of a flower on phanerogamous plants; composed of a filament and an anther.

Staminate: bearing stamens—longistaminate (having long stamens), mesostaminate (having average stamens), brachystaminate (having short stamens).

Stigma (*pl.* **stigmata)**: in phanerogamous plants, the part of a flower's female organ that extends from the ovary and style; the stigma provides the surface and the germination medium (fluid) for pollen growth.

Subterminal: located in an axillary position below the terminal bud.

Suckering: on a vine, the action of removing any sprouting buds located directly on old wood, as these would not bear fruit.

Sylleptic branching (*n.* **syllepsis**): branching that develops in the same year as the carrier branch. Also called "immediate branching" (*see* **Proleptic branching**; *see also fig. 4*).

Sympodial growth: growth whose axis develops from several meristems. This is caused either by the death or abscission of a terminal bud (apricot tree, chestnut tree, etc.) or by floral induction of the terminal bud (pear tree, apple tree, quince tree, etc.). In either case, apical dominance is high, and distal (axillary) buds are released for development (*see* **Monopodial growth**; *see also fig. 3*).

Tetraploid: *see* **Ploidy**.

Topping: on a vine, the pruning of branches (canes) before they hinder pathways between rows; on trees, pruning at the treetops, generally by mechanical means (*see* **Trimming**).

Trimming: removal of the skin from a nut (also called "blanching"). Trimming is also another word for pruning.

Triploid: *see* **Ploidy**.

Variety: a subdivision of a species. In a species, varieties are distinguished by their range of individual characteristics (e.g., the shape or color of fruit, or the amount and type of fruiting). If their ploidy allows, they may create hybrids between themselves and produce a new generation of offspring from which it is possible to select for new varieties (*see* **Cultivar**).

Veraison: the stage in fruit development (grape, olive, etc.) corresponding to the beginning of ripening, characterized by a change in color. Veraison most commonly describes color change in grapes. Other terms may denote similar color changes in other species (*ex.:* "color break" in sweet cherry).

Verticil: the arrangement of leaves, flowers, or branches in groups of two or more around an axis.

Wilting: the perishing or drying of leaves, generally in terms of the foliage's sensitivity to heat (as in pear trees). Wilting is caused by an imbalance between evaporation from the foliage and the rate of water absorption by the roots during extreme climatic demands (e.g., days of heavy evapotranspiration).

REFERENCES AND FURTHER READING

General Pomological References

Bailey, L.H. and Bailey, E.Z. (1976). *Hortus Third: A Concise Dictionary of Plants Cultivated in the United States and Canada.* New York: Macmillan.

Bailey, L.H. (1928). *The Standard Cyclopdia of Horticulture.* New York: Macmillan.

Bennett, W.F. (1993). *Nutrient Deficiencies and Toxicities in Crop Plants.* St. Paul, MN: APS Press.

Childers, Norman. (1990). *Modern Fruit Science.* Gainesville, FL: Norman Childers Publications.

Ferguson, Barbara. (1987). *All About Growing Fruits, Berries & Nuts.* San Francisco, CA: Ortho Books.

Fulbright, Dennis W. (2003). *A Guide to Nut Tree Culture in North America, Vol. 1.* Saline, MI: McNaughton and Gunn.

Jackson, D., Looney, N.E., and Morley-Bunker, M. (2010). *Temperate and Subtropical Fruit Production.* Wallingford, UK: CABI.

Janick, J. and Paull, R.E. (2008). *The Encyclopedia of Fruit and Nuts.* Wallingford, UK: Centre for Agricultural Bioscience International.

Morton, J.F. (1987). *Fruits of Warm Climates.* Miami, FL: Florida Flair Books.

Peterson, A.B. and Stevens, R.G. (1994). *Tree Fruit Nutrition.* Yakima, WA: Good Fruit Grower.

Rieger, Mark. (2006). *Introduction to Fruit Crops.* Boca Raton, FL: CRC Press.

Teskey, B.J.E. and Shoemaker, J.S. (1978). *Tree Fruit Production.* Westport, CT: The AVI Publishing Company, Inc.

Van Atta, M., Atta, M., and Wagner, S. (1993). *Growing Family Fruit and Nut Trees.* Sarasota, FL: Pineapple Press.

Westwood, N.M. (1993). *Temperate-zone Pomology: Physiology and Culture.* Portland, OR: Timber Press.

Williams, Kathleen. (1994). *Tree Fruit Irrigation: A Comprehensive Manual of Deciduous Trees Fruit Irrigation Needs.* Yakima, WA: Good Fruit Grower.

Almond

Grasselly, C. and Crossa-Raynaud, P. (1980). *L'Amandier.* Paris, France: Maisonneuve et Larose.

Grasselly, C. and Duval, H. (1997). *L'Amandier.* Paris, France: Editions CTIFL.

Micke, W.C. (1996). *Almond Production Manual.* Oakland, California: ANR Publication 3364.

Monastra, F. and Raparelli, E. (1997). *FAO Inventory of Almond Research, Germplasm, and References.* Rome, Italy: FAO.

Northern Nut Growers Association (www.nutgrowing.org)

The Almond Board of California (www.almondboard.com)

The Almond Doctor (www.thealmonddoctor.com)

Apple

Ferree, D.C. and Warrington, I. (2003). *Apples: Botany, Production, and Uses.* Wallingford, UK: Centre for Agricultural Bioscience International.

Forshey, C.G., Stebbins, R.L., and Elfving, D.C. (1992). *Training and Pruning Apple and Pear Trees.* Alexandria, VA: American Society for Horticultural Science.

Jones, A.L. and Aldwinckle, H.S. (1990). *Compendium of Apple and Pear Diseases.* St. Paul, MN: APS Press.

Lauri, P.E., Lespinasse, J-M., and Francis Delort (1994). "Le Raisonnement de la branche fruitière," in *Pomme Haute Définition,* special edition of the Revue Fruits et Légumes.

Lespinasse, J-M. (1997). *La conduite du pommier: Types de fructification, incidence sur la conduite de l'arbre.* Paris, France: INRA-INVUFLEC.

Lespinasse, Y. (1992). "Le Pommier" in A. Gallais, H. Bannerot (Eds.), Amélioration des espèces cultivées (p. 579–594). Paris, France: INRA Editions.

Lespinasse, J-M. (1980). *La conduite du pommier: L'axe vertical et rénovation des vergers.* Paris, France: INRA-CTIFL.

Trillot, M. and Lespinasse, Y. et al. (2002). *Le Pommier.* Paris, France: CTIFL.

Articles published by MAFCOT (Maîtrise de la fructification, concepts et techniques), Réussir Fruits et Légumes nos. 146, 147, 173, 182, 183.

Apricot

Bassi, D. (1999). *Apricot Culture: Present and Future.* Acta Hort 488: 35–40.

Gautier, M. (2001). La Culture Fruitière, Volume II, in *Les Productions Fruitières*. Paris, France: Tec & Doc.

Lichou, J. (1998). *Abricot, les variétés, mode d'emploi*. Paris, France: CTIFL.

Apricot Producers of California (www.apricotproducers.com)

Cherry

Claverie, J., Lauri, P-E., and Lespinasse, J-M. (1999). *Conduite du Cerisier: l'Arbre et sa Conduite, Nouveaux Concepts, in Réussir fruits et légumes* 177.

Edin, M., Lichou, J., and Saunier, R. (1997). *Cerise, les variétés et leur conduite*. Paris, France.

Lauri, P-E., Claverie, J. (2001). "Conduite du cerisier: Principes et Pratique de l'Extinction," in *Réussir fruits et légumes* 199.

Lichou, J., Edin, M., Tronel, C., Saunier, R., and Claverie, J. (1990). *Le cerisier*. Paris: France, CTIFL.

Webster, A.D. and Looney, N.E. (1995). *Cherries: Crop Physiology, Production, and Uses*. Wallingford, UK: Centre for Agricultural Bioscience International.

California Cherry Advisory Board (www.calcherry.com)

Northwest Cherries (www.nwcherries.com)

Cherry Marketing Institute (www.choosecherries.com)

Chestnut

Bouchet, M., Boutitie, A., and Ladrange, B. (2005). *Les Cahiers Pratiques: Votre Châtaigneraie*. Rodez, France: Éditions du Rouergue/Éditions Parc National des Cévennes.

Breisch, H. (1995). *Châtaignes et Marrons*. Paris, France: CTIFL.

Bruneton-Governatori, A. (1984). *Le Pain de Bois*. Toulouse, France: Eché.

Pitte, J-R. (1986). *Terres de Castanide*. Paris, France: Fayard.

Reyne, J. Marrons et Châtaignes d'Ardèche (2nd edition). Privas, France: Syndicat des Producteurs de Châtaignes et Marrons d'Ardèche.

Vossen, P. (2000). *Chestnut Culture in California*. University of California Division of Agriculture and Natural Resources Publication (ANR) 8010.

Chestnut Growers of America (www.wcga.net)

Fig

Anderson, P.C. and Crocker, T.E. (2009). *The Fig*. Gainesville, FL: University of Florida, Institute of Food and Agricultural Sciences Extension.

Condit, I.J. and Swingle, W.T. (1947). *The Fig*. Waltham, MA: Chronica Botanica Company.

Simms, C. (2004). *Nutshell Guide to Growing Figs: Everything You Need to Know in a Nutshell*. Port Orchard, WA: Orchard House Books.

Valdeyron, G. (1987). *Le Figuier*. Prades-le-Les, France: Éditions des Ecologistes de l'Euzière.

Vidaud, J. (1997). *Le Figuier*. Paris, France: CTIFL.

California Fig Advisory Board (www.californiafigs.com)

Hazelnut

Barnola, P. (1976). *Recherches sur la Croissance et la Ramification du Noisetier*. Ann. Sci. Nat. Bot. 17: 222–258.

Erdogan, V. and Mehlenbacher, S. (2000). *Interspecific Hybridization in Hazelnut (Corylus)*. J. Amer. Soc. Hort. Sci. 125(4): 489–497.

Germain, E., Sarraquigne, J-P., et al. (2004). *Le Noisetier*. Paris, France: CTIFL.

Olson, J. (2002). *Growing Hazelnuts in the Pacific Northwest*. Corvallis, OR: Extension Service, Oregon State University.

West Nut Growers Association (www.westnut.com)

Hazelnut Council (www.hazelnutcouncil.org)

Oregon Hazelnut Marketing Board (www.oregonhazelnuts.org)

Kiwifruit

Hennion, B. et al. (2003). *Le Kiwi*. Paris, France: CTIFL.

Ramonguilhem, M. (1986). *Formation et Conduite d'un Verger de Kiwi, in Revue Fruits et Légumes* 001.

Ryugo, K. and Stover, E. (2008). *Release of Hairless Kiwifruit 'Eldorado' and 'Nugget', and 'Early Bird' Pollinizer for Further Evaluation*. J. Amer. Pomol. Soc. 62(3):137–138.

California Kiwifruit Commission (www.kiwifruit.org)

Olive

Argenson, C., Régis, S., Jourdain, J-M., and Vaysse, P. (1999). *L'Olivier*. Paris, France: CTIFL.

Fernandez, A.G., Adams, M.R., and Fernandez-Diez, M.J. (1997). *Table Olives: Production and Processing*. New York: Springer.

International Olive Oil Council (1997). *World Olive Encyclopedia*. Barcelona, Spain: Plaza and Janes.

Loussert, R., and Brousse, G. (1997). *L'Olivier*. Paris, France: Maisonneuve et Larose.

Moutier, N. (2004). *Identification et Caractérisation des Variétés d'Olivier Cultivées en France*. Turriers, France: Naturalia Publications.

Sibbett, G.S. and Ferguson, L. (2005). *Olive Production Manual, Second Edition*. Oakland, CA: ANR Publication 3353.

Therios, Ioannis. (2009). *Olives*. Wallingford, UK: Centre for Agricultural Bioscience International.

University of California, Davis, Olive Center (http://olive-center.ucdavis.edu)

Peach

Giauque, P. (2003). *Conduite du Verger du Pêcher: Recherche de la Performance*. Paris, France: CTIFL.

Hilaire, C., and Giauque, P. (2003). *Le Pêcher*. Paris, France: CTIFL.

LaRue, J.H. and Johnson, R.S. (1989). *Peaches, Plums and Nectarines: Growing and Handling for Fresh Market*. Oakland, CA: ANR Publication 3331.

Layne, D.R. and Bassi, D. (2008). *The Peach: Botany, Production and Uses*. Wallingford, UK: Centre for Agricultural Bioscience International.

Monet, R. (1983). *Le Pêcher: Génétique et Physiologie*. Paris, France: INRA-Masson Édition.

Navarro, E. and Plénet, D. (2002). *Taille en Vert du Pêcher: l'Arrachage Manuel Précoce des Pousses Végétatives, Est-il une Technique Alternative?*, in *Réussir Fruits et Legumes* 209.

Ogawa, J.M., Zehr, E.I., and Bird, G.W. (1995). *Compendium of Stone Fruit Diseases*. St. Paul, MN: APS Press.

Proebstring, E.L. and Mills, H.H. (1978). *Synoptic Analysis of Peach and Cherry Flower Bud Hardiness*. J. Am. Soc. Hortic. Sci. 103: 842–845.

Roper, T.R., Mahr, D.L., and McManus, P.S. (2006). *Growing Apricots, Cherries, Peaches, and Plums in Wisconsin*. Madison, WI: University of Wisconsin Cooperative Extension.

Pear

Masseron, A. and Trillot, M. (1991). *Le Poirier*. Paris, France: CTIFL.

Mitcham, E. and Eklins, R. (2007). *Pear Production and Handling Manual*. Oakland, CA: ANR Publication 3483.

Ohlendorf, B. (1999). *Integrated Pest Management for Apples and Pears, Second Edition*. Oakland, CA: ANR Publication 3340.

Plum

Ames, G. (2001). *Low-Spray and Organic Plum Production*. Butte, MT: National Center for Appropriate Technology.

Audubert, A. and Chambonnière, S (1995). *La Reine-Claude*. Paris, France: CTIFL.

Blažek, J. (2007). A Survey of the Genetic Resources Used in Plum Breeding. In *Proceedings of the Eighth Annual ISHS Symposium on Plum and Prune* (E. Vangdal et al., Eds.), *Acta Hort* 734:31–46.

Norton, M.V. and Krueger, W.H. (2005). *Growing Prunes (Dried Plums) in California: An Overview*. Oakland, CA: University of California, Division of Agriculture and Natural Resources (ANR Publication 8264).

California Dried Plums (www.californiadriedplums.org)

Quince

Ghazarian, B. (2009). *Simply Quince*. Monteret, CA: Mayreni Publishing.

Gossetin, H-J. (1992). *Le Bon Jardinier, Volume II, Dictionnaire des Végétaux*. Paris, France: La Maison Rustique.

Leterme, E. (1995). *Les Fruits Retrouvés, Histoire et Diversité des Espèces Anciennes du Sud-Ouest*. Rodez, France: Éditions du Rouergue.

Masseron, A. (1989). *Les Porte-greffe Pommier, Poirier et Nashi*. Paris, France: CTIFL.

Table Grape

Creasy, G.L. and Creasy L.L. (2009). *Grapes*. Wallingford, UK: Centre for Agricultural Bioscience International.

Vidaud, J., Wagner, R. and Charmont, S. (1993). *Le raisin de table*. Paris, France: CTIFL.

University of California Integrated Viticulture (http://ucanr.org/sites/intvit/)

Walnut

Anderson, K.K. (2006). *Guide to Efficient Nitrogen Fertilizer Use in Walnut Orchards*. Oakland, CA. ANR Publication 3373.

Charlot, G. and Germain, E. (1993). *Le Noyer, Nouvelles Techniques*. Paris, France: CTIFL.

Germain, E., Prunet, J-P., and Garcin, A. (1999). *Le Noyer*. Paris, France: CTIFL.

Luedeling, E., Zhang, M., McGranahan, G. and Leslie, C. (2009). *Validation of Winter Chill Models Using Historic Records of Walnut Phenology*. Agricultural and Forest Meteorology 149:1854–1864.

Ramos, D.E. (1998). *Walnut Production Manual*. Oakland, CA: ANR Publication 3270.

Strand, L.L. and Clark, J.K. (2003). *Integrated Pest Management for Walnuts, Third Edition*. Oakland, CA: ANR Publication 3471.

Organizations

International Society for Horticultural Science (www.ishs.org)
American Society for Horticultural Science (www.ashs.org)
International Nut and Dried Fruit Foundation (www.nutfruit.org)
American Pomological Society (americanpomological.org)
United States Agricultural Information Network (usain.org)
National Sustainable Agricultural Information Service (www.attra.org)
California Rare Fruit Growers Association (www.crfg.org)
Edible Landscaping and Gardening (www.efn.org/~bsharvy/edible.html)
North American Fruit Explorers (www.nafex.org)

Newsletters & Quarterlies

The Fruit Growers News (www.fruitgrowernews.com)
Good Fruit Grower (www.goodfruit.com/)
American Fruit Grower (www.americanfruitgrower.com/)
Compact Fruit Tree (www.idfta.org)
Fruit Varieties Journal (Journal of the American Pomological Society; http://americanpomological.org/journal.html)

Extensions and University Resources

University of California, Davis
Home orchard: http://homeorchard.ucdavis.edu/

University of California, Riverside (subtropicals)
http://lib.ucr.edu/agnic/

Penn State University
http://horticulture.psu.edu/extension
http://consumerhorticulture.psu.edu/
Tree Fruit Production Guide: http://agsci.psu.edu/tfpg
Fruit production for the home gardener: http://agsci.psu.edu/fphg

Purdue University
https://mdc.itap.purdue.edu
www.hort.purdue.edu

Cornell University
http://www.fruit.cornell.edu/

University of Massachusetts
http://www.umass.edu/fruitadvisor

Michigan State University
http://web1.msue.msu.edu/fruit/

Clemson University
http://www.clemson.edu/extension/horticulture/

Iowa State University
https://www.extension.iastate.edu

Auburn/Alabama Extension Service
http://www.aces.edu/dept/peaches/

Colorado State University
http://www.cmg.colostate.edu/

New Mexico State University
http://aces.nmsu.edu/pubs/_h/

North Carolina State University
http://www.ces.ncsu.edu

Oregon State University
http://extension.oregonstate.edu

Texas A&M
http://aggie-horticulture.tamu.edu/

University of Georgia
http://www.caes.uga.edu/extension/

Virginia Tech/Virginia Extension Service
http://www.pubs.ext.vt.edu/category/fruits.html

Washington State University
http://www.tfrec.wsu.edu/
Crop-specific topics: http://www.wsulibs.wsu.edu/AgNIC/
Fruit publications: http://gardening.wsu.edu/text/treef.htm

Mid-Atlantic Regional Fruit Loop
http://www.caf.wvu.edu/kearneysville/fruitloop.html

PHOTO CREDITS

Numbers below refer to the photographs (not figures) in each chapter. Credit for chapter opening photos are preceded by "0". All illustrations (figures) are by Jean-Marie Lespinasse.

Introduction 1, 2: E. Leterme-CVRA; 3: J.-M. Lespinasse • **Almond** 3-5, 7: J.-M. Lespinasse; 0-2, 6: E. Leterme-CVRA • **Apple** 0: E. Leterme-CVRA; 1-16: J.-M. Lespinasse • **Apricot** 6, 11, 12: E. Navarro; 1-5, 7, 9, 10, 13-15: B. Hucbourg; 0, 8: E. Leterme-CVRA • **Cherry** 2, 4, 6-17, 19: J. Claverie-INRA; 0, 1, 3, 5, 18: E. Leterme-CVRA • **Chestnut** 4-9, 11: H. Breisch; 0, 10: J.-M. Lespinasse; 1-3: E. Leterme-CVRA • **Fig** 2-4, 6: Y. Caraglio-Amap-Cirad; 0, 1, 5: E. Leterme-CVRA • **Hazelnut** 0, 2, 4, 8, 9, 11, 16-31: ANPN; 5, 7, 12-15: J.-P. Sarraquigne; 6, 10: E. Germain-INRA; 1, 3: E. Leterme-CVRA • **Kiwi** 3-5, 7-9, 11, 13, 14: F. Dupèbe-Coop d'Amou; 0-2, 6, 10, 12, 15: E. Leterme-CVRA • **Olive** 0-4, 6-8: N. Moutier-INRA; 5: J.-M. Lespinasse • **Peach** 1, 4-8, 10: E. Navarro-GRCETA; 2, 3: E. Navarro; 0, 9: E. Leterme-CVRA • **Pear** 4, 5, 11, 13, 16: B. Florens-La Pugère; 0-3, 6-10, 12, 14, 15, 17-19: E. Leterme-CVRA • **Plum** 2, 6, 12, 14: M. Ramonguilhem; 4, 5, 13: E. Koké; 8, 9, 15: G. Adgié; 0, 1, 3, 11: E. Leterme-CVRA; 7, 10, 16: J.-M. Lespinasse • **Quince** 0-11: E. Leterme-CVRA • **Table Grape** 0-3, 5-11: G. Adgié-AOC Moissac; 4: E. Leterme-CVRA. • **Walnut** 0: F. Delort-INRA; 2-17: INRA Bordeaux; 1: E. Leterme-CVRA • **Appendix A** 1-5: E. Leterme-CVRA

ML

 2/12